Children's Museums, Zoos, and Discovery Rooms

CHILDREN'S MUSEUMS, ZOOS, AND DISCOVERY ROOMS

An International Reference Guide

Barbara Fleisher Zucker

Greenwood Press
New York • Westport, Connecticut • London

Library of Congress Cataloging-in-Publication Data

Zucker, Barbara Fleisher, 1936–
  Children's museums, zoos, and discovery rooms.

  Bibliography: p.
  Includes index.
    1. Children's museums—Directories.   2. Children's
zoos—Directories.   I. Title.   II. Title: Discovery
rooms.
AM8.Z83   1987   069'.088054'025   86-22793
ISBN 0-313-24538-X (lib. bdg. : alk. paper)

Library of Congress Catalog Card Number: 86-22793
ISBN: 0-313-24538-X

First published in 1987

Greenwood Press, Inc.
88 Post Road West, Westport, Connecticut 06881

Printed in the United States of America

The paper used in this book complies with the
Permanent Paper Standard issued by the National
Information Standards Organization (Z39.48-1984).

10 9 8 7 6 5 4 3 2 1

CONTENTS

PREFACE

Children's Museums, Zoos, and Discovery Rooms: An International Reference Guide contains 235 institutional profiles of children's museums or those that have special children's areas. Inclusion, therefore, is facility-based rather than program-based. Because museums do not easily fit into rigid categories, an operational definition was used with institutional identity an important factor. Furthermore, "museum" in contemporary usage encompasses zoos, aquariums, science centers, planetariums, botanical gardens, and arts centers.

Museums, zoos, and discovery rooms were identified through directories, the professional literature, conference attendance, and recommendation of colleagues. For U.S. institutions the primary sources were *The Official Museum Directory*, 1984 and 1985, and *Zoological Parks and Aquariums in the Americas 1984–85*. For non-U.S. institutions resources included *Museums of the World*, 3d rev. ed., 1981, the *International Zoo Yearbook*, and additional museum guides. Every directory entry was read carefully in order to identify those that were or had children's facilities. Each such institution was sent a cover letter explaining the scope and intended format of the book and a data form which outlined the kind of information being sought. The data sheet was both a way to collect information and a vehicle for initiating a dialogue with respondents, which yielded further information. The material provided by museums ranged from very brief notes to comprehensive summaries, and many sent brochures, packets, and other publications in response to the request for bibliographic information. References were by no means limited to those provided on museum data sheets, and extensive bibliographic searches were undertaken. Institutions that did not initially respond were sent a follow-up letter, and in a few instances telephone calls were made. During the final stages of preparing the manuscript in early 1986, the second request for information was discontinued.

All museums included in the volume responded to a call for information; each had an opportunity to verify its summary after it was written, and over 90 percent reviewed their profile. Each narrative is intended to provide a historical summary of the facility and information on current operations, including the circumstances leading to its establishment; when founded and by whom; information about the building, gallery, room, or area; collection strengths; exhibits; subject and program specialities, clubs, and classes; special facilities; staff, including the use of volunteers; audience and attendance; changes and trends within the institution; hours; sources of funding; and institutional publications and/or reference sources.

Entries are organized geographically and appear alphabetically by country, state or province (United States and Canada only), city, and finally institution. If it is a children's facility within a museum or zoo, the institutional name appears in the heading with the specific facility given at the beginning of the entry narrative. Institutional names in the original language are followed by an English translation in parentheses. Bibliographic sources were chosen both for their content and availability over time. Therefore, whenever possible, published sources rather than in-house material of an ephemeral nature were utilized. Also taken into consideration was the international character of the volume, and where possible, resources likely to be accessible worldwide were cited. The reference notes which appear at the end of the entry are specific to the children's museum or facility; and in a few instances where there are none, it is because nothing specific to the children's area was available. The selected bibliography at the back of the volume includes both general citations that did not appear with the entries and key works that relate to the entries but also highlight the overall development of children's museums, zoos, and discovery rooms. Appendixes list institutions in alphabetical order, in chronological order by date of establishment, and under 3 broad classifications: children's museums (including arboretums, exhibits, galleries, gardens, nature museums, planetariums, and theaters); children's zoos and aquarium touch tanks/children's coves; and discovery rooms, zoolabs, and educational/library resource centers. The index provides access to all institutions by name, translated name, or alternate name as well as references to a variety of topical items.

I wish to express my appreciation to those within the museum community who contributed information, granted access to library and archival collections, reviewed their entries, and provided encouragement. I am also grateful to Morris Library, Southern Illinois University at Carbondale, for its research support and to the Office of Museum Programs, Smithsonian Institution, for the opportunity to participate in the Visiting Professionals Program. Thanks are also extended to Mary Sive, Acquisitions Editor at Greenwood Press, who initially suggested the volume and helped shape its format and style, and to Cynthia Harris, Editor,

History, and Marilyn Brownstein, Editor, Humanities, who guided the volume to completion.

The book would not have been possible without the support of my sons, Jeff and Jon, and the unfailing understanding and encouragement of my husband, Stanley, to whom this volume is dedicated.

INSTITUTIONAL PROFILES

___ AUSTRALIA ___

CANBERRA

AUSTRALIAN SCIENCE AND TECHNOLOGY CENTRE, PO Box 65, Belconnen ACT 2616 (The Questacon Science Centre). Opened in September 1980, the Questacon Project was initiated in 1977 by Michael M. Gore. In 1979 he received a grant from the Commonwealth Schools Commission for an innovative project to establish a participatory science center on an experimental basis. The inspiration and model for the project was the Exploratorium in San Francisco (see entry under UNITED STATES/CALIFORNIA). Questacon is located in part of a disused school building with a main hall, 6 rooms, demonstration area, foyer, and other support facilities. It opened with 15 exhibits and currently has 100 continually changing exhibits based on the physical sciences and designed to involve the visitor, demystify science, and have practical applications to everyday life. Since its inception it has operated under the direction of Gore and Explainers, a group of senior high and tertiary students and adults, many of whom are retirees with varied backgrounds. Hours are Monday to Friday 10:30–4:30 and occasional weekends. Questacon stages regular science lecture series, sponsors special lectures in association with other science organizations, and hosts many community groups. Schools come from all over Australia for scheduled visits. During school holidays there are ''Kids 'n Science'' programs which encompass a wide variety of topics from biology to music. Questacon has more than 500 visitors a day. In 1985 Questacon initiated its mobile component, Science Circus, which travels thousands of kilometers around Australia. Support now comes from a variety of sources including government departments, industry, and scientific organizations. In 1984 the government agreed to establish a science centre in Canberra as a bicentennial project to open in 1988, and construction began on 30 May 1986. In addition to the building being constructed within the Parliamentary Triangle near the National Library, the centre is expected to have an extensive outreach component.

Dorothy Braxton, "A Touch of Science," *Panorama* (April/May 1983): 47–50; Michael Gore, "The Australian National Science Centre," *Australian Science Teachers' Association Journal*, forthcoming; "$14 Million Found for Canberra Science Centre," *Canberra Times*, 22 January 1986; Michael Gore, "Hands-On Science," *UNESCO Review* 8 (May 1983): 10–13; *Presenting the Australian Science and Technology Centre* (Canberra: Australian Government Publishing Service for the Department of Science, 1986); "Questacon Shows Why We Need a Science Centre," *Canberra Times*, 23 January 1986; *Workshop for Key Personnel Concerned with Out-of-School Scientific Activities by Young People: Report of a Regional Workshop* (Bangkok, Thailand: August 24–September 2, 1982), pp. 4–5: ERIC Document Reproduction Service, ED 237 360.

SYDNEY

TARONGA ZOO, SYDNEY, PO Box 20, Mosman, NSW 2088. The Friendship Farm, opened in 1975, is a 1-acre children's area with domestic animals. It evolved out of the old amusement and elephant ride sections at the zoo which were discontinued. After many board members and the general public expressed disappointment, the merry-go-round shelter was converted to a barn with stock pens radiating from it. Other exhibits were added, including poultry yards, an animal nursery, ponds, and farm machinery. Domestication is the theme of the area, and it is supported by graphics to help people understand the differences between domestic and nondomestic animals. Special events such as sheep shearing, wool carding, and weaving are held. Friendship Farm has a permanent staff of 5 and a corps of volunteers who oversee the exhibits and answer visitor questions. The zoo is open 9:30–4:00 daily, and there is an admission charge.

Taronga Zoo Guide (Sydney: Taronga Zoo, n.d.)

AUSTRIA

NATURHISTORISCHES MUSEUM (Natural History Museum), Burgring 7, 1014 Vienna. The Children's Hall, opened on 28 March 1977, is a 200-square-meter facility designed for children 4–14 years old. Developed over a 5-year period, the Hall provides opportunities for active participation appropriate to various developmental levels, including direct contact with objects, access to scientific equipment, walk-in dioramas, live animals, an audiovisual center, a computer, and a 500-volume science library. At the entrance to the installation are cases with representative samples from the museum's 8 departments designed to serve as an introduction to its collections. There is also a collection of large glass plates on various topics for visitor use on a specially designed viewing apparatus. This section is open to everyone, but the hall is reserved just for children and arranged into areas suitable for different age groups. A children's corner is reserved for 4–7 year olds, who may be left in the care of kindergarten assistants while parents view the museum exhibits. The corner has carefully selected groups of natural history objects, games, and books to be read by or to the children and can accommodate 20 children comfortably. For children up to age 10 there are the 2 walk-in dioramas with about 150 animals, a farmyard, and the forest, which are the main attractions of the Hall. The farm animals are arranged in natural poses, and some of them may be stroked. The forest re-creates a setting like that surrounding Vienna and includes almost all the mammals and birds native to the area, some of which may be touched. Each of the 20 birds is individually illuminated while its song and brief explanation are given during a 20-minute multimedia program. For children 8–14 there is a log house, 3 by 5 meters, built on a raised platform. It is equipped with microscopes, specimens embedded in polyster, a 500-volume library, and a well-outfitted audiovisual center with TV, video, slide projector, and overhead projector. Small and living objects and microscopic slides can be projected. Groups no larger than 20 can also use videotaped presentations, short films, slide/tape programs, and transparencies covering all fields of natural history. The log house can accommodate 30 children at a time. The Children's Hall has 10 teachers paid by the hour. Funding to develop the facility came from the Austrian Ministry of Science and Research, the Austrian National Bank, the President of the Friends of the Museum, and UNESCO. Support for the Hall comes from the Ministry of Science and Education. Hours are holidays 10:00–5:00, Saturday 1:00–5:00, and Sunday 10:00–5:00. The Children's Hall has 150,000 visitors a year.

Oliver E. Paget, "Vom 'Kindersaal' zur Erwachsenenbildung," *Theorie und Praxis* 1 (1978): 11–15; Oliver E. Paget, "Der 'Kindersaal' im Naturhistorischen Museum Wien," *Museumskunde* 43, no. 3 (1978): 148; Oliver E. Paget, "Der neue 'Kindersaal' im Naturhistorischen Museum in Wien," *Neue Museumskunde* 22, no. 2 (1979): 109–13; Oliver E. Paget, "The New Children's Hall at the Natural History Museum, Vienna," *Museum* [UNESCO] 30, no. 1 (1978): 55–58; Oliver E. Paget, "When Planning the New Children's Hall . . . ," *ICOM Natural History Museums Newsletter* 1 (1978), reprinted in *Museum Round-Up* 71 (Summer 1978): 24.

BELGIUM

BRUSSELS

LE MUSÉE DES ENFANTS/HET KINDERMUSEUM (The Children's Museum), 15, rue du Bourgmestre, 1050 Brussels. Founded by Kathleen Lippens in October 1976, the museum was inspired by the Boston Children's Museum (see entry under UNITED STATES/MASSACHUSETTS). An empty 500-square-meter house scheduled for demolition, 32, rue de Tenbosch, was rented by Lippens and 6 other women, and private donations were solicited. For the first 3 years the museum was run by volunteers, and the directors still serve without pay. After several years of planning, the museum moved to a larger, 700-square-meter building, formerly the Hôtel de Maître à Ixelles, in May 1986. The target audience is 4–12 year olds, and the museum is meant for all children regardless of language or social status. Every 2 years exhibits are completely changed; installations have included the city, the forest, the human body, the farm, space, dwellings, living together, water, and communication. Workshops relate to current exhibits. Discovery, participation, and fun are the basis for the displays and activities. The museum has a 5-member board, 1 designer (réalisator) and ten facilitators (animateurs). Weekdays 9:30–11:30 and 1:30–3:30 are reserved for school groups. Public hours are Wednesday, Saturday, and Sunday, 2:30–5:00. The museum's support comes 70 percent from donations, 28 percent from admissions, and 2 percent from subsidies. Approximately 35,000 people visit the museum each year.

"Children in Museums and Children's Museums," International Roundtable in Brussels on 17–18 February 1979 [Organized by the Brussels Children's Museum] (Typewritten);

Brigid Grauman, "The Museum That Children Love," *Bulletin*, 20 December 1982, p. 19; "Im Haus der grünen Hände: Das Kindermuseum in Brüssel," *Die Schöne Welt* (September 1983); "Vivre ensemble au Musée des Enfants," *Libre Belgique*, 24 January 1983.

CANADA

ALBERTA

Calgary

THE CALGARY ZOO, Box 3036, Station B, Calgary, Alberta T2M 4R8. The Children's Zoo, opened in 1970, has a farm animal theme and occupies about an acre. Many animals in the children's zoo may be touched under the supervision of volunteers. There is also an aviary with a variety of birds including some wading species. All educational programming, which is extensive, is conducted from the children's zoo. There are tours for school groups, classes, programs for preschoolers, family activities, outreach, and workshops for teachers. Plans are underway to renovate the children's zoo, and participatory activities connected with biological principles are being developed. The entire zoo is open daily 9:00–4:30 and has about 800,000 visitors per year, but no specific figures are available on visitors to the children's zoo. There is an admission charge but no extra fee for the children's zoo.

The Calgary Zoo Discovery Courses: 1984–85 Programs for School Groups (Calgary: The Calgary Zoo, [1984]); "Zoos Are News," *Woman's Day*, 23 October 1984.

Edmonton

THE EDMONTON ART GALLERY, 2 Sir Winston Churchill Square, Edmonton, Alberta T5J 2C1. The Margaret Brine Children's Art Gallery, opened in 1969, is an 800-square-foot exhibition space for the display of student art. This special gallery received financial support from the Junior League and was incorporated into the building plans when the new facility was being designed in the 1960s. The gallery initiated its education program in 1926 and its studio classes in 1934; today an extensive series of art courses are offered for children, teens, and adults. At present its financial support comes from the general gallery budget. The Margaret Brine Gallery has approximately 10 exhibits per year, which are seen by 90,000 visitors.

Kate Davis, "Difficult Challenges—Great Joys: History of the E[dmonton] A[rt] G[allery]," *Update* 6, no. 4 (July/August 1984): 12; "Art Education," *Update* 6, no. 4 (July/August 1984): 27, 28.

VALLEY ZOO, c/o 10th Floor CN Tower, 10004 - 104th Avenue, Edmonton, Alberta T5J 0K1. The Children's Zoo opened on 1 July 1959 as the Storyland Valley Zoo. Located in Laurier Park and occupying almost 5 acres, it was based on storybook themes. In 1975 a master plan was developed for the expansion of the Edmonton Zoo, and 65 acres adjacent to the original Storyland Zoo were developed. The new exhibit area became the Valley Zoo, and the children's area has remained a strongly tactile zoo based upon storyland themes. The children's zoo has a staff of 17, and there are 200,000 visitors each year. A small admission fee to the main facility includes the children's section. The zoo is open 10:00–6:00 during the summer and by appointment in the winter. It is municipally funded.

Rosl Kirchshofer, ed., *The World of Zoos: A Survey and Gazetteer* (New York: Viking, 1968), p. 231; "Storyland Zoo Opening May 1st," *Edmonton Journal*, 25 April 1960; "Valley Zoo Opens Gates," *Spokesman*, May 1977; "Valley Zoo to Re-Open in Early January," *Edmonton Examiner*, 5 November 1984.

BRITISH COLUMBIA

Kamloops

KAMLOOPS PUBLIC ART GALLERY, 207 Seymour Street, Kamloops, British Columbia V2C 2E7. The Children's Gallery, Young Art, opened in 1979 during the gallery's first year of operation. This small exhibition space displays a variety of art produced by children and youth, and the shows change approximately once a month. Even though there is a special place for children's art within the gallery, displays of children's art are not confined to this space. In addition to classes, tours, and special events, during the spring of 1983 a multimedia environment ALIVE! IN THE GALLERY was created by children K–12 from Kamloops School District 24. Four hundred children worked with 3 artists during a 3-week period using a variety of media and techniques. The event turned the gallery into an active place. It is hoped that the long-range effect will be to increase contacts with schoolchildren, some of whom may have works to show in the children's gallery. The gallery is open Tuesday through Saturday 11:00–5:00, Sunday 1:00–4:00, and closed Mondays and holidays. The gallery is a publicly supported educational organization, and there is no admission fee.

Alive! in the Gallery (Kamloops, British Columbia: Kamloops Public Art Gallery, 1983); *Look!* [Kamloops Public Art Gallery] (April-June 1984).

ONTARIO

Cambridge

AFRICAN LION SAFARI, RR #1, Cambridge, Ontario N1R 5S2. The Children's Zoo or Wildlife Bazaar opened in 1971 and is a 1-acre outdoor walk-through facility added to the 500-acre drive-through wildlife park. It was developed to provide a special place for children to interact with and explore the textures, scents, and sounds of animals and to be a teaching tool for the handicapped. Peafowl, young goats, llamas, lambs, guinea pigs, rabbits, and other domestic and exotic animals and birds can be observed at close range. Some animals may be petted, and feeding is allowed but controlled, with the food being purchased at the zoo. There is a "Birds of Prey" demonstration, and other demonstrations are also held in the Wildlife Bazaar The area is supervised by 2 attendants who are also available to answer questions. The zoo is open June to August 10:00–5:30 daily and during April, May, September, and October 11:30–4:30 weekdays and 10:00–4:30 weekends. There is an admission charge. Approximately 175,000 visitors walk through the children's area each year.

Antoinette M. Adey, G. D. Dailley, Jr., and Carole Precious, *Animals of the Wild: Official Guidebook of African Lion Safari* (Cambridge: Ainsworth Press, 1985), p. 18.

Hamilton

THE CHILDREN'S MUSEUM, 1072 Main Street East, Hamilton, Ontario L8M 1N6. After almost a decade of planning, the museum opened in 1978 with a part-time curator. The International Year of the Child and the growing interest in hands-on museums and education stimulated its development. The museum is situated in an old house donated by the city and located in Gage Park. About half of its 2,000 square feet is devoted to exhibits which create a total environment and change every 4 months. Artifacts and materials are acquired as needed for each installation. The primary audience is children 3–13, and exhibitions are planned with a specific age range in mind. Winter exhibits are for the junior level, spring exhibits for primary grades and preschoolers, and summer and fall exhibits are aimed at a mixed age group. Several of the exhibits have centered on self-awareness, with themes such as SENSES, WHAT IF YOU WERE (handicapped), ALL ABOUT ME, ME AND MY FEELINGS, and FITNESS AND ME. Other installations have dealt with careers, the natural sciences, other cultures, and the arts and architecture. Currently 8 kits, in both English and French, are available. Tours can be scheduled for groups, family participation is encouraged, and there are special events. There are 2 full-time and 2 part-time staff members who are assisted by grant-funded personnel, city staff, and about 20 volunteers. The Children's Museum is open Tuesday through Saturday 10:00–4:00, Sunday 1:00–4:00, by appointment, and closed Mondays. There are about 23,000 visitors annually. Support comes from admissions, kit rentals, the Corporation of the City of Hamilton, the Department of Culture and Recreation, and the Ministry of Citizenship and Culture, Museums Branch (operating grant).

David Dauphinee, "In Children's Museums, The Signs Say 'Please Touch,' " *Canadian Living* (April 1983): W15–16; "Games at Hamilton Museum Offer Lots More Than Mere Child's Play," *Globe and Mail*, 19 February 1983; "Hamilton Museum Misnamed but Children Love It Anyway," *Toronto Star*, 15 January 1983, p. E14; "Iroquois Heritage," *Hamilton Magazine* (October 1981): 79; "You Have To Drag Kids from This Museum," *Toronto Star*, 23 February 1980; Mike Walton and Al Toulin, "Cheap Thrills: For Young Urban Progeny," *Hamilton This Month* (Summer 1985): 15.

London

LONDON REGIONAL CHILDREN'S MUSEUM, 21 Wharncliffe Road South, London, Ontario N6J 4G5. The need for children to have a special place for educational fun and recreation activities led an interim planning board, established in 1975, to develop the Children's Museum. Starting with playground programs, the museum opened in 1976 in the Centre City Mall, and in late 1978 it moved to larger, temporary space and continued to grow. On 25 September 1982 the London Regional Children's Museum opened in a permanent, 30,000-square-foot facility in a renovated school building with 2 acres of grounds. There are 6 exhibit galleries designed to encourage hands-on discovery and 3 flexible programming galleries for special events. Artifacts relate to children's life-styles, both historic and ethnic, and the museum also collects natural history specimens. Currently the galleries include THE STREET WHERE YOU LIVE (a modern streetscape with cutaways of above and below ground), A CHILD LONG AGO (a re-creation of an 1800s town), INUIT (exploration of the Canadian Arctic), THINGS IN CAVES (with stalactites and stalagmites, mines, minerals, and dinosaurs), SCIENCE (areas for experimenting with sound and electricity), and the Lawson Planetarium. The flexible space is used for performances, workshops, craft activities, holiday celebrations, and community exhibits. Special 1-hour programs are offered for schools on Tuesdays through Fridays. The preferred group size is no more than 30 students, and an extra charge is added for groups up to the absolute limit of 35 pupils. On Mondays school groups may tour the museum on their own. Computer clubs are offered for preschoolers to adults and novice to experienced. Over 50 kits with authentic artifacts, costumes, audiovisual materials, and resource materials are available for rent. There are 12 full-time and 6 part-time staff members and over 100 volunteers including a junior corps. The museum is open Monday through Thursday and Saturday 10:00–5:00, Friday 10:00–8:00, and Sunday 1:00–5:00. There are approximately 100,000 visitors annually. Support comes from admissions, school programming, kit rentals, special events, public and private donations, and the government.

David Dauphinee, "In Children's Museums, The Signs Say 'Please Touch,' " *Canadian Living* (April 1983): W12–W13; David A. Young, "Touring Ontario's Museums: The London Regional Children's Museum," *Rotunda* 15, no. 4 (1983): 33–37.

Toronto

ART GALLERY OF ONTARIO, 317 Dundas Street West, Toronto, Ontario M5T 1G4. The Hands On environment, founded in 1974, was developed because the staff felt a place was needed where families could explore the visual arts. The primary objective of Hands On is to make the Art Gallery of Ontario, its collections, and basic concepts in the visual arts accessible to young people in a playful and participatory way. The audience is children 4–12, who must be accompanied by an adult. Three thematic exhibits a year are installed in the 35-by-35-foot Hands On environment. Each is designed to meet various developmental stages, create a stimulating but not overwhelming environment, and include participatory activities that can be completed in a limited time with readily available materials. The emphasis is on process rather than product, and the quiet activities require little explanation or supervisory intervention. Installations are the responsibility of the Hands On coordinator who consults with the staff of Elementary Level Programs. Such concepts as color, contrasts, portraiture, sculpture, line, and real and imaginary have been explored, and THE STAGE in Hands On complemented the gallery's HOCKNEY PAINTS THE STAGE exhibition. Hands On does not have its own staff but is one part of the programming offered by the Education Department. One full-time education officer acts as coordinator, and 4 part-time education officers, whose primary responsibility is to conduct school tours, supervise the Hands On program on a rotating basis. Hands On is open during the academic year most Sunday afternoons 1:00–4:00, in the summer months Tuesday through Saturday 11:00–4:00, and special programs are offered during school breaks. To prevent overcrowding, no more than 30 are permitted at each hourly session. Tickets are issued on a first-come, first-serve basis. Fifty percent of the visitors are K–2nd grade, 25 percent pre-K, and 25 percent 3rd–6th grade. Annual attendance is 8,500. Until June 1985 support for Hands On came from the Elementary Education Department's operational budget. In June 1985 a grant was received from a corporate donor exclusively to maintain Hands On for 1 year.

Hands On! (Toronto: Art Gallery of Ontario, [1983]), Portfolio; "Hands On Program," *The Gallery* 6, no. 8 (October 1984): 2.

ROYAL ONTARIO MUSEUM (ROM), 100 Queen's Park, Toronto, Ontario M5S 2C6. The Discovery Gallery, which opened in the summer of 1983, reinforces the museum's theme, "Mankind Discovering," and brings the visitor in closer contact with the museum's collections. ROM's original Discovery Room opened in July 1977 on an experimental basis and was used until the building closed for renovation 3 years later. The new Discovery Gallery is considerably larger, 2,765 square feet exclusive of storage and office space, but continues the intent of the original facility. It too is a place where visitors can explore, in an informal atmosphere, authentic specimens and artifacts which come from the museum's 19 science, archaeology, and art departments. A Touch Wall located outside the gallery entrance has tactile surfaces which provide an introduction to the gallery, and one square provides a description of the area in braille. Inside, Discovery Boxes, approximately 50 in number, provide visitors with an opportunity for independent learning and also refer to more extensive collections found elsewhere in the museum. Ten thematic Work Stations, an expansion of the Discovery Box, provide more sophisticated and challenging material in a setup similar to a study carrel. Intriguing objects are scattered about the gallery; a forest environment is created by the Discovery Trail; and identification drawers enable visitors to identify specimens and artifacts from their own collections. A small reference library and support equipment, such as magnifying lenses, microscopes, and ultraviolet lamps, encourage study and examination. Texts and labels are available in English, French, and braille. From time to time new material and displays are added or Discovery Boxes withdrawn for repair or revision. Children under 6 are not permitted in the Discovery Gallery, but discovery baskets and the Touch Wall are provided for them just outside the Gallery. Twenty-five visitors are admitted at a time, with the average stay lasting about a half hour. The room serves many age groups and provides an opportunity for both individual discovery and a shared learning experience, particularly between adults and children. During the peak seasons and weekends the average daily attendance is 200. The room is operated by a full-time coordinator, an assistant, 10 part-time weekend supervisors, and 80 volunteers. From time to time, students at various levels of education (secondary school and university) carry out projects for the Discovery Gallery as part of their course work. The general admission charge for the museum includes admission to Discovery Gallery. Groups may reserve the room weekday mornings, except Mondays, from 10:00 to 11:30, September through June. The room is open to the public 12:00–4:00 weekdays, September through June, 11:00–4:00 July and August, and weekends and holidays 1:00–5:00.

"Drawings That Trace History's Evidence," *Globe and Mail* 8 June 1985, sec. E, p. 16; Frances MacArthur, "The Discovery Gallery," *Rotunda* 16, no. 3 (Fall 1983): 16; "Museum Hopping in Toronto," *New York Times* 8 July 1984, sec. 10, pp. 9, 36; Royal Ontario Museum, *Hands On: Setting Up a Discovery Room in Your Museum or School* (Toronto: Royal Ontario Museum, 1979); Royal Ontario Museum, *Mankind Discovering*, vol. 2: *Evaluations for Planning* (Toronto: Royal Ontario Museum, 1979), pp. 5, 48–49, 106, 124–25, 127, 129, 131, 133, 134, 136–37, 187; Royal Ontario Museum, "A Teacher's Guide to the Discovery Gallery," Toronto, September 1985 (Mimeographed); Bette Shepherd, "Mankind Discovering: The Royal Ontario Museum's Discovery Room," *Rotunda* 10, no. 3 (Fall 1977): 2–3.

QUEBEC

Granby

GRANBY ZOO, 347 rue Bourget, Granby, Quebec J2G 1E8. The Little Farm opened in 1953 and occupies 2 of the zoo's 45 developed acres. Children may pet and feed farm animals or watch small creatures such as guinea pigs, rabbits, and weasels. Some animals in the children's area, such as a goat, rabbit, or donkey, are included in the zoo's adopt-an-animal program. One staff person supervises the area. The zoo is open from May to October 10:00–6:00. There is an admission charge, and group rates are available. Approximately 250,000 people visit the children's zoo each year.

"Communiqué: Adopt an Animal from the Granby Zoo," Granby, Granby Zoo, n.d. (Typewritten); "Communiqué: The Granby Zoo: A Child's Paradise," Granby, Granby Zoo, n.d. (Typewritten).

SASKATCHEWAN

Regina

MUSEUM OF NATURAL HISTORY, Wascana Park, Regina, Saskatchewan S4P 3V7. The Discovery Room, opened in 1983, was developed to provide children with direct tactile experiences with natural history materials that previously could only be observed. The museum's Tactile Aids room was available only to Regina Public Schools, but the Discovery Room is more extensive in both audience and content. The room is located in an area separate from the galleries and concentrates on providing programs to schools related to the curriculum. Fifteen students can use the room at one time, and museum staff members and trained volunteers are available to present any of 8 programs, each lasting about 30 minutes. Though these programs will change, they currently focus on winter survival tactics of Saskatchewan's birds and animals, the interdependence of marsh life, Saskatchewan dinosaurs, Plains Indian life-styles, and the Ice Age. Gallery guides and in-class study suggestions are mailed to the teacher when a tour is booked. Discovery Room programs are usually completely booked from October through June. In the summer Discovery Room programs concentrate on 2-week sessions called "Summer School for Kids." Admission is free.

"Children Get Feel for Museum Animals," *Star-Phoenix*, 10 September 1983, sec. D, p. 8; "Museum Profiles" and "Profils de musée," *Muse* 1, no. 1 (Spring/April 1983): 6–7.

FEDERAL REPUBLIC OF GERMANY

BERLIN

MUSEUM FÜR VÖLKERKUNDE (Museum for Ethnology), Arnimallee 27, 1000 Berlin 33–Dahlem. The Junior Museum (entrance Lansstrasse 8) opened in October 1970 and occupies 2 rooms, an exhibition area and a workroom, with 131 square meters of space. The facility was developed to confront children with other cultures and stimulate curiosity about ethnological questions. The idea for a junior museum resulted from a trip by Dr. Brigitte Menzel and her observations and appreciation of museum education departments in the United States. Since its inception the Junior Museum has installed 13 exhibitions including UNKNOWN INDIANS, HUNTING WITHOUT WEAPONS, PRAIRIE INDIANS, OTHER PEOPLE—OTHER CLOTHING, COLUMBUS, CORTES, AND PIZARRO: ERA OF DISCOVERY, and EVERYDAY LIFE FOR CHILDREN IN THE 3rd WORLD. The exhibition material comes from the other departments within the museum. Detailed information sheets for school children are developed, and another series is prepared for teachers. In May 1972 a support group including museum staff members formed to develop programs for disadvantaged children. The Junior Museum is open Tuesday through Sunday 9:00–5:00 with morning hours reserved for schoolchildren. Admission is free. There is a staff of 2, and the Junior Museum has approximately 32,000 visitors annually.

Peter Leo Kolb, *Das Kindermuseum in den USA: Tatsachen, Deutungen und Vermittlungsmethoden* (Frankfurt am Main: Haag and Herchen, 1983), pp. 290–94; Dharma Prakash and Ina Tautorat, "Kinderalltag in der 3. Welt und Bei Uns," *Berliner Museen*

(Beiheft 1983): 16–18; Jürgen Richter, "Das Junior Museum und Blindenmuseum im Museum für Völkerkunde," *Baessler-Archiv* (Neue Folge) 21 (1973): 385–93.

KARLSRUHE

STAATLICHE KUNSTHALLE KARLSRUHE (State Art Museum Karlsruhe), Hans-Thoma-Strasse 2, 7500 Karlsruhe 1. The Kindermuseum, established in 1973, occupies 300 square meters of gallery space in the State Art Museum. As part of the Department of Museum Education and Public Programs, the 6 professional staff members work in both the Kindermuseum and with the educational activities planned for other audiences. The exhibitions change about once a year and have taken various forms and themes, but each is planned to appeal to an audience of 5–14 year olds and includes hands-on activities. Some of the previous installations have included MUSEUMS ARE FUN—GREAT ART FOR LITTLE PEOPLE, CHILDREN SEE AND BUILD CITIES, HODGEPODGE—WHAT CHILDREN COLLECT, HERCULES AND SUPERMAN, FELIX KNITS AND KATRIN KICKS, DRAGONS THAT CRY AND LAUGH, PUPPET THEATERS AND PUPPETEERS, and KARLSRUHE CHILDREN IN THE THIRD REICH. There have been exhibit catalogs for most of the Kindermuseum installations. Tours for school classes are conducted during the first weeks of a new exhibition, and there are also tours to the other museum galleries. There is no admission fee; children may come alone, in groups, or with their families, but groups must arrange for their visit in advance. About 20 other staff members do the direct teaching in workshops held in an area separate from the gallery. The activities are related to the exhibits, which change every 3 months, and workshops meet weekly for a 1-hour session. The morning workshop hours are for kindergarten and special school classes, afternoons for school-age classes, and evening sessions are held for youth over 14 and adults. Established in 1969, the children's painting studio (150 square meters) is the oldest activity for children offered by the museum. Professional staff members are paid by the museum, while other staff members are supported by course fees, donations, and state subsidy. Additional support comes from a private foundation, Association for the Advancement of Youth in Museums, established in 1976. Since its inception the Kindermuseum has been under the direction of Anne Reuter-Rautenberg. Last year there were approximately 43,000 visitors.

Heide Grape-Albers and Anne Reuter-Rautenberg, "Staatliche Kunsthalle Karlsruhe: Kinder in der Kunsthalle," *Kunst und Unterricht* (Sonderheft 1976): 96–97; Peter Leo Kolb, *Das Kindermuseum in den USA: Tatsachen, Deutungen und Vermittlungsmethoden* (Frankfurt am Main: Haag and Herchen, 1983), pp. 304–19; Gert Reising, "Bilder behinderter Kinder: Erfahrungen mit einem Kurs und einer Ausstellung im Karlsruher

Kindermuseum," *Zeitschrift für Kunstpädagogik* 6 (1982): 54–57; Anneliese Reuter-Rautenberg, "Ein Kindermuseum in einer Gelmäldegalerie," *Museumskunde* 43, no. 3 (1978): 146–47; Staatliche Kunsthalle Karlsruhe, *Informationen zur Museumspädgogik* (Karlsruhe: Staatliche Kunsthalle Karlsruhe, 1983).

FRANCE

PARIS

CITÉ DES SCIENCES ET DES INDUSTRIES (City of Sciences and Industries), La Villette, 211, avenue Jean Jaurès, 75930 Paris. The Inventorium, opened in March 1986, is a 2,000-square-meter section especially for children in the new Cité des Sciences at La Villette. The facility offers a Small Children's Room for 3–6 year olds and Discovery Rooms for 6–12 year olds. Encompassing both science and technology, the Inventorium includes a broad range of subjects selected to appeal to children, and parents are encouraged to participate. There are interactive exhibits, workshops, and activities (animations) directed by a museum staff member. In addition, a resource center contains films, slides, books, and drawers with collections and activity cards. Three workshops offering activities to schools and other groups are available. At the opening there was a staff of approximately 20, but this is subject to change. The Inventorium is open to children 3–12 and adults who are accompanied by children. Initially the museum was open 2:00–7:00, but the hours were extended beginning in September 1986 to include morning hours. Support for the Inventorium comes from the government.

André Lebeau, "The Overall Conception of the National Museum of Science and Industry of La Villette," Paris, 8 December 1980, p. 3 (Typewritten); "French Center Is Dedicated to Science," *New York Times*, 29 April 1986, p. 16; "Les salles de découvertes," *Le Courrier de La Villette* 1 (December 1982): 5; "Science and Industry City," *ICOM News* 39, no. 1 (1986): 12–13.

GERMAN
DEMOCRATIC
REPUBLIC

BODE MUSEUM, Bodestrasse 1–3 (entance Monbijoubrucke), 1020 Berlin. The Kindergalerie of the State Museums at Berlin opened in May 1974 in the Altes Museum. In 1984 it was relocated in the Bode Museum and occupies 3 rooms on the 2nd floor with 70 square meters of space for exhibits and activities. Designed primarily for children between the ages of 5 and 10, the Kindergalerie was cooperatively developed by the National Gallery and the Museum Education Department to stimulate children's interest in art and foster pleasure from museum visits. Various exhibitions and programs oriented to the school curriculum are offered to appeal to different age levels. Children observe and interpret original works of art and then carry out creative activities. To acquaint children with the various museum departments there are small, special exhibits in the Kindergalerie, and visits may be taken to the permanent installations in the State Museums. The gallery can be used for teaching-related programs in aesthetic appreciation conducted by youth clubs and organizations. The staff of the Museum Education Department is responsible for the exhibitions and activities in the Kindergalerie. There have been over 25 thematic installations or exhibits of children's work in the Kindergalerie. These have included ANIMALS IN THE MUSEUM (animals from different collections of the State Museums), ON THE TRAIL OF THE ALCHEMIST, TOYS, PICTURES IN BOOKS, WHO IS PRETTY?, MY MUSEUM, GALLERY OF THE YOUNGEST CHILDREN (art by young children), and PINOCCHIO AND HIS FRIENDS. Catalogs have been prepared for some Kindergalerie installations. All the materials for the creative activities are provided by the museum. Groups must make appointments in advance; the maximum group size is 15; and usually 2 sessions are held per day, Wednesday through Friday. The Kindergalerie is open Wednesday through Sunday from 9:00 to 6:00 and has approximately 5,000 visitors annually.

Ruth Göres, "Fünf Jahre Kindergalerie der Staatliche Museen zu Berlin," *Neue Museumskunde* 23, no. 2 (1980): 100–08; *Die Kindergalerie im Alten Museum* (Berlin: Staatliche Museum zu Berlin, Abt. Museumspädagogik, 1976); Office of Museum Programs, Smithsonian Institution, *Proceedings of the Children in Museums International Symposium* [1979] (Washington, D.C.: Smithsonian Institution, 1982), pp. 217–19; Annerose Wittenberg, *Mit Kindern in der Bildergalerie: Ein Museumsführer fur Eltern und Erzieher* (Berlin: Volk und Wissen Volkseigener, 1983).

_ GREAT BRITAIN _

LANCASTER

JUDGES' LODGINGS MUSEUM OF CHILDHOOD, Church Street, Lancaster, LA1 1YS. The museum was established in 1976 after the County Museum Service bought a doll collection previously in private hands. A 17th-century building owned by the Lancashire County Council houses the 6-room Museum of Childhood on the top floor, and another collection is displayed on the first floor. Interested in all aspects of childhood in Lancashire, the museum collects and displays material on education, recreation, and child labor. There are over 1,000 dolls from the 18th century to the present day, a collection of school items, and some toys, clothing, and furniture. The photographic archive of regional childhood history is growing. The museum rooms include a bedroom of a well-to-do child, the day nursery which is a combination playroom and classroom, the doll exhibit, the c. 1900 schoolroom, and an exhibit room with various items connected with childhood. On the landing at the top of the stairs is a doll house with which children may play. There are no guided tours for school groups, but the information sheets for teachers on Victorian childhood and education provide background material, suggest lessons, and include a bibliography. A simple worksheet for children has also been prepared. Although all groups may sit in the desks and use the slates, it is sometimes possible by prior arrangement to conduct a lesson in the Victorian schoolroom. Groups must be limited to no more than 30 with 1 adult for each 15 children. Larger groups may split into smaller units, one visiting the museum and the other another attraction. There is a small admission with reduced rates given for groups of 25 or more booking in advance. During April, May, June, and October the museum is open 2:00–5:00 Monday through Friday. From July through September the hours are 10:30–1:00 and 2:00–5:00 weekdays and 2:00–5:00 weekends. A staff of 3 is assisted by 4 seasonal attendants. The Museum of Childhood has approximately 10,000 visitors a year. Support comes from admissions and the Lancashire County Council.

John Blundell and Edith Tyson, "Lancaster—A Museum Growth Area," *Museums Journal* 77, no. 1 (June 1977): 23–24; "Information for Teachers," Lancaster, Judges' Lodgings Museum, n.d. (Typewritten); "Judges' Lodgings, Lancaster: Gillow & Town House Museum/Museum of Childhood," Lancaster Judges' Lodgings, n.d. (Typewritten).

LONDON

BETHNAL GREEN MUSEUM OF CHILDHOOD, Cambridge Heath Road, London E2 9PA. Opened in 1872 as a branch of the South Kensington Museum, later the Victoria and Albert Museum, the museum's initial mission was to take some part of the national heritage to London's poorer side. Its first activities for children were organized in 1915. In 1923 the first Children's Exhibition was held, and out of this grew the permanent Children's Section. Gradually enlarged due to the interest of Queen Mary, it became the predominant part of the museum and in 1974 was renamed the Bethnal Green Museum of Childhood. As a branch of the Victoria and Albert Museum, it concentrates on the artifacts related to childhood. The largest collection is of dolls and toys, with other major holdings in children's dress and children's books. The history of toys as objects of design was the primary emphasis of the collection, and the social significance of toys was of lesser importance. The current priority is in displaying the collection. One gallery was completed in the late 1970s, and 2 others have just been rearranged. The collection of children's dress is being expanded to include nursery furniture, perambulators, and related material including graphics. In some recently vacated space, exhibits on children at home, in school, and at work will be installed. A large collection of children's books was given to the museum in 1970, and in the future they will be used to establish a research library and provide material for regular gallery and special exhibitions. The Education Department of the Victoria and Albert concentrates its children's activities at Bethnal Green. There are changing exhibits, workshops open to all children in the Art Room at 11:00 and 2:00 every Saturday, and special events in the summer, at Christmas, and at Easter. School groups can arrange for project mornings and special talks, but they do not need a reservation just to visit the museum. Teachers' packs are available. Bethnal Green has 8 curatorial staff members, 16 warders, 11 support staff members, 1 part-time educational officer who is on the staff of the Educational Department of the Victoria and Albert, and 1 volunteer. The museum is open Monday through Thursday and Saturday 10:00–6:00, Sundays 2:30–6:00, and closed Fridays and major holidays. As a branch of the Victoria and Albert Museum, it receives support from the government through the Office of Arts and Libraries. The Bethnal Green Museum of Childhood has approximately 6,000 visitors a week.

Bethnal Green Museum of Childhood Guide/Souvenir (London: Victoria & Albert Press, n.d.); "The Function of the Museum" [London: The Bethnal Green Museum of Childhood], July 1983 (Typewritten); "A London Wonderland: The Museum of Childhood Overflows with Period Toys," *New York Times*, 8 January 1984, sec. 10, pp. 9, 39; "Why Sir Derek Thinks the Toys May Have To Be Put Away for Good," *Times Educational Supplement* (London), no. 3447, 23 July 1982, p. 6.

SCIENCE MUSEUM, South Kensington, London SW7 2DD. The Children's Gallery, which opened on 12 December 1931, will be supplemented by Launch Pad in 1986. The new 1,000-square-meter area will take over and expand the role of the original gallery, which was unique when it opened in the basement of the museum. Models illustrated particular processes; there were push-button demonstrations; subjects were treated historically rather than as isolated achievements or events; a series of dioramas dealt with the evolution of transport; and a set of transparencies traced the evolution of medicine, astronomy, and human flight. Even though the Children's Gallery was intended for younger visitors, it was immediately appealing to adults. The major goal of the new gallery is to introduce young people to science and technology through exploration and experimentation with an emphasis on making learning fun. The design of the 100 to 150 fully interactive exhibits will focus on how and why things work. Three special types of exhibits will be playground-style displays allowing visitors to climb onto or into them, sets of take-apart and reassemble exhibits illustrating mechanisms, and a microcenter with computers and microprocessors. Explainers, who are full-time museum staff members, will always be available in the gallery to help run the exhibits and provide encouragement or information in a personal, informal way. Launch Pad is viewed as an experimental venture which will develop through experience and may eventually outgrow this location and move into a permanent, independent facility of its own. The exhibits are being designed with this in mind. Not only will this new gallery be well suited for young children, but it will appeal to visitors of all ages, levels, and backgrounds. The total staffing for Launch Pad will be about 11. Though the Science Museum is government-funded, additional support from grants and sponsorships has been obtained for Launch Pad. There is no admission charge to visit the museum.

"The Children's Gallery in the London Science Museum," *School and Society* 34, no. 887 (26 December 1931): 863–64; "The Children's Gallery at the Science Museum," *Museums Journal* 31, no. 10 (January 1932): 442–44; "A Children's Gallery in the South Kensington Museum," *School and Society* 32, no. 823 (4 October 1930): 447–48; Pam Gillies and Anthony Wilson, "Participatory Exhibits: Is Fun Educational?" *Museums Journal* 82, no. 3 (December 1982): 131–34; *Launch Pad* (London: The Science Museum, n.d.); *Launch Pad Information Sheet* no. 2 (London: Science Museum, April 1985);

Barbara R. Winstanley, *Children and Museums* (Oxford: Basil Blackwell & Mott, 1967), pp. 23–24.

PETERBOROUGH

LILFORD PARK, Nr. Oundle, Peterborough PE8 5SG. The Children's Farm was built in 1972 when the present Lord Lilford decided to reestablish a collection of animals in the park. The Lilford aviaries, created in the 1860s, were restored when the 280-acre park was developed. The farm includes ponies, pygmy goats, sheep, pigs, calves, rabbits, ducks, guinea pigs, and other domestic animals. There is a special emphasis on close contact with young animals. The aviaries have been restocked with native and exotic birds and include birds of prey, a 10-acre flamingo pen with other waterfowl, and owl aviaries; other birds are displayed inside a walled garden. There is an adventure playground with a large tree house. The park is suitable for school tours and other groups, and a variety of special events are held there. In 1983 craft workshops were opened, providing permanent space for a variety of artisans, and their shops are open to the public several times a week. There is a staff of 3. The park is open daily 10:00–6:00 and has about 80,000 visitors a year.

Lilford Park (Peterborough: Lilford Hall Ltd., [1984]).

INDIA

AMRELI

SHRI GIRDHARBHAI CHILDREN'S MUSEUM, Bal Bhavan, Amreli–364 601 (Gujarat State). The museum, founded on 1 April 1955, serves as an educational, cultural, and community center for the area. It is housed in the Rang Mahal building built in 1835 and situated in a spacious natural setting. The collection includes local antiquities, natural history and botanical specimens, and toys from other countries. There are also a children's zoo and planetarium. The galleries encompass the arts, archaeology, stamps, transportation, science, and famous people. There are special exhibitions and holiday installations, guided tours, lecture series and demonstrations, films, musical and meet-the-artist programs, and field study of local birds, plants, and the environment. Posters are circulated to the district schools, and extension projects are sent to rural areas. The museum holds interschool debate competitions and annual essay contests for primary and secondary school students concerning the museum galleries and exhibitions. Visits to historical sites are also sponsored. The Friends of the Museum Association helps guide children in various hobbies by sponsoring clubs for astronomy, painting, music, and natural science. The staff includes a director, curator of astronomy, educational officer, artist, workshop teachers, and attendants. Hours are 9:00–12:00 and 3:30–6:00 daily. The museum is supported by a grant from the state government and rent from the shopping center. There are 104,100 visitors a year.

B. S. Ranga, "Children's Museum in India—Its Scope and Functions," *Journal of Indian Museums* 36 (1980): 70.

CALCUTTA

NEHRU CHILDREN'S MUSEUM, National Cultural Association, 94/1 Chowringhee Road, Calcutta–700020. The museum opened in November 1972 to provide children with opportunities beyond the routine academic curriculum, transmit cultural heritage, and promote an awareness of modern science and the need for world unity. The state government leased a plot of land to the National Cultural Association, and funds for the 6-story, 18,000-square-foot building were provided by the government. The initial collection included dolls and toys donated by 62 countries, scientific models and equipment purchased with money provided by UNESCO, and working models donated by the government and industry. The first 4 floors are reserved for exhibitions with the doll gallery occupying 1,000 square feet, the models 4,000 square feet, the science gallery 2,300 square feet, history told through miniature models, and a variety of changing exhibits. The 5th and 6th floors are used for the various activities in the fine arts, performing arts, science, and a small children's library. Children are encouraged to enhance their skills through various classes and workshops, and every year the museum organizes contests in science and the fine and performing arts. TV and closed circuit TV are used, and films and slides are shown. Since the mid–1970s exhibitions to popularize science and stimulate an interest in scientific inquiry have been organized in collaboration with the Ministry of Education. Special efforts are made to get teachers and village children to participate. The museum also sponsors "Learn-to-Together" camps every year. There are 8 gallery staff members, 7 office people, 18 instructors, 6 maintenance workers, and 9 volunteers. The museum is open 11:00–7:00 daily except Monday. Over 3.2 million people have visited the museum since it opened, and 60 percent of these visitors were children. Support comes from government grants, the sale of tickets, and donations.

A. N. Bose, "India," in "Out-of-School Science Education in Asia and the Pacific," *Bulletin of the UNESCO Regional Office for Education in Asia and the Pacific*, Special Issue (Bangkok: UNESCO, 1982), p. 62: ERIC Document Reproduction Service, ED 226 989; *Nehru Children's Museum: A Prospective of History and Activities—1946–1980* (Calcutta: The National Cultural Association, [1980]).

LUCKNOW

CHILDREN'S MUSEUM, Motilal Nehru Marg, Lucknow–1. The museum was established in October 1957 at the urging of the Minister of State, Shri Chandra Bhanu Gupta, who believed children between the ages of 5 and 14 would benefit from museum galleries and informal classes and clubs. Beginning with only 2 small galleries, it now has 14 exhibition areas for permanent and temporary displays covering 2,323.52 square meters. The collection contains about 20,000 objects, including paintings, sculptures, geological specimens, and cultural artifacts. The permanent galleries focus on Indian culture, Buddha, foreign cultures, life in prehistoric times, geology, under the sea, man on the moon, the military, health, and the popular sciences with a new environmental study gallery. The temporary exhibits vary and are built to reflect the needs and interests of the children and the community. There is a big playground for outdoor games, and sometimes it is also used for setting up temporary large-scale special exhibitions. Adjacent to the museum there is a well-equipped auditorium which is available when needed. In addition, the museum has one of the largest children's libraries in the country, with more than 50,000 juvenile titles in the 4 leading languages of India. It also runs 12 mobile library centers for children. The museum conducts guided tours and talks, presents slide lectures, and children's movies. There are also after-school classes in the arts, hobbies and handcrafts, dolls and puppetry, movement and dance, music, sports and games, and judo-karate. Discovery Boxes for children/parents and loan boxes for the schools up to grade 10 are being developed. Training and refresher courses for child welfare workers are also held here. A staff of 8 is assisted occasionally by volunteers. The museum is open 10:30–5:30 daily except Mondays and public holidays and has about 350 to 400 visitors daily. Admission is free. The primary support for the Children's Museum comes from the Motilal Memorial Society with additional funding coming from donations, endowments, and government grants.

B. S. Ranga, "Children's Museum in India—Its Scope and Functions," *Journal of Indian Museums* 36 (1980): 70.

MADRAS

GOVERNMENT MUSEUM, Egmore, Madras–8. The Children's Gallery, opened to the public on 14 November 1960, was originally located on the mezzanine floor of the Geology Gallery. Its initial exhibits were displayed in 15 specially built cases and included models, dioramas, specimens, and other materials of interest to children. When a new building for the Bird Gallery was constructed in 1963, the Children's Gallery was transferred to this building and set up on the first floor. The 88-by-11½-foot gallery contains about 24 exhibits, including the solar system, prehistoric animals, classification and physiology of plants and animals, and minerals. It also includes the story of transportation, working models of trains, a telephone, a rocket, dolls showing Indian dances, and dolls in costumes of India and other countries. Tours and lecture demonstrations are conducted for schoolchildren of all ages. The curator of zoology is currently in charge of the Children's Gallery. It is open 8:00–5:00 daily and has about 1,500 visitors a day. Support comes from the State Government of Tamilnadu. A new building for the Children's Museum is nearing completion, and the 40-by-13.6-meter, 2-story facility will open early in 1986. Initially a costume dolls gallery and a history gallery will be set up. To be developed at a later date are galleries for natural history and the physical sciences. There will also be activity and hobby rooms for children.

B. S. Ranga, "Children's Museum in India—Its Scope and Functions," *Journal of Indian Museums* 36 (1980): 70; S. T. Satyamurti, "The Children's Gallery of the Madras Government Museum," *Studies in Museology* 6–8 (1970–72): 74–80; S. T. Satyamurti, "Modernization of the Madras Museum," *Curator* 9, no. 1 (March 1966): 71, 78.

NEW DELHI

NATIONAL CHILDREN'S MUSEUM, Bal Bhavan Society, Kotla Road, New Delhi–2. The museum, founded in 1961, was established to organize exhibits for and about children and to display their creative work. It is the major component of a complex named Bal Bhavan. A new 3-story building, with about 48,000 square feet of space, is now being built which will have exhibit galleries and work studios for children. The museum collects objects, artifacts, and specimens in all categories, with the main consideration being that they show promise, immediate or future, of being utilized in exhibitions designed for children. The collection includes more than 1,500 dolls, toys, sculptures, paintings, models, replicas, and photographs. The schools are intimately connected with the museum, as exhibitions are planned which relate to the curriculum, study kits are designed for classroom use, and schools visit the galleries. Every year there are usually 5 thematic exhibits from the sciences and humanities and about 800 study kits loaned to the schools by the school services program. A museum techniques club provides an opportunity for children to study objects, integrate subject matter, and develop skills related to exhibit preparation, such as modeling, making molds, casting metal, fiber glass, taxidermy, and script writing. There is a professional staff of 6. Every month about 4,000 children, 2,300 adults, and 10 school classes visit exhibitions. The museum is open 9:00–5:00 daily, admission is free, and support comes from the Ministry of Education.

Kenneth Hudson, *Museums for the 1980s: A Survey of World Trends* (New York: Holmes & Meier, 1977), p. 101; Renée Marcousé, "Changing Museum in a Changing World," in *Museums, Imagination and Education* (Paris: UNESCO, 1973), pp. 20–21; B. S. Ranga, "Children's Museum in India—Its Scope and Functions," *Journal of Indian Museums* 36 (1980): 71; Prabha Sahasrabudhe, *A Children's Museum for India* (Baroda: University of Baroda Press, 1965), p. 35.

NATIONAL MUSEUM OF NATURAL HISTORY, FICCI Museum Building, Barakhamba Road, New Delhi–110 001. The Discovery Room opened in 1979, the International Year of the Child, to provide an opportunity for hands-on informal learning. There are several Discovery Boxes which contain a variety of natural history specimens and question cards. Microscopes and lenses are available; there are scientific instruments for simple experiments and a small library corner. In another area children may model, paint, or do other creative activities. Aquariums, live birds, and small mammals provide an opportunity for direct contact with living things. Special 2-hour programs for the blind were initiated shortly after the museum opened and are conducted every month. Up to 30 children at a time visit the gallery and use the Discovery Room, which has braille scripts and embossed materials. To provide individual attention, the child-to-staff ratio is kept at 2 to 1. Pre-visit materials for classes are available, and the museum has published a variety of nature study and environmental education books and project kits for children. The Discovery Room is open 10:30–12:00 and 2:00–3:30 weekdays except Mondays, and 10:00–1:00 and 2:00–5:00 on weekends. There is no admission charge. Last year about 30,000 visitors used the room. The museum is fully funded by the government of India and was established in 1978 to promote an increased appreciation and understanding of the natural environment.

S. M. Nair, "The Museum and the Child in the United States and India," *Museum* [UNESCO] 31, no. 3 (1979): 164–67; S. M. Nair, "Special Programmes for Blind Children at the National Museum of Natural History, New Delhi," *Museum* [UNESCO] 33, no. 3 (1981): 174–75; *The Discovery Room—Where Learning Can Be Fun!* (New Delhi: National Museum of Natural History, n.d.).

ISRAEL

JERUSALEM

THE ISRAEL MUSEUM, PO Box 1299, 91012 Jerusalem. The Ruth Youth Wing opened in 1978 and is the successor to the museum's Youth Wing which opened in May 1966. The programs and services offered in the new wing—special exhibitions for youth, guided tours, and classes—are not different from those in the earlier facility, but they cater to a wider age range, are more varied, and incorporate the active involvement of the visitor. All of the activities which take place here continue to fulfill the Youth Wing's original purpose of educating all young people, not just the artistically talented. The Ruth Wing is about 4 times larger than the original facility and occupies 3,600 square meters, or 8 percent of the total museum area. This includes 500 square meters of exhibition space, 10 studios, an auditorium, teachers' orientation center, traveling exhibits department, recycling room, and a library. The Youth Wing collects toys and ethnographic materials connected to the child's world, and the museum educator has access to original works of art. There are 2 or 3 expository exhibits annually which focus on art, archaeology, ethnography, and the child's world and their needs. All shows have elements which require both the observation and the active participation of the visitor, and many have opportunities for creative expression. In planning exhibits the Youth Wing tries to design exhibits which will not only interest children but will also have the potential to be family-oriented learning experiences. The 10–14 year olds comprise the largest group of visitors. They usually come alone, or with siblings or friends, and only 25 percent visit with parents. This age group is the target audience for the exhibitions, their activities and explanations. The 6–10 year olds are the next largest visitor group, and they usually come with older brothers and sisters or with parents. Research at the museum has suggested that children under 5 may benefit from areas and activities separate from those in the exhibition. In addition, annually there are guided tours for approximately 2,000 classes, about 100 art classes for children 6 to 18, services for teachers, and 35 courses for adults. About 500 children per week attend performances or films. Children's books on art and archaeology are published in Hebrew, Arabic, and English. Thirty-five thousand children carry a Youth Wing membership card. Ayala Gordon has been chief curator since its inception; there are 6 other full-time staff members, about 60 part-time teachers, and only a few volunteers. The working hours of the Youth Wing extend beyond those of the museum. Three days a week the Youth Wing is open from 8:30 a.m. to 10:00 p.m. and from 8:30 a.m. to 5:30 p.m. other days. The Ruth Wing receives financial support from the museum, student payments, and municipal and governmental sources.

Ayala Gordon, "The Exploration Route in an Exhibition: A New Follow-up Technique Employed in the Ruth Youth Wing," *Israel Museum News* 1 (1982): 79–90; Ayala Gordon, "Ten Years of Work in the Youth Wing," *Israel Museum Journal* 11 (1976): 27–34; reprinted as "Ten Years of Work in the Israel Museum Youth Wing," *ICOM Education* (1975/76): 42–44, and "Dix ans de travail à l'Aile des jeunes du Musée d'Israël," ibid, pp. 45–47; Ayala Gordon, "The Youth Wing of the Israel Museum," *Museum* [UNESCO] 20, no. 1 (1967): 28–30, and "Le Pavillon des jeunes du Musée d' Israël," ibid, pp. 30–33; Israel Shenker, "Ayala Gordon and the Youth Wing," *Art News* 85, no. 4 (April 1985): 101–06; Yocheved Weinfeld, "An Experiment in Art Teaching with High School Students at the Youth Wing," *Israel Museum News* 13 (1978): 21–31.

___ JAPAN ___

HIMEJI

HIMEJI CITY AQUARIUM, Nobusue, Tegarayama, Himeji City 670. The Touch Tank, opened on 28 March 1981, was built by the aquarium to offer direct contact experiences with animals. This facility was developed as a direct response to experiences with 11- and 12-year-old children participating in a summer program who were distressed to handle animals. Though a touch tank had been considered before, it had not been attempted due to the difficulty in maintaining such exhibits. But this problem seemed to be outweighed by the need to provide children an opportunity to discover nature through the contact that increased urbanization has made more difficult. Facilities in the United States and Canada were visited during the planning stage. Installed in a separate 60-square-meter building, the tank at Himeji City is an ellipse measuring 4.15 by 2.55 by 0.46 meters and containing 3.8 cubic meters of seawater. The design of the facility was influenced by the need to have sides low enough so that children 3 and older could reach into the water without difficulty and animals could be touched as they moved about the tank; the interior should resemble a natural area with inaccessible hiding places out of the visitor's reach. An observation window was installed in the wall of the tank to give an alternative perspective on the activities of the animals. The number of species represented and the actual numbers of animals are more extensive than in many similar facilities. The wall behind the tank has graphic panels. On Sundays instructors explain how to handle and touch invertebrates, and during summer and winter vacations a special education program is offered for students. The staff includes

2 curators, 3 biologists, 2 keepers, and 4 assistants. Hours are 9:00–5:00 daily. The Himeji City Aquarium has 220,000 visitors a year. There is an admission fee, and support also comes from the Himeji Municipal Government.

Itaru Uchida and Mitsunori Asuke, "The Touch Tank at the Himeji City Aquarium," in *International Zoo Yearbook* 22 (1982): 271–76, ed. P.J.S. Olney (London: The Zoological Society of London, 1982).

HIROSHIMA

THE HIROSHIMA CITY CULTURE & SCIENCE MUSEUM FOR CHILDREN, 5–83 Moto-machi Nakaku, Hiroshima 730. In the early 1970s teachers, workers in social education, and citizens recognized the need for and undertook establishment of a children's museum as a project for the International Year of the Child. The building, opened on 1 May 1980, has 4 stories and 4,683 square meters of floor space. The 53 exhibits, most of which can be touched or operated by children, are designed to stimulate an interest in science and culture. They encompass city development, transportation, science in daily life, astronomy, and the measurement of physical strength. The museum provides leisure time activities and programs including use of the ham radio room, classes, clubs, concerts, plays, movies, and special exhibitions. In addition, there are Sunday and summer vacation parent/child classes for 3rd and 4th grade youth. The 345-seat planetarium is one of the largest in Japan, and a visit is part of the curriculum for 5th-grade students and those in the first year of the secondary school. Once the older students have a basic understanding of astronomy and have learned how to operate the planetarium's computer, they prepare their own show, which when completed is shown to the public. The staff, supported by volunteers, numbers 20. Support comes from the Hiroshima City Government. There is no admission fee for the museum, but there is a small fee for the planetarium unless it is part of the school curriculum. Visitors come from all over Japan and abroad; the museum has about 500,000 visitors a year and the planetarium 130,000. Approximately 70 percent of the visitors are younger than 14. The museum is open Tuesday through Sunday 9:00–5:00 and closed on Mondays. There are 4 or 5 planetarium shows daily with 1st and 2nd projection times during the weekdays sometimes reserved for school classes. The museum shares the building with the children's library.

A Guide to the Hiroshima City Culture and Science Museum for Children (Hiroshima City: Hiroshima City Culture and Science Museum for Children, n.d.); Hideo Ohashi, "Japan," in "Out-of-School Science Education in Asia and the Pacific," *Bulletin of the UNESCO Regional Office for Education in Asia and the Pacific*, Special Issue (Bangkok: UNESCO, 1982), pp. 90–91: ERIC Document Reproduction Service, ED 226 989; Takeshi Sato, "New Stars for Hiroshima," *Sky and Telescope* 61, no. 5 (May 1981): 392–93.

MORIOKA

MORIOKA CHILDREN'S MUSEUM OF SCIENCE, 13–1 Aza-Hebiyashiki Motomiya, Morioka, Iwate. Plans for the museum were initiated in 1979 during the International Year of the Child in response to the wishes of area children. The museum opened on 5 May 1983. There is a total floor space of 33,845 square feet, 27,225 of which is exhibit area and a planetarium. The 52 exhibits encompass optics, electronics, mechanics, and wave mechanics; and there are labs, classrooms, play tables, and a library. The 270-seat planetarium has a dome 18 meters in diameter. Classes in science and handcrafts are offered, and there is an inventors club. In addition, the museum offers special days for teachers. There are 6 technical and scientific staff members and 8 office workers. The museum is open Tuesday through Sunday 9:00–4:30 and closed Monday. The planetarium holds 5 shows on Sunday, and on the other days there are 4 showings with the 1st and 2nd projection times set aside for school classes. During the first 10 months the museum was open, there were 113,284 visitors to the exhibit halls and 91,689 who attended planetarium programs. There is a small admission. The science museum is municipally owned, operated and financed by the City of Morioka.

Morioka Children's Museum of Science (Morioka: The City of Morioka Children's Museum of Science, [1983]) (In Japanese).

SOTOME

SOTOME MUSEUM OF CHILD, 2749 Nishishustu-go, Sotome-cho, Nagasaki 7851–24. Opened on 31 March 1983, the museum is part of the municipal cultural village. It was developed to promote social education and give children an opportunity to grow intellectually and emotionally. One-third of the 813.43 square meters of floor space contains exhibits: water, solar, wind, and manpower as sources of energy; evolution; body development, including the nervous system and nutrition; TV and telephone learning booth; future of the town installation; children of the world map; and the island of coal mine. A robot, the museum's symbol, can guide visitors around. There is also a creative room for pottery and construction projects, a science room for experiments and an outdoor observation area, a laboratory, a children's theater to promote art and culture, and a library/ research room. Parents and children have a reading club. The museum is interested in exchanging toys and greetings with others around the world. The staff includes a director, a subdirector, a museum teacher, and a secretary. Hours are 9:00–5:00 Tuesday through Sunday and closed Monday, national holidays, and 29 December through 3 January. There is a small entrance fee, and the museum is municipally managed. Four thousand children 6–18 and 6,000 adults visit the museum each year. Future plans are to develop a nature center, botanical garden, and zoo.

Sotome Museum of Child (Sotome-cho Nagasaki: Sotome Museum of Child [1983]) (In Japanese).

TOKYO

NATIONAL SCIENCE MUSEUM (Kokuritsu Kagaku Hakubutsukan), Ueno Park, Tokyo. One section of the Discovery Room—a look, think, and try installation—opened in May 1985 and is about 800 square meters, half inside and half in the courtyard. The exhibit consists of 3 parts including the physical sciences (sound, light, magnets), natural history (life in the wood and plains, minerals, and fossils), and water (fall, spring, waterguns, watermills, and screwpumps). Children can observe or do various kinds of experiments and also have the opportunity to examine and touch stuffed animals and specimens of plants or minerals. Three to 6 instructors are available to answer questions and to give visitors advice about the exhibits. In the spring of 1986 a second section of 600 square meters was opened. The Discovery Room is open Tuesday through Saturday 9:00–12:00 for groups or school classes, 1:00–4:00 for individual visitors, and Sundays and holidays 9:00–4:00 to all visitors. There are from 5,000 to 6,000 visitors per month with an increase during summer vacations. In addition to the Discovery Room, there are regularly scheduled education activities on weekends for all age groups including child/parent classes. Children with similar interests are brought together in the Children's Center, where museum staff help them obtain information about classifying, studying, preparing, and exhibiting their collections.

Victor J. Danilov, "Discovery Rooms and Kidspaces: Museum Exhibits for Children," *Science and Children* 23, no. 4 (January 1986): 11; *Guide to the National Science Museum* (Tokyo: National Science Museum, 1982), pp. 42–43; "Outline of the National Science Museum 1877–1977," *Newsletter National Science Museum, Ueno Park, Tokyo* 10 (20 July 1977).

MEXICO

PARQUE ZOOLOGICO BENITO JUAREZ, APDO, Postal 92, C. P. 58000, Morelia, Michoacan. The Children's Zoo, founded in 1980, was developed to provide a special place to exhibit young animals. It also provides a setting to teach children and other visitors about animal care. The area, a little larger than half an acre, has become one of the most popular attractions of the zoo. There are 2 islands for baby monkeys, 4 indoor enclosures for baby cats, 10 pens for baby herbivores, 5 enclosures with controlled temperature, and a small fish pool. Animal breeding and raising of the young are studied in the children's zoo with a speciality in mammals and birds. Guided tours are given on an irregular basis, and sometimes food for feeding the animals is sold. Two keepers and 1 veterinarian are assisted by volunteers, usually teens at vacation time. The zoo is open 10:00–6:00 year round. Annual attendance is approximately 1,000,000, and almost all visitors come to the children's area. The zoo is government owned, and support comes from a subsidy and admissions.

THE
__NETHERLANDS__

AMSTERDAM

KINDERMUSEUM TM JUNIOR (Children's Museum TM Junior), Lin-
naeusstraat 2A, Amsterdam, Postcode 1092 CK. The Children's Museum TM
Junior, a department of the Royal Tropical Institute and Tropical Museum,
opened on 15 January 1975 and has 750 square meters of exhibition space. Its
special mission is to acquaint children from 6 to 12 with the Third World and
its relation to them. In order to have children utilize all their senses to experience
the exhibitions, it was felt that a separate children's area was needed. There are
semipermanent exhibits. By using a variety of techniques, including simulation
or drama which takes place in the museum "environment," children gain a
deeper understanding of cultural diversity. Prior to the museum visit, the school
classes work with their teachers for 2 months with educational materials prepared
by the staff of the children's museum. The schools receive booklets for the
children and a teachers manual which includes additional background information, stories, slide sets, and cassettes. Much of what is included corresponds to
what children will later experience at the museum. When groups come, the
teacher participates in the 3-hour program along with the children and museum
staff. Monday through Thursday 9:30–12:30 is reserved for school groups, and
there are also special programs for mentally or learning disabled students. Teacher
training colleges also come to the museum on weekdays to use the educational
materials and experience the stimulation. The museum is open to the general
public on weekends. Sunday afternoons and during holidays there are special
programs for children 6–12. There is a professional staff of 7 and approximately

25,000 visitors per year. TM Junior receives its financial support from the Ministry of Foreign Affairs and from donations.

Bernd Altgassen and Annette Matton, "Das Suriname-Project des Amsterdamer Tropenmuseums Junior," *Mitteilungen & Materialien der Arbeitsgruppe Pädagogisches Museum* 19 (1982): 28–52; Gerard Berlijn, "Bildungsarbeit am Amsterdamer Tropenmuseum," in *Museumspädagogik: Museen als Bildungsstätten*, ed. Wolfgang Klausewitz (Frankfurt am Main: Deutscher Museumsbund, 1975), pp. 75–84; H. de Boer, [Views on "Environmental Education"], Tropenmuseum, 26 September 1983 (Mimeographed); Henk Jan Gortzak, "The Museum, Children and the Third World," *Museum* [UNESCO] 33, no. 1 (1981): 51–56; Office of Museum Programs, Smithsonian Institution, *Proceedings of the Children in Museums International Symposium* [1979] (Washington, D.C.: Smithsonian Institution, 1982), pp. 66–67.

EINDHOVEN

EVOLUON, Noord Brabantlaan 1a, 5652 LA Eindhoven. Science Playground, formerly called Prelude to Technology, is a separate section of the science center designed for children. Opened on 24 September 1966, Evoluon was built by the industrial firm Philips on the occasion of its 75th anniversary. The 6,000-square-meter exhibition area is devoted to exploring how science and technology influence our daily lives. In Science Playground, which occupies probably no more than 5 percent of the total space, children come into contact with a variety of subjects and have a chance to explore scientific principles through active involvement. Like the other exhibition areas, the displays are continually updated, each lasting for probably no more than 5 to 7 years. Since the opening of the flying saucer–shaped building, there has been a special children's installation, and recently the 3rd total setup of Science Playground was completed. The staff of 40 is involved primarily with exhibit planning, design, and fabrication rather than a direct interpretive role. Presentations, labeling, and written materials are in multilingual format. Evoluon is open all year Monday through Friday 9:30–5:30, Saturday and Sunday 10:30–5:00, and closed Christmas and New Year's Day. Four hundred thousand visitors come to Evoluon annually. There is an admission charge, and the remaining support comes from Philips.

Victor J. Danilov, "European Science and Technology Museums," *Museum News* 54, no. 6 (July/August 1976): 71–72; Victor J. Danilov, *Science and Technology Centers* (Cambridge: MIT Press, 1982), pp. 6–7, 32, 36–37, 43, 140, 309–10; *Evoluon* (Eindhoven: Evoluon, 1985); *Evoluon* (Eindhoven: Evoluon, n.d.); John H. Wotiz, "Chemistry Museums of Europe," *Chemteck* 12, no. 4 (April 1982): 222, 226.

EMMEN

NOORDER DIERENPARK ZOO EMMEN, Hoofdstraat 18/Postbus 1010, 7801 BA Emmen. The zoo contains, among many other features, a children's zoo completely modernized in 1982. An educational theme lasting 2 years is planned by the zoo and is then carried out in its exhibitions, signs, and publications. Themes have included the senses, camouflage, and reproduction. The emphasis of the children's zoo is domestic animals. The collection includes cows, sheep, goats, rabbits, hamsters, chickens, pigs, pigeons, and parakeets. There are guided tours, demonstrations, and small exhibitions about keeping certain domestic animals such as hamsters, rabbits, and pigeons. The number of staff members varies, but the average is 4.

In the Museum of Natural History, which is intended for both adults and children, is a special project for groups concerning the use of the tactile sense. It consists of 24 boxes containing a variety of natural history specimens or parts of them, which can be touched but not seen. There are 3 types of boxes, each representing a different degree of difficulty. Each time the whole project is supported by a member of the educational staff. The exhibitions in the Natural History Museum include several quests which are made for children of various age groups. Schools can purchase a special activity box to prepare them for their museum visit. Summer hours are daily 9:00–6:30, and winter hours are 9:00–4:30. The zoo is private, and there is an admission charge. Separate attendance figures are not kept for the children's zoo, but the general zoo has 900,000 visitors a year.

Jeremy Cherfas, *Zoo 2000: A Look beyond the Bars* (London: British Broadcasting Corporation, 1984), pp. 51, 60–62; Rosl Kirchshofer, ed., *The World of Zoos: A Survey and Gazetteer* (New York: Viking, 1968), p. 307.

NORWAY

STAVANGER

VESTLANDSKE SKOLEMUSEUM (Western School Museum), Storgt 27, Postbox 3542, Tjensvoll 4001 Stavanger. The School Museum was founded in 1925 by an enthusiastic teacher, Johan Gjøstein; from the beginning it collected pedagogical literature and school items of historic interest and exhibited contemporary instructional media. This latter function has now been taken over by other institutions, and the museum concentrates on older materials. The collection has about 5,000 objects and 20,000 books. A support group formed in 1984, which annually publishes a book on school history *Skolemuseumslaget Årbok 1984*, promotes the museum, and actively seeks new acquisitions. Of particular interest are old photographs of children and school conditions, equipment, and oral history interviews. Currently in a building of 200 square meters, the museum would like to take over an old school building. Tours are conducted for school classes. The children have an opportunity to experience what it was like when there was no school building in small towns and the teacher came to the area with a box library, taught for a few weeks, and then moved on to another community. Items from the mid–19th century are of particular interest, and there are also models, handmade items demonstrating the practical arts, and an early 20th century classroom corner. The museum is funded by the province and has 1 part-time paid staff member. It is open on Tuesday 10:00–12:00, Thursday 11:00–2:00, and on some Sundays. The museum has approximately 750 visitors a year.

Årsmelding 1983 (Stavanger: Vestlandske Skolemuseum, [1984]).

SINGAPORE

SINGAPORE

SINGAPORE ZOOLOGICAL GARDENS, 80 Mandai Lake Road, Singapore 2572. The Children's Zoo, opened in 1973, was replaced by the Children's Zoo Adventureland in 1980. While the earlier version had large and full-grown animals, the new one features only small animals, including guinea pigs, tortoises, hamsters, poultry, parrots, pigs, pony, sheep, goats, and rabbits. To play on the child's sense of adventure, many of the animals are tucked away in trees, at the top of structures, and in tunnels. There are also contact areas which provide an educational experience for children growing up in an urban environment. A regular Adventureland feature is the Saturday afternoon 2:00–3:00 opportunity to meet young animals, new zoo babies, and learn the correct way to handle animals. There are also contests and special holiday events. Adventureland features bright graphic structures of Asian folklore and Western nursery rhymes, a tree house, and an obstacle course. Films on animal life are shown in the 100-seat zoo theatrette. Exhibits of animal artifacts have been mounted, and in 1984 the zoo installed "Education in Eggs" with 15 types of eggs, photographs of eggs hatching, and other egg facts. Seventy percent of the schools are registered as institutional Friends of the Zoo. Educational services include guidesheets for children, posters for school groups visiting the zoo, preparation of slide/tape programs, and workshops for teachers. The zoo's quarterly educational publication features articles on plants and animals that relate to the school syllabus, photographs are taken locally, and all animals featured are found in the zoo. Adventureland hours are 8:30–12:00 and 1:00–5:30. In 1984 there were 896,000 visitors to the 75-acre, open-concept zoo, but no separate figures were recorded for Adventureland. Support comes from government grants, gate revenues, adoption programs, and donations. There are plans to enlarge the children's area, and sponsors are now being sought.

"Adventure and Education at the Children's Zoo-Adventureland," *Zoo-Ed* 5 (1980): 1; *Annual Report 1983 Singapore Zoological Gardens* (Singapore: Singapore Zoological Gardens, [1984]), pp. 7, 17–18; "O. T.'s News Desk," *Zoo-Ed* 21 (1984): 5, 8; "Zoo Babies," *Zoo-Ed* 22 (1984): 3, 10.

___ SWEDEN ___

STOCKHOLM

SVERIGES TEKNISKA MUSEUM (National Museum of Science and Technology), Museivägen 7, S–115 27 Stockholm. Teknorama, opened in June 1985, is a department within the museum and is located in a building adjacent to the National Museum of Science and Technology. Teknorama is about 600 square meters and has approximately 50 exhibits modeled on designs from the Exploratorium (see entry under UNITED STATES/CALIFORNIA), other science centers, and ones constructed by the museum. All exhibits are hands-on and explore the physical sciences. There is also a small room used for demonstrations in physics and chemistry. Teknorama is open to school groups with reservations in the mornings from 10:00 to 12:00 and to the general public in the afternoons from 12:00 to 6:00. The facility has 1 chief executive, 4–6 Explainers, and 1–2 teachers; all are part-time during the hours that Teknorama is open. This new facility is now what most people come to the museum to see, and during its first year it had approximately 200,000 visitors.

Victor J. Danilov, "Discovery Rooms and Kidspaces: Museum Exhibits for Children," *Science and Children* 23, no. 4 (January 1986): 11; "New Developments Highlighted at CIMUSET Meeting," *ICOM News* 39, no. 1 (1986): 10.

THAILAND

BANGKOK

SCIENCE MUSEUM, 928 Sukhumvit Road, Bangkok 10110. The Discovery Room, opened on 10 August 1979, was incorporated into the plans for the new museum as a participatory facility for 1st to 6th-grade students. Survey research carried out prior to the establishment of the Science Museum, Bangkok, suggested the need for a participatory area where young visitors could have fun with science and develop process skills through interaction with objects. The Discovery Room is located on the 2nd floor of the Science Museum's main building and is 154 square meters. Forty visitors can be accommodated at one time. Schools may reserve the Discovery Room for a class visit, and individual children may get a free ticket on a first-come, first-serve basis for one of the 4 daily time periods. The Discovery Room collection has 200 scientifically oriented, colorful toys and games in the form of science kits, puzzles, creative toys, and models. The room has a series of 5 square tables; each contains a set of toys, and those utilizing the same process skills are grouped together. The tables are arranged to progress from the most basic process of observing to the controlling of variables. Exhibition changes occur quarterly with the installation of a new set of toys. The collections of the Discovery Room are also made available to the public by its school loan services, mobile kits, special exhibitions, workshops, seminars, and a nationwide contest on educational toys. Four museum staff members are involved with the Discovery Room. Attendance is about 30,000 annually, and the audience is composed primarily of school groups who attend during the week with their class. The Discovery Room is open Wednesday through Sunday for 4 time periods beginning at 9:00, 10:30, 1:30, and 3:00, and closed Monday, Tuesday, and national holidays. The museum is supported by the Thai government as a part of the Ministry of Education, Center for Educational Museums, Nonformal Education Department.

The Discovery Room (Bangkok: Center for Educational Museums, Ministry of Education, [1979]); "New Developments Highlighted at CIMUSET Meeting," ICOM News 39, no. 1 (1986): 10; Niched Suntornpithug, "Children and the Science Museum, Bangkok," Museum [UNESCO] 31, no. 3 (1979): 189–92; Workshop for Key Personnel Concerned with Out-of-School Scientific Activities by Young People: Report of a Regional Workshop, Bangkok, Thailand: August 24–September 2, 1982 (Bangkok: UNESCO, 1982), pp. 28–29; ERIC Document Reproduction Service, ED 237 360.

UNION OF SOVIET SOCIALIST REPUBLICS

ARMENIAN REPUBLIC: YEREVAN

NATIONAL CENTRE FOR CHILDREN'S AND YOUNG PEOPLE'S ART, Centre for Aesthetic Education, Abovian Street 13, 375001 Yerevan. Armenian S.S.R. The gallery for children's art, opened on 13 March 1970, evolved into the Museum of Children's Art. In 1978 it became the core of a centre for aesthetic education. The museum was created to collect, exhibit, and preserve children's art following a 1968 exhibit, THE WORLD THROUGH CHILDREN'S EYES. Eight hundred works by children were seen by 120,000 people in a 2-week period. The exhibition was organized by Zhanna Agamiryan, an art teacher in Yerevan, and it convinced her that children's art was worth saving. By 1975, the museum's collection contained over 100,000 children's drawings and paintings from various cities of the Soviet Union and other countries. It was then decided to establish a permanent exhibition which would display works selected from its acquisitions. By the mid 1980s the collection contained over a million works by children from 60 countries. Though Agamiryan was killed in a plane crash in 1975, her work has been carried on by her husband, art critic Genrich Igitian, director of the centre. Believing that every child has artistic gifts, the centre does not intend to produce professional artists but make the arts fundamental to life. It also linked the free artistic expression of children to the development of skills in the applied arts—ceramics, woodcarving, embroidery, carpet-weaving, mosaics—that can be used throughout life but are often not taught. The centre now has 3 branches and a staff of over 500 teachers and others who serve children throughout Armenia. There are theater groups performing drama, musicals, monologues, and puppetry, music and dance ensembles, and painting studios. Approximately 5,000 children are enrolled each year in the studio program and those between 3 and 16 are eligible for a one-man show. On May 20th of each year the Festival of Pavement Drawing is held in Yerevan's Theater Square. The centre conducts exchanges with institutions from all parts of the world and art by Armenian children has been shown in Asia, Europe, Canada, and the United States. In Yerevan, exhibitions are held about once a month and over a hundred shows have been organized. The Centre holds workshops for teachers and encourages the study of the creative process in children. The Centre for Aesthetic Education has become a national model within the USSR and established an international reputation. The museum is open daily from 10:00 to 5:00 and is visited by adults and children each year.

Sh. S. Agamirjan, "Die Organisation der Kinder-Bildergalerie in Jerewan und die allgemeine Charakteristik ihrer ästhetischen Arbeit," *Schule und Museum* 10 (1975): 76–91; "Bulletin Board: A Checklist of Recent Announcements," *American Libraries* 17, no. 7 (July/August 1986): 556; "The Edifying Nature of Beauty," *Sputnik* 18, no. 11 (November 1984): 134–42; Konstantin Sergeevich Mezhlumyan, "The Children's Art Centre in Yerevan," *Museum* [UNESCO] 36, no. 4 (1984): 199–203.

_ UNITED STATES _

ALABAMA

Birmingham

THE DISCOVERY PLACE, 1320 South 22nd Street, Birmingham, AL 35205. In 1977 4 area women saw the need for a hands-on museum, visited others, and initiated a local fund-raising effort. Beginning in temporary quarters in a small renovated house, the museum offered free tours for school groups by appointment weekdays from 9:00 to 12:00. On 4 October 1981 the museum opened in its own 7,700-square-foot building. The exhibits are designed to appeal to children 4–14 and to acquaint teachers and parents with participatory learning. Currently there are 5 major exhibits, a gallery, and an area with mind-boggling puzzles. MAGIC CITY explores city careers, the underside of a street, and a construction platform. INFORMATION PLEASE focuses on how we communicate, from body language to sophisticated equipment, and includes a TV studio and computers. WONDERFUL ME encourages learning about body systems and the senses and has a dentist office. Two exhibit-related books have been published; one helps discover Birmingham, and the other is designed to help children collect information about themselves. The museum also offers workshops, special events, and family Super Sundays. Five full-time and 6 to 9 part-time staff members are assisted by about 200 volunteers. Junior volunteers must be at least 12, and children under 8 must be accompanied by an adult. School tours are arranged during the morning hours by appointment. The Discovery Place is open Tuesday through Friday 9:00–3:00, weekends 1:00–4:00, and closed Monday and major holidays. The museum is also closed for several weeks in either August or September for major exhibit changes. There are about 51,000 visitors a year, and a nominal admission is charged with reduced rates for groups. Support comes 20 percent from city grants, 20 percent from admissions, 10 percent from federal grants, and the remaining 50 percent from private foundations and fundraisers.

"Discovery Place Celebrates Sunday," *Birmingham Post-Herald*, 1 October 1981; "Discovery Place Museum," *Birmingham News*, 15 November 1980, p. 2C; "Youngsters 'Discover' Learning Experience," *Shades Valley Sun*, 8 October 1981, p. 2.

ARIZONA

Mesa

ARIZONA MUSEUM FOR YOUTH, 35 North Robson, Mesa, AZ 85201. Founded in August 1978 by a group of Mesa citizens, this privately funded nonprofit art center for children opened in early 1981 in the Poca Fiesta Mall. The program was tested in this donated space where 5 shows were presented to 15,000 people. All the exhibits were designed for active viewing with hands-on experiences. The exhibits then were interrupted for over a year while the museum looked for a new location. In November 1983 a 17,000-square-foot former grocery store in downtown Mesa was selected for the permanent facility, and the city provided a grant to assist in its purchase. Following building renovation the museum reopened on 21 September 1985 with a multisensory exhibit, THE HEART OF CELEBRATION. Tours are conducted for school and community groups, and teachers are provided with follow-up materials. Four shows per year are planned. Classes and workshops for children, teenagers, and families are held in conjunction with the exhibitions in the 3 classrooms. There are 6 full-time and 10 part-time staff members. The center's public hours are Monday through Friday 12:00–5:00, Saturday 10:00–5:00, and Sunday 1:00–5:00. Group tours are available by appointment weekday mornings from 9:00 to 12:00. There is a small admission charge for those over 2, workshops charges vary, and the remaining support comes from private sources.

Catherine R. Brown, William B. Flessig, and William R. Morrish, *Building for the Arts* (Santa Fe, NM: Western States Arts Foundation, 1984), p. 15; "Handle with Joy: Museum Caters to Curious Kids," *Phoenix Gazette*, 20 September 1985, sec. F, p. 1; Bonnie Lewis, "The Museum for Youth: Art with Kids in Mind," *Arizona Museum Association Newsletter* (October/November 1984): 4; Karen Monson, " 'Neat Stuff' for Kids," *Phoenix Magazine* (August 1984): 73–74.

Phoenix

PHOENIX ART MUSEUM, 1625 North Central Avenue, Phoenix, AZ 85004. The Junior Museum, opened in 1965, was sponsored by the Junior League, which provided the funds for the Junior Museum's portion of the construction costs when the building was enlarged in 1964–65. The Junior League support continued for several years. In 1972–73 sponsorship was assumed by the Art Museum League. All exhibitions are designed to increase a child's understanding of the components of art. Each participatory or environmental installation is created by a member of the museum's curatorial staff or a consultant and remains in the 1,300-square-foot gallery about 2 years. Works of art were made in the Junior Museum's IMAGINATION CENTER; and COLOR, SHAPES, AND NUMBERS, a related exhibit in the changing gallery, was drawn from the permanent collection and designed to appeal to children and parents. Another format tied the 2 areas when the SHADOW ROOM in the changing gallery became a Junior Gallery installation. MAGNET MADNESS used common metal surfaces like a car door or refrigerator as canvases, and the installation included bilingual Spanish/English wall displays. The museum's visual and performing arts classes, programs, and special activities for children and parent/child are frequently related to the Junior Gallery. Museum and Junior Gallery hours are Tuesday, Thursday, Friday, and Saturday 10:00–5:00, Wednesday 10:00–9:00, and Sunday 1:00–5:00. There is an admission to the museum but no extra charge for the Junior Gallery. Businesses provide 26 percent of the museum's support, earned income 9 percent, government 9 percent, individual memberships and contributions 38 percent, support group fund-raising 11 percent, and other sources 7 percent. There are approximately 180,000 visitors a year to the museum.

Elsa Cameron, "The Junior Museum Orientation Gallery of the Phoenix Art Museum," Phoenix, 27 March 1974 (Typewritten); "Color, Shapes, and Numbers," *Phoenix Art Museum Calendar*, May-June 1980; "Magnet Madness Is More Than Child's Play," *Phoenix Art Museum Calendar*, May-June 1984; "New Children's Museum Open," *Phoenix Art Museum Calendar*, January-February 1982; Hazel Stone and Lisa Schleier, comps., "Phoenix Art Museum: A History," Phoenix, August 1984, pp. 4, 5 (Typewritten).

ARKANSAS

Little Rock

OLD STATE HOUSE MUSEUM, 300 West Markham Street, Little Rock, AR 72201. Granny's Attic, a hands-on exhibit room of 350 square feet, opened in 1981 and contains authentic items from the Victorian era that can be tried on, handled, and used. The artifacts in the room were selected to help children both enjoy the object and think about its modern counterpart. There is an ice box, a treadle sewing machine, a victrola, clothing, tools, and equipment. Available for school groups, Granny's Attic is limited to 30 students at a time and recommended for 4th- to 6th-grade students. An activity-oriented program in the room is designed to be led by the teacher with no set time limit. Following advance registration and prior to the museum visit, resource materials and a slide show are sent to the classroom. In addition, any teacher may borrow, free of charge, boxes with Victorian items for classroom use. Granny's Attic has also been used for 1-week, half-day summer activities for 4th- to 6th-grade children. Granny's Attic, when not in use by groups, is like any other exhibit hall. There is no staffing beyond the periodic checking by museum guards, and rarely have any objects been missing from the room. Two full-time program assistants conduct the staff-directed school programs. In "Legislative Process" 5th- to 12th-grade students use role-playing techniques to learn the legislative process and debate in the original House of Representatives. "Arches and Columns" introduces K–3 children to 19th-century architectural concepts. Volunteers from professional fields work with the program assistants in week-long summer classes. The Museum is open 9:00–5:00 Monday through Saturday and 1:00–5:00 Sundays. There is no admission charge. Support comes 90 percent from state appropriations and 10 percent from membership dues and grants.

"Discoveries in Granny's Attic," *Southern Living* 17, no. 12 (December 1982): 25; *Old State House Museum Educational Programs 1985–86* (Little Rock: Old State House, 1985).

CALIFORNIA

Bakersfield

LORI BROCK JUNIOR MUSEUM, 3801 Chester Avenue, Bakersfield, CA 93301. Opened on 6 October 1976, the museum grew from a Junior League project called Young Adventurers. The League started a building fund, and after constructing a building on county grounds, deeded the building to the county. The target audience is children 3–14. For the first 4 years displays were based on borrowed items, but now the museum's participatory, thematic exhibits utilize a collection that has gradually been acquired. Traditionally, a thematic exhibit has encompassed the entire 4,400-square-foot facility, but in 1985 the museum used 1 of its exhibit halls for the best of the previous shows. Installations have focused on petroleum, China, the human body, and communications. The museum emphasizes exhibit-related activities for school tours, which are available for classes preschool through junior high. In addition, there are Wild Wonderful Wednesdays throughout the year, enrichment class sessions 3 times a year, and Community Days with special displays and related activities twice a year. Three paid staff members are assisted by approximately 50 volunteers. The museum is open Monday through Friday 10:00–4:45 and Saturday 10:00–4:00. There is no admission charge, and workshop fees vary. The museum's self-generated support comes from fund-raisers, corporate and individual memberships, and grants and foundations. The 25,000 annual visitors are school tours, youth groups, and families including grandparents.

Lori Brock Junior Museum (Bakersfield: Lori Brock Junior Museum, n.d.); "Oil," *Sunset* 167 (October 1981): 42.

Berkeley

LAWRENCE HALL OF SCIENCE, University of California, Centennial Drive, Berkeley, CA 94702. Established by the Regents of the University of California in 1958, the Lawrence Hall of Science (LHS) opened to the public in 1968. It is dedicated to improving science education at all levels and to the dissemination of knowledge about the sciences. From its inception the LHS has functioned as a public science center, as a resource for schools, and as a developer of curriculum, science materials, equipment, laboratories, and model classrooms. A number of research projects on the processes of teaching and learning and on the uses of computers for instruction in science and mathematics have been conducted at Lawrence Hall, in collaboration with the University of California School of Education. Experimentation with TV and other media has also been of interest.

During its first year of operation 25,000 visitors attended programs or used the exhibits, although the LHS was open only on Saturday and Sunday for 4 hours each afternoon. Now, almost 2 decades later, the 4-level building features over 250 permanent exhibits, regularly scheduled temporary exhibits, thematic events, labs, a planetarium, 300-seat auditorium, 52-seat amphitheater, science education library, and exterior space suitable for public programs. A primary purpose of the participatory exhibits is to explore science as a dynamic process and encourage visitors to pursue their interests by further exploration, not just to convey factual information. In addition, the exhibits serve as prototypes and are the basis for additional research on visitor learning and exhibit design. The LHS serves a broad constituency that comprises preschoolers, school groups, children and youth, teachers, the disabled, and the general public. There are regularly scheduled workshops, family discovery labs, lectures, and LHS summer camp. Programs for teachers of all grade levels have over the years reached an estimated 100,000 educators. In addition, special events that are related to the science interests of the community have included inventors' fairs, science fairs for senior citizens, film programs, model rocketry, robotics month, weekend computer fair, dinosaur days, and whale celebration. The LHS Discovery Van, now the LHS Science Shuttle, began serving Bay Area schools in 1972. Science exhibits to shopping malls began in 1979, the inflatable LHS Traveling Star Theater planetarium in 1980, and informational science programming via cable TV in 1981.

As an innovator of science curricula, the LHS has developed several programs and related resource materials that are widely distributed. They are being utilized not only by schools but also by other museums. The Health Activities Project (HAP), for 4th- to 8th-grade students, includes 12 modules on science, current health, and physical education topics that were field-tested in San Francisco area schools and later in selected trial centers including museums. Outdoor Biology Instructional Strategies (OBIS), designed for youth 10–15 years old, consists of 27 programs on ecological relationships, and activities within a program last about an hour. Designed for adult leaders who are not scientists, this approach has made the OBIS materials accessible to a wide audience, including scouts, camps, and classroom teachers. The LHS Science Curriculum Improvement Study (SCIS) for children 5–13 is being used in 20 percent of the nation's elementary schools. The CHEM STUDY textbooks, translated into several other languages, and HAP, OBIS and SCIS have been adopted for use internationally. Great Explorations in Math and Science (LHS GEMS) is currently underway to publish some of the best science and mathematics activities, assembly programs, and exhibits developed at LHS for use in schools, science centers, museums, and community groups. In addition, over 200 planetariums worldwide use participatory programs developed for the LHS's Holt Planetarium.

In 1970 the LHS initiated its Math and Computer Education Project (MCEP) with a conference for local teachers and public-access computer classes for 9–14 year olds. With continued expansion the program now includes a public-access computer education center with over 120 microcomputers in 5 labs and a schedule of over 100 courses per year. MCEP has produced software and in 1984 began exploring the linking of computer technology and personal robots. To aid California teachers in using the latest computer software and instructional television programs in teaching science and mathematics, LHS has produced resource guides relating these new technologies to the state's teaching objectives.

There are approximately 250 professional staff members; about half are full-time, and 66 hold academic positions. The LHS has over 250,000 visitors each year, and an additional 50,000 people, preschoolers through adults, are reached by its outreach programs. The LHS is open to the public 7 days a week, 360 days a year, from 10:00 to 4:30 and on Thursday evening until 9:00. All exhibits are open during museum hours. There is an admission charge, and fees for workshops, labs, and classes vary. Support for public programs and museum activities is derived 4 percent from federal grants and contracts, 9 percent from private gifts, 17 percent from the University of California, 18 percent from foundation and corporate grants and gifts, and 52 percent from income. Following the organization of the Friends of the Lawrence Hall of Science in 1982, financial support from the community has increased. The LHS Members' Association provides additional financial support and encourages participation in LHS programs.

Victor J. Danilov, "Science Museums as Education Centers," *Curator* 18, no. 2 (June 1975): 92–94; Ann Jensen, "A Strictly Science Summer at Lawrence Hall," *School*

Library Journal 31, no. 5 (January 1985): 22–23; *LHS Bulletin* 1, no. 1 (Spring 1984); "Museums to Teach By," *Mosaic* 10, no. 4 (July/August 1979): 17, 19–20, 22, 23; Bonnie Pitman-Gelles, *Museums, Magic & Children: Youth Education in Museums* (Washington, D.C.: Association of Science-Technology Centers 1981), pp. 42, 66–67, 92, 98, 118, 125, 128, 149, 181, 197, 204, 231; Cary I. Sneider, Laurie P. Eason, and Alan J. Friedman, "Summative Evaluation of a Participatory Science Exhibit," *Science Education* 63, no. 1 (1979): 25–36.

La Habra

LA HABRA CHILDREN'S MUSEUM, 301 South Euclid Street, La Habra, CA 90631. In the early 1970s the city purchased and renovated a 1923 railroad depot for a participatory museum, which opened in December 1977. The primary audience is children through the 6th grade. Collection strengths are in the sciences, local history, and culture. Permanent exhibits in the 3,500-square-foot building include a NATURE GALLERY (touchable specimens and artifacts and a bee observatory), MODEL TRAIN VILLAGE, and PLAYSPACE. There are 2 changing exhibits galleries and workshop space. Previous exhibits have included THE OLYMPIC SPIRIT, MICROKIDS (history of computers and hands-on), A VISIT TO THE HOSPITAL, BIG TOP, and RISING STARS (the theater arts). The museum has take-out trunks, multimedia exhibits which are available for a 2-week loan period for a small fee. Three trunks on disabilities are adapted from a 1981 installation, ANOTHER WAY TO BE. Other trunks include FOOD FUNTRITION and FESTIVAL JAPAN. Cable TV programming is another museum activity. There is a Kids Council, and the museum publishes a newspaper 3 times a year which is distributed free to area schoolchildren through their elementary schools. Adjacent to the museum are several retired railroad cars to explore. Guided tours are available on weekdays during the school year and self-guided tours at anytime, but groups of more than 10 are required to make a reservation. Two full-time and 2 part-time staff members are assisted by approximately 100 volunteers. The museum is open Tuesdays through Saturdays 10:00–4:00 and closed Sundays, Mondays, and national holidays. Support comes 15 percent from local government, 20 percent from grants and foundations, and 10 percent from contributions and outside employment programs. Revenues come 20 percent from admissions, 20 percent from benefit events, 7 percent from marketing projects, and the remaining 8 percent from memberships, interest, and the gift shop. Most of the 64,000 annual visitors come from southern California.

"It's Reruns Time," *Daily Star-Progress*, 14 October 1985, p. 9; "Step Right Up! It's Circus Time!" *Daily Star-Progress*, 28 December 1984, p. 9; "Youngsters Learn to Be 'Rising Stars,' " *Highlander Publications: La Habra 3*, 5 June 1985, p. 13.

La Jolla

THE CHILDREN'S MUSEUM OF SAN DIEGO, 8657 Villa La Jolla Drive, La Jolla, CA 92037. Opened on 22 August 1983, the museum was founded in

December 1980 by a group interested in establishing a hands-on facility for children in the San Diego area. In December 1982 the museum acquired a site when 5,000 square feet of rent-free space in the La Jolla Village Square (shopping mall) was donated for a 5-year period. The museum acquired another 3,800 square feet in 1985. The target audience is children 4–14. Exhibits are designed to give children contact with real materials, are centered around a body of content, and allow choice in open-ended situations to foster creativity. Exhibit areas currently include THE HEALTH CLINIC, KKID TV STUDIO, SELF IMAGES, HANDICAPPED AWARENESS, SENSORY TUNNEL, ART STUDIO, and BACKSTAGE THEATER (scenery, props, and a puppet stage). There are frequent special events, programs, and workshops. The museum has a Recycle Center. Five full-time and 8 part-time staff members are assisted by about 100 volunteers and a Kids' Advisory Council. Hours for groups with reservations are Tuesday all day and Wednesday through Friday 9:30–11:30. Public hours are Wednesday through Friday and Sunday 12:00–5:00, Saturday 10:00–5:00, and closed Mondays. Support comes 30 percent from admissions; 11 percent from memberships; 17 percent from group visits, programs, and special events; 16 percent from the store; 19 percent from corporate and individual donations; and 7 percent from grants and miscellaneous sources. The museum has about 55,000 visitors a year.

Handprints [The Children's Museum of San Diego Newsletter] 3, no. 2 (Summer 1984); "A History of the Children's Museum," La Jolla, July 1984 (Typewritten); "Milestone for Children's Museum," *The Tribune*, 2 April 1985, p. B–6; "The Top 10 for Kids: From Boston to L.A.," *USA Today*, 6 October 1983.

Los Angeles

THE LOS ANGELES CHILDREN'S MUSEUM, 310 North Main Street, Los Angeles, CA 90012. Perceiving the need for a hands-on facility for children in an urban setting motivated 2 teachers to enlist support for their idea. After a year of preparation the Los Angeles Children's Museum opened in June 1979 in a city-owned shopping mall site with 17,000 square feet of space. Once the initial burst of enthusiasm passed, the museum was faced with finding a secure financial base to pay rent and complete the partially finished exhibits. The museum closed in the fall of 1980 for a period of reevaluation and completion of necessary work. It reopened 3 months later. For a time the museum also operated a 3,100-square-foot satellite gallery. From the single downtown facility, 16 permanent exhibit areas, outreach activities, and performance programs serve its 260,000 annual visitors, mainly families with children under 12. The museum is separate from the shopping areas, and its visitors are generally not shoppers making a sidetrip to the museum but people visiting the museum specifically. The emphasis is on learning by doing, with full-scale environments which reflect the urban world: CITY STREETS (view under the street, bus, policeman's motorcycle, and occupational clothing), HELP (health education learning project with health facilities and equipment), STICKY CITY (Velcro-covered foam blocks for constructions), BEFORE YOU AND ME (grandma's attic with try-on clothing, toys, and tools), a recording studio, and a Recycle Center. A rotating ethnic exhibit allows families to explore multicultural issues. The 60 full-time and part-time paid staff members are assisted by volunteers who donate some 10,000 hours annually. The museum receives about half of its yearly income from contributions and half from admissions and fees. Daily summer hours are 9:30–11:00 for groups and 11:45–5:00 for the general public. In the winter the museum is open Monday through Friday 9:30–1:45 for school groups, with general public hours on Wednesday and Thursday 2:30–5:00 and Saturday and Sunday 10:00–5:00.

William R. Anderson and Herbert Sprouse, "Museums in the Marketplace," *Museum News* 63, no. 1 (October 1984): 59–67; "Fourth-Graders Meet the Top 40: Children's Museum Demystifies the Recording Studio," *Los Angeles Times*, 25 November 1985, sec. V, p. 5; "New Director for Children's Museum," *Los Angeles Times*, 29 August 1981, sec. 2, p. 10; Bonnie Pitman-Gelles, *Museums, Magic & Children: Youth Education in Museums* (Washington, D.C.: Association of Science-Technology Centers, 1981), pp. 44, 185, 210; "Power of Positive Organizing," *Los Angeles Times*, 5 April 1979, sec. 4, pp. 1, 6; JoAnne Van Tilburg, "Los Angeles Children's Museum," *Design for Arts in Education* 81, no. 4 (April 1980): 8–15.

Monterey

MONTEREY BAY AQUARIUM, 886 Cannery Row, Monterey, CA 93940. Touching pools are part of the aquarium opened on 20 October 1984 to interpret Monterey Bay marine life and its shoreline. A group of 4 marine biologists proposed the facility in 1977, and the following year the Monterey Bay Aquarium Foundation was formed by David and Lucile Packard. Built on the former site of Monterey's largest sardine cannery, the innovative 177,000-square-foot building on a 2.3-acre site has 3 main exhibits, THE KELP FOREST, MONTEREY BAY HABITATS, and SEA OTTERS. There are also over 80 other smaller exhibits, including MARINE MAMMALS GALLERY, COASTAL STREAM, THE SLOUGH, SANDY SHORE, and OCTOPUS AND KIN. The tactile tidepools and bat ray pool are designed to provide an opportunity to learn by touching and to foster a greater appreciation of marine shore natural history. The aquarium includes a 273-seat auditorium and 2 classroom/labs which serve about 100,000 school children per year. Some of the 50-minute programs for K–12 students utilize the tidepools and labs. Materials are available for teachers prior to their visit and include suggestions for follow-up activities. About 50 teachers and administrators serve as advisors to the marine educators. In addition, the aquarium offers courses, workshops, field trips, lectures, and film series. Family workshops are available for different age groups/parents including 3–5 year olds, grades 1–3, 4–6, and 7–12. The education department has 18 paid staff members who are assisted by 400 docents and 25 junior guides. The aquarium is open daily 10:00–6:00 except Christmas. Support comes from admissions, corporate sponsorships, private donations, and memberships.

Marquis Childs, "A Novel Aquarium Depicts the Story of Monterey Bay," *Smithsonian* 16, no. 3 (June 1985): 94–98, 100; *Monterey Bay Aquarium Shorelines* 1, no. 2 (Spring 1985); "Monterey Bay and Its Astonishing New Aquarium," *Sunset* 173 (November 1984): 92–95, 99–101; Eleanor Smith, "Monterey's Natural Aquarium," *Oceans* 17, no. 6 (November/December 1984): 12; Steven K. Webster, "Interactive Exhibits at the Monterey Bay Aquarium," *AAZPA 1985 Annual Conference Proceedings*, pp. 63–68: ERIC Document Reproduction Service, ED 265 038.

Pasadena

KIDSPACE, 390 South El Molino Avenue, Pasadena, CA 91101. The museum, founded by the Junior League, opened in February 1980 at the Rosemont Pavilion near the Rose Bowl. The idea for a children's museum was introduced to the community in 1979 with a 6-week exhibition at the Baxter Art Gallery, California Institute of Technology. In April 1981 Kidspace moved to its present 5,700-square-foot facility, formerly the gym of the McKinley Junior High School. Exhibits and programs, planned for a target audience of children 2–12, encompass the arts, humanities, technology/medicine, and science. Currently the participatory areas include a TV studio KKID and a disc jockey booth KFUN; health and anatomy at OUTSIDE/IN; an occupational area GROWN-UP TOOLS with a variety of uniforms and equipment; the exploration of light, color, and shadows in ILLUSIONS; and the HUMAN HABITRAIL where children move through a labyrinth of carpeted curves and act out the world of ants. In addition to the permanent exhibits, the museum offers drop-in workshops, children's film festivals, and special events. The 6 administrative staff members are assisted by 15 museum teachers and 25 junior volunteers. During the school year Kidspace is open to the public Wednesday 2:00–5:00 and weekends 11:00–4:00; tours for groups with advance reservations are given Monday through Friday morning. Public hours in the summer are Wednesday through Sunday 1:00–5:00, and tours for groups with advance reservations are given in the mornings Monday through Friday. The museum is closed on major holidays and each year at the end of September for repairs. There is an admission charge. Support comes 56 percent from earned income, 29 percent from contributions, 10 percent from the annual benefit and memberships, and the remaining 5 percent from various sources. Kidspace has about 80,000 visitors a year.

"Children's Museums: Learning the Fun Way," *Family Weekly*, 26 May 1985, p. 12; "Kids Get Their Own Space to Play and Learn," *Los Angeles Herald Examiner*, 6 September 1984, pp. 1, 8; "Kidspace: It's Getting Better Every Year," *Star-News*, 14 June 1985, p. B–5; *Kidspace Museum Annual Report 1984–85* (Pasadena: Kidspace, [1985]); "Kidspace Museum Boasts Fun, Involvement for All Ages," *Butterfield Express & Valley Times*, 14 August 1985, pp. 2, 5.

Sacramento

SACRAMENTO SCIENCE CENTER AND JUNIOR MUSEUM, 3615 Auburn Boulevard, Sacramento, CA 95821. The museum was founded on 15 March 1951 after a group of citizens accepted the assistance of John Ripley Forbes to establish a facility for natural science education. Forbes served as the first director of the museum, which was initially called the California Junior Museum. It became the first west coast natural science center and junior museum established under the auspices of the National Foundation for Youth Museums. With additional support from the Junior League, the museum opened on 27 August 1951 in a building on the State Fair Grounds as a fair exhibit. Soon thereafter a building for live exhibits was added, and in 1953 a planetarium was donated by a member of the museum board. Besides the exhibits, clubs, classes, planetarium shows, and an animal lending program, there was an outreach program, which in the early 1960s added a mobile unit. In 1976 the Sacramento Science Center, which had been founded at another location, united with the Junior Museum; the museum then moved to its present 12-acre site in a city park. Both the landscaping and the live animal hall stress what is native to California. The museum has a natural history collection of 6,500 specimens, of which 99 are live animals available for exhibition, programs, research, and loan material for teachers. The recent adding of a planetarium; refurbishing of the exhibits addition; and additional programming have increased participation in the museum. In addition to the various on-site activities, there are a wide variety of outreach programs and field trips. The 8 full-time and 19 part-time professional staff members are assisted by approximately 100 volunteers. Hours are Monday through Saturday 9:30–5:00 and Sunday 12:00–5:00. Support comes from admissions, memberships, program fees, school contracts, governmental support, and corporate contributions. Approximately 70 percent of the walk-in visitors and 90 percent of the total 120,000 annual visitors are children.

Marilyn Hilliard Geraty, ''Museum on Wheels,'' *Education* 83, no. 3 (November 1962): 179–81; Selina Tetzlaff Johnson, ''Museums for Youth in the United States: A Study of Their Origins, Relationships, and Cultural Contributions'' (Ph.D. dissertation, New York University, 1962), p. 187; Natural Science for Youth Foundation, *A Natural Science Center for Your Community* (New York: Natural Science for Youth Foundation, [1960]); *Programs 1980–81* (Sacramento: Sacramento Science Center and Junior Museum, [1980]).

San Francisco

CALIFORNIA ACADEMY OF SCIENCES, Golden Gate Park, San Francisco, CA 94118. The Discovery Room at the Academy opened on 15 September 1978. This facility was suggested and underwritten by Janet Nickelsburg, a naturalist and museum docent, who had seen tactile areas for children functioning in other museums. Continuing support for the Discovery Room comes from royalties from a book written by the benefactor. The 18-by-30-foot carpeted room encourages direct contact with a variety of natural history objects and materials. Although the room was designed specifically for children through the 6th grade, adults also enjoy the hands-on experience. All objects are labeled with both large type and braille, tables are wheelchair-accessible, and a variety of sensory experiences are provided for visitors. Disabled persons are encouraged to participate. Larger objects are found on partitioned open shelving, while the discovery boxes contain small objects centered around a theme. There are about 18 boxes on topics such as fur, shells, match a sound, seashore life, nests, feel and guess, fossils, and insects and spiders. Personal discovery is encouraged by the availability of science books, and a costume cupboard contains clothes from around the world. The room has a supervisor, an assistant coordinator, a part-time preparator who assists with the upkeep and development of new materials, and approximately 45 volunteers. The Discovery Room is open Tuesday through Friday 10:00–12:00 for groups with advance reservations. Everyone is welcome on a first-come, first-serve basis Tuesdays through Fridays 1:00–4:00 and on weekends 11:00–3:30. The general admission charge includes admission to the Discovery Room. The number of people permitted at one time is limited to 20. Last year approximately 93,000 people visited the Discovery Room.

A touch tank was incorporated into the Steinhart Aquarium at the California Academy of Sciences when it opened its Fish Roundabout in 1977. Located on the main floor, the tank simulates a California tidepool, and under docent supervision visitors of all ages are allowed to handle the animals. The tidepool is often included in guided tours, and a docent manual for tidepool volunteers has been developed. There are about 60 tidepool volunteers. The touch tank is open the same hours as the academy, daily 10:00–5:00 with extended hours until 7:00 from July 4 through Labor Day. The general admission charge includes the aquarium.

Kerry Mahar and Lloyd E. Ullberg, "Academically Speaking: The Discovery Room," *Pacific Discovery* 32, no. 6 (November/December 1979): 27–30; John E. McCosker, "The Steinhart Aquarium Fish Roundabout," *Pacific Discovery* 30, no. 3 (June 1977): 4–6; Janet Nickelsburg, *Nature Activities for Early Childhood* (Menlo Park: Addison-Wesley, 1976).

THE EXPLORATORIUM, 3601 Lyon Street, San Francisco, CA 94123. Opened in October 1969, the Exploratorium was conceived and developed by Frank Oppenheimer, its director from 1969 to 1985. He articulated his plans for this innovative science center prior to its opening, and the initial funding came from a grant given by the San Francisco Foundation in May 1969. The Exploratorium leases from the city 100,000 square feet of space in the reconstructed Place of Fine Arts. The museum, multidisciplinary in nature, integrates science, technology, and the arts. Exhibits are fabricated by Exploratorium staff, demonstrate basic scientific principles, and involve the visitor in self-discovery. The more than 600 hands-on installations are meant to satisfy several levels at the same time, from casual observation to in-depth understanding. The use of displays and visitor feedback are important aspects of exhibit design. The Exploratorium has produced 2 *Cookbooks* which provide construction plans for over 130 of its exhibits. These *Cookbooks* have received worldwide distribution, and Exploratorium exhibits are being built by many other institutions both here and abroad. In 1986, 80 Exploratorium displays were brought to the IBM Gallery of Science and Art in New York for an exhibition SEEING THE LIGHT.

To facilitate an understanding of the various scientific principles, the Exploratorium initiated the Explainer program in 1969. It pays high school students, who serve as floor staff during public hours, to answer questions and demonstrate exhibits. Explainers undergo 50 hours of training prior to beginning and receive staff guidance throughout their tenure. They have been effective with both young visitors and adults. Students are chosen for their ability to communicate and capacity to learn, not for their specific scientific knowledge. With San Francisco being an ethnically diverse area, attention is paid to ethnic and gender balance, with special incentives given to young women. Full-time Explainers work whenever the museum is open to the public and receive academic credit for their 20 hours. Part-time Explainers work 10 hours on the weekend. All Explainers receive the same hourly salary and serve for a 4-month term. A few are hired for a 2nd term to avoid having 100 percent turnover every 4 months. The Explainer program has been underwritten by grants and has become a model which many other institutions have used.

Programs for schools and teachers are provided but not the usual school tour, which is inconsistent with the nature and philosophy of the Exploratorium. School classes have exclusive use of the exhibits during several mornings a week, and it is estimated that 700–800 children visit with their teachers on any given morning. Adult Explainers are available to assist, encourage, and demonstrate. An intensive program for 4th- to 6th-grade students known as SITE (School in the Exploratorium) began in the fall of 1972. Since its inception there have been changes in SITE, and currently it is oriented toward upper elementary and junior high school teachers. This program is designed to affect attitudes toward science and provide teachers with practical information, including Idea Sheets, applicable to their classroom science instruction. There is also an extensive lending library of miniature exhibits and resource material which teachers may check out for school use. In addition, once or twice a year the museum conducts 15 to 30-hour courses for teachers in training. In the winter of 1984 privately funded training institutes for middle school science teachers, many of whom have no formal science training began. The participants concentrated on various physics topics. In the summer of 1984, with funds from the National Science Foundation, a 3-year program for experienced high school teachers was started, and the group continued meeting during the school year. In the fall of 1984 the Exploratorium received state funds for a pilot program to develop training for science and math teachers; such funding implies that the museum's curriculum fits well with that of the schools. Classes on various topics are held for children and adults. There is an artist-in-residence program, a concert and performance series, and free weekend movie matinees. Special events are also held throughout the year. Through its Dissemination Program, initiated in 1979, the Exploratorium has provided internships to more than 100 people from 75 institutions and sponsored conferences attended by more than 250 participants. These activities, in addition to its publications, have provided information about interactive exhibits and effective displays to other museum professionals. The first 5 years of the program were underwritten by the Kellogg Foundation.

There are over 63 full-time staff members, more than 78 high school and college-age Explainers, and an active volunteer program. Those under 18 are admitted free, and there is free admission every Wednesday evening and the first Wednesday of every month. Support comes 39 percent from earned income; 21 percent from city, state, and federal grants; and 40 percent from corporate and foundation grants and contributions. Summer public hours are Wednesday through Sunday 10:00–5:00, Wednesday evening 5:00–9:30, and closed Monday and Tuesday. Winter public hours are Wednesday through Friday 1:00–5:00, weekends 10:00–5:00, Wednesday evening 5:00–9:30, and closed Monday and Tuesday. Annual attendance is about 500,000. More than half the visitors are adult age; about 65 percent come from the Bay area, and the remaining 35 percent come from around the world.

Raymond Bruman, *Cookbook I*, 2d ed. with revisions (San Francisco: The Exploratorium, 1984); Commission on Museums for a New Century, *Museums for a New Century* (Washington, D.C.: American Association of Museums, 1984), pp. 57, 94; Judy Diamond, Terry Vergason, and Gaile Ramey, "Exploratorium's Medical Technology Series," *Curator* 22, no. 4 (December 1979): 281–98; Ron Hipschman, *Cookbook II* (San Francisco: The Exploratorium, 1980); Barbara Y. Newsom and Adele Z. Silver, eds., *The Art Museum as Educator* (Berkeley: University of California Press, 1978), pp. 268–69, 270, 271, 272, 299–305, 402, 404, 440–42, 697–98; Frank Oppenheimer, "Exploration and Culture: Oppenheimer Receives Distinguished Service Award," *Museum News* 61, no. 2 (November/December 1982): 36–45, with an Introduction by Kenneth Starr; Frank Oppenheimer, "A Rationale for a Science Museum," *Curator* 11, no. 3 (1968): 206–09; Paul Preuss, "Education with an Edge: An Introduction to Educational Programs at the Exploratorium," *The Physics Teacher* 21, no. 8 (November 1983): 514–19; "A Science Show That Brings Back the Wonder," *New York Times*, 31 January 1986, sec. C, pp. 1, 24.

JOSEPHINE D. RANDALL JUNIOR MUSEUM, 199 Museum Way, San Francisco CA 94114. The San Francisco Recreation Commission opened the museum in February 1937 under the name Junior Recreation Museum. Initially the museum occupied one wing of an old wooden building, but success soon demanded that it use the entire building. From the beginning a comprehensive program was offered which included exhibits, nature study, clubs, arts and crafts, and field trips. The need for a fireproof and centrally located structure was recognized by the Recreation Commission, and in 1941 a 14-acre site in the

Corona Heights section was purchased. In a 1947 bond issue funds were approved for a new building, and in September 1951 the new facility was dedicated. At this time the name was changed to the Josephine D. Randall Junior Museum in honor of the superintendent of recreation, who was a major force in the museum's development. The site is now 16 acres and includes a 30,000-square-foot building with exhibit areas, classrooms, computer lab, live animal room, seismograph, auditorium, and library. The target audience is 9–12 year olds, but there are activities which appeal to younger children and adults. School groups may schedule a single visit lecture/demonstration or multiple-visit workshop on a first-come, first-serve basis. Programs encompass a wide variety of arts and science topics. All lecture programs are free; most workshops have a fee, and charges vary. In addition, there are family films, parent/child courses, and clubs specifically for children or adults. The classes last 5 or 6 weeks and are in the broad categories of physical and natural sciences, arts and crafts, and industrial arts. The museum also sponsors science fairs, field trips, and campouts. There are 10 full-time staff members and many volunteers. During June, July, and August the museum is open Monday through Friday 10:00–5:00, and September through May it is open Tuesday through Saturday 10:00–5:00. The museum is a hands-on learning center that has maintained its central location and serves approximately 25,000 people per year, mainly from San Francisco. Support comes from the city and the County of San Francisco Recreation and Parks Department.

Richard A. Chase, "Learning Environments," *Museum News* 54, no. 1 (September/ October 1975): 38; Monique Durieux, *A Guidebook to the Operations and Background of the Josephine D. Randall Junior Museum of San Francisco* (San Francisco: The Museum, July 1973); Josephine D. Randall, "Junior Museum," *Recreation* 40, no. 9 (December 1946): 467–68; Josephine Dows Randall, "A Recreation Museum for Juniors," *Recreation* 32, no. 1 (April 1938): 27–29, 53–54; "San Francisco's Junior Museum," *Recreation* 31, no. 7 (October 1937): 415–16; Bert Walker, "A Municipal Children's Museum," *Museum News* 9, no. 7 (April 1961): 30–33.

SAN FRANCISCO ZOOLOGICAL GARDENS, Zoo Road and Skyline Boulevard, San Francisco, CA 94132. The Children's Zoo, opened in the mid–1950s, had a storyland theme and was located adjacent to the San Francisco Zoo. In 1963 the San Francisco Zoological Society began running the area. It operated as a semimobile unit in 1964 and by 1968 was converted to a permanent facility with a main barn, nursery, and waterfowl exhibit. In 1971 the Society and the city shared the cost for the construction of an animal contact area. Expansion continued with the addition of exhibits with natural settings for North American mammals and local wildlife. In the early 1970s, with the cooperation of the Board of Education, the zoomobile expanded its services to local schools. After a visit groups are encouraged to come to the zoo. In the mid–1980s the Children's Zoo occupies 7 acres and has a large contact yard with domestic animals, a nursery for hand-raising young animals, and about 25 other exhibits of domestic and exotic animals, including a waterfowl pond, small aviaries, a hatchery, and an insect zoo. A nature trail, begun in the mid–1970s, is a walk-through area open in the summer which displays animals used during the school year in the zoomobile program. Teenage volunteers are stationed at several locations along the wooded trail as animal handlers and interpreters. Programs lasting 20 minutes are held throughout the day during the summer months and on weekends during the rest of the year on livestock care, parrots, and insects. The staff of the zoo's education department uses the small outdoor theater in the Children's Zoo for demonstrations of birds of prey and reptiles. In addition, docents lead tours for school groups, and there is a farmhands summer program. The Children's Zoo has a manager, 4 keepers, 1 year-round and 1 summer intern, 1 insect zoo manager and keeper, and about 100 volunteers. In the summer the Children's Zoo is open daily 10:30–4:30. Winter hours are weekdays 11:00–4:00 and weekends 10:30–4:30. There is a small admission charge, which provides 90 percent of the zoo's support, with the remaining funds coming from the sale of animal food and concessions. The Children's Zoo has approximately 300,000 visitors annually.

"The Children's Zoo," *The San Francisco Zoo* (San Francisco: San Francisco Zoological Society, [1974]); Roger Hoppes, "The Children's Zoo: Providing an Intimate Experience," *Animal Kingdom* 87, no. 2 (April/May 1984): SF1–4; Roger Hoppes, "Educating Humpty Dumpty at the San Francisco Children's Zoo," *AAZPA Regional Conference Proceedings 1985*, pp. 147–52; Roger Hoppes, "Life at South Pond," *Animal Kingdom* 84, no. 5 (October/November 1981): SF2–3.

San Jose

CHILDREN'S DISCOVERY MUSEUM OF SAN JOSE, PO Box 9433, San Jose, CA 95157. Founded in 1982 to enhance the educational and cultural opportunities for children of the South Bay area, the museum started outreach programs in 1984. "Stage Door Stories" (a dramatics program) and "One Way or the Other" (about handicaps) are being presented to a target audience of children 8 to 12 years old. Construction of the museum will begin in 1986, and opening is anticipated in 1987. The new 40,000-square-foot building with 17,000 square feet of exhibit space will occupy a prime downtown park site along the Guadalupe River. More than half of the projected funds needed have been raised, including one-fourth of the total amount from the San Jose Redevelopment Agency. Plans call for 30 full-time, 20 part-time staff members, and about 50 volunteers. Current programs in the arts and sciences reach more than 10,000 children per year.

"Kids Get Chance to See How Disabled Live," *San Jose Mercury News*, 13 November 1985, pp. 1, 5; "Kids Learn Drama in Stories Program," *East San Jose Sun*, 7 November 1984, pp. 1, 4; "Stage Door Stories Let Kids Act Out Their Own Tales," *Oakland Tribune*, 19 June 1985, pp. 1, 2.

Walnut Creek

ALEXANDER LINDSAY JUNIOR MUSEUM, Larkey Park, 1901 First Avenue, Walnut Creek, CA 94596. In the spring of 1955 a group of Walnut Creek residents headed by Alexander Lindsay organized the Diablo Junior Museum. In his honor the museum became the Alexander Lindsay Junior Museum after his death in 1962. For a period of 10 years a local elementary school was used in the summer for natural history classes, and field trips were taken. By 1965, feeling the need for a year-round facility and program, museum members sought a permanent location and sponsor. About this time the City Parks and Recreation Department was enlarged. In 1966 Walnut Creek took over the operation of the museum, which moved into the 12,000-square-foot Larkey Park building. The museum developed an active program, including changing exhibits, classes, field trips, a wildlife rehabilitation program, outreach service, specimen checkout, and an extensive pet-lending library. A membership card allows 6–18 year olds to check out a domestic animal for 1 week, and teachers may borrow for a 2-week period. Approximately 40 docents either teach and tour or work as museum technicians assisting with exhibits and record keeping. In addition, about 130 6th through 12th-grade youth act as aides and interpretive guides. Tours are conducted by reservation only. There is no admission charge to the museum. Summer hours are Wednesday through Sunday 11:00–5:00; winter hours are Wednesday through Friday 1:00–5:00 and weekends 12:00–4:00; and the museum is closed Monday and Tuesday. The junior museum involves the entire community, and last year 100,000 people visited the museum and participated in its programs.

John Paul Eddy, "The Alexander Lindsay Junior Museum," *Science Activities* 9, no. 1 (February 1973): 36–37; Yvonne Keck Holman, "An Investigation into the Dynamics of Children's Museums: A Case Study of Selected Museums" (Ph.D. dissertation, Northern Illinois University, 1982), pp. 56, 68, 76, 81, 83, 85, 87, 92, 94, 99, 101, 103–04, 114.

COLORADO

Denver

CHILDREN'S MUSEUM OF DENVER, 2121 Crescent Drive, Denver, CO 80211. A group of educators and parents saw the need for a hands-on, experiential facility for area children. In March 1973 a planning group formed, and in June 1973 it received money from the Department of Health, Education, and Welfare (HEW) to test the feasibility of a participatory museum for children. Volunteers constructed a series of hands-on exhibits and traveled to various metropolitan locations during the summer of 1973. After 2 years of presenting traveling exhibits, the organizers were convinced that there was a community interest in having a permanent facility. The museum opened on 25 January 1975 in an inner-city, renovated turn-of-the century dairy. In mid–1976 with a new director, Richard Steckel, the museum began to develop products and services specifically designed to achieve financial self-sufficiency. Besides a variety of displays and activities at the museum, an aggressive off-site, income-generating program was initiated which included traveling exhibits, promotions, and publications. In 1978 the museum began publishing a monthly children's newspaper, *Boing!*, which was distributed free to thousands of Denver families. Furthermore, other children's museums bought the newspaper, included their local information, and sold advertising which appeared along with national material. In 1981 the museum became self-supporting, generating 95 percent of its budget by admissions and the sale of its products and exhibits including SENSORIUM (senses), JIM SHORT'S HEALTH CLUB (nutrition and fitness), SCIENTOYFIC (science), and FIGURE IT OUT (everyday math). Planning began in 1981 for a new 24,000-square-foot building in Gates-Crescent Park that would more than double the space available in the original Bannock Street location. The new family-oriented facility opened in January 1984. Children and adults must accompany each other, and neither may attend independently. The target audience is children preschool to 12. Exhibits change annually and encompass a variety of participatory learning activities. Installations have included URBAN WILDLIFE (animals from the Platte River environment), WHY ME? (birth and growing up), COLLECTIONS (things kids collect and kids' collections), a mini grocery store, MONSTER IN MY CLOSET (children's fears), FREE WHEELIN' (handicap awareness obstacle course), and KIDS AND PETS. Workshops are offered, performances are held in the museum's 1,900-square-foot theater, and there are outreach programs. Fourteen full-time and 3 part-time staff members are assisted by about 115 volunteers. Admission is charged, but fees vary. The museum is open to the general public Saturday 10:00–5:00, Sunday 12:00–5:00, and Tuesday through Friday 12:00–5:00. Tuesday morning 9:30–12:00 is for preschoolers and their parents only, and the museum is closed Monday. Groups of more than 10 may visit the museum by reservation only. The museum is closed in early September for 2 weeks for its yearly change of exhibits. Annual attendance is approximately 250,000.

Educational Facilities Laboratories, *Hands-on Museums: Partners in Learning* (New York: Educational Facilities Laboratories, 1975), pp. 22–23: ERIC Document Reproduction Service, ED 113 832; Yvonne Keck Holman, "An Investigation into the Dynamics of Children's Museums: A Case Study of Selected Museums" (Ph.D. dissertation, Northern Illinois University, 1982), pp. 241–74, 282–83, 285, 286, 288, 290–91, 292–93, 295, 296, 297, 298, 299–301, 303, 304, 305, 306, 318; Lisa Farber Miller, "Making Museum Education Programs Self-Supporting: A Marketing Approach to Fund Raising," in *Museum-School Partnerships: Plans and Programs*, Sourcebook #4, ed. Susan Nichols Lehman and Kathryn Igoe (Washington, D.C.: George Washington University, 1981), pp. 103–07: ERIC Document Reproduction Service, ED 216 945; Office of Child Development (DHEW), *A Museum for Children, Final Report* (Washington, D.C.: DHEW,

1976: ERIC Document Reproduction Service, ED 130 958; Bonnie Pitman-Gelles, *Museums, Magic & Children: Youth Education in Museums* (Washington, D.C.: Association of Science-Technology Centers, 1981), pp. 94, 113–14, 193, 230.

Manitou Springs

MIRAMONT CASTLE, 9 Capitol Hill Avenue, Manitou Springs, CO 80829. The Song of Sixpence Children's Museum opened on 29 May 1982 in a 1,038-square-foot area in a historic house. Besides an opportunity to play with Victorian toys and games, there are exhibits of costumed dolls from around the world, a pioneer schoolroom, and a puppet theater. The room is supervised by a paid staff of 4. The museum is open 10:00–5:00 daily from Memorial Day through Labor Day and can be rented for parties. About 2,500 children visit each season. As a memento, each child receives period paper dolls or baseball cards. The museum is supported by a small admission charge.

Pikes Peak Journal, 7 May 1982, p. 1.

CONNECTICUT

Manchester

LUTZ CHILDREN'S MUSEUM, 247 South Main Street, Manchester, CT 06040. Founded in 1953 by Hazel Lutz, a school art supervisor, the museum was initially sponsored by the Manchester Parent-Teacher Association (PTA) Council. Her idea was to bring real things into the classroom for children and their teachers. Items were donated by local citizens, and collections were catalogued and organized into school loan kits. After a few years the school museum required more than PTA financial support, a volunteer staff, and limited space. In 1958 it became a community museum, moved into an 1859 historic school building, and a full-time director was hired. Loan kits continued to be circulated, audiovisual materials were added to the delivery, classes could make an appointment to visit the museum, and children could visit the museum alone or in small groups after school. In 1982 the museum moved into a new home— formerly an elementary school—that doubled its space, and in 1985 it constructed a large Playscape area on the grounds behind the museum. Currently the museum offers kits, resource lessons, teaching tours, classes, and family trips. Services are designed to supplement the curriculum and meet the needs of a variety of educational organizations from nursery schools to convalescent homes, teachers, and youth group leaders. There are about 200 loan kits in art, history, natural history, science, and social studies. Kits must be reserved in advance and picked up by the borrower, except for Manchester schools, which may use the school delivery service. Throughout the school year resource lessons are taught in classrooms or other educational settings by museum staff members and volunteers. Teaching tours at the museum emphasize participatory learning and can be arranged by prior appointment. Exhibits are planned around the collections, which include over 20 live animals. The museum participates in the wildlife rehabilitation program. Museum public hours are Tuesday, Wednesday, and Friday 2:00–5:00, Thursday 2:00–8:00, weekends 12:00–5:00, and closed Monday and holidays. Hours are extended in July and August. There are 5 full-time and 3 part-time staff members and 80 volunteers. In the mid–1980s about 35 towns in Connecticut use the loan kits each year. There are fees for museum services, and Manchester Public Schools are covered by a prepaid agreement with the Manchester Board of Education. Support comes 37 percent from donations, 28 percent from earned income, 12 percent from the town of Manchester, 10 percent from the United Way, 8 percent from admissions, and 5 percent from membership fees.

Yvonne Keck Holman, "An Investigation into the Dynamics of Children's Museums: A Case Study of Selected Museums" (Ph.D. dissertation, Northern Illinois University, 1982), pp. 20, 77, 82, 84, 87, 96, 101, 105, 109, 117, 119, 125, 127; Hazel Lutz, "Museum Visuals Vitalize Teaching," *School Activities* 33, no. 3 (November 1961): 75–77; "Museums That Come to the Classroom," *Grade Teacher* 83, no. 9 (May/June 1966): 44; Beatrice Parsons, *Museums and Schools: Partners in Education*, audiotape of panelists Janice Goffney, Philip Hanson, and Steven Ling, presented at meeting of the American Association of Museums, Detroit, June 1985 (Shawnee Mission, KS: Vanguard Systems, 1985).

New Britain

NEW BRITAIN YOUTH MUSEUM, 30 High Street, New Britain, CT 06051. Founded in 1956 by the Service League of New Britain (now the Junior League), the museum opened in the basement of the Hawley Memorial Children's Library on 10 March 1957 with donated natural history and cultural artifacts. Adult volunteers assisted by junior curators ran the museum until 1961, when a full-time director was hired, but volunteers of all ages have continued to play an important role. Known as the Children's Museum for about a decade, the museum then changed its name to Youth Museum. Exhibits, programs, and field trips were organized by the museum, and later live animals were added. By the late 1960s more space was needed, and in 1974 plans were made to keep the museum in the center city and build a new facility. In October 1975 the museum opened in its new 2-story, 6,000-square-foot building. Exhibits are prepared by museum staff and are based on the collection or themes of current interest to children. The museum has a permanent collection of about 12,000 specimens and artifacts, approximately 150 loan kits, and about 35 live animals. In addition, the museum is a rehabilitation station for immature or injured wildlife. In 1975 the Junior League funded a Discovery Room which became the museum's hands-on space, and themes changed about 3 times a year. In the early 1980s the discovery-oriented displays were moved into the larger main exhibit room, and the former discovery area is being used for exhibits based on items from the permanent collection. Interviews conducted as part of a needs assessment indicated a continued interest in information about the care of live animals, and museum staff members have noted an increasing need to provide special programming for preschool children. A direct result of a comprehensive, 4-year study started by the museum in the late 1970s was the opening in July 1984 of the 30-acre Hungerford Outdoor Education Center. Programs are tailored to specific groups, including preschool, special needs groups, teachers, families, and adults. Activities are offered both during and after school, in the evening, and on the weekend. Museum public hours are Tuesday through Friday 1:00–5:00 and Saturday 10:00–4:00. Nature center hours vary with the season. Spring 1986 public hours were Tuesday through Friday 1:00–5:00, Saturday 10:00–5:00, and Sundays in April 1:00–5:00. In 1985 the museum had 9,600 visitors and the nature center 25,500 visitors. There are 7 full-time and 3 part-time staff members who are assisted by volunteers of all ages. There is no admission to the museum, but there is a small admission to the nature center. Seventy-five percent of the museum's support comes from the city and the remaining 25 percent from membership, grants, and contributions.

An Approach to Master Planning (New Britain: New Britain Youth Museum, 1981): Yvonne Keck Holman, "An Investigation into the Dynamics of Children's Museums: A Case Study of Selected Museums" (Ph.D. dissertation, Northern Illinois University, 1982), pp. 68, 78, 81, 85, 86, 95, 97, 101, 104, 105, 108, 114, 122, 125, 127; *Master Plan: New Britain Youth Museum* (New Britain: The Board of Trustees, 1982); Bonnie Pitman-Gelles, *Museums, Magic & Children: Youth Education in Museums* (Washington, D.C.: Association of Science-Technology Centers, 1981), pp. 180–81; *Youth Museum-Hungerford Outdoor Center Ramblings* 1986 (March/April).

New Haven

CONNECTICUT CHILDREN'S MUSEUM, 567 State Street, New Haven, CT 06510. The museum was founded on 1 May 1973 to provide cultural activities for young children because nothing was available in the area specifically for them. The 3,600-square-foot building was originally designed as a small village for role-playing what it is like to be an adult. Over the years the places and activities have changed and reflected the strengths of the staff. Currently there are a health center, post office, store, TV station, employment office, boat, and trolley. The collection is strongest in objects from the Victorian era. In addition, there is an outdoor education area with a garden. Programs are conducted for school groups and families, with the target audience being children 2–8. The museum has its own day-care program and full-day kindergarten for preschoolers, Kidspace, which serves 18 children. In April 1985 the museum opened a branch facility, Artcart, at the Primary Care Waiting Room at the Yale/New Haven

Hospital. This branch is supported by the Hospital Auxiliary and admission is free to the neighborhood users. A full-time staff of 3 is assisted by 12 contracted personnel and 10 student volunteers, who are high school seniors and Yale undergraduate and graduate students. The museum is open in July and August Monday through Friday 9:00–1:00, October through April Tuesday through Thursday 2:30–4:30 and weekends 12:30–4:30, and May and June Tuesday through Thursday 2:30–4:30. The museum has approximately 12,000 visitors annually. Support comes from Kidspace, the New Haven Foundation, program fees, and donations.

"Artcart Helps Visitors Be 'Patient,' " *New Haven Register*, 23 April 1985; "Children to Learn about Adoption," *New York Times*, 10 November 1985, sec. 23, p. 18; Don Cyr, "The Children's Museum: Learning to Play and Playing to Learn," *Arts and Activities* 83, no. 2 (March 1978): 22–25, 64; Yvonne Keck Holman, "An Investigation into the Dynamics of Children's Museums: A Case Study of Selected Museums" (Ph.D. dissertation, Northern Illinois University, 1982), pp. 78, 82, 84, 88, 102, 106, 108, 115, 133; "Sick Kids Have Fun While They Wait," *New Haven Register*, 27 April 1985, p. 26.

West Hartford

SCIENCE MUSEUM OF CONNECTICUT, 950 Troutbrook Drive, West Hartford, CT 06119. The museum was founded as the Children's Museum of Hartford in June 1927 by a group of citizens. It opened as a nature center museum in 1 room of the Elizabeth Park Pond House, with Delia Griffen as director, and soon moved to a 9-room house on Farmington Avenue. The collection started with donated or loaned natural history materials and items illustrating life in foreign countries. Exhibits changed frequently, programs for school classes were offered, and there were after-school activities. The museum also organized field trips and sponsored clubs that met on Saturdays or during school vacations. In 1929 a 225-seat auditorium was built for slide shows, films, and lectures. Besides its activities for children, the museum also tried to stimulate the interest of adults in science and cooperated with area natural science clubs. Jane Cheney became director in 1946, and under her direction the museum continued to serve both area children and adults. Closed-circuit television for area schools using museum staff and collections began in 1957, and later programs were used by many other stations. In 1959 the museum moved to its present 25,000-square-foot site; a planetarium was added in 1967 and an aquarium in 1974. In 1973 the museum merged with the 117-acre Roaring Brook Nature Center, which has a 6,000-square-foot building with classrooms, a small exhibit area, and an auditorium. Both the building and the trails were built to be accessible to the handicapped. Most of the center's programs for grades K–9 are held outdoors, and there is also a complete schedule of in-school programs. Always strong in the natural sciences and later environmental education, the museum expanded in the late

1970s to include the physical sciences. A 2,500-square-foot Discovery Room opened in the early 1980s; it will be modified in 1986 to include more exhibits and will again use prototypes developed by the Exploratorium in San Francisco (see entry under UNITED STATES/CALIFORNIA). Several kinds of museum programs are given for schools including multimedia, stage, and hands-on. They encompass health, zoology including the minizoo and aquarium, the physical sciences, the social sciences, and the planetarium. In 1983 the museum won an award from the National Science Teachers Association for its science enrichment program for inner-city youth initiated in the mid–1970s. In 1985 the museum received 2 grants for a new program designed to keep minority students in the Hartford Public Schools in precollege math and science courses. There are 55 full-time and part-time staff members and approximately 100 volunteers. The museum changed its name in 1984 to the Science Museum of Greater Hartford and in January 1985 to the Science Museum of Connecticut to increase its appeal to adults as well as to serve children. Based on studies undertaken in 1984, the museum initiated a fund-raising campaign to expand services and upgrade facilities. Currently annual attendance is about 65,000 schoolchildren in groups and 100,000 public visitors, about two-thirds of them adults. Hours are 10:00–5:00 Monday through Saturday, 1:00–5:00 Sunday, and closed major holidays. Support comes 75 percent from earned income, including admissions, fees for services (classes), memberships, store sales, and building rentals; 10 percent from grants; and 15 percent from contributions and gifts.

Jane Burger Cheney, "Focus on Children's Museums," *Museum News* 39, no. 7 (April 1961): 14–19; *The Children's Museum of Hartford and Roaring Brook Nature Center Are Becoming . . . The Science Museum of Connecticut* (West Hartford: Science Museum of Connecticut, [1985]); Educational Facilities Laboratories, *Arts and the Handicapped: An Issue of Access* (New York: Educational Facilities Laboratories, 1975), pp. 25–26; ERIC Document Reproduction Service, ED 117 829; Delia I. Griffen, "Children's Museum of Hartford (Conn.)," *Museums Journal* 31, no. 4 (July 1931): 149; "Supporting Science and the Schools," in *Museum-School Partnerships: Plans and Programs*, Sourcebook #4, ed. Susan Nichols Lehman and Kathryn Igoe (Washington, D.C.: George Washington University, 1981), pp. 108–09: ERIC Document Reproduction Service, ED 216 945.

DELAWARE

Greenville

DELAWARE MUSEUM OF NATURAL HISTORY, PO BOX 3937, Greenville, DE 19807. The Discovery Room, opened in 1981, serves as a teaching facility for schools and other groups, and as a participatory activity for families and the general public. It focuses on natural history topics and sensory awareness by using actual specimens and activity stations. Changes are made throughout the year to highlight museum exhibits and events. Approximately 30 specimens and 10 activity stations are in the 80-by-30-foot area at any one time. Programs

1/2 hour in length form part of the 2-hour museum group visit and are tailored to the age, interest, and abilities of the group. The Discovery Room is a popular part of the museum experience for visitors 4 years through adult, including special education and disabled students. Reservations are required, and group rates are available. Discovery is open to the public on weekend afternoons and for museum special events. Usually at least 1 special public activity, such as a workshop or game, is offered each month. A small staff, assisted by volunteers, supervises the facility. An admission fee provides about 10 percent of the museum's support, which is supplemented by memberships, gifts, and grants. Last year the Discovery Room had approximately 25,000 visitors.

Bill Baughman, ed., "Our Museum World: Delaware Museum of Natural History," *Explorer* 22, no. 2 (Summer 1980): 12; "Our Museum World: Delaware Museum of Natural History," *Explorer* 23, no. 1 (Spring 1981): 8; Mary Timchick, ed., "Our Museum World: Delaware Museum of Natural History," *Explorer* 25, no. 4 (Winter 1983): 19; "Our Museum World: Delaware Museum of Natural History," *Explorer* 26, no. 1 (Spring 1984): 18.

Hockessin

DELAWARE NATURE EDUCATION SOCIETY, PO Box 700, Hockessin, DE 19707. The Discovery Room, designed by the Junior League of Wilmington, opened in 1982 in a converted loft at the Society's Ashland Nature Center near Wilmington. It serves as a facility for specific interpretive programs as well as a place for families with small children. Animal tracks painted along the staircase lead visitors into the room where the ceiling is an evening sky with constellations. An Indian lodge, dugout canoe, costumes, and tools introduce children to local tribal life. A panorama of rolling fields and forests is brought closer by a pair of binoculars. The Discovery Room also includes games, puzzles, books, and a fish tank. Other exhibits are added on a seasonal basis. Admission is free. Another facility, Abbotts Mill Nature Center, is maintained at the opposite end of the state. The Society uses its two facilities to develop an awareness and appreciation of the environment through a wide variety of programs for all age groups and families.

Delaware Nature Education Society News 19, no. 2 (Spring 1983): 5; *Humane Education Projects Handbook* (Ogden, UT: Junior League of Ogden, 1982), pp. 81–82: ERIC Document Reproduction Service, ED 229 247.

DISTRICT OF COLUMBIA

CAPITAL CHILDREN'S MUSEUM, 800 Third Street, NE, Washington, D.C. 20002. Called the Center for Inquiry and Discovery when it was incorporated in April 1974, the museum was renamed the Capital Children's Museum in September 1977. It was established because a group, mostly from the Junior League, believed that Washington needed a hands-on facility for children 4–14. Ann White Lewin was hired as director in 1975. Before a site for the museum was found, 2 editions of a calendar for kids, "Ask Me Annual," were published, volunteers were trained, and the staff participated in city celebrations and events. With initial seed money donated by several local foundations and space in the underenrolled Lovejoy Elementary School given rent-free by the Washington Board of Education, the museum opened on 4 October 1977 in 4 classrooms. Soon after opening, the museum started to look for a larger facility. In October 1978 the U.S. Department of Housing and Urban Development (HUD) announced a matching grant for the purchase of a permanent site. The 3 Victorian brick buildings and 3.2-acre grounds were formerly a convent and nursing home belonging to the Little Sisters of the Poor. The museum opened in its new location on 13 February 1979 with 40,000 square feet of exhibit space. Some displays and activities from the Lovejoy School were moved to the new museum building. The first major installation at the new facility, MEXICO, has an archaeological site, an open-air market, a live goat, houses, and opportunities to cook and do native crafts. In 1981 a computer center, FUTURE CITY, opened, and in 1982 the museum produced award-winning software, *Paint*. Related to the computer center is the rest of the communications exhibit of the history of messages and information transfer, containing a print shop, a radio production studio, a switchboard and telephones, and a film theater. CHANGING ENVIRONMENTS shows what's under the street, has opportunities to role-play many of the jobs needed to keep a city moving, and has an eye doctor's office, simple machines, and a factory. In October 1985 the NEK CHAND GARDEN opened at the entrance to the museum. In addition to the exhibits and classes, the museum has regularly scheduled demonstrations, workshops, children's theater performances, special events, courses for teachers, and intergenerational activities. METKIDS was developed to provide after-school and weekend enrichment activities and training programs for children in neighborhood elementary and junior high schools. In 1983 the Capital Children's Museum reorganized as the National Learning Center with two operating units, the museum and a new school, Options. The school is an experimental instructional program for students who have not benefited from traditional educational programs. The Capital Children's Museum has 40 full-time and 40 part-time staff members and over 200 volunteers, many over 60 years of age. There is an admission charge, and rates are available for groups larger than 10 with a reservation. The Capital Children's Museum has 250,000 visitors a year. Support comes from admissions, fees, contributions, and grants.

" 'Ask Me' Calendar Full of Fun for Kids," *Potomac Current*, 20 November 1975; "A Capital Museum That Invites Kids to Participate," *New York Times*, 12 April 1981, sec. 10, p. 1; "Children's Museum: It's a Place for Kids to Play and Learn," *Montgomery Journal*, 14 April 1978, sec. B, pp. 1, 8; "Grant for Children's Museum," *Washington Post*, 2 June 1979, p. C7; Yvonne Keck Holman, "An Investigation into the Dynamics of Children's Museums: A Case Study of Selected Museums'' (Ph.D. dissertation, Northern Illinois University, 1982), pp. 21, 34–35, 47–48, 56, 77, 82, 84, 87, 93, 94, 95, 98–99, 100, 103, 106, 115–16, 118, 120, 123, 124; Edwards Park, "Around the Mall and Beyond," *Smithsonian* 16, no. 10 (January 1986): 22; Bonnie Pitman-Gelles, *Museum, Magic & Children: Youth Education in Museums* (Washington, D.C.: Association of Science-Technology Centers, 1981), pp. 44, 134, 213–14.

THE CHILDREN'S MUSEUM OF WASHINGTON, 4954 MacArthur Boulevard NW, Washington, D.C. 20007. Opened on 28 February 1942, the museum initially occupied the Villa Rosa at 4215 Massachusetts Avenue. The District Commissioners allowed the museum to use the mansion rent-free. Set on a large wooded site, the museum had a nature trail, a bird sanctuary, and a small zoo. The museum collected foreign dolls, mounted changing exhibits, sponsored clubs, and had a library. Open afternoons after school, on weekends, and during the summer, the entire museum was staffed by volunteers and directed by Matilda Young. In 1945 the museum was evicted to make way for the construction of an apartment house. After an unsuccessful search for a permanent location for a few years, it converted temporarily to a trailer-coach museum with history and natural history exhibits. In 1948 the Children's Museum acquired its first toy theater from the revived Pollack's of London. Since that time it has continued its interest in and promotion of the use of toy theaters. After 2 decades without a permanent home, the museum moved in 1980 into the last 1-room school in the District, the Conduit Road School. The 26-by-40-foot 1864 schoolhouse is the original building on its original site. The building was placed in the National Register of Historic Sites in 1973 and is the responsibility of the National Park Service. The museum offers conversational classes in Spanish and French, maintains a collection of children's library books in different languages, and gives toy theater presentations. In addition, there are study clubs, lectures, and films. The director is assisted by other staff members as needed. There is no admission to the museum, but there is a fee for classes. From July through September hours are 10:30–4:00 Tuesday through Friday, and the rest of the year the museum is open 10:30–4:00 Tuesday through Friday and 10:30–3:00 Saturday.

E. J. Applewhite, "It's Not All on the Mall: A Personal Look at Washington's Other Museums," *Museum News* 62, no. 4 (April 1984): 23, 27; "Needed: Another Imaginative Museum Just for Children," *Washington Post*, 2 January 1966, sec. F, p. 22; "The Old Conduit Road Schoolhouse," *Northwest Current*, 31 January–13 February 1985, pp. 3, 5; "Washington Children's Museum Opened," *The Museum News* 21, no. 18 (15 March 1942): 1; Matilda Young and Marguerite B. Gleysteen, "Penny Plain or Twopence Coloured," *Historic Preservation* 22, no. 2 (April-June 1970): 4–10.

DAR MUSEUM, 1776 D Street NW, Washington, D.C. 20006–5392. A Touch of Independence, opened on 1 December 1984, was organized and sponsored by the Daughters of the American Revolution docents. They identified the need for a special place in the museum where children visiting with parents or other adults could learn about 18th and early 19th century American life. Located on the 3rd floor of the Memorial Hall outside the New Hampshire Toy Attic, the 30-by-8-foot discovery area is designed for children 4–11 years old. A Touch of Independence was inspired by the Discovery Room at the National Museum of Natural History (see entry under UNITED STATES/DISTRICT OF COLUMBIA) but is set up to accommodate only a few people at a time. Children are encouraged to touch the authentic items, which are not rare or unique, and reproductions are used. Some objects are found on open shelves, and others are in thematic discovery boxes which focus on topics such as early American toys, colonial drinking vessels, trade goods shipped to America, and the belongings of a Revolutionary War soldier. The text cards in the boxes are designed for children who can read and for adults who help children learn about the contents. The room also includes a collection of child-sized chairs representative of the different styles popular a few centuries ago. These chairs are similar to the ones found in the period rooms elsewhere in the museum. Docents staff the area, and 2 or 3 are always on duty. A Touch of Independence is open Monday through Friday 10:00–3:00. Support for the installation comes from the DAR docents, and admission is free. There were about 500 visitors during the first year.

"An Attic Any Little Girl Would Love," *Washington Post and Times Herald*, 7 October 1956, sec. F, p. 8; "Playthings from the Past at the DAR," *Washington Post*, 11 December 1985.

DISCOVERY THEATER OF THE SMITHSONIAN INSTITUTION,
Room 1235 Arts and Industries Building, 900 Jefferson Drive SW, Washington, D.C. 20560. The Discovery Theater, part of the Smithsonian's Resident Associate Program since 1983, opened in 1977 in redesigned space that was formerly used by the Smithsonian Puppet Theater. Prior to 1983 the theater was part of the Smithsonian's Division of Performing Arts. Washington's only continuously running theater for young audiences, it presents 9 or 10 productions per season (October to June) selected to appeal to a variety of age groups from preschool through junior high school. The theater is accessible to people in wheelchairs, and with 72-hours advance notice oral interpretation, sign language, and loop amplification are available. There are 2- to 4-week runs of a particular performance—puppetry, mime, dance, storytelling, and original plays. Currently about 40 percent of the performances involve puppets. The theater holds about 175 people, who are seated on carpeted risers in an intimate setting close to the performers. Performances run 45 to 60 minutes and are usually followed by an informal question-and-answer session with the cast. A free learning guide, specific to the show, is provided to groups of more than 20. In addition to the performances, Discovery Theater has sponsored writing and art contests for elementary school children with the winning pieces being incorporated into works presented at Discovery Theater. During the summer an intensive 3-week basic course in theatrical skills has been offered to young people. There are 3 full-time and 2 part-time staff members. Performance times are Tuesday through Friday 10:00 and 11:30, and Saturday 1:00 and 3:00. There is an admission

charge, and special group rates are available. Yearly attendance is approximately 60,000 children and their families.

"Discovery Theater," *The Smithsonian Associate*, monthly column; *Learning Guide: Discovery Theater—October 1984–June 1985* (Washington, D.C.: Smithsonian Institution Resident Associate Program, [1984]); Paul H. Oehser, *The Smithsonian Institution* (New York: Praeger, 1970), pp. 172–73; Edwards Park, "Around the Mall and Beyond," *Smithsonian* 16, no. 6 (September 1985): 30.

NATIONAL MUSEUM OF AMERICAN HISTORY, Smithsonian Institution, 14th Street and Constitution Avenue, NW, Washington, D.C. 20560. Hands On History, opened on 18 November 1985, is a discovery facility incorporated into the museum's new permanent exhibition hall, AFTER THE REVOLUTION: EVERYDAY LIFE IN AMERICA, 1780–1800. The 20-by-25 foot installation is an outgrowth of the Discovery Corners and related audience research conducted at the museum. It is an attempt to involve adults in discovery learning, and at present, schoolchildren without adults are not encouraged to visit. But it is suggested to children that they come back with their families. Participatory opportunities focus on the lives of everyday Americans in the last 20 years of the 18th century. Assembling a reproduction of a Philadelphia Chippendale chair and constructing a small bucket convey the notion of the difficulty of a craftsman's work. Seneca baskets can be examined to determine weaving patterns, and women's stays and a man's waistcoat can be tried on to get the feel of posture. Trunks have other interesting objects including toys. A board game simulates an archaeological dig of slave quarters, and artifacts give information about slave life. There is also a game for preschoolers on how wool is used to make yarn. Visitors also have a chance to try the methods historians employ by using the papers and artifacts of a Delaware farm family. The largest artifact is a 17th-century house, inhabited until the 1950s, which has 1 wall stripped away, revealing the layers of construction. Twenty people are allowed in the installation at any one time, groups are not admitted, and the time limit is a half hour. The half-time coordinator and half-time exhibits manager are assisted by approximately 40 docents. Hands On History is open Tuesday through Sunday 12:00–3:00 and closed Monday and major holidays. There is no admission charge. Free tickets, good only the day of issue, are available at the door 11:45 each day the room is open. It is recommended that visitors secure their tickets early. Although the room has been open only a short time, the staff has already noticed return visitors.

"Lancaster Talent to Highlight Smithsonian Museum Display," *Sunday News*, 11 August 1985, sec. E, p. 1; Faith Davis Ruffins, "The Exhibition as Form: An Elegant Metaphor," *Museum News* 64, no. 1 (October 1985): 55, 57; "What It Was Like in Early U.S.," *Burke/Braddock Connection* [Fairfax, VA], 21 November 1985, p. 46; Robert Wolf, Mary Ellen Munley, and Barbara L. Tymitz, *The Pause That Refreshes: A Study of the Discovery Corners in the National Museum of History and Technology Smithsonian*

Institution (Washington, D.C.: Office of Museum Programs, Smithsonian Institution, 1979): ERIC Document Reproduction Service, ED 196 772.

NATIONAL MUSEUM OF NATURAL HISTORY, Smithsonian Institution, 10th Street and Constitution Avenue, NW, Washington, D.C. 20560. The Discovery Room opened on 5 March 1974. It was initially developed by Caryl Marsh, with Judith White as project assistant, for the museum's Office of Exhibits to study visitor response to tactile displays. Now it is part of the museum's Office of Education. The purpose of the Discovery Room is to encourage close-up observation, self-discovery, and tactile experiences in an informal atmosphere. Therefore, only 30 visitors at a time are allowed in the 36-by-28-foot facility. The objects in the room come from throughout the world of natural history, and selection is based primarily on visual and tactile interest and durability. Those placed around the room on open display are meant to catch the visitor's attention and are called "stumpers" because they challenge the imagination and stimulate curiosity. Of the 50 "stumpers" scattered about the Discovery Room, some are of a seasonal nature, and virtually all relate to other exhibits in the museum. Minicollections containing 8 to 12 specimens make up the thematic discovery boxes. There are about 25 boxes, 17 by 12 by 4 inches, made of birch and divided into compartments to protect the objects and facilitate the checking-in process. Boxes are designed to appeal to a variety of ages and have encompassed fossils, beetles, Eskimos, a Swahili kitchen, touch a sound, teeth, reading a tree, Chesapeake Bay, braille, color in shells, minerals, Middle Eastern Bazaar, North American Indian dolls, and toys of the world. New themes are added periodically, and the boxes are continually being refurbished. Plasticized information cards are included in each discovery box, and others are available which relate to the "stumpers." The room contains a small library where visitors are encouraged to find answers to their questions. Due to the interest expressed in objects from other cultures, a costume corner with try-on clothing was added in the early 1980s. The Discovery Room staff includes 80 volunteers (docents) who work approximately 3 hours a week, 3 part-time employees, 2 volunteer coordinators (weekdays and weekends), and an exhibit manager who is responsible for developing and maintaining the exhibit. Volunteers do not serve as instructors but greet visitors, maintain security of the room, and encourage learning through discovery. Although 100,000 visitors per year use the room, only about 3,000 are members of a school group, which prior to 1982 had to be 2nd grade or above. Now classes of preschool children are allowed to make a class visit, and the Discovery Room is easily adapted for the disabled. Most visitors come in family groups where a close relationship between adult and child fosters a sharing of discoveries. The room is open 7 days a week but with limited hours, and there is no admission charge. Monday through Thursday mornings 10:00–11:45 October-May are reserved for school groups with a written reservation. Public visiting hours on a first-come, first-serve basis are Monday through Thursday 12:00–2:30 and Friday through Sunday 10:30–3:30. On weekends and holidays free passes, available from the Information Desk, are required. No school groups are allowed during public hours.

The Discovery Room of the National Museum of Natural History serves as both a model and a source of technical information for other museums interested in developing their own discovery rooms. Staff members have participated in workshops and produced a slide/script program, and a manual is forthcoming.

The Discovery Room: An Introduction (Washington, D.C.: Office of Education, National Museum of Natural History, Smithsonian Institution, 1985), Slides/Script; Vincent J. Gabianelli and Edward A. Munyer, "A Place to Learn," *Museum News* 53, no. 4 (December 1974): 32–33; Joan C. Madden, "The Discovery Room: A Place for Learning," *Children Today* 11, no. 5 (September/October 1982): 7–11; Barbara Y. Newsom and Adele Z. Silver, eds., *The Art Museum as Educator* (Berkeley: University of California Press, 1978), pp. 80, 108–10; Bonnie Pitman-Gelles, *Museums, Magic & Children: Youth Education in Museums* (Washington, D.C.: Association of Science-Technology Centers, 1981), pp. 27, 35–36; Peggy Thomson, "Please DO Touch These Exhibits," *Smithsonian* 5, no. 2 (May 1974): 92–95.

NATIONAL ZOOLOGICAL PARK, Smithsonian Institution, 3001 Connecticut Avenue, NW, Washington, D.C. 20008. The learning labs at the National Zoo, Zoolab, Birdlab, and HERPlab, were developed under the direction of Judith White following her involvement with the Discovery Room at the National Museum of Natural History in 1974 (see entry under UNITED STATES/ DISTRICT OF COLUMBIA). When she became head of the zoo's Office of Education in 1975, she suggested that the zoo develop interactive learning spaces for its visitors, especially families. Zoolab opened in the Education Building the fall of 1977 and contains a variety of natural history materials, including skins, skeletons, horns, feathers, plants, activity boxes, books, and 8mm-film loops which were later converted to video. There are tables, chairs, and seating platforms, and the room is designed to appeal to visitors of all ages and encourage family learning. School groups may schedule visits to Zoolab from October through May, classes receive a 30-minute time slot, and no more than 15 children may use the room at one time. Public hours are June through August, Tuesday through Sunday, 12:00–3:00, and October through May, Friday through Sunday, 12:00–3:00. The lab can accommodate 25 to 30 visitors at a time, and free tickets are available on a first-come, first-serve basis at the information desk in the lobby. Zoolab is staffed by volunteers. In 1978 Zoolab won the Education Award from the American Association of Zoological Parks and Aquariums (AAZPA).

Birdlab, located within the Bird House, opened in October 1978. Smaller than Zoolab and with materials specifically related to birds, the lab is open to visitors of all ages but not available to school groups. It can accommodate 15 visitors at a time, tickets are required, there is no admission, and it is staffed by volunteers. The materials, including activity boxes, 8mm-film loops which were converted to video cassettes, and books, are designed to be interactive and encourage both shared learning and independent investigation. Research indicates that visitors who use Birdlab come for specific information on birds. Hours are Friday through Sunday 12:00–3:00 with extended hours in the summer.

HERPlab, opened in October 1982, is both an expansion and a refinement of the other labs and was developed through a 3-year grant from the National Science Foundation. It is integrated into the renovated Reptile House, developed around conceptional themes, and contains materials of interest to a multigenerational audience. Families tried out the materials during the developmental stages; the John Ball Zoo in Grand Rapids, Michigan, and the Philadelphia (PA) Zoo served as field-test sites; and the project had an advisory board of science and education specialists. The 676-square-foot facility contains activity boxes, live animals housed in specially designed clear plastic boxes to facilitate viewing from all sides, skeletons, tanks with live lizards, an area devoted to the job of reptile keeper with try-on clothing and equipment, microscopes, video cassettes, and a library. From HERPlab, visitors can also observe the behind-the-scenes work of the keepers. HERPlab is open Wednesday through Sunday 12:00–3:00, and a ticket system is used to limit the number of visitors in the lab to 25 at a time. HERPlab is not available to school groups. There is no admission fee. In 1983 HERPlab received the AAZPA's Education Award.

Zoolab, Birdlab, and HERPlab are prototype facilities. A manual has been published as a guide for others interested in starting a similar learning lab and documenting its development.

Deborah A. Besch, "HERPlab," *Animal Kingdom* 86, no. 3 (June/July 1983): 17–18; Melinda Young Frye, "A Spring Quintet: Five Washington Area Exhibits You Won't Want to Miss [HERPlab]," *Museum News* 62, no. 5 (June 1984): 64–65; Judith S. King, "A Chicken Is Not a Bird: Visitor Programs at the National Zoo," *AAZPA Regional Workshop Proceedings 1979*, pp. 100–103; Judith White and Sharon Barry, *Families, Frogs, and Fun: Developing a Family Learning Lab in a Zoo—HERPlab: A Case Study* (Washington, D.C.: Smithsonian Institution, 1984); Judith White and Dale Marcellini, "HERPlab: A Herpetology Learning Center," *Herpetological Review* 14, no. 3 (September 1983): 62–65; Judy White and Signe Girgus, "The How-to-Build-a-Better-Box Book," *Roundtable Reports* (Fall 1977): 11–17.

ROCK CREEK NATURE CENTER, Rock Creek Park, 5000 Glover Road NW, Washington, D.C. 20015. The Rock Creek Nature Center, part of the National Park Service, opened on 7 October 1956 in a 19th-century stone mansion. Immediately it became evident that the building was inadequate. But it did help to introduce the nature center concept to the area and served as a pilot project for designing the new building, planning programs, and creating displays. In particular, participatory exhibits were found to be very effective, and they were interspersed with other displays and live animal exhibits. The present interpretive building, dedicated on 4 June 1960, has 11,000 square feet of floor space. There are exhibit areas, an auditorium, a 90-seat planetarium, a patio which is used as an outdoor classroom, and 2 self-guiding nature trails. The Center is located on an 1,800-acre woodland site. Prior to having a building constructed to meet the Center's needs, park naturalists gave programs in area schools, led field trips, developed a training course for junior naturalists, and sponsored a Junior Audubon Club. Currently the Center features natural science exhibits which highlight the park's resources, and nature study activities and programs planned for a specific age group or audience. There is an environmental education/nature study package that includes a full-day orientation workshop for leaders; parent/child activities; special planetarium shows for 4–7 year olds accompanied by adults and more advanced shows for children over 7; nature walks; and orienteering. There are 6 full-time and 1 part-time staff members who serve about 40,000 visitors annually. The Center is open 9:00–5:00 Tuesday through Sunday and closed Mondays and federal holidays. Support comes from governmental appropriation, and admission is free.

W. Drew Chick, Jr., "The Place of a Children's Museum as a Part of a Specialized Service," *Museum News* 45, no. 4 (December 1966): 36–37; Berne Teeple, ed., *Children's Interpretative Programs: National Park Service, National Capital Region 1978–79* (Washington, D.C.: National Park Service, 1979), pp. 24–25: ERIC Document Reproduction Service, ED 175 597.

FLORIDA

Cocoa

THE BREVARD MUSEUM, 2201 Michigan Avenue, Cocoa, FL 32926. The Discovery Room, opened in 1980, was created by the Junior League of Cocoa–Titusville. They staffed it with 2 volunteers for the first 2 years and have continued their support by providing funds for the facility. The 18-by-20 foot carpeted room has 12 Discovery Boxes, "stumpers," collection shelves, microscope, try-on clothes, a reading gazebo, and a reference collection including audiotapes, an aquarium, and an active beehive. The boxes, self-guided and multisensory, encompass Indians, weights and scales, magnets, minerals, spices, visual experiences, and other topics. The open shelves contain natural history materials that can be touched and held, such as bones, teeth, shells, birds, reptiles, fossils, rocks, and plant products. Programs in the room are offered for school groups, preschool through high school, and the handicapped. They can be on a specific subject or open-ended, and the items used depend on the focus of the presentation. Seventy-five percent of those using the room come in school groups and 20 percent are families. Fifty percent of those visiting are K–2nd grade and 30 percent 3rd–6th grade. The Discovery Room has 1 part-time paid staff member. Hours are Tuesday through Saturday 10:00–4:00, Sunday 1:00–4:00, and closed Monday. In 1985 there were more than 3,000 visitors.

"The Best Kept Secret in the County: Brevard Museum in Touch with Our History," *Today*, October 1984, sec. D, p. 1.

Fort Lauderdale

THE DISCOVERY CENTER, 231 S.W. Second Avenue, Fort Lauderdale, FL 33301. The Junior League provided the impetus for a youth museum, which opened to the public in April 1977. In November 1973 a planning grant was funded; the city agreed to rent for a dollar a year the historic (1905) New River Inn building, now listed in the National Register of Historic Places; and the cost for the renovation was covered by the Junior League, the National Park Service, and the city. In June 1976 the League made a 3-year commitment to supply personnel and provide financial support. The Center now occupies 3 historic buildings with a total of approximately 15,000 square feet, and most recently an 800-square-foot reconstructed schoolhouse was added. It is a hands-on museum of art, science, and history with participatory exhibits on the Everglades and the Seminoles, a pioneer home, perceptions, energy, computers, and an exploration of the 5 senses. In addition, there are zoos for insects, reptiles, and fish, a planetarium, and art studios. The museum's collection is strongest in turn-of-the-century household items, clothing, and shells. Since its inception there has been an outreach service which goes to schools, community and recreation centers, condominiums, and nursing homes. Programs are "Star Reach" (a portable planetarium), "Snake Reach" (Florida reptiles), and "Art Reach" (art and history of silk screen). The museum also sponsors classes, special activities, and programs targeted for the handicapped and the frail elderly. Ten full-time and 12 part-time staff members are assisted by 40 volunteers who work regular hours, and many others work as needed. Summer hours are Tuesday through Saturday 10:00–5:00 and Sunday 1:00–5:00. During the school year weekday mornings are for school groups visiting by prior reservation. Public hours are Tuesday through Friday 2:00–5:00, Saturday 10:00–5:00, Sunday 1:00–5:00, and closed Monday. Financial support comes 26 percent from local government, 12 percent from school board contract, 13 percent from admissions and tours, 4 percent from fees for outreach and classes, 10 percent from state and federal grants, 22 percent from corporate donations, and 13 percent from membership fees, individual giving, fund-raising, and the museum store. The Discovery Center Museum has about 60,000 visitors per year, 16,000 of which are schoolchildren on organized tours.

"Center's Discovery: How to Succeed at Marketing Culture," *Miami Herald*, 28 April 1985, pp. 1BL, 2BL; "Discovery Center Exhibit Putting Light on Science," *Fort Lauderdale News/Sun-Sentinel*, 20 August 1982, p. 3B; "Discovery Is a Delight in Children's Museum," *Miami News*, 27 May 1985, p. 2B; "Her Museum's No Fossil," *Fort Lauderdale News/Sun-Sentinel*, 4 June 1982, p. 3D; "Youngsters Learn about Reptiles by Getting Chance To Touch Them," *Fort Lauderdale News/Sun-Sentinel*, 21 February 1985, p. 12.

Gainesville

FLORIDA STATE MUSEUM, Museum Road, University of Florida, Gainesville, FL 32611. The Object Gallery, opened on 9 July 1974 as a pilot project, was created to provide opportunities for self-directed study and continuing education. Its development was aided by a grant from the National Endowment for the Arts. The 2,700-square-foot area contains more than 200 trays with thousands of objects drawn from the museum's collection, primarily archaeological, ethnological, and natural history materials. The specimens and artifacts can be viewed closeup, and many can be handled. While there are synoptic collections, in general they refer to other museum exhibits and are concept-oriented. In addition, there are aquariums, cages, and terrariums for study. Supplementary written and audiovisual materials for various age and interest levels are available within the gallery. Collections in the Object Gallery are continually being revised, and the facility also mounts special exhibits such as one on endangered species. Display panels and audiovisual materials developed for use in the gallery are made available to a wider audience when circulated through various outreach programs. The gallery is a multiple-use space under the Department of Interpretation; a number of staff members and volunteers are often involved. The Object Gallery is used with school groups, and about 14,000 students in scheduled programs visit the museum annually. Equally popular with the general museum visitor, the gallery is visited by about 90 percent of the 225,000 annual visitors to the museum. The museum is open Monday through Saturday 9:00–5:00 and Sunday 1:00–5:00. There is no admission charge. The museum, a college of the University of Florida and the State Museum of Natural History, is supported by the State of Florida and private granting agencies.

Educational Facilities Laboratories, *Arts and the Handicapped: An Issue of Access* (New York: Educational Facilities Laboratories, 1975), p. 24: ERIC Document Reproduction Service, ED 117 829; Vincent J. Gabianelli and Edward A. Munyer, "A Place to Learn," *Museum News* 53, no. 4 (December 1974): 28–31; "The Object Gallery Opens," *Florida State Museum Newsletter* 3, no. 4 (July/August 1974); Bonnie Pitman-Gelles, *Museums, Magic & Children: Youth Education in Museums* (Washington, D.C.: Association of Science-Technology Centers, 1981), pp. 36, 203.

Jacksonville

JACKSONVILLE MUSEUM OF ARTS AND SCIENCES, 1025 Gulf Life Drive, Jacksonville, FL 32207. The Marshroom, designed as an environmental exhibit/classroom, provides an opportunity for discovery learning and continues the initial intent of the museum. The 600-square-foot room contains a 200-gallon saltwater hands-on tank, live animals, many of which are reptiles native to Florida, and regularly scheduled live animal demonstrations. The Marshroom staff consists of a curator of natural sciences, 2 assistants, and an active teenage intern program. When the room is open to the public, it is staffed by a trained interpreter. Association for Childhood Education members who wanted to use specimens and artifacts in their classes started the museum in 1935; they later made window displays in a local bank. Though the Jacksonville Children's Museum was officially chartered in 1945, it wasn't until 1948, with the help of the Junior League, that it opened in a renovated 19th-century Victorian house. As the city grew, so did demands on the museum, and by the mid–1960s it was evident that a new building was needed. Again the Junior League along with others provided support, and in December 1969 the museum moved into its new downtown location with 32,000 square feet of interior space including a planetarium. In order to reflect its more general family orientation, the name was changed in 1977 to the Jacksonville Museum of Arts and Sciences. Thirty-four full-time and part-time staff members are assisted by 300 volunteers. During the summer the museum is open Monday through Friday 9:00–5:00, Saturday 11:00–5:00, and Sunday 1:00–5:00. During the winter it is closed on Monday. There is a small admission fee. The museum has approximately 150,000 visitors a year.

Educational Facilities Laboratories, *Hands-On Museums: Partners in Learning* (New York: Educational Facilities Laboratories, 1975), pp. 14–15: ERIC Document Reproduction Service, ED 191 755; Bonnie Pitman-Gelles, *Museums, Magic & Children: Youth Education in Museums* (Washington, D.C.: Association of Science-Technology Centers, 1981), pp. 81, 122, 161; Michael Webb, "New Children's Museum in Florida," *Museum News* 49, no. 7 (March 1971): 12–14; "Where Curiosity Begets Wisdom," *Southern Living* 10, no. 11 (November 1975): 36, 38.

Miami

METROZOO, 12400 SW 152 Street, Miami, FL 33177. The Children's Zoo, opened in 1981, is styled after a Malayan village called Sulewesi. The 1-acre area houses birds of prey, parrots and macaws, ostrich, emu, servals, lemurs llamas, and domestic animals. Visitors may buy food for the sheep and goats kept in the contact area. Educational talks on natural habitats and the status of the wild are given by 4 staff members throughout the day. Docents assist in the children's zoo on days when there are a large number of visitors. Hands-on experiences for zoo visitors increased in December 1985 when the "Zoo Close-Ups" program began. With docents on hand Thursday through Sunday from 12:00 to 3:00, visitors are able to observe close up and touch ferrets, snakes, hedgehogs, and a monkey. In addition, a wide variety of animal artifacts, including shells, hides, eggs, snake skins, horns, and claws, are available for firsthand examination. Open 10:00–5:30 daily, the zoo has about 800,000 visitors a year. Support comes 35 percent from county subsidy and 65 percent from earned income. The Metrozoo was developed following a county bond issue to replace the original Crandon Park Zoo, opened in 1948 on Key Biscayne. Its children's zoo, opened in 1957, was a 2-acre farm with domestic animals and a contact enclosure, silo, working windmill, and tropical bird aviary which could be entered. In 1980 the 47-acre Crandon Park Zoo was replaced by the 740-acre Metrozoo. Currently 280 acres are developed.

Rosl Kirchshofer, ed., *The World of Zoos: A Survey and Gazetteer* (New York: Viking Press, 1968), p. 244; Janet Ross, "Metrozoo Close-Ups Provide Hands-On Experience"

(Miami: Metrozoo Press Release, [December 1985]); Janet Ross, "Metrozoo Facts" (Miami: Metrozoo Press Release, 17 December 1985).

MIAMI YOUTH MUSEUM, The Bakery Centre, 5701 Sunset Drive, Miami, FL 33143. Opened on 16 February 1985 in 2,030 square feet of donated space, it was designed specifically as a cultural arts hands-on museum for children 18 months through high school. Besides visiting other museums prior to opening, the director and assistant director attended a seminar in 1984 offered by the Boston Children's Museum and the Children's Museum of Rhode Island, "How to Start/Not to Start a Children's Museum." To introduce the concept of a hands-on museum to the community, an introductory event, "Art in the Park," was held and a hospital outreach program initiated. Exhibits reflect a focus on art, music, drama, dance, literature, and related careers; each remains for a few months and includes many hands-on activities. Educational packets are also produced. INTO THE WOODS explored wood sculpture, collage, paper furniture, and violin making and showed woods from around the world; BEHIND THE SCENES featured the theater arts; and UNDER CONSTRUCTION, the art of architecture and related careers in the building trades. In April 1986 the museum moved from its original Sunset Strip Plaza location to a larger donated space in a newly developed shopping complex. The first exhibit in the larger 4,500 facility, ONCE UPON A PICTURE, was on book illustrations and illustrators. In addition, there are art classes, special events, and a Recycle Shop. The Kidz Council, comprised of 12–18 year olds, helps with fund-raisers and volunteers in the museum. There are also about 50 adult volunteers who assist the full-time director, an assistant director, and a part-time volunteer coordinator. The museum is open Tuesday, Wednesday, and Friday 10:00–5:00, weekends 12:00–5:00, Thursday only for tours in the morning, and closed Monday. Support comes 25 percent from the state and county councils, 25 percent from corporations, 25 percent from memberships, and 25 percent from admission fees and donations. The museum's 20,000 visitors during its first year were mainly families, school groups, and tourists.

"Discovery Is a Delight in Children's Museums," *Miami News*, 27 May 1985, p. 2B; "New Museum Is a Hit with Young Patrons," *Miami Herald*, 16 September 1985, sec. B, p. 1; "New Youth Museum Has Creativity Built In," *Miami Herald*, 16 September 1984; "Unveiling a Mystery Museum," *Miami Herald*, 16 February 1985, sec. C, pp. 1, 4; Bernie Ward, "Touch Me!" *Sky* 14, no. 7 (July 1985): 14, 16.

Punta Gorda

YOUTH MUSEUM OF CHARLOTTE COUNTY, 260 Retta Esplanade, Punta Gorda, FL 33950. The museum was founded in 1969 by mothers from the community who wanted a place for cultural and creative activities outside a formal school setting. Classes in drama, art, and music were taught and have continued to be a part of the museum's program. The first part-time director, hired in 1975, initiated the collection of natural history materials, cultural artifacts from around the world with an emphasis on dolls and costumes, and objects of local historical interest. Displays change every 3 months and focus on science and art, and the museum plans to create more interactive exhibits for families. The museum occupies a 3,000-square-foot building and has traveling exhibits it sends to schools and other public facilities. In addition, there are classes, clubs, field trips, and special events. In 1983 the museum became a public institution when it became a part of the county library system. The museum now has a full-time professional as coordinator, 2 other staff members, several volunteers, and 4 individuals who teach various classes. The museum is open Tuesday through Saturday 10:00–5:00 and serves all ages. Situated in a large retirement community, the museum is visited by many grandparents and grandchildren during the summer, while during the rest of the year school groups and younger families attend. About 6,000 people visited the museum last year, and many others were served by outreach programs. In addition to the support from the county, funds come from local corporations and state sources.

"Students Pull Some Strings for Art Exhibit," *Sarasota Tribune*, 16 March 1985; "Weaving: Museum to Display Looms, Raw Silk, Flax," *Fort Meyers News-Press*, 23 December 1984, pp. 1B, 2B; "Youth Museum Introduces Traveling Manatees," *Fort Meyers News-Press Charlotte*, 9 September 1984; "Youth Museum Receives Arts Grant," *Daily Herald News*, 25 October 1985.

Tallahassee

TALLAHASSEE JUNIOR MUSEUM, 3945 Museum Drive, Tallahassee, FL 32304. Founded in 1957 by the Junior League and teachers who were members of the Association for Childhood Education, the museum opened downtown in 1958. Additional support was provided by the National Foundation for Junior Museums. In 1960 a 50-acre site was purchased and buildings were constructed, and on 24 March 1962 the museum moved from a donated house to its new, spacious location southwest of the city. Although always providing a variety of hands-on exhibits, the museum has undergone a subtle shift from an initial emphasis on supporting the school curriculum to family-oriented learning and environmental education. Four facilities make up the main building complex and house the permanent exhibits which remain for 2 or 3 years, temporary exhibits which change monthly, classrooms, and natural science displays including a feeding window for birds. There is an emphasis on 19th-century clothing and artifacts, local history, and native plants and animals. Four historic buildings have been moved onto the museum grounds as representative of the area and for preservation. A re-creation of an area pioneer farm from the 1880s contains buildings that have been transferred from nearby communities, a crop garden, farm animals, and special activities related to farm life. A self-guided nature trail moves through a variety of north Florida habitats. Since 1980 the museum has greatly expanded its programming and now offers a nature-oriented pre-school, classes taught at the museum, summer day camp, in-school programs, outreach Treasure Chests, and seasonal special events. There is a regular staff of 14, 2 part-time people, a few volunteers, and a large support group dedicated to fund-raising. Twelve percent of the museum's income comes from the city, county, and school board, with the remaining 88 percent being generated by memberships, admissions, fund-raising, and grants. Hours are Tuesday through Saturday 9:00–5:00, Sunday 2:00–5:00, and closed Monday. Last year approximately 70,000 people visited the museum.

Rodney Allen, David LeHart, and Joel Dawson, *Community Leaders' Training in Environmental Studies: A Cooperative Community Project Funded under Title I of the Higher Education Act of 1965. Ways to Environmental Education. Final Report: 1974–1975* (Tallahassee: Florida State University, 1975): ERIC Document Reproduction Service, ED 107 583 and other project volumes ED 106 213, ED 107 579, ED 121 671; Educational Facilities Laboratories, *Arts and the Handicapped: An Issue of Access* (New York: Educational Facilities Laboratories, 1975), p. 24: ERIC Document Reproduction Service, ED 117 829; Helen T. Grissett, "Touch-Feel Learning at the Tallahassee Junior Museum," *Childhood Education* 47, no. 5 (February 1971): 261–64; "Museums That Come to the Classroom," *Grade Teacher* 83, no. 9 (May/June 1966): 44–45; Carolyn Schultz, "Here's the 'Critter Lady'!" *Science and Children* 22, no. 8 (May 1985): 49–51.

Tampa

THE TAMPA MUSEUM, 601 Doyle Carlton Drive, Tampa, FL 33602. The Lower Gallery, named because it is the only one on the ground level, is the scene of participatory and children's exhibits. Many of the installations are companion presentations to the exhibitions of fine arts in the 5 other galleries. The museum was formed from the union of the Tampa Junior Museum, founded in 1958, and the Tampa Bay Arts Center, founded in 1923. Since the museum's inception in 1979, the Lower Gallery has focused on exhibits for family interaction by presenting GAMES KIDS PLAY, ARM CHAIR ARCHAEOLOGY, FAMILY TIME, COVERED-ALBUM ART, and COMPUTER ART. Approximately 4 exhibits per year are mounted with an expository approach to the humanities. Pre-and post-visit activities for school groups and curriculum guides for certain exhibitions are available as part of the museum's programs for students in grades K–12. The lower level also contains the classroom and together with the gallery occupies 1,600 square feet. There are 1 full-time and 1 half-time staff member. Over 32,000 children and their families participate annually in Lower Gallery exhibitions and the special programs presented for children. Hours are Tuesday, Thursday, and Friday 9:00–6:00, Wednesday 9:00–9:00, Saturday 9:00–5:00, Sunday 1:00–5:00, and closed Monday. There is no admission fee. The Lower Gallery is supported by the museum budget, which comes 33 percent from the City of Tampa, 18 percent from fund-raising, 8 percent from grants, 24 percent from private sources, 14 percent from corporate sources, and 3 percent from sales.

"Crayons Outclassed by Computer Art," *Peninsula Tribune*, 17 May 1984, p. 3PE; "The Domino Theory: The Tampa Museum's 'Games Kids Play' Exhibit Is Designed to Get Kids off the Bench," *Tampa Tribune*, 18 June 1982, p. 10; "An Exhibit for Children of All Ages," *St. Petersburg Times*, 3 August 1982; "Museum Exhibit Gives Kids a Feel for the Old West," *Tampa Tribune*, 21 January 1983, sec. D, pp. 1, 2; Inez S. Wolins, "Educating in the Museum with Television," *Museum Studies Journal* 1, no. 2 (Fall 1983): 52–57.

West Palm Beach

THE SOUTH FLORIDA SCIENCE MUSEUM, 4801 Dreher Trail North, West Palm Beach, FL 33405. Tolerton Hood Discovery Hall opened in September 1982 and provides hands-on activities which are an extension of the museum's many participatory exhibits. The 25-by-35-foot Hall is designed for individual discovery and scientific investigation. No more than 15 students at one time are permitted, and reservations by schools are required for the 45- to 60-minute visit. Entrance fees for the county schools have been prepaid, and private schools pay according to group size. Started by the Junior League in 1959 as the Junior Museum of West Palm Beach, it became the Science Museum and Planetarium of Palm Beach County in 1964, signaling its evolution from a children's museum to a community science center. In 1985 the name was changed to the South Florida Science Museum, reflecting its regional natural history orientation. Still strong in exhibits and programming for children, the museum also offers classes for adults, family activities, and events for senior citizens. Of the 100,000 yearly visitors about 27,000 come in school groups. There are 14 full-time and 4 part-time staff members and approximately 150 volunteers. The Discovery Hall and the museum are open Tuesday through Saturday 10:00–5:00, Sunday and Monday 12:00–5:00, and Friday evenings 6:30–10:00.

Selina Tetzlaff Johnson, "Museums for Youth in the United States: A Study of Their Origins, Relationships, and Cultural Contributions" (Ph.D. dissertation, New York University, 1962), p. 189; "The Junior Museum of West Palm Beach in Florida," *Museum News* 37, no. 4 (June 1959): 32; "The Science Museum's SPLASH Jump into Fun: Opening of the South Florida Aquarium and New Science Museum," *Supplement to the Post* [Palm Beach, FL], 20 November 1983.

GEORGIA

Atlanta

HIGH MUSEUM OF ART, 1280 Peachtree Street, NE, Atlanta, GA 30309. The High Museum's Junior Activities Center and Junior Gallery opened in 1968 following 5 years of active involvement by the Junior League of Atlanta, who provided volunteers and financial support. These Junior areas became the base for all young people's activities at the museum. COLOR/LIGHT/COLOR (1968– 1971) explored the nature, properties, and uses of color, and SHAPES (1971– 1974) offered a variety of ways to learn about shapes in everyday life and in works of art. The multimedia environment THE CITY (1974–78) focused on what a city could be by looking at urban spaces. In May 1976 the museum extended its exploration of the city to the outdoors with the opening of PLAY-SCAPES, a children's play environment designed by sculptor Isamu Noguchi. During the summer months arts awareness activities for preschool and elementary children are held at PLAYSCAPES. Opening in September 1978, CHILDREN IN AMERICA (1978–1979) exhibited images of children from colonial times to the present and included artifacts, books, toys, and clothing. SPACES AND ILLUSIONS (1979–1983) focused on real everyday space and space that was imagined, distorted, recorded, or translated in paintings, photographs, and other ways. Traveling suitcase exhibitions were based on the exhibition themes and distributed to schools throughout Georgia. SENSATION (1983–1988) opened in the new High Museum facility and occupies 3,000 square feet. The most complex installation to date, it uses art, music, science, and technology in structured and open-ended experiences to explore the senses. The Department of Education, Student Programs, has 5 full-time and 4 part-time staff members and 150 volunteers. Since its inception a variety of school tours and workshops have been developed for the school-age audience, including a program for inner-city 4th-grade students, an outreach project for hospitalized children, a multipart program focusing on interdisciplinary learning, tours for children with physical handicaps and learning disabilities, and participatory tours for various age groups. During the school year SENSATION is reserved for prearranged tours and programs during school hours. Public hours are Tuesday through Friday 2:00–4:30, Saturday 10:00–4:30, Sunday 12:00–4:30, and closed Monday. During the summer the Junior Gallery is open Tuesday through Saturday 10:00–4:30, Sunday 12:00–4:30, with extended hours on Wednesday evenings until 8:30, and closed Monday. Children younger than 9 must be accompanied by an adult. Admission to the Junior Gallery is included in the regular museum admission, and approximately 25,000 schoolchildren and 250,000 public visitors tour annually. Support comes 50 percent from the museum budget and 50 percent from corporate contributions, private donations, and grants.

James T. Black, "Art Rises to a New High in Atlanta," *Southern Living* 19, no. 2 (February 1984): 116; Pamela Bray and June Schneider, "How the Arts and Technology Can Extend the Senses," *Art Education* 38, no. 3 (May 1985): 11–12; *HMA: A Report Covering the Period August 1, 1983, to July 31, 1984* (Atlanta: High Museum of Art, 1984), pp. 2, 13, 16–18; *Handbook for Guides*, rev. ed. (Atlanta: High Museum of Art, 1983), pp. 7, 15, 16–17; Rosamond Olmsted Humm, "Children in America: Images as History," *Design for Arts in Education* 80, no. 4 (March/April 1979): 8–13; Barbara Y. Newsom and Adele Z. Silver, eds., *The Art Museum as Educator* (Berkeley: University of California Press, 1978), pp. 388–94, 701; Bonnie Pitman-Gelles, *Museums, Magic & Children: Youth Education in Museums* (Washington, D.C.: Association of Science-Technology Centers, 1981), pp. 38, 91, 160.

Marietta

COBB COUNTY YOUTH MUSEUM, 649 Cheatham Hill Drive, PO Box 78, Marietta, GA 30061. The museum, founded in 1964, opened in 1970 after the Junior League of Marietta raised funds from the community, purchased land, and built the building. Surrounded by 10 acres, the museum has approximately 3,400 square feet of exhibit space and a puppet theater. Every 2 years the exhibits and programs change completely. Themes are taken from the sciences and social studies and have included CAREERS IN COBB—A CENTURY OF WORK, PADDLES TO PLANES, AMERICAN FRONTIERS, JOURNEYS TO DISCOVERY, AMERICAN INVENTORS, and BECOMING AMERICAN: THE IMMIGRANT EXPERIENCE. There is no emphasis on collecting, but children participate by dressing in period costumes and acting out the history involved in the exhibition. Classes are scheduled twice daily for 2-hour tours during the school year, and the summer program is open to the public. The director, tour coordinator, and office staff are assisted by 50 volunteers, who act as docents and puppeteers. The museum is open Monday through Friday 8:30–2:00 and on 5 Sundays a year from 2:00 to 4:00 for viewing the exhibitions. Financial support comes from the Cobb and Marietta School boards, the Public Library, the Friends' fund drive, and private corporate donations. The 15,000 annual visitors are schoolchildren and community groups.

"Students Live the 'Old Days,' " *East Cobb Neighbor*, 24 October 1985.

Savannah

OATLAND ISLAND EDUCATION CENTER, 711 Sandtown Road, Savannah, GA 31410. Opened on 1 September 1974, this environmental education facility occupies a 175-acre site that was formerly used by the federal government's Center for Disease Control. In 1973 the General Services Administration declared the property surplus and accepted proposals for its use. Tony Cope, director of the center, developed the Savannah-Chatham Public Schools' plan for utilizing the site as an outdoor classroom. The area is made up of 75 acres of salt marsh, 60 acres of coastal forest, and 40 acres of cleared land with a large 2-story brick building, built in 1927 as a home for retired railroad conductors, and 15 outbuildings. Students have blazed trails and built docks, observatories, a marine lab, 10 habitats for animals indigenous to Georgia, a 520-foot marsh walkway, a TV studio, cabins, and outbuildings. They have also reconstructed 2 19th-century cabins. Programs are closely tied to the school curriculum, and teachers receive pre-visit materials and activities, along with objectives and suggestions for post-visit activities. The Center has developed more than 35 different programs ranging from an hour-long kindergarten barn trip to a 3-day/2-night environmental education program for upper elementary and middle school students. Classes in television communication are held for high school youth, and there is an alternative program for middle school students who have been unsuccessful in regular school programs. A staff of 14 includes the director, assistant director, 7 teachers and 2 teachers aides, secretary, carpenter, and custodian/carpenter, who are assisted by approximately 25 regular volunteers. The Center is open 8:30–5:00 Monday through Friday throughout the year. Special programs are held the 2nd Saturday of the month October through May. The Center is closed during the seasonal holidays. Support for the staff, utilities, and maintenance of buildings comes from the public school system, and funding for new programs, trails, and animals areas comes from grants, gifts, and donations. Admission to all programs is a can of dog food, which is used to help feed the animals. The Center has approximately 35,000 school-age visitors and 15,000 other visitors each year.

"Island off Savannah Gets a Classroom Aura," *Christian Science Monitor*, 18 July 1977, p. 20; *Program Guide: Oatland Island Education Center* (Savannah: Savannah-Chatham County Board of Public Education, [1984]; "Where the Marsh and Forest Are School," *Christian Science Monitor*, 31 March 1975, p. 11; "Where You Feed the Animals, " *Southern Living* 15, no. 2 (February 1980): 72, 74.

HAWAII

Honolulu

BERNICE PAUAHI BISHOP MUSEUM, 1525 Bernice Street, PO Box 19000-A, Honolulu, HI 96817–0916. The Hall of Discovery, opened to the public on 7 October 1979, was designed to be the hands-on part of the museum. Installations were cooperatively developed by education and exhibit department staff and members of the museum's various research departments, including botany, ethnology, entomology, and zoology. Items from the collection are interspersed with creative activities designed to appeal to children 4–13. Included are natural history specimens and artifacts from various cultures. The primary audience served by the Hall are 4th and 5th grade students. Since its inception, the 2,000-square-foot Hall of Discovery has been visited by thousands of schoolchildren and families and last year by more than 14,000 schoolchildren. In addition, every month there is a Family Sunday, which attracts between 1,500 and 2,000 people. Plans for a major renovation of the Hall are currently being drawn and include the development of new interactive exhibits, discovery boxes, and activities. The redesigning will tie the Hall more closely to the mission of the museum and bring into public view more of the collection. The education department has 6 full-time staff members, 2 full-time volunteers, and 30 docents.

Educational programs take into consideration the 2 distinct audiences, local residents and visitors, that the museum serves. The Hall of Discovery is open daily except Sunday from 9:00 to 5:00 and the first Sunday of the month. There is an admission charge to the museum but no extra charge for the Hall of Discovery. Support comes 25 percent from investments, 24 percent from dues and contributions, 20 percent from grants and contracts, 12 percent from admissions, 6 percent from state government, and the remaining 13 percent comes from sales, services, and tuitions.

"Where Children Can Discover Hawaii," *Sunset* 174, (January 1985): 53.

ILLINOIS

Bloomington

MILLER PARK ZOO, PO Box 3157, Bloomington, IL 61702. The Petting Zoo opened in 1972, and its development coincided with the organization of the Junior Zookeepers program initiated that same year. The junior keepers were active participants in the effort to enlarge the zoo, and in September 1975 ground was broken for the new zoo. The Petting Zoo has always maintained a hoofstock collection, but with expansion the contact yard is now 30 by 65 feet and includes a barn. Exhibits have varied over the years, there are year-round and seasonal additions, and various small animals are included. The Petting Zoo has a "Morning at the Zoo" program in the summers for preschoolers, and many traveling zoos go out to the public year-round. Participants in the Junior Zookeepers program may begin anywhere between the ages of 8 and 13 and remain for as many years as they wish. With registration in the fall, the first-year juniors attend Saturday morning sessions and take a field trip. Upon successful completion of the first year, the junior keepers are expected to volunteer in the children's zoo during the summer months. Advanced junior keepers have graduated the first-year course and attend sessions geared to a more advanced level. The Miller Park Zoological Society sponsors the junior program in cooperation with the Bloomington Parks and Recreation Department. The Petting Zoo is open daily 10:00–7:00 from Memorial Day through Labor Day and has 3 seasonal paid staff members, Junior Zookeepers volunteers, and a few adult volunteers. Support comes from the city, a small admission, an occasional private donation, and additional purchases from the Junior Keepers Association and the Miller Park Zoological Society. Although no attendance figures are kept for the children's area, it is estimated that 45,000 visitors a year come to the Petting Zoo.

Randall E. Carney, "Miller Park Zoo Renovation," *AAZPA Regional Conference Proceedings 1981*, pp. 256–60; Randall E. Carney et al., "You Can Get Here from There: A History of the Miller Park Zoo," Bloomington, [1976] (Typewritten); Dianne M. Jedlicka, "Junior Zoo Keepers Association of America," *AAZPA Regional Conference*

Proceedings 1982, pp. 441–43; "Junior and Advanced Zookeepers Schedule 1985–1986," Bloomington, [1985] (Typewritten).

Brookfield

BROOKFIELD ZOO, 3300 Golf Road, Brookfield, IL 60513. The Children's Zoo opened in August 1953, and during its first full year of operation (1954), it had a half million visitors though it was open only in the spring, summer, and fall months and charged a small admission. Established as part of the education program and special exhibits, it provided a supervised opportunity to feed, pet, and observe both wild and domestic animals. After Gail Schneider became superintendent of the Children's Zoo in 1969, thematic exhibits were developed and stress given to fostering visitor understanding of man's relationship to both domestic and native wild animals. In 1970 the Children's Zoo started to stay open year round, and until 1981 admittance was free from late fall until early spring. Controlled animal feeding was introduced in 1976, and in 1977 the Children's Zoo eliminated visitor feeding. In its 2 acres are several contact areas, including the pet-and-learn circle and a walk-in farmyard, where visitors are encouraged to meet and touch animals and talk to a keeper. The Seabury Arena houses the "Animals in Action Program," where throughout the day animals show their herding, hunting, and other skills and demonstrate how they work with people. There is a hatchery, a barn where cows and goats are milked and butter is churned, a Clydesdale yard, dog and horse shows, and an Illinois animal exhibit. The wild animals in the Children's Zoo are orphaned or disabled and would not be able to survive on their own. A sensory corner has touch boxes and other participatory activities. The zoo staff is readily available, and programs can be arranged for special populations. In addition, there are a work-study program for local high schools and junior colleges and a 4-H program. The Children's Zoo participates in a wide variety of community parades and parties. Besides a visitor guide, a wide variety of handouts are available, and many are produced in large print and braille. There are 14 full-time and an average of 15 (per day) seasonal staff members, 20 volunteers, 2 work-study students, and 1 intern. It is open every day 10:00–5:45 in the summer and until 4:45 during the other 3 seasons. Sixty percent of the 450,000 to 550,000 visitors per year are adults, and Children's Zoo visitors account for 27 percent of the total zoo attendance. Support comes from the main zoo budget, which is reimbursed by a separate admission to the Children's Zoo, donations, and grants.

The Brookfield Zoo 1934–54 (Brookfield: Chicago Zoological Society, 1954), pp. 71–74; Davida Kalina, "Getting Involved in Children's Zoo: An Interview with Gail Schneider," *Docent Journal* [Brookfield Zoo], 1982, pp. 4–5; Gail Schneider, "Children's Zoo in Action: Kinetics of a New Zoo Force," *Brookfield Bison* (June/July 1979): 1–8; Gail Schneider, "Children's Zoo Grows Up," *Brookfield Bandarlog* 42 (Spring 1975): 3–5; Gail Schneider, "A New View of the Zoo," *Brookfield Bison* (October/November 1978): 5–8.

Chicago

THE ART INSTITUTE OF CHICAGO, Michigan Avenue at Adams Street, Chicago, IL 60603. The Junior Museum, a division of the Department of Museum Education, opened on 14 February 1964 after several years of planning by the Women's Board of the Art Institute and the Junior League of Chicago. The need for a children's facility was recognized by area teachers and women's organizations, but it was not until the early 1960s that 14,500 square feet of space on the museum's lower level became available. The educational planning and training of volunteers was conducted by the museum staff. Currently the children's section is divided into a 50-by-35-foot gallery, 2 corridor galleries, 2 small auxiliary gallery spaces, a library, auditorium, reception area, meeting room for docents, student cloakrooms, and other support areas. Designed to introduce the arts to children in contexts they can understand, the installations and programs are also suitable for families. The Junior Museum draws on the collections of the Art Institute for its exhibitions, and original art is used in the large gallery. Reproductions are generally used in the smaller galleries, and 1 permanent installation, TOUCH OF ART, is a hands-on exhibition with objects installed at wheelchair height and labels in braille, accessible to and used by all ages. Guided or self-conducted tours are available during the school year for grades 1–12, and admission is free to all Illinois student groups with a confirmed reservation. Tandem tours conducted in cooperation with 4 other cultural organizations, the Chicago Historical Society, the Chicago Symphony, the Field Museum, and a live performance at the Art Institute followed by a visit to a related gallery, are also offered. Student work is displayed in the picnic room and changed bimonthly. In addition, the Junior Museum conducts workshops for teachers and families, artists give demonstrations on Saturday and Sunday year round, and programs are held throughout the summer. Gallery games like "I Spy" are available, and the library distributes 5 booklets, *Heritage Hikes I-IV* and *Forms in Space*, written by museum staff, which are self-guided tours of Chicago Loop architecture and sculpture. Lois Raasch, director of the Junior Museum since its inception, is assisted by 2 part-time exhibit preparators, a full-time volunteer coordinator, an appointment secretary, 70 trained docents, 10 greeters, and 6 library volunteers. Staff salaries come from the Department of Museum Education, and other expenses including publications come from a Women's Board endowment. Last year the Junior Museum had approximately 60,660 schoolchildren on school tours, 16,580 in self-guided groups, 5,000 family program participants, 2,000 teachers in workshops, and 5,000 users of gallery games or self-guided walks. The Junior Museum is open weekdays except Tuesday 10:30–4:30, Thursday 10:30–7:00, Saturday 10:00–4:30, and Sunday 12:00–4:30.

"Chicago's Art Institute Spawns an Offspring: The Junior Museum Designed by Architect Arthur Myhrum," *Interiors* 124, no. 4 (November 1964): 70–73; Jane Clarke, "The Junior Museum's Tenth Birthday," *Bulletin of the Art Institute of Chicago* 68, no. 1

(January/February 1974): 12–15; "The Junior Museum," *The Art Institute of Chicago Quarterly* 58, no. 2 (Fall 1964): 22–33; Barbara Y. Newsom and Adele Z. Silver, eds., *The Art Museum as Educator* (Berkeley: University of California Press, 1978), pp. 310–14, 385, 688; Bonnie Pitman-Gelles, *Museums, Magic & Children: Youth Education in Museums* (Washington, D.C.: Association of Science-Technology Centers, 1981), p. 123.

BALZEKAS MUSEUM OF LITHUANIAN CULTURE, 6500 South Pulaski, Chicago, IL 60629. The Children's Museum opened in July 1981 to promote and preserve Lithuanian culture and occupies 2,000 square feet. Exhibits and programming, designed for preschoolers to 12 year olds and families, emphasize historical and cultural information and ethnic arts activities. With artifacts from the museum's collection, children have an opportunity to dress up in Lithuanian costumes, touch a variety of objects including an ancient string instrument called kankles, handle scratch-carved Easter eggs, use puppets based on characters from Lithuanian folklore, and explore the rest of the museum with a treasure hunt sheet which highlights the collection. A brief introductory tour of the museum is available to groups and includes information on the Lithuanian-American settlement in Chicago. Special demonstrations and school workshops are offered, depending on staff availability, for an additional fee. Outreach exhibits are also circulated. One staff member is assisted by 8 volunteers. The Children's Museum is open during regular museum hours, 1:00–4:00 daily, and support comes from the Balzekas Museum's general operating budget and grants. In 1984 the Children's Museum received a program grant from the Illinois Arts Council for "Lithuanian Folk Art Demonstrations" and in 1985 a Chicago Council on Fine Arts program grant for "Offshoot from Ethnic Art Roots: A Child's Introduction to Ethnic Folk Art." In mid–1986 the museum moved from 4012 South Archer Avenue to its present larger facility on South Pulaski.

"The Children's Museum," *Lithuanian Museum Review* 98 (July/August 1984): 1; "The Children's Museum," *Lithuanian Museum Review* (September/October 1985): 2; "Children's Museum Awarded City Arts II Challenge Grant—Museum Needs to Raise $1800 in Matching Funds," *Lithuanian Museum Review* 102 (March/April 1985): 4; "Polish Paper Cuts: 'Wycinanki,' " *Lithuanian Museum Review* 103 (May/June 1985): 4.

CHICAGO HISTORICAL SOCIETY, Clark Street at North Avenue, Chicago, IL 60614. The Marx Education Gallery, opened in 1972, serves as the Society's participatory center. In the late 1950s programs for children began using duplicate items from the collection, and following a building renovation a small space on the lower level was created for hands-on and role-playing activities. Initially the gallery served preschool and primary children; the theme was the Illinois pioneer era. In 1977 the gallery moved into a larger space at the rear of the 1st floor and is now used by all age groups. The 1,078-square-foot facility has both thematic settings and changing display areas which reflect late 19th- and early 20th-century life in Chicago. All artifacts are chosen to appeal to a broad age range and offer information through handling, manipulation, and active involvement. Material is still acquired by deaccessioning, but a small budget is also available for additional purchases. The permanent displays include a pioneer home setting with fireplace, household artifacts, and a loom; and a 1920–30s living room with radio corner and player piano. Three other areas change to focus on a timely topic, season, or era or to complement an exhibit at the Society. Recent installations were GIFTS TO THE BRIDE IN 1900, FUN AND GAMES ON PORCH AND SIDEWALK, and WHO WON? (presidential campaigns). In addition, a workshop using primary sources and focusing on early broadcasting has been developed for gifted 7th and 8th-grade students from the Chicago schools. A museum educator spends about one-third time coordinating the Gallery and is assisted by about 35 volunteers. Following renovation due to begin in 1986, the Marx Gallery will be enlarged to 1,550 square feet and relocated at the front of the building. A third to a half of the 100,000 schoolchildren who visit the Society annually are able to visit the Marx Gallery. Once the new facility is available, it is hoped that all groups can be accommodated. The Marx Gallery is open weekdays 10:00–12:00 and 1:00–3:00 on selected afternoons and weekends. Admission is free with membership in the Society. Support comes from the budget of the Department of Education and Public Programs.

"Chicago Historical Society," *The Quarterly: Midwest Museums Conference* 44, no. 1 (1984): 9; Carole Krucoff and Hilarie Staton, "Tuning in to the Past: A Workshop on Old-Time Radio Helps Gifted Junior High Students Learn about Chicago History," *History News* 40, no. 11 (November 1985): 27–31; "Museum Doors Open on Learning Cornucopia," *Chicago Tribune Sunday*, 24 November 1985, sec. 18, p. 4; Judy Weisman and Nancy Lace, "Education and Public Programs," *Chicago History* 10, no. 3 (Fall 1981): 186.

EXPRESS-WAYS CHILDREN'S MUSEUM, Lincoln Park Cultural Arts Center, 2045 Lincoln Park West, Chicago, IL 60614. The museum opened in October 1982, with Junior League support, in 2,500 square feet of donated space on the 4th floor of the Chicago Public Library Cultural Center. It developed as a direct response to the lack of financial support for arts programs in many area schools. Express-Ways provides participatory activities that focus on problem solving and learning through the arts for children up to 14, their families, and schools. The inaugural exhibit, GETTING TO KNOW HUE, explored color from many perspectives. In the fall of 1983 the museum expanded its exhibit space by another 2,000 square feet with the opening of its 2nd installation, AMAZING CHICAGO, a minicity. Buildings 3 to 10 feet high were grouped into 4 clusters and stimulated learning about architecture, city sounds, journalism, and occupations. Later a city hospital was added. The first outreach exhibit, GOOD FIB'RATIONS (about fibers), opened at the museum in October 1984 and began traveling to schools in January 1985. It can be rented and is set up by museum personnel; teacher in-service sessions are provided, and there are pre- and post-exhibit materials for classroom use. Also in 1985 a tactile tunnel,

TOUCHY BUSINESS, opened. School groups are accommodated weekday mornings with advance reservation, and there is a program fee. Express-Ways drop-in hours are weekday afternoons and weekends. Children must be accompanied by an adult and a donation is requested. The museum also has a Recycle arts center, in-service workshops for teachers, family activities, and monthly special events. Two-thirds of the groups come from schools within Chicago, and the remaining third from suburban and outlying area schools. In 1985 the museum served 67,000, one-fourth of which was through its outreach services to schools, community centers, shopping malls, and arts festivals. The museum moved in April and reopened in May 1986 in its new 7,500-square-foot facility in a Chicago Park District facility on the city's near northside. There are 6 full-time and 3 part-time staff members, 85 volunteers, and several exhibit designers and workshop leaders. More than half of the museum's support comes from foundations, corporations, and grants; about 10 percent comes from fees and contracts, and the remaining funds come from memberships and other miscellaneous sources.

"Children's Museum Locates in Lincoln Pk," *North Loop News*, 10 October 1985; Annette Faber, "A Green Light Museum: Express-Ways Children's Museum," *Design for Arts in Education* 85, no. 5 (May/June 1984): 38–43; "Fiber Exhibit Blends Learning and Fun for Kids," *Southtown Economist*, 6 February 1985; "A Kid's Museum with the Right Touch," *Chicago Tribune*, 12 April 1985, sec. 7, pp. 3, 8; Jean Morman Unsworth, "Express-Ways," *School Arts* 82, no. 9 (May 1983): 26–27.

FIELD MUSEUM OF NATURAL HISTORY, Roosevelt Road at Lake Shore Drive, Chicago, IL 60605. The Place for Wonder, opened in December 1976, was developed to provide multisensory experiences for the general public and meet the needs of the handicapped more effectively. The 1,240-square-foot room contains touchable specimens and self-directed learning activities in anthropology, botany, geology, and zoology, which are the major subject areas of the museum. Low wooden cabinets spaced about the room have a display area on top for larger specimens, free-access drawers filled with smaller items, and shelving for books related to the collection. The anthropology materials center around a particular country, currently China, and are changed every 2 years. Included in this area are clothing to try on, games, toys, musical instruments, and household items. The layout was designed to provide wheelchair access, and the cabinets are labeled in braille. In 1983 a new dimension was added when demonstrations of craft projects were initiated. A full-time staff person is responsible for maintaining the collections, training and scheduling the 20 volunteers, and planning the special events. The 2 volunteers who work each day provide visitor orientation, facilitate exploration, and care for the room and its collections. On weekdays between 10:00 and 12:15 school groups may schedule a 45-minute visit, and the room is open to the general public from 1:00 to 3:00. On weekends Place for Wonder is open on a first-come, first-serve basis 10:00–12:00 and 1:00–3:00. Attendance is limited to 30 people at any one time. The number of visitors has averaged about 135,000 per year with 80 percent representing the general public and the remaining 20 percent preregistered school groups. Funding for Place for Wonder comes from private gifts, and operating funds are provided by the museum.

Mary Bishop, "Man in His Environment: A Discovery Approach," *Curriculum Review* 16, no. 4 (October 1977): 245–47; Victor J. Danilov, "Discovery Rooms and Kidspaces: Museum Exhibits for Children," *Science and Children* 23, no. 4 (January 1986): 7–8; Educational Facilities Laboratories, *Arts and the Handicapped: An Issue of Access* (New York: Educational Facilities Laboratories, 1975), p. 27: ERIC Document Reproduction Service, Ed 117 829; "New Discovery Room," *Roundtable Reports* (Summer 1977); Bonnie Pitman-Gelles, *Museums, Magic & Children: Youth Education in Museums* (Washington, D.C.: Association of Science-Technology Centers, 1981), pp. 27, 37.

LINCOLN PARK ZOO, 2200 North Cannon Drive, Chicago, IL 60614. The Children's Zoo, opened in the early 1950s, started as a small contact area which operated only during the summer months. Popular with both children and adults, it was expanded in 1959 with the opening of a year-round children's zoo building. The facility housed young animals that had recently come to the zoo, those that the mother was not able to care for, and young hoofed mammals. An outdoor section was open only during the summer months. Volunteers, called zoo leaders, were available to answer visitors' questions. In addition, the children's zoo was available to the handicapped. The Traveling Zoo started operating in the late 1950s, and each summer it visits locations all over the city. In the late 1970s improvements to the Lincoln Park Zoo included an expansion of the Children's Zoo. The waterfowl lagoon was enlarged with an all-season glazed dome for winter observation. An outdoor amphitheater for informal programs accommodating about 50 children was added. Adjacent to the petting area for goats, llamas, and deer an enclosed pavilion was built and used as a contact area with handicapped children and as a classroom. There are 4 full-time regular keepers during the year and about 20 full- and part-time staff members during the summer. After 25 years of service the Children's Zoo is being renovated. It was closed in April 1986, and construction is expected to take a year. The building will have a new central island with animal habitats; staff will have a concealed management area in the middle; the zoo nursery will be expanded and include a skylight and an exercise area; and a learning center/auditorium for small groups and classes will be added. This area will be suitable for serving the handicapped and elderly. The support areas for the Traveling Zoo and outdoor classroom will be improved. The children's garden and petting area will be transformed from a playground design to a midwestern forest community with wooded pathways, animal habitats, petting areas including a special one for the handicapped, and educational displays. Following renovation, some of the outdoor area will remain open year-round.

In 1965 the Lincoln Park Zoo opened its 5-acre Farm-In-The-Zoo to provide urban children experiences with domestic animals. It is a working replica of a midwest farm and was developed cooperatively with the Chicago Park District and the University of Illinois College of Agriculture. The 5 main areas include the steer barn, horse stable, dairy barn, poultry and egg building, and the main barn, which houses the sheep and swine and is also used as an exhibit area for educational displays, machinery, and equipment. There are daily farm activities and demonstrations. There is a staff of 6 to 8 keepers. The Farm-In-The-Zoo will also soon undergo renovation.

Both the Children's Zoo and the Farm-In-The-Zoo are used by the Department of Education for their programs and activities. All school programs are free of charge, and there is no admission to the zoo, which is operated by the Chicago Park District. The zoo is open 9:00–5:00 daily, and the Children's Zoo is open from 10:30 daily. Each year about 3 to 4 million people come to the zoo, and most go to the children's zoo. The Farm-In-The-Zoo has about 2 million visitors annually.

"Children's Zoo Construction Update," *Lincoln Park Zoo Review* 1, no. 1 (Spring 1986): 6; "The Farm-In-The-Zoo," *The Ark* 3, no. 2 (Summer 1975): 2–5, 14; Judith Rena Kolar, "Hands On Zoo: An Educational Program about Animals for the Blind and Partially Sighted Learner," *AAZPA Regional Conference Proceedings 1981*, pp. 214–19; "The Lincoln Park Zoo Improvement Program," *The Ark* 5, no. 1 (1977–1978): 7–9; Rhoda Musfeldt, "Children's Zoo Open Year Round," *Parks & Recreation* 42, no. 7 (July 1959): 330–32; Mark Rosenthal, "The Two Zoos in the Zoo," *The Ark* 2, no. 2 (Summer 1974): 2–4; "Work Set to Begin on Children's Zoo," *Landmark News* 2 (Winter 1986): 3.

MUSEUM OF SCIENCE AND INDUSTRY, 57th Street and Lake Shore Drive, Chicago, IL 60637. The Kresge Library Science Education Center, opened on 2 January 1984, made accessible to the public a facility inactive for over 40 years. In the mid–1970s the museum's director, Victor J. Danilov, initiated the idea of revitalizing the library and expanding its services to visitors of all ages. In 1981 a substantial matching grant was received from the Kresge Foundation, and the museum made the renovated and expanded library one of its 50th-anniversary funding priorities. The 10,500-square-foot multilevel facility is high-tech in an Art Deco setting with a general browsing area, a 2,300-square-foot youth section, an adult science collection, and a teacher's resource collection that includes commercial and museum-produced materials. The youth area, a long rectangle, is divided by use rather than walls so that preschoolers are at one end and teens at the other. For younger visitors there is a freestanding unit with carpeted risers forming a minitheater on one side that provides shelving on the other. Preschool story hours on science themes are given in the theater area, which is also used for school group orientation and film viewing. The shelves around the other side are filled with books, activity boxes, and puzzles of interest to young children. Adjacent to this area is a parents' section with a collection of child development material. Nearby is a youth section with books and other materials arranged around topics of interest. At the far end of the room is a partially enclosed computer learning area with microcomputers, software, and printed material related to computer technology. There is no charge to use the library or its computers. Materials are noncirculating, but public domain software may be copied by users. Since 1973 the museum has sponsored the Annual Children's Science Book Fair, and in 1985 a basic list of the best books from 1973 to 1984 was published. The library's regular public hours are Sunday through Friday 1:00–4:00 and Saturday 9:30–4:30. Group visits may be scheduled mornings Monday through Friday. Three professional staff members are assisted by 3 nonprofessionals and 15 volunteers. Support for the library comes from private sources, and it has about 80,000 visitors per year.

The Curiosity Place, a 2,000-square-foot permanent science exhibit for children through age 6, opened in November 1984 and has 4 areas with interactive devices. Planning for the facility began in the mid–1970s, and 29 prototype units were developed in 1979, when the museum received a grant from the National Science Foundation (NSF). The testing phase was carried out between February 1980 and May 1981, and then major funding was solicited. The sturdy play units are designed for children to explore, without adult assistance, sound, light, forces and motion, and water. The Curiosity Place also includes a resource room, an area for adults to interact with children and other adults, which includes periodicals, reference books, free take-home sheets, discovery boxes, and children's books. The facility is open to the public Saturday and Sunday 10:00–5:00 year-round and weekdays during the summer 10:00–4:00. School-year hours are Monday through Friday 11:15–3:30 for the general public and for school groups with reservations from 9:45 to 11:15. It is closed on major holidays. To control the number of children and adults during busy times, a ticket system is used, allowing no more than 20 children inside at a time. Tickets are free, and visits are limited to 40 minutes. There are 1 full-time supervisor, 2 part-time assistants, and about 50 volunteers. Initial funding came from the museum, the NSF, and several foundations, and support now comes from the museum. The Curiosity Place had 85,000 visitors during its first year.

"A Curious Place," *Progress* 36, no. 2 (March/April 1985): 8–9; Victor J. Danilov, "Early Childhood Exhibits at Science Centers," *Curator* 27, no. 3 (September 1984): 181–83; "Form, Function Blend in a Unique Library and Science Center," *Chicago Tribune Magazine*, 10 March 1985, p. 30; Carla D. Hayden, "Museum of Science and Industry Library," *Science and Technology Libraries* 6, nos. 1/2 (1985): 47–53; "Kresge $$ Will Build for Chicago a Children's Science Library," *Library Journal* 106, no. 16 (15 September 1981): 1683; Museum of Science and Industry, Department of Education, "An Interactive Science Exhibit for Preschoolers: Development, Design and Evaluation," Chicago, January 1982 (Typewritten); Bernice Richter and Duane Wenzel, comps., *The Museum of Science and Industry Basic List of Children's Science Books 1973–1984* (Chicago: American Library Association, 1985).

Peoria

GLEN OAK ZOO, Glen Oak Park, 2218 North Prospect Road, Peoria, IL 61603. The Children's Zoo opened in 1956 as a small contact area with farm animals and now includes domestic and foreign farm animals and pony rides. With new management in 1974, an education department was established and several outreach programs initiated. The World of Wonder, a 15-by-45-foot hands-on discovery center, with activities for visitors of all ages, opened in January 1985. Exhibits will change about once a year and currently include a live animal area, microscopes, and touchable animal biofacts related to the current displays on birds, fish, animal diets, and endangered species. There are also animal stamps for making imaginary creatures. Based upon the 20-year master plan that was developed in 1985, many other future exhibits will have some participatory feature. THE AFRICAN PLAINS exhibit, scheduled to open in the spring of 1986, includes a replica of an African termite mound that visitors will be able to enter and through which they will be able to view the animals. The Glen Oak Zoo and World of Wonder are open daily 10:00–4:00 except Thanksgiving, Christmas, and New Year's. The zoo has 8 full-time and 4 part-time staff members who are assisted by 40 docents. In peak season there are additional part-time staff members. The zoo is owned and operated by the Peoria Park District. Sixty-five percent of its support comes from admissions and sales and 35 percent from county taxes, donations, and an endowment. The zoo has about 131,000 visitors a year.

Earl F. Davis, ed., "Peoria Zoo Has 'Animal Fair,' " *Parks & Recreation* 38, no. 10 (October 1955): 23–24; Jim Ellis, "The Re-Development of the Glen Oak Zoo through Education," *AAZPA Regional Workshop Proceedings 1977–78*, pp. 564–67; *Glen Oak Zoo: World of Wonder* (Peoria: Glen Oak Zoo, [1985]).

Rockford

DISCOVERY CENTER MUSEUM OF ROCKFORD, 401 South Main Street, Rockford, IL 61101. Founded in 1981 by the Junior League of Rockford and the Rockford Council for Arts and Sciences, the museum was developed to be a resource for the children of northern Illinois. Located downtown in the Old Post Building with 14,000 square feet of gallery space and additional office, storage, and class space, the Discovery Center specializes in science and perceptual exhibits with arts-related installations. The target audience is children K–6. Originally open only for school groups, the museum gradually began to have public hours. After its first year and a half it introduced Sunday family programs, a Friday afternoon series in the summer, and after-school classes. Many of the 50 hands-on exhibits were built locally, are unique, and are rotated so that new things are on the floor for return visitors. The Discovery Center did purchase SENSORIUM and GETTING TO KNOW HUE from other children's museums and rented GOOD FIB'RATIONS. In February 1985 a 24-seat planetarium was added. Each year there are 2 major traveling exhibits and 1 special program each month during the school year. The executive director is assisted by a part-time secretary, a weekend employee, 30 docents, and 2 volunteer planetarium operators. Professional instructors are hired for classes and a 7-member Junior League committee is involved with program planning and implementation. Group tours are given daily by reservation only, and public hours during the school year are Saturday 11:00–4:00 and Sunday 1:00–4:00. Summer hours are Wednesday through Sunday 1:00–4:00. The museum is closed all major holidays and the last 2 weeks of August for refurbishing. There is a small admission. Support comes 25 percent from admissions, family memberships, and class fees; 10 percent from grants; 20 percent from a corporate fund drive; 25 percent from earned income; and the rest is in-kind donations. Last year the Discovery Center Museum had 240 children enrolled in classes and 12,000 visitors.

"Eyes West: Rockford State's Fun Capital? No. 2 Trying to Change Image," *Daily Courier News*, 19 October 1984, p. 10; "Get a Peek at the Stars: Planetarium Opens Sunday at Discovery Center," *Rockford Register Star*, 2 February 1985, p. 1B; Peggy Dahlberg Jensen, "The Discovery Center—Where Curiosity Is Rewarded," *Illinois Magazine* 25, no. 1 (January/February 1985): 30–32.

Springfield

ILLINOIS STATE MUSEUM, Spring and Edwards, Springfield, IL 62706. A Place for Discovery opened on 27 March 1982 to provide a special area where artifacts and specimens could be handled and self-directed learning encouraged. The 804-square-foot room contains a variety of objects from the worlds of natural history and anthropology, over 30 discovery boxes, a changing variety of learning games, and about 6 live animals. The room is accessible for use by the handicapped and includes braille labels. Classes and other groups may arrange for a special 45-minute program. A Place for Discovery is under the direction of the curator of education and is managed by a coordinator whose position has been supported by a foundation grant. The more than 20 volunteers who assist in the room come from the Illinois State Museum Society, the Springfield Association of Retired Teachers, and the Junior League. Many learning activities have been developed by the volunteers in conjunction with the scientific staff. Hours are Tuesday through Saturday 8:30–5:00, Sundays 1:45–4:45, and closed Mondays. The target audience is children and families, but a Place for Discovery is also enjoyed by adults. Last year approximately 52,000 visitors used the Discovery Room.

Bill Baughman, ed., "Our Museum World: Illinois State Museum," *Explorer* 24, no. 2 (Summer 1982): 15; Edward A. Munyer, "Exhibits, Education and Technical Services," *The Living Museum* 44, no. 5 (1983): 71–74; "Exhibits, Education and Technical Services," *The Living Museum* 44, no. 5 (1983): 71–74; "Exhibits, Education and Technical Services," *The Living Museum* 45, no. 5 (1984): 74–77; "Exhibits, Education and Technical Services," *The Living Museum* 46, no. 5 (1985): 90; Edward A. Munyer, "Museums and Their Discovery Rooms," *The Living Museum* 44, no. 3 (Summer 1982): 43–45.

Wilmette

KOHL CHILDREN'S MUSEUM, 165 Green Bay Road, Wilmette, IL 60091. Founded on 1 February 1985, the museum was developed by the Kohl Educational Foundation staff in Wilmette and Jerusalem. Planning for the 10,000-square-foot facility began in 1984 and is a larger working model of the interactive learning activities that have been carried out in the United States and Israel by the Kohl Teacher Centers since 1974. The initial staff installations included A WALK THROUGH JERUSALEM and THE DINOSAUR FOREST. These were supplemented by exhibits purchased from the Denver Children's Museum and 25 computers designed to travel. The exhibits include FIGURE IT OUT (everyday math), SCIENTOYFIC (science toys), WHO AM I? (pretend and fantasy), BUBBLEMANIA (all about bubbles), THE JIM SHORTS HEALTH CLUB (aerobics and nutrition), A WALK THROUGH MOROCCO (sights, sounds, and crafts of a Middle East market), KIDS AND PETS (care of pets), STAY TUNED (making a commercial), and WOOLLY MAZE (production of wool). Outreach is an important museum activity, and there are weekend workshops for families. The primary audience is children 2–11, but the majority of visitors are 3–6. Programming reflects a teacher/parent/child resource center philosophy. The director is assisted by 5 consultants and 10 docents. Monday through Friday the museum is open for group visits by appointment, and public hours are Tuesday through Sunday 10:00–4:00. Support comes 67 percent from admissions and rentals, 13 percent from memberships, and 20 percent from the Delores Kohl Educational Foundation.

"Kohl Teacher Center and Kohl Jewish Teacher Center," *Directory of Teacher Centers in Illinois* (Springfield: Illinois State Board of Education, n.d.), p. 11; "Museum Features Hands-On Fun," *Milwaukee Journal*, 17 March 1985, p. 3; "New Museum for Children Mixes Learning and Fantasy," *Chicago Tribune*, 18 January 1985, sec. 7, p. 4; "Rx for Summer Blahs," *Wilmette Life*, 27 June 1985, pp. 22, 36.

INDIANA

Bloomington

HILLTOP, THE BLOOMINGTON YOUTH GARDEN–NATURE CENTER, Department of Biology, Indiana University, Bloomington, IN 47405. Established in 1948, Hilltop is jointly sponsored by Indiana University, the City Department of Parks and Recreation, and the Bloomington Garden Club.

The 1-acre facility has 90 plots, 9 by 9 feet, and accommodates 150 children per year. Registration for the annual season is open to any 9–12 year old, and there is a small membership charge. The fee covers a full year's use of tools, seeds and young plants, plot, 38 instructional meetings, project materials, field trips, social activities, and produce which children take home. The gardening season begins in late February with indoor lessons, moves to the outdoors by mid-April, and concludes in mid-August. While school is in session, the youth gardeners meet on Saturday mornings for a 1 1/2-hour period, divided into veterans and beginners. During the summer months meetings are held Tuesday, Thursday, and Saturday mornings. The lessons cover soil management, crop production, ecology, nutrition, and decorative gardening. Learning to work with others is another aspect of the program. Besides the vegetable plots, there are small flower and herb beds, a greenhouse, classroom, library, toolroom, and amphitheater. Hilltop serves as both a leisure science program for youth and a vital component of the university's science education curriculum. Barbara Shalucha, cofounder and director of Hilltop, is a member of the university's Department of Biology, and 15 to 40 hours of work per week are provided by department students. In the summer the city supports a science education coordinator, 2 grounds keepers, and 3–4 university interns. Since its inception over 10,000 youth gardeners and 1,000 university-student interns have been involved with Hilltop.

Barbara Shalucha, "Garden, Hilltop Leadership Training Center: Its Function," *Symposium Report of the National Civic Garden Centers* (Bloomington: Indiana University Publications, 1975), pp. 35–51; Barbara Shalucha, "People Want to Become Self-Sufficient Gardeners: The Beginnings with Youth," *Acta Horticulturae* 105 (December 1981): 23–31.

Evansville

MESKER PARK ZOO, Bement Avenue, Evansville, IN 47712. The Children's Contact Area and Petting Zoo opened in 1975 and covers approximately 1 acre. It focuses on domestic animals and is the only area within the 67-acre zoo, established in 1929, where visitors are allowed to feed the animals. The contact area is visited by school groups at the zoo, and the outreach program uses some of its animals. In addition, there are many special events for children during the year, and the Summer Safari Day Camp stresses hands-on and uses the children's zoo. Each safari session lasts 1 week, is planned for a particular age group, and 1 week is for handicapped youth. Fridays, the last day, parents are invited to a safari session. The summer program is due to expand, with 2 weeks being planned especially for disadvantaged children. Volunteers and docents use the contact zoo for tours and educational demonstrations. There is 1 keeper in charge of feeding and cleaning, and 2 seasonal employees sell animal food during the peak season. Support comes from admissions, the city, the Evansville Zoological Society, and special fund-raising. The zoo is open 9:00–

4:00 daily and has approximately 200,000 visitors a year. No separate attendance figures are kept for the children's contact area and petting zoo.

Mesker Park Zoo (Evansville: Rowe & Field, n.d.).

Fort Wayne

FORT WAYNE CHILDREN'S ZOO, 3411 Sherman Avenue, Fort Wayne, IN 46808. The zoo, opened on 3 July 1965, was developed by local citizens who wanted to have a zoological facility in the community for its children and families. Originally 11 acres, it increased to 33 acres in 1971 with the opening of the 22-acre AFRICAN VELDT, exhibiting several species and re-creating a natural African savannah. Visitors can see the veldt from an elevated boardwalk or by taking safari rides to the Ugandan and Kenyan sections. The animals are free to roam, but visitors must remain on the pathways and roadways. A new office/education building houses the Discovery Center, a 1,500-square-foot room containing participatory exhibits. It includes ARE YOU SENSE-ABLE (comparing human senses with those of animals), INVENT AN ANIMAL (rubber stamps with various animals heads, bodies, and legs), fish tanks, a woodland turtle habitat, glass beehive, and incubators to watch eggs hatching. Numerous microscopes and magnifiers are available to examine animal artifacts. In the barnlike atmosphere of the contact area, visitors can feed and pet animals, and in the amphitheater there is an opportunity to touch animals and ask questions in the volunteer-run program, "Meet the Animals." A zoomobile takes outreach programs into the community, and Zoo Activity Packets for grades K–8 help teachers prepare their students for zoo field trips. Special events are held throughout the summer, and a winter film series is offered to zoological society members. In 1987 a new 5-acre exhibit, the AUSTRALIAN ADVENTURE, will open. An orientation center will acquaint visitors with the people, animals, and environments of Australia, and will feature a 24-foot-long Great Barrier Reef tank. Australian mammals and birds will be exhibited in a nocturnal jungle building, a walk-through aviary, and an outback area. There are 7 full-time, permanent and 40 seasonal staff members, who are assisted by 80 adult and 75 teenage volunteers. The zoo is open from late April through mid-October 9:00–5:00 Monday through Saturday, and until 6:00 on Sunday and holidays. It is also open during the last 2 weeks in October for the Great Zoo Halloween and 3 weeks in December for Christmas Time at the Zoo. Support comes 40 percent from gate admissions, 40 percent from concessions, 10 percent from donations, and 10 percent from zoological society memberships. Approximately 385,000 visitors of all ages, primarily from northeastern Indiana, southern Michigan, and western Ohio, come to the zoo annually.

"The Biggest Little Zoo in America," *Fort Wayne Magazine* (August 1978): 65; David M. Jenkins, "A Survey of Interactive Technologies," *AAZPA 1985 Annual Conference Proceedings*, pp. 74, 75, 77, 80: Eric Document Reproduction Service, ED 265 038; Cynthia L. Vernon, "The Great Zoo Halloween Party," *Fort Wayne Today* (Fall 1985): 2; "Your African Veldt," *Zoo Tails* (March 1971): 1; "Zoos Are News," *Woman's Day*, 23 October 1984.

Indianapolis

THE CHILDREN'S MUSEUM, 30th & Meridian, PO Box 3000, Indianapolis, IN 46206. Founded in 1925, the museum was established due to the enthusiasm of Mrs. John N. Carey, who had visited the Brooklyn Children's Museum (see entry under UNITED STATES/NEW YORK) in 1924. She was able to mobilize the interest of other civic-minded women in the community, and they worked in cooperation with the Progressive Teachers Association. An exploratory meeting was held in December 1924, and in April 1925 the Children's Museum Association organized with 32 charter members. A tiny carriage house at 126 East 14th Street, behind the Indianapolis Propylaeum, was the museum's first home. Immediately the donated collections started to accumulate, and in January 1926 the museum moved to the south wing of the city's Garfield Park Building. Arthur B. Carr, named curator in May 1926, guided the museum's move to its third home, the former Carey residence at 1150 North Meridian, where it opened on 16 April 1927. Carr was interested not only in collecting artifacts but in making the museum a vital part of the community's educational system. The collection, mostly donated, now includes over 130,000 objects in natural history, paleontology, geology and archaeology, ethnology, and history.

Many of the programs and services initiated during the 1930s have continued into the 1980s. Starting in 1931 the Board of School Commissioners began to make an annual appropriation to the museum and appointed 1 member to the museum's board of trustees. The city schools still make a yearly contribution, and other school systems also provide support. In 1932 a lending service began circulating small exhibits using duplicate items in the collection. This service took the museum to those who were unable to make a visit. In 1980 the Children's Museum began to participate in a cooperative outreach program which serves elementary-age hospitalized children. The Resource Center currently circulates more than 800 portable exhibits to schools and other child-centered organizations such as scouts, day-care centers, and church groups, making approximately 6,000 loans per year. In 1933 the Children's Museum Guild was formed, and since then its young women have provided both services and financial support. Today there are 80 active members and more than 200 associate members, who contribute more than 18,000 volunteer hours and a sizable sum through fund-raising projects each year. Grace Blaisdell Golden, who joined the museum in 1928, succeeded Carr as director in 1942 and served until 1964. During her tenure the museum continued its growth, purchased and moved into another building, the Parry house at 30th and Meridian, and increased its programming and services. There were performing arts groups, scout badge classes, weekly TV shows, and crafts demonstrations in the museum galleries.

Mildred Compton became the museum's third director in 1964. During her 18-year tenure the museum successfully raised money for a new facility, including a substantial pledge from the Lilly Endowment. On 2 October 1976 the museum opened its new 203,000-square-foot, 5-level building on a 5-acre site. The building now encompasses 228,000 square feet following an expansion project in 1983. There are 8 major galleries, a 350-seat theater for music, drama, dance, music, and puppet performances, and an operating carousel. Although the museum has traditionally been rooted in the social and natural sciences, it opened a physical science gallery in 1979 which was expanded in 1982. There are 40 hands-on exhibits and an 80-seat demonstration theater. There is also a computer lab with more than 50 terminals and printers and classes for all age groups. The museum is beginning to incorporate the computer into exhibits using it as an interpretive device. PLAYSCAPE, a special gallery with 7 areas for young children 2–7 years old, opened in 1980. MYSTERIES IN HISTORY, opened in June 1985, gets the visitor involved in the process of history using primary sources to learn about the past. In addition, there are classes for members and the general public, guided tours for school groups, a junior curator and junior historian program, and a neighbors program for those in the immediate neighborhood. With Peter Sterling as director, the Children's Museum has 80 full-time and 70 part-time staff members, who are assisted by over 500 volunteers. The museum is open Tuesday through Saturday 10:00–5:00 and Sunday 12:00–5:00. From Memorial Day through Labor Day it is also open Monday 10:00–5:00. Support comes 66 percent from endowment income; 19 percent from contributions, grants, and memberships; and 15 percent is earned income from the gift shop and program fees. There is no admission charge, and about half of the museum's 1.3 million annual visitors are adults.

Mildred S. Compton, "A Training Program for Museum Volunteers," *Curator* 8, no. 4 (1965): 294–98; George Gonis, "The Children's Museum of Indianapolis Emphasizes Historical Processes Rather than Historical Facts in Its New Gallery," *History News* 40, no. 7 (July 1985): 12–15; Grace Golden, "Financing a Private Children's Museum," *Museum News* 37, no. 7 (April 1961): 26–29; Nancy Kriplen, *Keep an Eye on That Mummy* (Indianapolis: The Children's Museum of Indianapolis, 1982); Judy Otto, "Learning about 'Neat Stuff': One Approach to Evaluation," *Museum News* 58, no. 2 (November/December 1979): 39–45; Bonnie Pitman-Gelles, *Museums, Magic & Children: Youth Education in Museums* (Washington, D.C.: Association of Science-Technology Centers, 1981), pp. 8, 25, 43, 89, 92, 101, 113, 121, 135, 193, 201, 220, 230; John Vanausdall, "The Computer as Interpreter," *Museum News* 64, no. 3 (February 1986): 73–82.

Muncie

MUNCIE CHILDREN'S MUSEUM, 306 South Walnut Plaza, Muncie, IN 47305. The museum was founded in February 1976 by a small group of women; the planning committee received financial support from the Kappa Kappa Kappa sorority. The museum opened on 27 December 1977 in a converted storefront at 519 S. Walnut and in 1981 moved to a 9,500-square-foot building, formerly a drugstore. The Ontario Corporation pays the rent, and utilities are paid out of museum revenues. The museum is designed to provide hands-on opportunities for children 18 months to 12 years old. There are 8 main semipermanent exhibits, a few smaller areas, and room for seasonal displays. Installations include MY GRANDFATHER'S MIDDLETOWN (Muncie and central Indiana in the 1920s and 1930s), LEARN NOT TO BURN (fire safety), BRAINBOW (functions of the brain), INTERMEDIA SPACE (a theater area for all kinds of shows and participatory activities), ANT WALL (a sideways maze), and the farm area with live animals and growing plants. The museum offers workshops, tours for groups, curriculum packets, summer programs, parent/child projects, and special events. There are a full-time director, 4 part-time staff members, and 100 regular volunteers. The museum is open Tuesday through Saturday 10:00–5:00 and closed Sunday and Monday. About half of the annual 20,000 attendance is made up of school groups. Support comes from a small admission charge, fees, memberships, contributions, and grants.

"Children's Museum Plans Arts Program," *Muncie Star*, 17 June 1985; Yvonne Keck Holman, "An Investigation into the Dynamics of Children's Museums: A Case Study of Selected Museums" (Ph.D. dissertation, Northern Illinois University, 1982), pp. 76, 81, 83, 86, 94, 95–96, 99, 101, 105, 108, 113–14, 120, 121, 124–25, 127, 128; "Muncie Children's Museum Historical Sketch," Muncie, n.d. (Typewritten); Eileen Wallen, "Children's Museums Come of Age," *Museum News* 58, no. 2 (November/December 1979): 47–48.

IOWA

Des Moines

DES MOINES SCIENCE CENTER, 4500 Grand Avenue, Greenwood-Ashworth Park, Des Moines, IA 50312. The Discovery Room was a Junior League project initiated in 1980 by its Science Center Impact Group. The design and development of the 1,600-square-foot area was a cooperative effort between the League and the Science Center staff. The room opened in July 1982, and in the fall of 1983 the Science Center took over the project and added elements of its own to the facility. There is a tactile tree, Discovery Boxes with collections of experiments, Foucault pendulum, and a theremin (electronic keyboard-like musical instrument). The emphasis is on interactive learning through experimentation. The 20 different learning packages available have been very popular with families. The room is not manned on a permanent basis and uses primarily part-time staff and volunteers. It is open the same hours as the Science Center, Monday through Saturday 9:00–5:00 and Sunday 1:00–5:00. Support for the Discovery Room comes from general revenues, which include admissions, memberships, classes, and gifts. The audience is family-oriented, and 45,000 people a year use the Discovery Room.

Paul Hoffman, ed., *American Museum Guides-Science* (New York: Macmillan, 1983):108.

KANSAS

Topeka

TOPEKA ZOOLOGICAL PARK, 635 Gage Boulevard, Topeka, KS 66606. Kids Kraal, opened in 1981, was developed to provide hands-on experiences with live animals and to generate additional revenues for the zoo. Originally known as AnimaLand, it was situated outside the grounds and across the street from the zoo. It housed goats, sheep, chickens, turkeys, macaws, turtles, and a burro and was cared for by 2 part-time keepers and volunteers. In 1983 it moved into the zoo and became known as Kids Kraal. The 20-by-50 foot area, surrounded by a wire-mesh fence, has an outdoor exhibit yard and an off-exhibit holding area. The animals are now cared for by a keeper who also maintains other areas of the zoo. Contact is through the fence; therefore, the area does not require full-time supervision. Animal food is available for purchase. Hours are 9:00–4:30 daily. The zoo is supported by the city, and Kids Kraal is funded by the zoo budget. There is a small admission charge to the zoo, and about 130,000 people visit annually.

Nancy Cherry, "Kids Kraal," *Zoo Magazine* 21, no. 2 (1985): 21.

Wichita

WICHITA ART ASSOCIATION, 9112 East Central, Wichita, KS 67206. The Children's Theater, opened in October 1971, has 500 seats and is suitable for all types of performances. The theater was the final addition to the 15-acre Wichita Art Association complex. Presentations of live theater and classes in drama and dance are held in this facility year round. The 30 classes for children 5–18 offered annually by the School of Children's Theater encompass singing, vocal skills, dance, choreography, acting, scenery techniques, and set design. There is a registration fee for classes, but tuition scholarships are available. Children give 3 performances in the theater each year with a maximum attendance of 1,500. The performing arts for children have been an integral part of the Association's program for 4 decades.

Barry Paris, "Children's Theater Is Dream Come True," *Children's Theater Review* 21, no. 1 (1972): 12–14; *School of Art/School of Children's Theater* (Wichita: Wichita Art Association, Fall 1985); *School of Children's Theater* (Wichita: Wichita Art Association, [1984]).

WICHITA ART MUSEUM, 619 Stackman Drive, Wichita, KS 67203–3296. The Hands-On Gallery, founded in 1980, was developed following a well-received 5-week exhibition SCULPTURES TO TOUCH. After this 1978 installation the Volunteer Alliance of the Friends of the Wichita Art Museum, in consultation with the museum's education department, initiated plans for developing a permanent touch gallery. In April 1980 a fund-raising benefit was held, and the Friends presented the first piece for the 775-square-foot gallery. Since then more than 20 additional works of original art in a variety of media, many especially commissioned, have been added. The wood, stone, fiber, blown glass, 19th-century, and folk art pieces are selected for both the visual and tactile experiences they provide. All works have clearly printed and braille labels. Used on almost all children's tours, the gallery is popular with visitors of all ages, including special education classes and handicapped adults. The education department has a curator, administrative assistant, and about 50 docents. The Hands-On Gallery is open the same hours as the museum, Tuesday through Saturday 10:00–4:50, Sunday 1:00–4:50, and closed Monday. Attendance averages about 270 visitors per day. Support comes from the Friends of the Wichita Art Museum.

"Museum Offers 'Touchable' Art," *Wichita Eagle-Beacon*, 9 September 1980, pp. 7A, 8A; "Please Touch," *Wichita Eagle-Beacon*, 14 November 1980; " 'Please Touch' Gallery to Open at Art Museum," *Wichita Eagle-Beacon*, 31 August 1980, p. 1C; *Please Touch: The Hands-On Gallery* (Wichita: Wichita Art Museum, n.d.).

WICHITA PUBLIC SCHOOLS, Office of Museum Programs, 640 North Emporia, Wichita, KS 67214. Established in 1975 by the Superintendent of Schools with federal bicentennial grant money, the Office of Museum Programs is part of Curriculum Services. The museum was created to provide a more experience-centered education for students. Two- and 3-dimensional exhibits and media are circulated to area public schools, and the Office of Museum Programs coordinates the activities of students in the 15 area museums. Initially there was a 10-by-60-foot mobile pioneer history museum, and mobile museums of pioneer crafts and natural science were later added. Pioneer history was discontinued in 1981, and currently the 3 mobile museums are crafts, science, and trading post. Instruction in each mobile unit lasts 30 to 45 minutes, and every 18 to 24 months the exhibits are changed. The mobile museums have also traveled to public locations and community festivals. In addition to the traveling vans, the Office of Museum Programs sends to classrooms about 50 different exhibits, 40 kits, slide/tape programs, videotapes, photographic exhibits, and resource documents. There is a descriptive catalog, the loan period is from 2 to 4 weeks, and deliveries are by school truck. Since 1982 the museum has used a classroom in the oldest remaining school building in Wichita for a half-day 1890s school experience for elementary age groups. The McCormick School, listed in the National Register of Historic Sites in 1978, also provides a unique introduction to historic preservation and architecture. The Office of Museum Programs actively collects historical and ethnic group artifacts for future use, and the location of a permanent site for the Wichita Public School Museum is being explored. There are 1 supervisor, a staff of 4, an occasional volunteer, and summer youth employees. The Office of Museum Programs is open Monday through Friday 8:00–5:00 and serves the entire school population of 45,000 students. Support comes from public school funds, grants, and private donations.

Bonnie Pitman-Gelles, *Museums, Magic & Children: Youth Education in Museums* (Washington, D.C.: Association of Science-Technology Centers, 1981), pp. 81–82, 93, 232; "Schools Sponsor Office of Museum Programs, Wichita, Kansas," in *Museum-School Partnerships: Plans and Programs*, Sourcebook #4, ed. Susan Nichols Lehman and Kathryn Igoe (Washington, D.C.: George Washington University, 1981), pp. 99–100: ERIC Document Reproduction Service, ED 216 945; *Tenth Annual Report 1984–1985, Office of Museum Programs* (Wichita: Curriculum Services, Wichita Public Schools, July 1985); *Wichita Museum News* 10, no. 1 (Fall 1985).

KENTUCKY

Lexington

THE LIVING ARTS AND SCIENCE CENTER, 362 Walnut Street, Lexington, KY 40508. In 1965 the Junior League perceived a need for enrichment programs and educational opportunities in the arts and sciences and spearheaded the movement to establish the Center. Three years later art classes for preschoolers and workshops and creative programs for all ages were offered on a limited basis. In 1970 the Center moved to its present location, the Kinkead House, a large antebellum mansion built in 1847 and listed in the National Register of Historic Landmarks. The house was leased from the heirs from 1970 until 1981, when they donated the building and grounds to the Center. The move to the house in 1970 allowed for expanded programming, and until 1977 the Center was able to secure grants. When these major funding sources cut back, financial problems caused the Center to vote to close its doors in February 1980. Immediately public hearings were held, and a fund drive was initiated to enlist community support. In August 1980 the Center reopened and offered classes and installed exhibits. The 7,000-square-foot building, repaired and renovated, contains 3 20-by-28-foot galleries, a darkroom, 5 classrooms, and staff support areas. There is no permanent collection. The Center has 4 temporary science and 9 art exhibits per year. The exhibits are free and designed to be self-guided, but if requested a staff member will conduct a tour for schoolchildren or small groups. In addition, there are 4 class sessions per year which are held at the Center, in elementary schools, and in communities nearby. There is a small fee for the workshops to cover the instructor's salary and cost of supplies. There are 4 full-time and 4 part-time staff members, who are assisted by 150 volunteers and up to 25 part-time teachers per session. The Living Arts and Science Center receives 7 percent of its support from memberships, 17 percent from city and state grants, 41 percent from corporate and private donations, 16 percent from fund-raising events, and 19 percent from tuition. It is open Monday through Friday 9:00–4:00, and about 30,000 children use the Center each year.

Educational Facilities Laboratories, *Arts and the Handicapped: An Issue of Access* (New York: Educational Facilities Laboratories, 1975), p. 31: ERIC Document Reproduction Service, ED 117 829; Barbara Y. Newsom and Adele Z. Silver, eds., *The Art Museum as Educator* (Berkeley: University of California Press, 1978), p. 737; "Review Summer 1984: The Living Arts & Science Center," *Lexington Herald-Leader*, 20 May 1984.

Louisville

LOUISVILLE ART GALLERY, 301 York Street, Louisville, KY 40203. The gallery opened in 1950, with Junior League support, as the Junior Art Gallery to provide a visual arts museum for children. As a reflection of its expanded audience it became the Louisville Art Gallery in 1980, but exhibitions are still planned to be of interest to children. There are also workshops, special events, lectures, and demonstrations for all ages, but more workshops are offered for children 4 and older than for adults. Located on the 2nd floor of the main library, the gallery has 1,200 square feet of gallery space and another 1,800 for workshops, storage, and offices. There is no permanent collection due to limited space. Six thematic exhibits of contemporary art are held each year, and artists with national and regional reputations are invited to exhibit along with local professionals. Frequently the work has not been shown previously. Although the gallery program revolves around the current exhibition, the workshops are not limited to exhibit themes. Five full-time staff members are assisted by 10 volunteers. The gallery is open Monday through Saturday 9:00–5:00 and has approximately 36,000 visitors a year. Admission to the gallery is free. Support comes from membership fees, the Greater Louisville Fund for the Arts, corporate contributions, and state and federal grants.

Selina Tetzlaff Johnson, "Museums for Youth in the United States: A Study of Their Origins, Relationships and Cultural Contributions" (Ph.D. dissertation, New York University, 1962), p. 190; Sue McWhirter Thurman, "Louisville's Junior Art Gallery," *Junior Arts Activities* 33, no. 4 (May 1953): 38–41, 45; Barbara Y. Newsom and Adele Z. Silver, eds., *The Art Museum as Educator* (Berkeley: University of California Press, 1978), pp. 363, 737.

LOUISVILLE ZOOLOGICAL GARDEN, 1100 Trevilian Way, Box 37250, Louisville, KY 40233. A seasonal children's zoo, one portion of the total 75-acre zoo, opened in 1969. It had a farm motif and included domestic and small exotic animals, many of which could be petted. In 1976 this section was renamed the Small Animal Area and now is one of the 4 major components of the zoo, housing small exotic animals and the nursery. Babies that have been rejected by their mothers are frequently hand-raised by keepers in this area. Currently there are 167 animals in 31 exhibits including 2 endangered species. The Small Animal

Area has 1 curator, 5 keepers, and approximately 2 winter and 10 summer volunteers. The zoo's new 4,000-square-foot education center, the MetaZoo, opened on 7 August 1981. Added on to an existing amphitheater, the 1-story year-round facility combines living animals and sophisticated museum display techniques. It has 4 major components and a library for docents and education staff. Used in formal educational programs and by the general public, the MetaZoo's participatory exhibits are designed to encourage interaction between adult and child and provide enjoyable learning for all ages. Young Discovery Room, a classroom and exhibit area designed for children preschool–grade 1, has a variety of small live animals and a collection of touchable biofacts. The Central Display area is devoted to endangered species and combines living animals with biofacts. Also included are magnified displays, an oscilloscope to explore animal sounds, and a giant insect head to see how the world looks to an insect. In the pond room a 35-foot, glass-fronted tank re-creates a Kentucky pond with waterfall and gives visitors an underwater view of a variety of fish, amphibians, and aquatic plants in a naturalistic setting. The theater/gallery area seats 100 and is used for audiovisual shows, as a classroom, and houses drawings with related information. Signs and written displays are used throughout the MetaZoo and are carefully designed to ask questions, suggest observation, and stimulate curiosity. In 1984 the adjacent amphitheater was renovated and now includes covered seating for 1,000. The education department offers classes for school groups of various academic levels, teacher-guided tour kits, weekend classes and films, teacher workshops, summer day camp, and outreach to hospitals, schools, and senior citizens. MetaZoo staff consists of a curator, 3 educators, 2 part-time and 5 summer counselors, and 62 docents. Funds for MetaZoo construction came 40 percent from corporations, and approximately 20 percent each from the state, the private sector, and the Zoo Society and Commission. Twenty thousand people participate in MetaZoo education programs, and 50,000 students use the entire zoo each year. The zoo is open year-round, 10:00–5:00, Tuesday through Sunday, September through April, and 10:00–6:00 daily May through August. There is an admission charge. The zoo generates approximately half of its income, with the remainder of its support coming from the city and the county.

Robert B. Bean, "The Louisville Zoological Garden-A 20 Year Plan," *AAZPA Regional Conference Proceedings 1983*, pp. 371–77; "A Better Operation through Participation," *Tourist Attractions and Parks* (Spring 1983): 9–15; Ann Clayton Brandt, "What Makes Flamingos Pink?" *EdNews: Kentucky Department of Education* (September 1982): 1, 9; David Jenkins, "The Louisville Zoological Garden MetaZoo: A Dual Function Education Center," *AAZPA 1982 Annual Conference Proceedings*, pp. 215–25; Ivo Poglayen-Neuwall, "The Birth of a Zoo," in The World of Zoos: A Survey and Gazetter, ed. Rosl Kirchshofer (New York: Viking, 1968), pp. 201, 203; "The Tiny Animal World of MetaZoo," *Southern Living* 18, no. 8 (August 1983): 48.

LOUISIANA

Baton Rouge

LOUISIANA ARTS AND SCIENCE CENTER, Riverside Museum, 100 South River Road, PO Box 3373, Baton Rouge, LA 70821. Discovery Depot, the children's gallery, opened on 4 October 1983 after 2 years of research by the Junior League. There was no established art education program in the local parish schools, and the program was created to fill this gap. The 3,000-square-foot space is used for participatory exhibitions and activities in the visual arts and has an orientation area, discovery room, and group activity room. A reproduction rack with activity trays, which encourages children and parents to explore works of art through creative activities, is a special feature of the Discovery Room. Large drawing and magnetic surfaces, a building-block table, a sound sculpture, a color-light table, a texture wall, and a geo-board are other exhibits available in the Depot. These exhibits are added to and/or changed regularly. There are also special programs, "Artists in Action," held in conjunction with the Center's exhibitions, Saturday workshops, and summer classes. Discovery Depot has an education curator and 20 to 25 volunteer gallery teachers. Tours are conducted for children ages 4–11, and classes are held for students up to 16. Tuesday through Friday 10:00–12:00 is for school groups with reservations. Public hours are Tuesday through Thursday 12:00–4:30, Saturday 10:00–4:30, and Sunday 1:00–4:30. There is no admission charge. Support comes from local and state arts and humanities councils, and private, business, and corporate donors. Twenty thousand children a year come to Discovery Depot.

" 'All Aboard' at Riverside Museum," *Southern Living* 20, no. 8 (August 1985): 31; *Discovery Depot* (Baton Rouge: Louisiana Arts and Science Center, [1983]); Educational Facilities Laboratories, *Hands-On Museums: Partners in Learning* (New York: Educational Facilities Laboratories, 1975), pp. 30–31: ERIC Document Reproduction Service, ED 113 832; *LASC Calendar* (Baton Rouge: Louisiana Arts and Science Center, September-November 1984).

New Orleans

AUDUBON PARK AND ZOOLOGICAL GARDEN, 6500 Magazine Street, PO Box 4327, New Orleans, LA 70178. The Wisner Children's Village, opened in 1980, created a special area for children as a part of an institutional revitalization. It occupies 2 of the zoo's 58 acres. The village had a farm theme, was built around existing buildings constructed by the Works Progress Administration (WPA), and was funded with a substantial contribution from the Wisner Fund. Animals were selected for their ability to interact with children and included a prairie dog exhibit, rabbit circle, and contact yard. A nocturnal house and a discovery area were added later to give visitors close contact with domestic and exotic animals. In 1984 renovations moved the Children's Village away from the farm theme and towards participatory exhibits. GIANTS OF THE PAST (life-size replicas), ENDANGERED (graphics), ANIMAL ATHLETES (children compare their skills to those of selected animals), and Zoolab opened in July 1985. Zoolab contains 4 marine aquariums, a fact wheel to find the life-style and habits of 30 popular zoo animals, discovery boxes are being developed, and a table with microscopes for demonstrations using live animals and artifacts will be added. Other recent additions include computer-controlled cricket feeders for bat-eared foxes and an opportunity for visitors to try fiber glass fox ears which simulate the acuity of the foxes' hearing. An Australian nocturnal animals exhibit was added to the existing animals of the night installation. The Wisner Children's Village has 7 full-time staff members, 1 additional person during the summer months, and a volunteer corps of about 95. Junior keepers are 14–16 years old and the program has about 14 members. There is an admission charge for the zoo but no extra charge for Wisner Children's Village. The McDonald's operators of New Orleans provided the funds for the new exhibits. Operating support for the zoo comes 92 percent from earned income and 8 percent from the city. Capital support comes 50 percent from the state and federal government and 50 percent from corporate and private sources. Hours are 9:30–5:00 daily with extended hours 9:30–6:00 on summer weekends. The Audubon Zoo has approximately 900,000 visitors a year.

Reginald Hoyt, "Underwater Zoo," *At the Zoo* (Winter 1986): 8–11; Reg Hoyt, "Wisner Children's Village Phase II: An Exhibit with Purpose," *At the Zoo* (Autumn 1985): 10–11; "Kids Can Meet Animals Face to Face," *New Orleans Times-Picayune*, 3 May 1981, sec. 1, p. 10; "New Wing to Open at Audubon Zoo Children's Village," *New Orleans Times-Picayune*, 14 July 1985; "Touch' n' Talk Nose to Snout at the New Zoo," *New Orleans Times-Picayune*, 19 April 1981, sec. 4, p. 1.

LOUISIANA NATURE AND SCIENCE CENTER, 11000 Lake Forest Boulevard, New Orleans, LA 70127. The Discovery Loft, a 1,000-square-foot mezzanine area visible from the 1st floor, opened in March 1980 as a feature of the original exhibits building. The Nature Center, a major community effort, started as a project of the Junior League, which provided the initial funding. The Center emphasizes the natural history of the Mississippi River delta region. The Loft has 36 Discovery Boxes filled with shells, skins, skulls, seeds, leaves, bark, and other interesting materials. There are also "stumpers," a tree-root system installation, a cloud exhibit, and fish, snakes, and turtles in aquariums. New materials are added as they become available. All the exhibits in the Loft and elsewhere in the Nature Center are hands-on and have discovery components. In addition to the programs for children, the Center offers workshops for teachers including a few specifically focused on discovery learning, and a university course on a practical approach to biological education through discovery is taught by the director of the Center. Family activities are offered; there are outreach programs to schools, films, field trips, and 86 acres with 3 nature trails. The Center has 6 teaching staff members and 7 administrative and maintenance personnel. Hours are Tuesday through Friday 9:00–5:00, weekends 12:00–5:00, and closed Monday and major holidays. The Loft is open at the same hours and is accessible by stairs or elevator. There is a small admission, and support is one-third self-generated, one-third from government sources, and one-third from corporate and other donations. Separate attendance figures are not kept for the Discovery Loft, but the Center has approximately 100,000 visitors a year.

"Junior League of New Orleans: Louisiana Nature Center Project," *Humane Education Projects Handbook* (Ogden, UT: Junior League of Ogden, 1982), pp. 71–72: ERIC Document Reproduction Service, ED 229 247; "Louisiana Naturally," *New Orleans Times-Picayune Dixie Magazine*, 23 March 1980, p. 10.

MAINE

Portland

CHILDREN'S MUSEUM OF MAINE, 746 Stevens Avenue, Portland, ME 04103. Founded in March 1977 by the Junior League of Portland, the museum opened in 2 rooms of a vacant school building in the town of Cape Elizabeth. In September 1977 it moved to larger quarters where it remained until September 1980, when it relocated in Portland on the campus of Westbrook College. The hands-on learning environment occupies 15 rooms in a 1,520-square-foot building. The participatory exhibits include SNUG HARBOR (Maine sea life), medical center, radio/TV station, FIRE ROOM (what it's like to be a fireman), THE SWITCHBOARD (calling someone in another exhibit area), post office, and theater arts room. Workshops and special events occur throughout the year. Schools and other groups may book tours. Two full-time and 1 part-time staff members are assisted by approximately 22 youth (ages 12 to 18) and 18 adult volunteers who perform more than half of the work at the museum. In 1983 a grant from the Junior League helped to establish this volunteer program. Admissions provide half of the museum's support, fund-raising about one-third, with the remaining income coming from memberships and grants. Hours are 10:00–5:00 Tuesday through Friday, weekends 11:00–4:00, and closed Monday. About 13,000 children and 7,000 adults come to the museum annually.

Yvonne Keck Holman, "An Investigation into the Dynamics of Children's Museums: A Case Study of Selected Museums" (Ph.D dissertation, Northern Illinois University, 1982), pp. 76, 81, 83, 85, 87, 95, 100, 101, 104, 105, 109, 112, 120, 131; *Kitetales* [The Children's Museum Newsletter] (Spring 1984).

MARYLAND

Baltimore

CYLBURN NATURE MUSEUM, 4915 Greenspring Avenue, Baltimore, MD 21209. The museum opened in 1954 in a Victorian structure, originally a private summer home, that had become Baltimore city park property in 1952. In 1972 the Cylburn Arboretum and Mansion were entered in the National Register of Historic Places. The museum, located on the 3rd floor of the mansion, has 3 display rooms and a workroom. There are 2 large dioramas with animals, a Maryland woodland scene and a Maryland Eastern Shore marsh, fossils, skulls, and a map depicting Maryland's ecological zones and natural resources. Besides specimens, an active beehive, and games, there are hands-on exhibits of natural history materials. Mounted specimens of common birds, nests, simple feeders, and other nature materials may be borrowed for classroom use. The museum director is assisted by 15 volunteers who also conduct tours. Open 8:30–3:30 weekdays and by appointment, the museum has about 3,000 visitors annually. Support comes from a small requested contribution, the Cylburn Arboretum Association, and the Maryland Ornithological Society.

"Birds and Nature Study for School Classes at Cylburn Arboretum," Baltimore, Maryland Ornithological Society, n.d. (Typewritten).

NATIONAL AQUARIUM IN BALTIMORE, Pier 3, 501 East Pratt Street, Baltimore, MD 21202. The Children's Cove, one of the exhibit areas incorporated into Baltimore's new aquarium, opened on 8 August 1981. Influenced by a visit to the New England Aquarium in Boston (see entry under UNITED STATES/MASSACHUSETTS), the mayor of Baltimore initiated a campaign to build a similar facility. The same architect designed both aquariums, and the popularity of the touch tank in Boston was well-known. The Cove at the National Aquarium is irregularly shaped, averages about 55 by 13 feet in size, and holds 5,000–5,800 gallons of water. Built to simulate the rocky Maine coast, the main pool includes a variety of marine invertebrates that children can handle and explore. Several smaller aquariums contain animals too delicate to handle or of special interest but from geographic areas other than the one the Cove represents. During public hours the exhibit is usually staffed by 2 volunteer guides, and 1 full-time aquarist is responsible for the Cove's animals among other duties. The greatest use is by children, especially school groups, but most visitors spend some time in the Cove. Education Department statistics indicate that 98,000 schoolchildren visited with groups in 1985. Those from Maryland enter free, and all school groups must have a reservation. There are no guided tours, but special programs can be scheduled, and an educator's guide to the aquarium is available. Winter hours are 10:00–5:00 daily with extended hours on Friday until 8:00. Summer hours are Monday through Thursday 9:00–5:00 and Friday through

Sunday 9:00–8:00. There is an admission to the aquarium, and support for the Children's Cove comes from the First National Bank of Maryland, its annual corporate sponsor, with additional funding from the general operating budget of the aquarium.

In 1986 the Children's Cove will be remodeled but will retain its major purpose as a tidepool touchtank. Redesigned to feature 2 different tidepool habitats, a North Atlantic and a Pacific Northwest, it will enable visitors to compare and contrast species from 2 different areas. The modification will also improve filtration and visitor flow and will make the area more accessible to the handicapped. A mural will also be added. The area will retain the 2 volunteer guide stations. The renovation is expected to be completed in early 1987.

"Citation: Architectural Design—Cambridge Seven Associates, Inc.," *Progressive Architecture* 60, no. 1 (January 1979): 83; *Humane Education Projects Handbook* (Ogden, UT: Junior League of Ogden, 1982), pp. 55–56: ERIC Document Reproduction Service, ED 229 247; Daniel M. Kehrer, "A Symphony of Fish," *Science Digest* 91, no. 2 (February 1983): 66; "The National Aquarium in Baltimore: Cambridge Seven Associates," *Architectural Record* 170, no. 6 (May 1982): 89, 90; Thorgunn R. Stevens, "Water Wonderland," *Animal Kingdom* 85, no. 1 (February 1982): 9.

Frederick

ROSE HILL MANOR CHILDREN'S MUSEUM, 1611 North Market Street, Frederick, MD 21701. Founded in 1972, the 43-acre site was acquired by Frederick County for an urban park. The 1790s mansion, an example of rural Georgian architecture, was restored and the site was developed further in cooperation with the County Board of Education as a children's museum for hands-on interpretive activities. In addition to the 6-room mansion, there are a blacksmith shop, log cabin, ice house, 18th-century country garden and orchard, restored carriage and sleigh collection, farm museum exhibit building with agricultural implements, and barns. The interpretive program emphasizes early 19th-century life in Frederick County and Maryland. There are 2-hour tours for school groups. Hands-on experiences at Rose Hill encompass carding wool, weaving, soap making, candle dipping, apple butter boiling, quilting bees, and barn raisings. Special events programming includes crafts demonstrations, blacksmithing, an annual Fall Festival, Historical Carriage Drive, Needlework Show, and Children's Christmas Open House. There are also an urban 4-H program which incorporates Future Farmers of America (FFA) and the disabled, crafts classes, and summer day camps for Girl Scouts on colonial history. The staff includes a curator, 12 part-time tour guides, 6 docents, 12 committee members working on special events, 20 volunteers, and 4 grounds staff. Walk-in tours are conducted Monday through Saturday 10:00–4:00 and Sunday 1:00–4:00 from April 1 through October 31. During March, November, and December the museum is open only on weekends, and it is closed during January and February. Group tours are available March through December by appointment. The annual attendance of 35,000 consists of 9,500 children on tour, 14,000 attending special events, and 21,500 general visitors. There is an admission charge. The museum is operated by the Frederick County Parks and Recreation Commission with additional support coming from the Rose Hill Children's Museum Committee, the Needle Show Committee, and Project Open Space.

Rose Hill Manor Children's Museum (Frederick: Frederick County Parks and Recreation Commission, n.d.).

MASSACHUSETTS

Acton

THE CHILDREN'S DISCOVERY MUSEUM, 177 Main Street, Acton, MA 01720. Established in December 1981, the museum opened to the public in a 100-year-old Victorian house with 3 acres of ground in October 1982. The founder of the museum, Donald Verger, felt a place was needed where suburban families with young children could share an educational and creative time together. All of the installations are hands-on, and the majority have been conceived by the staff. Nine discovery rooms are spread over 1,300 square feet of exhibit space. New components are added throughout the year, and annually 1 major area is completely changed. Current themes are dinosaurs, dominoes, magnets, water discovery, gears, legos, whales, and quiet play. The museum is appropriate for children 1–10 but is most frequently visited by those 2–4 and their families. Tuesday, Thursday, and Friday mornings during the school year are for groups with reservations. Each class has an hour and a half, which includes time to explore the museum and a 15-minute informal workshop taught in small groups of 10 to 15 children. There are weekly workshops, occasional guest performers, and 2-week summer camp sessions for 4–5 and 6–7 year olds. Ten full-time staff members, 2 part-time educators, and 10 high school or college student part-time Explainers are assisted by 40 volunteers. From Labor Day through June public hours are Wednesday and weekends 10:00–4:30; Tuesday, Thursday, and Friday 1:30–4:30; and closed Monday. Summer hours are Tuesday through Sunday 10:00–4:30 and closed Monday. The museum extends its hours during school vacations and holidays and closes the first 2 weeks of September for an annual updating. There is an admission charge. Thirty-eight percent of the museum's support comes from admissions; 22 percent from the state; 12 percent from family memberships; 18 percent from individual, corporate, and foundation contributions and/or grants; and the remaining 10 percent from other sources. The Children's Discovery Museum has about 50,000 visitors a year, including 7,000 children in school groups.

In 1986 construction began on a 7,500 square foot Science Discovery Museum.

Completion is anticipated in the fall of 1987. Planned for children/youth 6–16, the new facility will have interactive exhibits in the physical and natural sciences.

"Discovery in the Suburbs," *Boston Globe Calendar*, 10 May 1984, p. 6; "A Growing Phenomenon," *Boston Globe Calendar*, 18 April 1985, pp. 14–15; "Museums for Kids Say 'Please Touch,' " *USA Today*, 6 October 1983, p. 3D; "Optical Illusions Fascinate the Young," *Beacon*, 2 February 1984.

Boston

CHILDREN'S MUSEUM, Museum Wharf, 300 Congress Street, Boston, MA 02210. The museum, founded in 1913 by the Science Teachers' Bureau, was installed in a city-owned park building in Pine Bank, Jamaica Plain, on 1 August 1913. In 1914 it was chartered as a separate organization. With natural history and ethnological collections donated by individuals and area museums, programs and services in support of the curriculum were started by the director, Delia Griffen (1913–1927). Exhibits, lectures, clubs, loan kits, and lantern slide presentations were offered and a library organized. In 1915 the 1st annual meeting of the Children's Museum was held and a support group, the Museum Aid Association, established. It initiated a series of benefit lectures that continued for at least 20 years, even though the association had disbanded in 1920. In addition to its field trips, the museum exhibited aquariums and terrariums, and in 1916 started classes for children who were blind or deaf. A branch museum, the Barnard Memorial, opened in November 1919 and offered activities similar to those at Pine Bank. After 3 years, the group owning the facility decided to use it to meet their own needs, and the branch closed. In 1925 it reopened for a year. Mildred Manter, director from 1927 until the mid–1940s, was followed by Elsie M. Boyle. In 1936 the museum moved into a house at 60 Burroughs Street, Jamaica Plain, and later expanded to an adjacent building.

Michael Spock became director in 1962 and led the museum for the next 23 years. Almost immediately, an institution that had changed little for years began to show new vitality. The 1963 hands-on participatory exhibit, WHAT'S IN-SIDE, became the first of many pioneering installations. The following year the museum received a grant to develop instructional materials that could be displayed in classrooms and manipulated by children. Sixteen different MATCH (Materials and Activities for Teachers and Children) kits with 9 copies of each were initially developed, tested, and made available to schools for a modest rental fee. The MATCH project was funded from 1964 to 1968 by the U.S. Office of Education, and later commercial versions were developed by the museum in cooperation with a company that marketed them. The Workshop of Things, a center to introduce real things into classroom learning and an opportunity for teachers and museum staff to review them, opened in 1967. With grant support the workshop evolved into the Resource Center, a multidimensional library which provides in-depth information, consultations, training, workshops on children and learning, and manages the kit-rental department. It also includes Recycle, a much emulated source of industrial scraps that offers an ever changing variety of material for children's creative energy. Even though the museum remodeled a former auditorium into an exhibit area in 1968, it was beginning to consider relocating its facilities to a more central location in order to become accessible to all Boston-area residents. In 1973 the museum started looking for a new site and in 1975 purchased, with the Museum of Transportation, a 150,000-square-foot abandoned wool warehouse on the Boston waterfront. In July 1979 the Children's Museum moved into its shared building, tripling its exhibit area to 21,000 square feet and occupying 78,800 square feet of building space. In 1982 the museum bought the portion of the building owned by the Museum of Transportation and in 1983 sold it to the Computer Museum. Renovating the 1880s building, designing proper storage for the museum's 50,000-item collection of 30,000 cultural artifacts and 20,000 natural history specimens, and developing of exhibits took 4 years. Tried in the older facility and incorporated into the new is the study-storage concept. Now more of the collection is available to the public and grouped into categories of availability. Green, yellow, and red are color cues to indicate touch, handle, and look only. Permanent exhibits like CITY SLICE, GRANDPARENT'S HOUSE, and the JAPANESE HOUSE have been models for other institutions. PLAYSPACE, an indoor play area for children under 5 years old and a resource area for parents, was developed over several years and serves as a prototype for the development of similar spaces in other public facilities. Equally influential have been many of the museum's temporary installations where children have role-played different workplaces, including a factory, supermarket, and garage; visited the health clinic; used computers; experimented with bubbles; become broadcasters at WKID-TV; and learned about how movies move. The exhibits WHAT IF YOU COULDN'T? (handicaps), WE'RE STILL HERE (native Americans), MEETING GROUND (ethnic diversity), and ENDINGS: AN EXHIBIT ABOUT DEATH AND LOSS have become landmarks because of their content. The targeting of different audiences has included Detours, a program initiated in 1981 to help the 11–16 year old explore Boston, special tours for the disabled, and an after-school program for 8–14 year olds started in 1984.

The museum has the equivalent of 85 full-time staff members and about 40 volunteers. Through its interpreter program 10–20 interns train for 3 to 10 months. Approximately 450,000 visitors come to the museum each year, and another 250,000 are reached by its outreach services. The 6–9 year old is the most frequent age group, but visitors are toddlers to teens, and almost half of all who come to the museum are adults. Groups must have reservations, and visits by in-state nonprofit schools and community groups are funded by the Massachusetts Council on the Arts and Humanities, a state agency whose funds are recommended by the governor and the legislature. Groups make up 15 percent of the museum's visitors. Eighty percent of the museum's income comes from earned sources, including admissions, memberships, leases, workshop fees, service contracts, and shop sales, with the remaining 20 percent coming from grants, foundations, corporations, and individuals. Hours September through June are 10:00–5:00 Tuesday through Sunday and until 9:00 Friday evening, and closed Monday except school holidays and vacations. Hours from July until Labor Day are 10:00–5:00 daily and until 9:00 Friday evening. The museum is closed on Thanksgiving, Christmas, and New Year's. There is no admission on Friday evening from 5:00 to 9:00.

Since the 1960s, the influence of the Children's Museum has been far-reaching. With its themes and installations it has affected not only other children's museums but all kinds of institutions both here and abroad. In addition, it has become a center for the training of museum professionals.

Enid Farmer and Tom Farmer, "A Boston Museum Where Children Can Cavort at Will," *Smithsonian* 12, no. 7 (October 1981): 158–62, 164, 166–67; Elaine Gurian, "Adult Learning at Children's Museum of Boston," in *Museums, Adults and the Humanities: A Guide for Educational Programming,* ed. Zipporah W. Collins (Washington, D.C.: American Association of Museums, 1981), pp. 271–96; Janet Kamien, *Sensitive Subjects: Museums and Controversy,* audiotape of panelists Linda Downs and Michael Howfield, presented at meeting of the American Association of Museums, Detroit, June 1985 (Shawnee Mission, KS: Vanguard Systems, 1985); Barbara Y. Newsom and Adele Z. Silver, eds., *The Art Museum as Educator* (Berkeley: University of California Press, 1978), pp. 121, 123–31, 234–35, 270, 406, 463, 468, 502–04, 691–62; Bonnie Pitman-Gelles, *Museums, Magic & Children: Youth Education in Museums* (Washington, D.C.: Association of Science-Technology Centers, 1981), pp. 13, 28–29, 44, 45, 81, 87, 91–92, 99, 102–03, 123, 129, 146, 193; Jeri Robinson and Patricia Quinn, *Playspace: Creating Family Spaces in Public Places* (Boston: Boston Children's Museum, 1984); Adelaide B. Sayles, *The Story of the Children's Museum of Boston* (Boston: George H. Ellis, 1937).

MUSEUM OF SCIENCE, Science Park, Boston, MA 02114–1099. The Discovery Room, opened on 18 October 1978, was originally called the Eye-Opener Room. It was developed at the suggestion of the Education Advisory Committee, which noted that although the museum was participatory, not much was oriented toward young children. The 350-square-foot facility was designed to include materials which relate to the museum's permanent exhibits and are appropriate for the developmental level of younger visitors. Originally, the target audience was children K–4 and their families. Space studies indicated better use of the room, and it has been rearranged twice. Materials in the discovery boxes are evaluated annually and redesigned based on use and effectiveness. In addition, the contents of the room reflect interests expressed by its audience. The collection is strongest in natural history materials. Programs are conducted for school groups, which can reserve 45-minute programs at 10:00, 11:00, and 12:00 Tuesday through Friday. Local colleges also use the Discovery Room to supplement early childhood science curriculum courses. There is a full-time supervisor who is in charge of staff and materials. The room is staffed by a paid intern and about 30 volunteers. During the summer the room is open daily 12:00–4:00 and

Wednesday and Friday evenings 6:00–8:30. During the rest of the year it is open Tuesday through Friday 10:00–1:00, weekends 10:00–4:00, and closed Mondays. Since the fall of 1985, due to the popularity of the facility, Friday evenings from 6:00 to 8:30 are reserved for members and their children. The Discovery Room was initially funded by a grant from the Arthur D. Little Company, but it is now supported by the museum's operating budget. The museum has an admission charge, but there is no additional fee for the room. Approximately 5,100 children in school groups and 50,000 other visitors use the Discovery Room annually.

Victor J. Danilov, "Childhood Exhibits at Science Centers," *Curator* 27, no. 3 (September 1984): 174–75; Victor J. Danilov, "Discovery Rooms and Kidspaces: Museum Exhibits for Children," *Science and Children* 23, no. 4 (January 1986): 9; "Discovery Room for Members Only," *Museum of Science Newsletter* 35, no. 1 (October/November 1985): 4; Paul Hoffman, ed., *American Museum Guides—Science* (New York: Macmillan, 1983), pp. 127–29.

NEW ENGLAND AQUARIUM, Central Wharf, Boston, MA 02110. The Children's Tidepool was incorporated into the original building design and opened in June 1969. It was the first of several participatory aquatic environments built to revitalize urban waterfronts. The 300-square-foot tidepool simulates the rocky shore environment found locally and includes many of the animals found there. Children are encouraged to pick up the creatures that survive the extreme daily tidal changes. Around the walls are 25 child-high tanks which illustrate a variety of behaviors and adaptations. A school program, "Life on Rocky Shores," is available by prior reservation, and a curriculum packet with pre-trip, trip, and post-trip activities has been developed. All age groups enjoy the children's gallery, but it is especially popular with the 35,000 schoolchildren who visit during the school year. A 1981 study of present and former aquarium members indicated they held very favorable opinions of the children's tidepool exhibit. The tidepool was remodeled in the early 1980s. A biologist is responsible for collecting and maintaining the animals, and volunteers interact informally with children as they examine the creatures. The aquarium is supported by admissions and donations, and there is no extra fee to visit the tidepool. The summer hours are Monday, Tuesday, and Thursday 9:00–6:00; Wednesday and Friday 9:00–9:00; and Saturday, Sunday, and holidays 9:00–7:00. The winter hours vary slightly.

"Boston's Underwater Environment: Cambridge Seven Associates' First Major Building Is a Sensational Participatory Aquatic Environment," *Progressive Architecture* 50, no. 12 (December 1969): 96–107; "Citation: New England Aquarium, Boston, Mass.," *Progressive Architecture* 46, no. 1 (January 1965): 152–53; *Life on Rocky Shores* (Boston: New England Aquarium Education Department, n.d.); *New England Aquarium Annual Report 1981* (Boston: New England Aquarium, 1982): Bonnie Pitman-Gelles, *Museums, Magic & Children: Youth Education in Museums* (Washington, D.C.: Association of Science-Technology Centers, 1981), pp. 9, 30, 191, 232.

Sandwich

THE THORNTON W. BURGESS MUSEUM, 4 Water Street, Sandwich, MA 02563. The Discovery Room, opened in March 1984, is a 64-square-foot room with participatory exhibits. Included are puppets for acting out stories, a saltwater aquarium, and a variety of touch-and-learn activities. During July and August natural history story times are offered daily at 1:30 on the museum grounds. The Discovery Room is open seasonally from April to December and has about 60,000 visitors a year. Admission to the museum is by donation. In July 1984 the Society dedicated its Green Briar Nature Center, where a variety of educational programs for young people are offered. In addition to classes for children, the Society also sponsors field trips and nature-related activities for children, families, and adults.

Nancy A. Kaiser, "The Thornton W. Burgess Museum," *Science and Children* 17, no. 6 (March 1980): 13; "Museum Notes," *Thornton W. Burgess Society Newsletter* 8, no. 2 (Spring 1984): 4.

South Dartmouth

THE CHILDREN'S MUSEUM, 276 Gulf Road, South Dartmouth, MA 02748. The museum was founded in 1952 by a group of local women who wanted to stimulate children's interest in the arts, natural sciences, and humanities. It remained a small natural science center until 1965, when the first full-time director was hired, and in 1973 it opened a second center. After the museum was destroyed by fire in 1982, its collections and staff were moved to a renovated 1935 dairy farm complex. In 1983 it reopened with over 12,000 square feet of temporary and permanent exhibit space. The collection is strong in geological specimens, invertebrates, and mounted ornithological and mammalian specimens, Native American artifacts, photographic collections related to children, and antique dolls and toys. Exhibits focus on local ethnic groups and their traditions, contemporary and historical technology, health, nutrition and the human body, the fine and performing arts, and live animals. There are temporary and traveling exhibitions, a wide variety of educational services offered to schools and community groups, and a growing membership. The museum, surrounded by 58 acres of natural habitat, conducts outdoor environmental education programs using an interpretive shelter, a 10-inch observatory telescope, and a wind-driven generator that demonstrates alternative energy. A current priority, and the museum's original mandate, is to restore the balance of the arts, sciences, and humanities. There are 7 full-time and 4 part-time staff members who are assisted by over 40 volunteers. The museum is open Tuesday through Saturday 10:00–5:00, Sunday 1:00–5:00, and closed Monday. Support comes from admissions, program fees, and private and public funding. The museum has about 75,000 visitors annually.

Yvonne Keck Holman, "An Investigation into the Dynamics of Children's Museums: A Case Study of Selected Museums" (Ph.D. dissertation, Northern Illinois University, 1982), pp. 78, 82, 84, 85, 86, 87, 94, 96, 102, 105, 107, 108; Selina Tetzlaff Johnson, "Museums for Youth in the United States: A Study of Their Origins, Relationships, and Cultural Contributions" (Ph.D. dissertation, New York University, 1962), p. 191; Rene Laubach, "An Invitation to the World of Children," *New Bedford Magazine* 4, no. 2 (1984): 40–45.

MICHIGAN

Ann Arbor

THE ANN ARBOR HANDS-ON MUSEUM, 219 East Huron, PO Box 8163, Ann Arbor, MI 48104. After 4 years of volunteer effort the museum opened on 13 October 1982 in a century-old central firehouse. The need for a participatory museum for children and the existence of an unused landmark prompted a group to organize, enlist community support, carry out the renovation, and build the exhibits. Seven traveling displays, some modeled on successful ones designed by other museums, were fabricated and taken to public locations and schools as demonstrations of the hands-on concept. Currently the museum is using about 10,000 square feet of space on 2 floors, half for exhibits, and there are areas for classes and special events. A fund drive for expansion into the 3rd-floor attic area was initiated in late 1984. Plans include additional exhibit space, classrooms, office and storage space, and an elevator for the handicapped. The 65 participatory exhibits explore interrelationships and connections. THE SUBJECT IS YOU promotes self-awareness with opportunities to measure heart rate; test strength, visual perception, reaction time, and hearing; and analyze meals on a computer. THE WORLD AROUND YOU explores the natural and social sciences, mathematics, art, and the humanities. The cultural exhibits are built around a pastime or bond that is shared by many people like tops and puppets. In addition, there is a Discovery Room with about 30 activities and games involving natural history specimens, objects, miniexhibits, microscopes, and a live beehive. There are Saturday workshops and classes, a special series of science classes for preschoolers, weekend demonstrations, films, and special events throughout the year. A full-time director is assisted by 5 part-time employees. There are over 50 volunteers who work about 3 hours per week, 40 of them as Explainers. The museum appeals to all ages and last year had 32,000 visitors. Public hours are Tuesday through Friday 1:30–5:30, Saturday 10:00–5:00, Sunday 1:00–5:00, and closed Monday. Morning hours are for groups by appointment only. The Ann Arbor Public Schools have contributed money to the museum each year and school groups pay half the normal entrance fee. Admissions provide 40 percent of the museum's support, memberships 20 percent, classes and sales 8 percent, and the remaining 32 percent comes from benefits, gifts, and grants.

"Hands-On Museum—Educational Fun for Children of All Ages," *Ann Arbor News*, 5 June 1983, p. G3; "Learning Comes Alive at the Ann Arbor Hands-On Museum," *Ann Arbor News*, 6 March 1984, p. B1; "Physics Professor Uses Toys to Teach," *Ann Arbor News*, 19 September 1984, p. F1; "Popular Hands-On Museum Seeks Funds for Expansion," *Ann Arbor News*, 30 December 1984, p. A3.

Bloomfield Hills

CRANBROOK INSTITUTE OF SCIENCE, 500 Lone Pine Road, Box 801, Bloomfield Hills, MI 48013. The Discovery Room, opened in 1982, was initially a seasonal summer program. It originated as an exhibit offshoot and in 1984 became a permanent facility housed in a separate nature center building with 1,500 square feet of space. There are no boxes but discovery drawers with natural history specimens, including bones, shells, minerals, nests, and furs. The room also has a microscope corner, live animal exhibits, observation beehive, articulated horse skeleton, giant tortoise shell, whale vertebra, and mastodon femur. The "stumper" concept is used with interactive, hidden exhibit labels. In addition, the Discovery Room has been an adjunct to the museum's exhibits and special events. Eskimo tools, toys, and clothing were added to the room at the time of Cranbrook's INUA exhibition. Programs on reptiles, mammals, birds, and bones and fossils are presented. In a conscious shift towards a preschool audience, sensory awareness activities are also conducted. The Discovery Room is the responsibility of a nature programs specialist, who is assisted by approximately 25 volunteers. During the school year the Nature Center is open 9:00–5:00 weekdays for scheduled groups only. The Institute's kindergarten, 3rd-, and 6th-grade programs also use the room. On weekends and in the summer it is open to the public from 1:00 to 5:00. Visitors are primarily school groups and families, and the annual attendance is 35,000. There is an admission, with the remaining support coming from private sources.

"Hands-On Discovery," *Birmingham Eccentric*, 14 July 1983, p. 3A; "Hands-On Fun at Cranbrook," *Detroit Free Press*, 24 July 1984, p. 2C; "Nature Nook," *Newsletter/Cranbrook Institute of Science* 54, no. 5 (January 1985): 2; "Please Touch—and Listen, Smell, Watch—in Discovery Room," *The Cranbrook Journal* 1, no. 2 (March 1985): 3.

Detroit

CHILDREN'S MUSEUM, Detroit Public Schools, 67 East Kirby, Detroit, MI 48202. The museum began in 1917 as a cooperative undertaking between the Detroit Museum of Art and the Detroit Board of Education and was initially housed in 2 basement rooms in the Art Museum. They donated the original collection, and the schools paid the salary of the curator, Gertrude Gillmore, who served as head of the museum until her retirement in 1939. Remaining in its first location until 1925, the museum used one of its rooms for monthly changing exhibits and the other as a workroom and space to manage the loan department which sent collections to the schools. In 1925 the Board of Education made the museum an instructional unit of the public schools and assumed full responsibility for its operation. At this time it moved into the Farr Residence at 96 Putnam Avenue in what is now known as the Cultural Center. For the next decade the museum expanded its staff, collections, and services until they were curtailed by the severe economic conditions of the mid–1930s. In 1936 when the lease on the building housing the museum expired, the museum moved to a smaller facility, the Kelsy residence at 5202 Cass Avenue, where it remained for the next 20 years. Margaret Brayton became head of the museum in 1939 and served in that capacity until her retirement in 1963. Under her leadership changing exhibits replaced permanent installations, the lending department was revised and new catalogues prepared, Saturdays became activity days at the museum, and a comprehensive series of information publications for children, parents, and teachers were produced.

By the early 1950s, as the museum expanded its collections and services, the need for a larger facility became obvious. But the situation which forced the schools to secure another site was created when the Cass Avenue building, located on the Wayne University campus, was needed for the university's use. In 1957 the museum moved into the first permanent home, a 3-story brick building purchased by the Board of Education, at 67 East Kirby Street in the Cultural Center. Included in the renovation of the building was the addition of a planetarium. The 8,500 square feet of space were divided in equal amounts between exhibits, the lending department, and offices, workrooms, and storage facilities.

Under the leadership of Beatrice Parsons, who became director of the Children's Museum in 1963, it now occupies 20,000 square feet of space and provides a comprehensive program. It offers 42 classes at the museum related to the school curriculum for grades K–12 and special education groups. Museum staff members also go to schools, and loan collections provide a variety of materials, including specimens, objects, models, reproductions, and other pictorial items. Ten subject-area and special catalogs are available. The collection is strongest in the areas of American Indians, ethnology, folk crafts, dolls and toys, musical instruments, natural history, textiles, and writing and printing. Approximately 60,000 children, parents, and teachers come to the museum annually for its after-school activities, which include clubs, classes, planetarium demonstrations, Saturday and vacation-day programs, changing exhibits, and teachers workshops. In 1972 a Children's Museum Friends group was organized; a junior members group is a vital part of the organization. Two of their activities are printing a newsletter, *The Hoof Beat, For and By Children*, and funding special programs and activities on Saturdays and vacation days. The current staff of 19 includes the director, 5 teachers, 2 artists, 4 in the lending department, and 7 support personnel. In addition, 10 to 15 volunteers work on fund-raising, collections, and special projects. Hours are Monday through Friday 9:00–4:00 for classes and 1:00–4:00 for the general public. It is open Saturday, October through May, 9:00–4:00. The museum is supported by the Detroit Board of Education. The Children's Museum, which began in borrowed space with objects from a storeroom, has evolved over the years into a dynamic institution serving an entire school system and the metropolitan area. With a comprehensive collection and a wide variety of programs it has functioned as a model to others interested in establishing museums for children.

Margaret M. Brayton, "School Board Develops a Children's Museum," *Museum News* 39, no. 8 (May 1961): 32–35; Gertrude A. Gillmore, "The Work of the Detroit Children's Museum and Its Relation to the Schools," *Museum Work* 4, nos. 3 and 4 (November/ December 1921–January/February 1922): 135–39; Migs Grove, Sybil Walker, and Alexandra Walsh, "The Use of Adversity," *Museum News* 61, no. 3 (February 1983): 28; Beatrice Parsons, "Children's Museum," in *Improving Learning in the Detroit Public Schools: A History of the Division for Improvement of Instruction 1920–1966*, ed. Paul T. Rankin (Detroit: Detroit Public Schools, 1967); Beatrice Parsons, "The Place of a Children's Museum in the Public Schools," *Museum News* 45, no. 4 (December 1966): 34–35; Bonnie Pitman-Gelles, *Museums, Magic & Children: Youth Education in Museums* (Washington, D.C.: Association of Science-Technology Centers, 1981), pp. 8, 158, 179–80, 230.

Grand Rapids

JOHN BALL ZOOLOGICAL GARDENS, 201 Market SW, Grand Rapids, MI 49503. The children's zoo opened with a circus theme in 1953, and in 1977 the 2-acre area was remodeled. Open from May to September, it includes a petting corral staffed by 4 to 6 seasonal staff members and 45 teen volunteers who work 1 day per week after successfully completing a training program. Zoolab opened in March 1980 under the sponsorship of the Smithsonian Institution (see entry under UNITED STATES/DISTRICT OF COLUMBIA) as part of its Regional Associates Program. The 30-by-40-foot lab, located in the Education Building, contains 15 to 20 Discovery Boxes, games, puzzles and discovery sheets keyed to these boxes, animal artifacts, microscope, several brief slide/tape programs, and a library. Discovery Boxes have also been incorporated into programs for the disabled. Zoolab is open on scheduled weekday afternoons and on the weekends. HERPlab was established in October 1982 as a field site by the National Zoo (see entry under UNITED STATES/DISTRICT OF COLUMBIA), which is part of the Smithsonian, with money from the National Science Foundation. When the new herpetarium opened at the zoo in April 1983, a wedge-shaped area 12 feet deep by 12 –20 feet was set aside for HERPlab. Although the contents of the lab are similar in structure to those found in Zoolab, those in HERPlab focus solely on reptiles and amphibians. This lab has also been used in a program for school classes called "Herptile," which includes an hour of preparation at school followed by a 2-hour program at the zoo. The Children's Zoo, Zoolab, and HERPlab are under the direction of a full-time zoologist assisted by volunteers. The zoo is open daily 10:00–4:30 in the winter and 10:00–7:00 in the summer. There is a small admission charge to the zoo, which also receives support from the city of Grand Rapids and the John Ball Zoological Society. Approximately 200,000 people visited the children's zoo or Zoolabs last year.

Deborah A. Besch, "HERPlab," *Animal Kingdom* 86, no. 3 (June/July 1983): 17–18; Roe Ellen Froman and Carol Gray, "An Education Program for the Mentally and Emotionally Impaired," *AAZPA Regional Conference Proceedings 1982*, pp. 409–12; Melissa Gaulding, "HERPlab: A Cooperative Venture," *AAZPA Regional Conference Proceedings 1984*, pp. 9–11; Frederick C. See, "The Grand Rapids Children's Zoo," *Parks & Recreation* 40, no. 1 (January 1957): 17, 19; Judith White and Sharon Barry, *Families, Frogs, and Fun: Developing a Family Learning Lab in a Zoo—HERPlab: A Case Study* (Washington, D.C.: Smithsonian Institution, 1984), pp. 12, 17.

Lansing

CARL G. FENNER ARBORETUM, 2020 East Mount Hope, Lansing, MI 48910. The park opened in August 1959 after the city of Lansing purchased the site, formerly the property of the Turner family, for use as a nature park and arboretum. The facility is used primarily by preschool and school classes, guided interpretive programs are offered year-round, and a nature day camp is operated by the Lansing Parks and Recreation Department during the summer for children K through junior high. The arboretum contains approximately 5 miles of trails covering a variety of habitats and special-use facilities including a group camp area, picnic sites, and amphitheater which seats 100. In addition, there are a nature center with meeting rooms, a library for young and adult readers, exhibits including interpretive displays, and live animals. The center also includes a children's corner with a "touch table," discovery boxes, and Golden Guide Field Guides attached to the child-sized tables and benches. Currently the 49-by-32-foot basement is being converted into usable public meeting room space. A full-time naturalist is assisted by part-time staff as needed, and there is an active Friends group which provides volunteer support. The park is open all year from 8:00 until dark and the nature center weekdays 9:00–4:00 and Sundays 12:30–4:30. Groups with prior reservations can arrange their own time schedule. The park is city funded. Last year about 10,000 people came to arboretum programs, but there is no accurate estimate of those who used the site.

Friends of Fenner Arboretum (Fall 1984).

Midland

CHIPPEWA NATURE CENTER, 400 South Badour Road, Midland, MI 48640. The Discovery Room opened in 1978 and is located in the Interpretative

Building, which also includes a museum, classrooms, auditorium, meeting rooms, a project room, darkroom, and library with over 2,000 volumes. The Discovery Room is 1,200 square feet and contains aquariums, terrariums, hands-on natural history materials, quizzes, and an automated weather station. During 1985 and 1986 the Discovery Room is scheduled for revamping and remodeling. The center, which now occupies 1,200 acres, was initiated by volunteers as a natural history day camp that met in a borrowed school building. A nature observatory building was dedicated in 1968 and the Interpretative Building in 1975. The mission of the institution is to serve as a center for natural history outdoor education for the Saginaw Valley. The staff of 10 still depends on substantial volunteer effort to maintain its varied programs year-round. Approximately 30,000 people used the center last year and about 40 percent, or 12,000, visited the Discovery Room. The facility and its activities are funded by memberships, day use fees, and foundation support.

A Decade of Discovery: 1966–1976 (Midland: Chippewa Nature Center Annual Report, 1976); *On the Move* (Midland: Chippewa Nature Center Annual Report, 1983), p. 6.

Plymouth

PLYMOUTH HISTORICAL MUSEUM, 155 South Main Street, Plymouth, MI 48170. The Then and Now Center opened in 1982 to help children discover and compare the Victorian era with today. It is located in a 12-by-15-foot corner on the museum's lower level and enclosed by a white picket fence. The center has 6 hands-on stations: the general store, remedies, school, toys and games, clothing, and Victorian rooms and furnishings. Everything in the center is to be handled, tried on, and examined. This area was developed by the Museum's Education Committee and built by members of the Historical Society, all of whom are volunteers, for those children who visit the museum without their school class. But everyone visiting the museum enjoys the center. About 500 students per month participate in organized social history activities, and teachers may arrange for classes Wednesday through Friday. Built on the site of a farmhouse constructed in the early 1870s which included the village blacksmith shop, the museum has 15,000 square feet of exhibit space and an archive. It is open to the public Thursday, Saturday, and Sunday 1:00–4:00. There is a small admission. Fees for local students attending social history classes are underwritten by the Kiwanis Clubs of Plymouth.

Samuel Hudson, "A Child's Place," *Michigan History* 67, no. 5 (September/October 1983): 18–21.

Saginaw

SAGINAW CHILDREN'S ZOO, 1730 South Washington, Saginaw, MI 48601. Founded in 1967, the zoo is 7 1/2 acres with winding paths and greenery.

There are farm and exotic animals, free-roaming birds, a large cement whale which houses aquariums, an ark which houses small reptiles and mammals, and a contact yard. In addition, there are pony rides and a miniature train with a 1-mile scenic ride. There are 2 full-time staff members, 16 temporary staff members, and 2 volunteers. Open every day 10:00–5:00 from the 3rd week of May through Labor Day, the zoo is owned and operated by the City of Saginaw Parks and Recreation Department. There is a small admission charge. The zoo has about 100,000 visitors per year.

MINNESOTA

Minneapolis

JAMES FORD BELL MUSEUM OF NATURAL HISTORY, University of Minnesota, 10 Church Street SE, Minneapolis, MN 55455. The Touch and See Room opened in 1968 after the museum, asked to prepare an exhibit for the state fair, put out a variety of expendable objects accompanied by staff interpreters. Due to the success of this display the concept was incorporated into the museum itself, first in a temporary space and later a permanent one. The early design was planned cooperatively by a staff person from the museum and one from the University of Minnesota College of Education interested in nontraditional learning. The 4,000-square-foot room is considered to be both an exhibit and an ongoing education program. The natural history specimens used in the Touch and See Room are selected for their durability and grouped to elicit comparison and categorization. There are common and exotic animals and animal parts, tables of assembled objects including bones, wings, feet, skulls, shells, rocks, and a dissecting microscope. The staff interacts with visitors as they seek to understand the specimens. Few labels are used to encourage visitors to follow their own interests. Though the room is suitable for all age groups, its primary audience is preschool through grade 6, special education groups, and the handicapped elderly. Staffed with 2 part-time staff members, who are trained and supervised by the permanent staff, it is open Tuesday through Saturday 9:00–5:00, Sunday 1:00–5:00, and closed Monday and major national holidays. Financial support comes from a special legislative allocation to the University of Minnesota with additional building and support services from the university. Seventy-five thousand visitors use the Touch and See Room annually.

Victor J. Danilov, "Discovery Rooms and Kidspaces: Museum Exhibits for Children," *Science and Children* 23, no. 4 (January 1986): 7; Paul Hoffman, ed., *American Museum Guides—Science* (New York: Macmillan, 1983), p. 66; Helenmarie Hofman, "Touch and See," *Science and Children* 11, no. 3 (November 1973): 16–17.

Saint Paul

THE CHILDREN'S MUSEUM, 1217 Bandana Boulevard North, Saint Paul, MN 55108. The Children's Museum, Minnesota's Awarehouse, was founded in April 1979 and opened on 12 December 1981. Three women spearheaded the movement to establish a hands-on museum in the Twin Cities, and it was established without municipal or institutional support. The museum was installed in a renovated 1887 brick warehouse in downtown Minneapolis near the Mississippi River. The primary audience for the participatory exhibits and programs is children 6 months to 12 years old and their parents and teachers. The original building soon became too small, and in February 1985 the children's museum moved into the old blacksmith shop of the Northern Pacific Railroad in Saint Paul, constructed in 1886. The newly renovated 2-level plus basement 17,000-square-foot facility is almost 3 times larger than the first museum site. More than half of the first floor is devoted to Main Street, with operating devices, businesses, and services. The traffic lights and fire hydrants work, kids can pump gas, operate an electromagnetic crane, or become involved in participatory activities in the bank, store, TV and radio studio, kid's clinic, service station, railroad station, and lego construction area. This level also has an orientation area, the shop, and a developmental environment for children 3 and under. The upper floor has current and future technology, gallery space for changing visual arts exhibitions, and an area for public programming such as classes, workshops, and presentations. Groups specializing in performances for children have found an enthusiastic audience here. There are 11 full-time and 4 part-time staff members and about 100 volunteers. During the school year the museum is reserved for school groups Tuesday through Friday 9:30–2:00. Public hours are Tuesday through Friday 2:00–5:00 with extended hours on Thursday until 8:00, Saturday 10:00–5:00, and Sunday 11:00–5:00. Hours during July and August are Monday through Saturday 10:00–5:00 with extended hours until 8:00 on Thursday and Sunday 11:00–5:00. About 150,000 people visited the museum the first year in its new building. Support comes 70 percent from admissions, 14 percent from foundations and corporations, 7 percent from the store, 5 percent from fundraising events, and 4 percent from memberships and individual contributions.

Miriam Feldman, "High Tech for Tots," *Minnesota Monthly* (December 1983): 20; "Kids Run Things at the Enlarged New Children's Museum," *Minneapolis Star & Tribune*, 16 February 1985; "Museum Offers Kids Fun, Magic," *St. Paul Pioneer Press & Dispatch*, 15 February 1985, sec. D, pp. 1, 3; "New Children's Museum Caters to Young Crowd," *Minneapolis Star*, 11 December 1981, p. 5C; Mary Bader Papa, "Kids' Museum for Exploring, Not Boring," *Twin Cities Magazine* (September 1981): 20–21.

MINNESOTA HISTORICAL SOCIETY, 690 Cedar Street, Saint Paul, MN 55101. The Chautauqua Room was established around 1970 as part of the Society's effort to revitalize its exhibition program. Originally the room was designed to have extensive hands-on opportunities with historical materials; the emphasis was on having a wide variety of artifacts and different experiences. Initially the 1,200-square-foot room had a trading post stocked with goods used by traders and explorers, an Indian cultures area, a Minnesota settlers section, and carpeted risers for student seating which could be removed to satisfy other program needs. Over the years the number of touchable objects decreased, and the room became more thematically arranged. The risers, which can seat 30 6th-grade students, have remained. Currently it is organized around a series of biographies of Minnesotans from across the state who represent diverse experiences. There still are manipulative materials but fewer objects, permitting the room to be open to the public without a staff person present. The Chautauqua Room serves as a sampler, reflecting the major collections held by the Historical Society, and includes objects, photographs, maps, newspapers, census data, manuscripts, and artwork. The materials span the time from 1850 to 1930. The room is also the home base for the museum's education program and the setting for hour-long thematic lessons in Minnesota history. Students are actively involved by a museum teacher and use materials from the Society's collections. Early Indians, the fur trade, logging, the immigrant experience, the simultaneous development of Minnesota farms and towns, and the use of historical sources are some of the topics currently explored. The lessons are not tied to a specific grade level but are suitable for diverse groups. Scheduled only on weekdays between 9:00 and 4:00, groups must make reservations 2 weeks in advance and are limited to 30 students per session. Programs are revised yearly to reflect changes in exhibits and a critical evaluation of current lessons. Special programs are also arranged on topics requested by teachers. The room has 1 full-time and 2 three-quarter–time staff members, and there are no volunteers. The Chautauqua Room is open Monday through Saturday 8:30–5:00 and Sunday 1:00–4:00. There is no admission charge. Approximately 17,000 children in scheduled groups and 50,000 other visitors, especially families, come to the Chautauqua Room each year. Support comes from state appropriation.

Ann Bay, *Museum Programs for Young People* (Washington, D.C.: Smithsonian Institution, 1973), pp. 133–45: ERIC Document Reproduction Service, ED 090 116; *Catalog of Educational Services 1985–86* (Saint Paul: Minnesota Historical Society, 1985), pp. 4–6; Bonnie Pitman-Gelles, *Museums, Magic & Children: Youth Education in Museums* (Washington, D.C.: Association of Science-Technology Centers, 1981), p. 150; Thomas Thompson, "Teaching in Museums," Parts 1, 2, 3. *Minnesota History Interpreter* 12, no. 9 (September 1984): 4–5; 13, no. 1 (January 1985): 3–6; 13, no. 4 (April 1985): 3–5.

MISSISSIPPI

Jackson

JACKSON ZOOLOGICAL PARK, 2918 W. Capitol Street, Jackson, MS 39209. The Children's Zoo, opened in 1977, occupies 3 1/2 acres with 4 800-

square-foot barns built facing each other, forming a courtyard. A contact area has small domestic animals and a changing collection of a few exotic young animals. Feeding is allowed with food purchased in the zoo. Children may climb on a tractor and other farm equipment. Flowers are planted in the children's zoo each spring, and some years vegetables have been grown. Visitors may enter the contact yard or walk around the outside of the children's zoo to observe the animals. The area has a staff of 1 keeper and 2 keeper attendants. The children's zoo is included on most docent-led tours. The zoo is open Memorial Day to Labor Day 9:00–6:00 and the rest of the year 9:00–5:00. Support comes from admissions, the city of Jackson, and the Zoological Society. The zoo has approximately 242,000 visitors a year, and almost all come to the children's zoo.

Gary D. Ford, "The Zoos Rise Again," *Southern Living* 18, no. 4 (April 1983): 134; Penny O'Prey, comp., "Zoo-Aquarium Reports: Jackson Zoological Park," *Animal Kingdom* 81, no. 1 (February/March 1978): 30; James L. Swigert, "New Expansion Program at Jackson, Mississippi Zoo," *AAZPA Regional Conference Proceedings 1975–76*, pp. 353–55.

MISSOURI

Saint Louis

THE EUGENE FIELD HOUSE AND TOY MUSEUM, 634 South Broadway, Saint Louis, MO 63102. The house opened to the public in December 1936 following a public campaign to save the historic 1845 federal rowhouse, the birthplace of the children's poet Eugene Field. It was initially administered by a division of the Saint Louis Public School System, the Saint Louis Educational Museum (now Audiovisual Services). Operation of the site was transferred to the Landmarks Association in 1968, although the Board of Education retained title to the property. With the transfer came financial contributions to make building repairs and donations of antique toys, dolls, and furniture to re-create life as it was when Eugene Field lived there. In 1981 the Landmarks Association formed the Eugene Field Foundation and assumed control of the property and its interpretation. The building is now listed in the National Register of Historic Sites. The 7-room, 3,000-square-foot house exhibits a large collection of antique toys, dolls, photographs, and Field memorabilia. Group tours are given, and the house is available outside museum hours for private social events. The curator is assisted by about 20 volunteers. The museum is open Tuesday through Saturday 10:00–4:00, Sunday 12:00–5:00, and closed Mondays and holidays. The house has approximately 30,000 visitors a year. There is a small admission charge, and support comes from private sources.

"Eugene Field: City's Best Loved Poet," *St. Louis Globe-Democrat Magazine*, 25 November 1956, pp. 7–10; "Eugene Field House: Sturdy and Staunch It Stands," *St. Louis Post Dispatch*, 29 June 1969, pp. 1H, 7H; *The Eugene Field House and Toy Museum*

(Saint Louis: Eugene Field House Foundation, n.d.); "Historic House Refurbished," *St. Louis Post Dispatch Pictures*, 22 November 1964, pp. 12–13.

THE MAGIC HOUSE, 516 South Kirkwood Road (Lindbergh Boulevard), Saint Louis, MO 63122. The Magic House opened to the public on 16 October 1979 with over 40 hands-on exhibits. Two young women recognized the need for a children's participatory museum in Saint Louis. They spent 3 years raising funds, overseeing the renovation of a 6,000-square-foot, 3-storied Victorian mansion with 15 rooms, and designing exhibits. Initial development was underwritten by foundations, corporations, and individuals, but since opening it has relied solely on admission fees. There are no collections but an ever increasing number of exhibits, now more than 80, all locally built. On the 1st floor visitors can work their way through a human-size maze, experiment with pulleys and mechanical arms, and test their reaction time. The 2nd floor has a tone memory machine and other audio exhibits, Morse code cubicles, a shadow wall, perpendicular mirrors, reaction time cars, computers, and a pitch-black touch tunnel. The 3rd level has experiments of vision and smell, electrostatic generator, heartbeat monitor, gravity exploration, and calculator games. A birthday party room can be reserved for weekend use. There are also monthly events, many of which center around seasonal themes. On 17 December 1985 the Magic House expanded with the opening of a new 3,000-square-foot area, A Little Bit of Magic, designed specifically for young children 1–7. This area has a puppet wall, a variety of light switches and doorbells, sand area with pendulum, gross motor activities, book nook, and computers with preschool programs. Morning hours in the new wing are reserved for preschool groups, and public hours begin at 11:00. The museum has a full-time director and assistant director, who are assisted by 20 part-time staff members. During the school year the Magic House has public hours Tuesday through Thursday 3:00–6:00, Friday 3:00–9:00, Saturday 10:00–6:00, and Sunday 12:00–6:00. School groups visiting before 3:00 must have reservations, a minimum of 15 per group, and 1 adult for each 5 children. Summer hours are Tuesday through Thursday 10:00–6:00, Friday 10:00–9:00, Saturday 10:00–6:00, and Sunday 12:00–6:00. Mondays in the summer are reserved for groups. The museum attracts about 200,000 visitors per year from metropolitan Saint Louis and the surrounding area, mostly families with preschool and elementary school children.

Hedy Ehrlich, *A Guide to the Magic House* (Saint Louis: The Magic House, 1982); "Keep in 'Touch' at Magic House," *St. Louis Globe-Democrat Magazine*, 5–6 September 1981, pp. 4–5, 12; "The Magic House: A Museum Where It's Fun to Play," *St. Louis Post Dispatch Sunday Pictures*, 14 October 1979, pp. 14–19; "The Magic House Teaches Kids about Science in Fun Ways," *Belleville News-Democrat Sunday Magazine*, 27 January 1985, pp. 8–9; "Making More Magic: The Magic House Sets Its Sights Younger Than Ever," *St. Louis Post Dispatch Sunday Magazine*, 15 December 1985, pp. 9–11.

SAINT LOUIS SCIENCE CENTER, Forest Park, Saint Louis, MO 63110. The Discovery Room, opened in 1983, was developed on a very limited budget using a 500-square-foot space. The movement for the facility was spearheaded by an education staff member. Due to its enormous success a larger Discovery Room, 2,900 square feet with a substantial budget, was installed in the museum's new facility which opened in July 1985. All the exhibits are participatory and designed for small groups and families, with the primary audience children 3–12. Highlights of the new facility include a medical area with a doctor's black bag and an opportunity to explore disabilities, an Indian section with 3 types of dwellings and clothing, a walk-through cave, a fossil area, physics and technology exhibits, Discovery Boxes, and "stumpers," intriguing objects that are mainly natural history items. The Discovery Room has a full-time coordinator, 3 part-time assistants, and approximately 30 volunteers. The room is limited to 45 visitors per 45-minute session. For preschool through 7th-grade students, an adult must accompany each 4 children, and each toddler must be accompanied by an adult. The Discovery Room is open Monday through Saturday 10:00–4:45 and Sunday 12:00–4:45. From Labor Day to Memorial Day the room is reserved for school groups Monday through Friday 10:00–1:00. Groups must make reservations 2 weeks in advance. There is a small admission charge per person. Approximately 5,000 people visit the Discovery Room each month.

Adventures for Your Mind: The New St. Louis Science Center (St. Louis: St. Louis Science Center, 1985); "Science Center Makes Learning Fun," *St. Louis Post Dispatch*, 21 July 1985, sec. D, pp. 1, 14.

SAINT LOUIS ZOOLOGICAL PARK, Forest Park, St. Louis, MO 63110. The Charles H. Yalem Children's Zoo opened on 14 June 1969 and is 3 1/2 acres. There is a 2,800-square-foot indoor facility open year-round where visitors can observe the hand-rearing of animals in the nursery, see food preparation and animal feeding in the kitchen, and changing exhibits that are mounted and arranged at a height convenient for visitors of all ages. In addition, the indoor area includes a number of mammals, birds, reptiles, an egg incubator, and a bird brooder. From October through April the children's zoo keepers conduct classes for prescheduled school groups. These 20- to 25-minute sessions, available for preschool through 3rd-grade children, include a talk and animal contact. Approximately 6,500 children attend these classes each year. The outdoor section, open from mid-May through September, contains a variety of animal displays, contact areas, and play spaces. Included in this area is a walk-through bird cage and a tunnel which gives a below-the-surface view into a 15,000-gallon pool containing native fish and aquatic turtles. There is a large contact area with sheep and pygmy goats, and a keeper is always on hand to both supervise and answer questions. Guinea pigs are always available for contact, and on the half hour keepers bring out a reptile, bird of prey, or mammal which visitors are encouraged to touch and ask questions. In the summer of 1982 3 new educational components, an amphitheater, a tree house, and spider web, were added to the outdoor section. The 50-seat amphitheater is used for hourly animal demonstrations, and these 20-minute presentations are similar to those given indoors for school groups during the winter months. Different keepers give the talks, and a variety of animals are used. The programs are well attended and visitors participate in the sessions. A trilevel tree house with displays of arboreal animals, including opossums, screech owls, chameleons, and snakes, was built around the porcupine enclosure. The 3rd addition was a child-sized, climbable spider web constructed near the tarantula display. The children's zoo has 7 year-round keepers, 14 additional summertime keepers, and a number of volunteers. The zoo is open every day of the year 9:00–5:00. Admission to the zoo is free, but there is a small fee for the children's zoo after 10:00. Support comes from city and county tax revenues. The Charles H. Yalem Children's Zoo has about 400,000 visitors each year.

"Children's Zoo Displays Winter Exhibit," *Zudus* (April/May 1984): S4; "Easter Parade and Children's Zoo Exhibit Herald the Arrival of Spring," *Zudus* (July/August 1985): S7; Jack Grisham, "Children's Zoo Philosophy at the St. Louis Zoo," *AAZPA Regional Conference Proceedings 1983*, pp. 387–89; Cynthia Pappas, "A Day at the Zoo," *St. Louis* 18, no. 5 (May 1986): 40–41; Ingrid Porton, "The Charles H. Yalem Children's Zoo: Fifteen Years of Adventure and Learning," *Zudus* (July/August 1984): S1-S2; "Zoo Story," *Industrial Design* 17, no. 9 (November 1970): 58–61.

NEBRASKA

Lincoln

UNIVERSITY OF NEBRASKA STATE MUSEUM, 212 Morrill Hall, Lincoln, NE 68588–0338. The Encounter Center, opened on 23 June 1980, was created to encourage interaction between the public and natural history objects. The museum contains over 3.5 million specimens, only a small percentage of which are on display to the public. The Encounter Center has 1,450 square feet of display area with exhibits representing each of the 6 scientific divisions: anthropology, botany, entomology, invertebrate/vertebrate paleontology, and zoology. The displays are actually activity centers that involve the use of touch, sight, sound, and smell. Finding and identifying a fossil, testing one's strength, petting a Madagascar hissing cockroach, and handling a variety of mounted specimens are a few of the activities for visitors. The Encounter Center was initially created to interest elementary school children in natural science. The center has evolved into a resource for educators across the state, a tourist attraction, and an adult education center. Resource materials that supplement the science curriculum of Nebraska schools include activity kits, mounted specimens, and slide/tape programs that may be checked out for classroom use. Special events emphasizing an area of the museum's research collections are held bimonthly. Recent programs have included "Misunderstood Bats," "Nine-Mile Prairie Walk," and "Oceans of the Past and Present." The Encounter Center is staffed by a coordinator and assistant, who plan the programs for school groups and other visitors. The student staff members, 6 college students, are caretakers and facilitators. However, the 55 volunteers make it possible to offer special programs, interact one-on-one with visitors, and maintain a diverse educational environment. In 1985 over 50,000 individuals visited the Encounter Center. Eighteen percent of this total were scheduled groups and teachers. The other 82 percent included 40 percent adults and 42 percent children. The Encounter Center is open during the summer for the public, Tuesday-Friday 10:00–12:00 and 1:30–4:30 and weekends 2:00–4:00. During the winter the center is open to the public Tuesday-Friday 2:30–4:30 and weekends 2:00–4:00. The remainder of the days are for prescheduled school groups. Support for the Encounter Center comes from the University Administration, Lincoln Public Schools, Junior League, Community Volunteers, and public visitors. A small admission is charged per student for reservations, but there is no admission charge during public hours.

"Background Information on 'Encounter Center': Its History, Activities, and Equipment," Lincoln, [1980] (Typewritten); *The Encounter Center: A Hands-On Learning Room* (Lincoln: University State Museum, 1985).

Omaha

OMAHA CHILDREN'S MUSEUM, 551 South 18th Street, Omaha, NE 68102. Started in 1975 by the Junior League and a group of local educators, the museum was initially a program of traveling art activities and exhibits which were circulated to local schools and libraries. In 1977 the museum obtained a temporary site and remained there for 2 years before relocating downtown in a 10,000-square-foot facility. Currently the museum is not a collections-oriented institution but is looking for a larger site which will include space for proper collections maintenance. The hands-on exhibits, which change every 3 to 6 months, are in the arts (40 percent), science (25 percent), the humanities (20 percent), and creative play (15 percent). There have been a Discovery Room, a TV station, color exploration, creative arts workshop, ARCHITECTURE: THE FIGHT AGAINST GRAVITY, KITE TALES, INSECT ZOO, MY BODY: A MARVELOUS MACHINE, NUMBER NAMES/NUMBER GAMES (math in other cultures), KIDS AT WORK (occupational clothing and a chance to role-play different jobs), an exhibit on Japanese culture, SOMEONE LIKE ME (the lives of Third World children), and exhibits to demystify the world of doctors and dentists. In addition to festivals and special events, the museum has 4 workshop series per year with 10 to 20 different offerings per session. There are also field trips, outreach programs, classes for parents, and programs planned specifically for teachers. There are 4 full-time and 11 part-time staff members and a corps of about 200 volunteers. The target audience is children 3–12 and their families. In 1984 38,000 people visited the museum, and 28,000 attended special events. Two-thirds were children and one-third were adults. From September through May the museum is reserved for groups or classes Monday through Friday 10:00–2:30. Public hours are Monday through Friday 2:30–5:00, Saturday 10:00–5:00, and Sunday 1:00–5:00. June through August hours are Tuesday through Saturday 10:00–5:00 and Sunday 1:00–5:00. The museum is closed Monday and major holidays. There is an admission charge. Support comes 33 percent from earned income, 17 percent from grants, 17 percent from fundraising efforts, and 33 percent from the United Arts Organization, a corporate funding agency.

Experience [The Omaha Children's Museum] 3 (Fall 1984); *Experience* 3 (Summer 1985); *Experience* 4 (Winter 1985); "Omaha Children's Museum; Overview of Programs and Operations," Omaha Children's Museum, [1985] (Typewritten).

NEW HAMPSHIRE

Portsmouth

CHILDREN'S MUSEUM OF PORTSMOUTH, The South Meeting House, 280 Marcy Street, Portsmouth, NH 03801. Opened on 30 July 1983 following 2 years of planning, the museum resulted from community interest in developing an educational resource for schools, groups, and families. The 1863 building, listed in the National Register of Historic Sites, is leased from the city for a dollar a year. The 6,000-square-foot facility has 2 floors plus a loft, exhibits are hands-on, and the museum has no collection. Permanent spaces include an arts area with daily projects, science section with frequently changing exhibits, computer center, WFUN-TV and WFUN-Radio, play space called THE YELLOW SUBMARINE, and a newly restored clock tower which serves as an exhibit hourly. Rotating areas now include GROWING MY WAY (handicaps), LIFE EXPERIENCE (a hospital room), and THE WORK PLACE (a grocery). A current exhibit looks at New England's Native Americans, and another offers adventures in geography. There are also workshops, weekend and summer courses, and performances. Two full-time and 3 part-time staff members are assisted by 65 volunteers. Summer hours are Tuesday through Saturday 10:00–4:00 and Sunday 1:00–4:00. Winter hours are Tuesday through Sunday 1:00–4:00 with mornings available for school groups and special classes. During school vacations there are extended hours. Sixty-six percent of the museum's support comes from admissions, memberships, and the shop, and 34 percent from corporations and foundations. Most of the 32,000 annual visitors are from the seacoast tristate region within a 60-mile radius of Portsmouth.

"After One Year It's Become Part of Portsmouth," *Foster's Daily Democrat*, 6 July 1984; Meredith Gregg, "Childless at the Children's Museum," *Portsmouth Magazine*, 13 February 1985; "Museums Can Be Fun," *Manchester Journal*, 31 July 1985; "Please Touch: That's the Only Restriction at Portsmouth's Children's Museum," *Concord Monitor*, 23 May 1985, p. 33.

NEW JERSEY

Lincroft

MONMOUTH MUSEUM, Newman Springs Road, Lincroft, NJ 07738. The Junior Gallery, opened in September 1978, is 35 by 60 feet. It was developed after it was observed that many of the visitors to the museum were children. The Junior League was contacted to provide research support and develop the children's facility. Initially a large, open area, which proved to be noisy and disorganized, the gallery was redesigned after a few years into smaller spaces. There is no permanent collection. Exhibit material is either created at the museum or borrowed from other institutions. Developed around a concept or theme, the presentations remain for 1 to 2 years and have included LOOK—TOUCH—DISCOVER, EVERYBODY (from the Staten Island Children's Museum (see entry under UNITED STATES/NEW YORK)), HABITATS, DO YOU READ ME, and BUILD YOUR OWN WORLD. In 1980 paid guides were hired who improved the quality of the museum experience. Traveling trunks based on previous exhibitions are developed, and there are workshops for teachers. The Junior Gallery has an education curator, outreach coordinator, exhibit designer and preparators, and part-time docents who are assisted by volunteers. Guided tours can be arranged with advance reservation. The museum and gallery are open Tuesday through Saturday 10:00–4:30, Sunday 1:00–5:00, and closed Monday. Support comes 30 percent from the county, 20 percent from donations, 15 percent from memberships, 10 percent from admissions, 10 percent from grants, 10 percent from interest, and 5 percent from the state. The Junior Gallery has 30,000 visitors a year.

" 'Anti-Monopoly' Game Lets Children Practice Resource Management," *Star Ledger*, 23 October 1984, p. 41; "Exhibit Teaches Students Impact of Development," *Advisor* 25, no. 41 (10 October 1984): 1; "Museums Cater to Children," *Asbury Park Press*, 15 May 1984.

Newark

THE NEWARK MUSEUM, 49 Washington Street, PO Box 540, Newark, NJ 07101. The Junior Museum originated in the Newark Public Library under John Cotton Dana when, in 1913, a room on the 3rd floor was set aside for exhibitions labeled and designed to appeal to young people. In 1916 a museum club was organized for high school–age collectors, who planned exhibitions and programs and ran their own membership campaign. Due to lack of space the children's museum was discontinued in 1919 and the club disbanded in 1920. Since the opening of the museum building in 1926, an area has been designated as the Junior Museum. Initially one large room, 55 by 55 feet, it displayed art, social science and natural history materials, including live animals, and had activity areas. Clubs were an important part of its programming and school classes were frequent visitors. With the new facility came the rejuvenation of the Junior Museum Club, which since 1926 has offered a life membership for 10 cents. Currently there are 5,000 active Junior Museum members on the mailing list. In 1980 the Junior Museum introduced a 1,200-square-foot Junior Gallery to serve its growing weekend audience. Utilizing the Newark Museum collections, its exhibitions DESIGN FACTORY, HELLO JAPAN, and WEATHER WHYS have each remained 2 years. The Junior Museum offers art and science workshops for children 3–18 years. During the week there are preschoolers art workshops for Newark-based organizations, after-school enrichment activities for Newark schoolchildren, community outreach programs, Saturday morning art and science workshops, special events workshops and holiday festivals, and hospital outreach. There are 11 studios, each 15 by 15 feet, and spring and summer gallery shows of workshop exhibits. The Junior Museum has 4 full-time staff members, 1 receptionist, and 14 part-time instructors. There is no admission, and support comes from the museum general fund. The Junior Museum, open Tuesday through Friday 9:00–5:00 and Saturday 9:00–1:00, serves about 200 on weekdays and 150 on Saturday mornings. The Junior Gallery, open Tuesday through Sunday 12:00–5:00, offers special Discovery Center sessions Wednesday-Friday from 3:30 to 4:30 and weekends from 2:00 to 4:00. The Junior Gallery has approximately 60,000 visitors annually.

"The Activities of a Junior Museum," *The Museum* [Newark] 3, no. 9 (October 1931): 179–81; "Art on the Ward," *Goodlife Magazine* (May 1985): 22–23; John Carr Duff, "Improving on Barnum: Plans for a Children's Museum," *The Nation's Schools* 14, no. 5 (November 1934): 21–26; "Exhibit Explains the 'Whethers' behind Weather," *Home News*, 1 July 1985; "Little Children Get Taste of Big Ideas at Newark Museum Junior Program," *Star Ledger*, 15 July 1985, pp. N2-N3; "Newark Museum Is Reaching Out to Kids," *Belleville Times*, 19 July 1984, p. 6; Persis Motter, "The Junior Museum Retrospective Exhibition at the Newark Museum," *School Arts* 48, no. 7 (March 1949): 224; "A Visit to the Junior Museum," *The Museum* [Newark] 1, no. 11 (February 1928): 168–70.

Paramus

BERGEN MUSEUM OF ART AND SCIENCE, East Ridgewood and Farview Avenues, Paramus, NJ 07652. The Discovery Room opened in March 1982 and was renovated in March 1985. The 15-by-25-foot facility is designed for children preschool through 8th grade and the handicapped. An audiotape is available at the entrance to the room to aid the visually impaired. School groups use the Discovery Room as part of their guided tour, and docents instruct children how to use the displays, which include print material. The 10 Discovery Boxes with natural history materials are changed every 6 months, and additional artifacts and specimens are accessible on tables. There are different kinds of mirrors, "What-Is-It" flip pictures of magnified objects to compare to the complete picture, a light tree covered with different colored bulbs which light according to the frequency voiced, a sound column, and a music corner. For the blind, there are a picture to feel and a touch sculpture with accompanying recording. The Discovery Room is open the same hours as the museum, and it is not staffed on a scheduled basis. Hours are Tuesday through Saturday 10:00–5:00, Sunday 1:00–5:00, and closed Monday. The museum has about 60,000 visitors annually; separate attendance figures for the Discovery Room are not recorded. Admissions provide 13 percent of the museum's support, the real fund 30 percent, grants 24 percent, fund-raisers 17 percent, and a variety of other sources provide the remaining 16 percent. Maintaining the Discovery Room and enlarging its scope continue a long-standing commitment to both children and the arts and sciences. The museum owes its origin to Selina Johnson, who founded the Leonia Youth Museum in 1950. The closing of that museum in June 1956 coincided with the establishment of the Bergen Community Museum in May 1956, which became the Bergen Museum of Art and Science in 1984.

Selina Tetzlaff Johnson, "Museums for Youth in the United States: A Study of Their Origins, Relationships, and Cultural Contributions" (Ph.D. dissertation, New York University, 1962), pp. 173, 191; "Museum Celebrates Discovery Room Reopening on March 31," *Bergen News*, 20 March 1985.

Short Hills

THE CORA HARTSHORN ARBORETUM, 324 Forest Drive South, Short Hills, NJ 07078. Opened in 1962, the arboretum was the result of a bequest from the estate of Cora Hartshorn to Millburn Township. The 16 1/2 acres of wild woodland has hiking trails and a nature museum located in the Stone House. Completed in 1933, it was renovated in 1962 when the nature museum was established, and added on to in 1974. The house is the focal point of arboretum activity, which includes changing exhibits, a small collection of live animals, an active beehive, mounted animals and specimens, a weather station, quiz games, a reference library, and a meeting room. The junior program includes an annual series of classes for elementary school students from the Millburn Public Schools, workshops, junior arboretum club, badge classes and programs for scouts, preschool program, and family activities. Adult programs encompass lectures and workshops, nature walks, trips, and special senior citizen events. In the spring the maple trees are tapped, and later honey is tasted fresh from the hive. There are 2 museum coordinators, a coordinator of youth programs, a corps of docents, and volunteers who help maintain the arboretum. The museum is open to the public during the school year on Tuesday, Wednesday, and Thursday 2:30–5:00, Saturday 9:30–12:00, and Sunday 3:00–5:00 during the fall and spring only. The trails are open year round during daylight hours. There is no charge for Stone House or the arboretum, and fees for workshops and other activities vary. Approximately 2,000 children and 500–800 adults participate in programs annually.

Program of Activities: Winter/Spring 1984 (Short Hills: Cora Hartshorn Arboretum and Bird Sanctuary, [1984]); Ginger Wallace, "Cora Hartshorn Arboretum: Nature's Classroom," *New Jersey Outdoors* 11, no. 2 (March/April 1984): 14–15.

Stone Harbor

WETLANDS INSTITUTE, Stone Harbor Boulevard, Stone Harbor, NJ 08247. Wetlandia, opened in 1972, is a touch museum supporting the institute's mission of furthering public understanding and appreciation of the coastal zone. The 18-by-30-foot facility exhibits preserved butterflies, shells, saltwater aquariums, preserved native fish and invertebrates, and includes games like the Shell Game and Quiz Boards. There are also microscopes. A raptor exhibit is in process of construction with completion anticipated in June 1986. Surrounded by a salt marsh and 6,000 acres of publicly owned coastal wetlands, the institute uses the outdoors for exploration with a self-guided or guided trail, birding expeditions, and field trips. Programs for groups are available by appointment; there are family activities, teacher workshops, and 5-day miniecology classes for children in the summer. A fall festival, Wings 'n Water, is the big fund-raiser of the year and attracts over 5,000 people. There is a staff of 6 assisted by 20 volunteers. The museum is open October to May on Tuesday, Thursday, and Saturday 10:00–4:30 and May to October on Tuesday through Saturday 10:00–4:30. During the summer months there are about 100 visitors per day. A small donation fee is requested at the door, and support comes from private donations, gifts, memberships, and fund-raisers.

"Wetlands Institute Offers Museum, Tours, Nature Education Programs," *Avalon Magazine* (Fall 1985): 14–15; "Wings 'n Water Festival," *Cape May County Herald Supplement*, 18 September 1985.

NEW MEXICO

Albuquerque

RIO GRANDE ZOOLOGICAL PARK, 903 Tenth Street SW, Albuquerque, NM 87102–4098. The Children's Zoo, opened in 1961, is a half-acre contact area open in the summer. Some of the animals found there include alpacas, Cameroon goats, Sardinian donkeys, and dwarf zebu. There is also a very popular prairie dog colony. Discovery Stations, where the alpacas and donkeys are walked and groomed, storytelling hours, and supervised visitor feeding of some animals are special activities of the petting zoo. One year-round staff person is assisted by 60 teenage and adult volunteers in the summer. There is an admission charge for the zoo but no extra fee for the children's zoo. Support for the zoo comes from the city. Hours are 9:00–5:00 weekdays and 9:00–6:00 weekends. The children's zoo has about 444,000 visitors a year.

Catherine Hubbard, "The Zoo as a Community Resource," *AAZPA Regional Conference Proceedings 1983*, pp. 331–34; "If You Have Time to Give or Want to Learn: Petting Zoo," *Kudu Review* (April/May 1985): 6; *Yours to Explore: Rio Grande Zoological Park* (Albuquerque: Rio Grande Zoological Park, [1984]).

NEW YORK

Binghamton

THE DISCOVERY CENTER OF THE SOUTHERN TIER, 164 Hawley Street, Binghamton, NY 13902. Opened in March 1984, the facility was developed through the combined efforts of a group of parents and the Junior League. Both wanted to have a hands-on science center for children in the area. Started as an all-volunteer endeavor, it has received strong business and community support. The center is located in the State Office Building Annex, formerly an elementary school, and has 4,000 square feet of exhibit space in the old school gym. Installations include a Boeing 747 Jumbo Jet cockpit with taped take-off and landing instructions and real controls, a 1930s grandma's kitchen, slice of a city with an occupational focus, medical/health area, light-mirror, shadows, and a nature section. There are also many smaller exhibits. Mini science lessons, Science Scoops, are given to tour groups, and there are special monthly events, Discovery Days. A paid staff of 3 is assisted by volunteers including teens and university interns. The target audience is schoolchildren 3–13 and family groups. Attendance doubled during the center's second year and now averages about 3,500 a month including school groups from a 100-mile radius. Expansion in 1987 is anticipated and will include classroom space. Hours have gradually increased, and the center is now open 30 hours per week, Tuesday through Saturday. There is a small admission charge. Additional support comes from the State Arts Council through the local arts council and some local industries and businesses.

Carol Snyder, "A Major Discovery," *New York Alive* 5, no. 5 (September/October 1985): 22; "Where Kids Can Learn from Play," *Press & Sun-Bulletin*, 3 October 1985, pp. 1D, 7D.

Bronx

BRONX ZOO, 185th Street & Southern Boulevard, Bronx, NY 10460. The Children's Zoo, opened on 21 May 1941, had a storybook theme and provided an opportunity for children to pet domestic animals. It was an immediate success, with 230,000 visitors during its first year. Gradually farm animals in realistic settings replaced the nursery rhymes, but the hands-on aspect remained. In 1970 the original Noah's Ark was converted into a game with chances to look, touch, smell, and listen. Participatory began to mean something more than just contact, although this continues to be popular with zoo visitors. In 1981, a new, 3.5-acre Children's Zoo with 56 exhibits in 5 main areas opened. Four are natural environments with wild North American animals, and the 5th is a domestic farmyard. Each wild animal area stresses an ecological concept and has a biological principle related to it. To encourage learning, animals are alongside interactive devices. Animal homes at the woodland-edge feature night herons perched in trees and nests, and children climb into nests of their own. After their descent they observe prairie dogs, go into a child-sized burrow, through a grotto where the occupants are snakes that don't build but find homes, and finally onto a 20-foot climbable web fashioned after the garden orb spider. The marsh helps children discover locomotion—swimming, wading, diving, and crawling—with the special chance to wear a shell and move like a snail. Animal defenses are exhibited in the forest where there is the opportunity to observe, escape from predators, and be a box turtle. The last habitat is the desert, where the senses are introduced. Children can hear like a fox, see like an owl, and view other desert animals. The final area within the Children's Zoo is the farmyard, where feeding and petting are allowed, and animals may be viewed in the nursery. There is also a 100-seat theater in which 15- to 20-minute programs on animal biology are held 5 times a day. The average daily staff in the Children's Zoo is 3 supervisors, 13 keepers, 10–15 volunteers, and a theater instructor. It is open every day April through October 10:00–5:00. The area appeals to all ages, has a ratio of 1 adult to 1 child, with 600,000 visitors per season. A number of foundations and donors provided the support for the redevelopment of the Children's Zoo, which is maintained by an admission fee.

The Bronx Zoo served as a model for others with its early development of a children's zoo and, most recently, with its emphasis on wild animals, naturalistic habitats, and innovative educational activities. The Children's Zoo won an exhibit award from the AAZPA in 1981.

Robert A. Brown, "Why Children's Zoos?," *International Zoo Yearbook* 13 (1973): 258–61, ed. Nicole Duplaix-Hall (London: The Zoological Society of London, 1973); Ruth Dauchy, "Where Adults Are Not Admitted—Unless Accompanied by a Child," *Recreation* 36, no. 7 (October 1942): 381–83; "Exploring the Children's Zoo," *Animal Kingdom* 75, no. 2 (April 1972): 2–7; Richard Lattis, "The New Children's Zoo," *Interpreter* 12, no. 3 (1981): 14–17, reprinted as "The New Children's Zoo," *Children's Environments Quarterly* 1, no. 3 (Fall 1984): 40–42; Richard L. Lattis, "Our Public Image: Starting with Children," *AAZPA 1983 Annual Conference Proceedings*, pp. 95–104; Susan Normandia, "Exhibit Effectiveness in the Children's Zoo," *AAZPA Regional Conference Proceedings 1983*, pp. 557–64; Harry Sweeny, Jr., "The Children's Zoo," *Bulletin New York Zoological Society* 44, no. 4 (July/August 1941): 99–107.

Brooklyn

BROOKLYN BOTANIC GARDEN, 1000 Washington Avenue, Brooklyn, NY 11225. The Children's Garden, established in 1914 as an educational experiment under the direction of Ellen Eddy Shaw, has been in continuous existence since its inception. Miss Shaw retired as curator of children's education in 1945 and was succeeded by Frances M. Miner. For several years after Miss Miner's retirement in 1974, various program changes occurred, and there was a gradual return to a more structured format. Each year approximately 250 children between the ages of 9 and 17 learn gardening, botany, and horticulture by doing. The 1-acre living exhibits include an herb garden, an annual border, and a vegetable garden. Planning by the staff occurs during the winter months, and the youngsters in the spring program begin their garden experience with indoor sessions held on 3 Saturday mornings in March. Groups are formed according to age, 12 in the younger group and 16 in the older one, each group with an instructor and a junior instructor. Two children share a 4-by-15-foot plot designed by the coordinator of the Garden and grow the crops selected for them. Older children design for themselves larger 8-by-15-foot plots and choose their vegetables. Planting day is usually the end of April, and on the following Saturdays until the end of June a variety of garden activities take place. If time permits, miniclasses are held on various topics. Harvest time begins in late May, and each gardener gets to take home his/her produce. There is also a summer program for children 2 mornings per week. One day is used for gardening and the other for classes or visits to nature centers. The gardening season concludes in September with a Harvest Fair. There are 4 full-time and 5 part-time staff members, 1 volunteer instructor, and 10 teenage junior instructors. There is a minimal fee for each session, and scholarships are available for those unable to pay. Operation of the Children's Garden is supported in part by corporate contributions, the Institute of Museum Services, and the Natural Heritage Trust. Since it began more than 70 years ago, over 15,000 children have participated in the program. The Children's Garden has served as a model for others, and its staff has provided leadership in the youth gardening movement.

Brooklyn Botanic Garden, *70th Anniversary of the Children's Garden, Brooklyn Botanic Garden, 1984* (Brooklyn: Brooklyn Botanic Garden, 1984); C. Stuart Gager, "Brooklyn Botanic Garden's Cooperation with Public Schools," *School Science and Mathematics* 40, no. 351 (October 1940): 614–18; Bonnie Pitman-Gelles, *Museums, Magic & Children: Youth Education in Museums* (Washington, D.C.: Association of Science-Technology Centers, 1981), p. 200; Ellen Eddy Shaw, "A Children's Garden in the City," *Library Journal* 65 (15 March 1940): 243–45; Doris M. Stone, "Children's Gardening at BBG," *Plants & Gardens, Brooklyn Botanic Garden Record* 40, no. 3 (Autumn 1984): 6–10.

THE BROOKLYN CHILDREN'S MUSEUM, 145 Brooklyn Avenue, Brooklyn, NY 11213. The world's first children's museum was established in 1899 as a branch of the Brooklyn Museum and became an independent institution in 1979. Initially housed in a Victorian mansion, the museum expanded in 1928 by acquiring an adjacent building. Although a new facility had been discussed and planned since 1907, movement in that direction did not take place for another 60 years. In 1967 these century-old mansions, now badly deteriorated, were condemned, closed, and soon razed. The following spring, after thoroughly examining the area's needs, the Brooklyn Institute of Arts and Sciences again became a pioneer and tested a new museum concept, the neighborhood museum. In May 1968 the Brooklyn Children's Museum reopened in the Bedford-Stuyvesant section of Brooklyn in a former garage. While officially named the Bedford Lincoln Neighborhood Museum, it was known as MUSE. Architectural plans for the new children's museum were unveiled in May 1971, and ground was broken on 13 June 1972. The staff moved into the nearly completed building early in 1975, but it was 2 more years before the museum was ready due to last-minute construction problems and a city financial crisis. The Brooklyn Children's Museum reopened its doors on 17 May 1977 in a 30,000-square-foot, participatory learning environment hailed as translating the museum's philosophy into an architectural reality. It also reaffirmed the museum's own heritage, as the high-tech facility was built on the original site.

Besides the continuity in the physical site, the current statement of purpose reasserts some of the original goals set by the trustees more than three quarters of a century ago. They desired to create an attractive educational center that would stimulate a child's power of observation, instruct, and delight. Museum curator Anna Billings Gallup, who was appointed in 1902 and served until 1937, helped transform these goals into reality. She believed that children should feel the museum was created for them and have full use of its facilities. Gallup developed an innovative program which included visually attractive collections that expressed a basic concept or principle. Brief descriptive labels utilized easily readable type. Not only did exhibits show relationships, but children were encouraged to use, touch, and manipulate them. Live animals began to appear inside the museum alongside stuffed ones. Teachers were welcome to use the museum's resources, and later more formal relationships developed with teacher-training institutions. Loan collections were available to schools. By the end of the first decade (1908) the museum's library held over 5,000 volumes. Clubs were formed to bring together children with similar interests. And finally, one of the staff's missions was to assist visitors.

In 1938, in her first curatorial report, Jane Wilson Garrison described the museum as having withstood 39 years of wear and tear with remarkable fortitude. More than 9 million children had passed through its doors, representing not so much a building as the spirit of childhood. Under her leadership and that of her successors, Margaret De Wolf Tullock (1945–1958) and Helen Vought Fisher (1958–1967), new programs were developed to meet changing needs. Interest clubs continued to be an important aspect of the museum's program, trips were organized, and by the late 1950s teenage youth vied for the few year-long unpaid junior curator positions made available. Yet, in 1960, Fisher felt compelled to clarify the museum's purpose. She said that although the Brooklyn Children's Museum looked like a standard museum with collections and exhibit galleries, as a children's museum it emphasized interpretation and had as its prime function education.

On 1 February 1967 the Brooklyn Children's Museum was temporarily closed to the public, its collections stored, and in the spring an experimental in-school program was initiated. Richard A. Madigan served as director for a brief time but was succeeded later in 1967 by Emily Dennis. As the museum's acting director, Dennis conceived the idea for MUSE. The directorship of the Brooklyn Children's Museum and of MUSE was assumed on 1 July 1968 by Lloyd Hezekiah. The pilot project MUSE not only brought the museum to the neighborhood, but residents also had an active voice in its programs and policies, which included substantial volunteer involvement. At MUSE the activity-oriented programs and tuition-free workshops were supplemented with exhibitions, although space was limited. More than 50 loan or traveling cases with authentic material were available to teachers. About 100,000 people per year, adults as well as children, participated in the museum's educational and cultural programs. In 1979 the MUSE facility was separated from the Brooklyn Children's Museum and converted into a community-oriented cultural center.

Once the Brooklyn Children's Museum reopened in its new building in 1977 with Hezekiah as director, it returned to a more child-centered emphasis. One-fifth of the full-time staff of 50 is involved in direct teaching activities. The museum hired a volunteer/intern coordinator in 1984 and has significantly expanded training and volunteer opportunities throughout the museum. The 50,000 objects in the museum's collection, primarily in the areas of natural history, technology, and ethnology, are used chiefly for interpretation, which is viewed as more the institution's mission than preservation. There is a small library for children. After-school clubs, organized in response to current interests and needs, attract children mainly from the immediate vicinity. A recently expanded school loan program makes artifact kits complete with teaching materials available at a minimal fee to classes unable to visit the museum. A new program offers schools assistance in developing and maintaining their own museums. Museum instructors also visit hospitalized youngsters with collections, objects, and live animals as part of the Hospital Outreach Program. Throughout the year a variety of film series, musical events, and theater activities are held. A major festival, the June Balloon, is held each year to celebrate urban family life.

On 1 July 1984 Mindy Duitz succeeded Hezekiah as director. In the mid–1980s the museum serves about 150,000 people, with school groups accounting for about 20,000. Approximately 40 percent of the visitors are from Brooklyn. A shift to younger children is noticeable, with the museum seeing more pre-schoolers and fewer teenage youth. Roughly 12 percent of the school groups consist of disabled children. Until the 1960s municipal financial support was supplemented by the museum's auxiliary and civic organizations. In 1984 New York City provided about 60 percent of the museum's operating expenses, and the rest of its support came from foundations, corporations, and state and federal sources. Beginning in July 1985, the museum instituted a voluntary admission program with a suggested contribution.

The Brooklyn Children's Museum has served as a prototype in its 3 major phases: the first children's museum, a neighborhood center called MUSE, and now an environment designed for children.

"The Children's Museum of the Brooklyn Institute," *Scientific American* 82 (12 May 1900): 296; Educational Facilities Laboratories, *Arts and the Handicapped: An Issue of Access* (New York: Educational Facilities Laboratories, 1975), pp. 12–14: ERIC Document Reproduction Service, ED 117 829; "Esprit Grows in Brooklyn," *Progressive Architecture* 59, no. 5 (May 1978): 62–67; Helen V. Fisher, "Children's Museums: A Definition and a Credo," *Curator* 3, no. 2 (1960): 183–91; Anna Billings Gallup, "The Children's Museum as an Educator," *Popular Science Monthly* 72 (April 1908): 371–79; Lloyd Hezekiah, "Reflections on MUSE," *Museum News* 50, no. 9 (May 1972): 12–14; "Neighborhood MUSE," *Architectural Forum* 129, no. 2 (September 1968): 86–89; Gabrielle V. Pohle, "The Children's Museum as Collector," *Museum News* 58, no. 2 (November/December 1979): 32–37.

NEW YORK AQUARIUM, Boardwalk & West 8th Street, Brooklyn, NY 11224. The Children's Cove, opened in 1972, featured touch tanks, boxes with tactile material, and displays and was staffed by docents. Although the Cove was popular with children, aquarium staff noticed that adults did not fully participate with children. This perception led to an extensive study of how people, especially families, learn at the aquarium. Years of research by Karen Hensel, curator of education, in conjunction with Columbia Teachers College staff provided a theoretical base for a new facility. Children's Cove was closed in late 1985, and the site will be taken over by a major new building, Discovery Cove, opening in 1988. The new facility, a 2-story, 60,000-square-foot prototype learning center, is planned for the general public with exhibits designed for a multigenerational audience. The building entrance will focus attention on the physical qualities of water and ecosystems with a linked-series exhibit simulating a sandy shore, salt marsh, and rocky shore, all coastal areas of the northeastern United States. Adaptation will feature feeding, respiration, locomotion, protection, and the senses of sight, sound, smell and taste. A transitional section will draw attention to the importance of water as the visitor moves into the area with ministorefronts, each devoted to a different product or resource from oceans, rivers, streams, and lakes. Docents will be on hand to answer questions, and several activities including using microscopes will be available. There will be an educational wing with a separate entrance for groups attending classes. It will house a simulated rocky coast, ecological vivarium, artifacts, and specimens. There will also be a Discovery Room for more detailed study, a classroom capable of 3-screen projection, access to behind the scenes of Discovery Cove, which is another form of instructional space, and a library/resource center. School groups will be able to schedule 1-hour programs in the alcoves; kits will be included in the exhibits and made available. A toddler and infant club for parents will be offered during the week. The staff will include a curator of education, 3 full-time and 2 part-time instructors, 1 reservationist, and 1 general secretary. The docent program is expected to grow, and the use of junior volunteers in the summer, who must be at least 16 years old, will continue. Capital funds were provided by the city of New York for construction of the building. The New York Zoological Society provided the funds for the interior of the building, and the city of New York provided funds for the classroom. It will be open 7 days a week 10:00–6:00. Discovery Cove will provide hands-on, thematic, self-discovery learning opportunities for all ages, with the family being the target audience.

Discovery Cove at the New York Aquarium (New York: New York Zoological Society, n.d.); Karen Hensel, "Creating Enabling Contexts," *Current/Journal of Marine Education* 5, no. 2 (Winter 1984): 6–9; Karen Astrid Hensel, "Displays at Displays: Looking at the Family as Educator in the Context of a Living Museum—An Aquarium" (Ph.D. dissertation, Columbia University, in progress); Karen Hensel, "Marinating the Family," *Outdoor Communicator* 13, no. 2 (Fall 1982): 9–14; Karen Hensel, "A New Look at Our Largest Audience (Ethnographic Analysis of the Family Unit)," *AAZPA 1982 Annual Conference Proceedings*, pp. 261–67; "How Visitors View Exhibitions," *Newsday*, 20 February 1983, sec. II, pp. 21–22.

Buffalo

BUFFALO MUSEUM OF SCIENCE, Humboldt Parkway, Buffalo, NY 14211. The Discovery Room opened on 5 January 1980 and replaced the children's room which existed from June 1968 to July 1975, when it was closed during building renovation. The first children's facility at the museum began in July 1923 and existed until the fall of 1928. Funds for the Discovery Room facility came from the Women's Committee and the Junior League, who worked with the museum staff to develop the 29-by-15-foot hands-on area. It is now supported with funds from the museum's general operating budget. Although the target audience is children 5–12, the room is open to everyone and used on an informal basis except when included in tours or used for magnet school minicourses or children's classes by science instructors. There are approximately 15 Discovery Boxes and a variety of objects around the room, including clothing, mounted specimens, rocks and minerals, plant and sea life, bones, horns, and shells, wood samples, and a series of field guidebooks. Visitors may stay for a half hour, and no more than 25 people can be in the room at a time. On school days the Discovery Room is available by appointment only from 10:00 to 2:30 and to anyone from 2:30 to 4:30. Saturday hours are 10:00–5:00 and Sunday 1:30–5:00. One regular museum staff person devotes roughly one-third time to the Discovery Room and is assisted by a student on weekends in the winter, a full-time teenage helper in the summer, and approximately 37 volunteers from 7th grade to adult. Of the 29,000 annual visitors about one-third are preschoolers, one-third from grades K–6, and one-third adults.

Robert A. Martin, Victoria J. Best, and Anni Praetorius, "Discovery Room Article," Education Department, Discovery Room File, Buffalo Museum of Science, 1980–81

(Typewritten); "A Place for Curious Kids," *Niagara Gazette*, 10 January 1980, p. 1-C; "Smithsonian-Inspired Discovery Room Opens Here," *Courier-Express*, 6 January 1980, sec. E, p. 1.

BUFFALO ZOOLOGICAL GARDENS, Delaware Park, Buffalo, NY 14214. The Children's Zoo, opened in 1966, occupies 1 acre and displays sheep, goats, ponies, donkeys, zebu, and birds. The area will undergo renovation during the first half of 1986 and then reopen to the public. The collections will remain the same, but the exhibits will be updated and set in more naturally landscaped enclosures. An elevated walk-through aviary (birdwalk) opened in April 1985 following renovation and features a variety of indigenous birds and plants. There are 3 to 5 seasonal staff members who care for the animals. The children's zoo is open 10:00–4:00 in the summer and 10:00–2:00 in the winter. A small admission charge to the zoo includes the children's area.

In February 1984 a Children's Resource Center building was completed and houses the Buffalo School's Science Magnet School. The zoo component of the magnet school program was initiated in 1981 and serves junior high students. Initially housed at the nearby school with shuttle-bus service to the zoo, the program now shares the new building with the zoo's education department. The 2-story building is jointly owned by the city and the Zoological Society, and contains a fully equipped animal room for the teaching collection, science classroom, zoomobile/zootruck garage, 340-seat lecture/dining hall, 5 regular classrooms, 2 science lab classrooms, computer room, greenhouse, junior high library, and facilities for the docents, offices, kitchen, and other support areas. The on-site school staff consists of 7 full-time and 3 part-time teachers, 3 teachers aides, an office clerk, and an assistant principal. There are also 2 zoo education staff members assigned to work with the magnet school students. Enrollment is approximately 225 students. In 1983 the Science Magnet School Zoo Satellite was awarded the Search for Excellence in Science Education Award from the National Science Teachers Association. In 1984 the Zoo School was chosen along with 212 other public secondary schools as "outstanding" by the United States Department of Education. Through the scientific disciplines, the program emphasizes gathering and organizing knowledge, problem solving, and critical thinking skills. Lab and fieldwork are a regular part of the curriculum. This science-oriented program, which already has components in the elementary school, may be extended to include the high school level.

Buffalo Zoological Gardens Educational Programs 1984–85 (Buffalo: Buffalo Zoological Gardens, [1984]), pp. 3–4, 6; "The Children's Zoo Renovation," *Zoolog* (January/February 1986): 2; Patricia M. Dailey, "Buffalo's Science Magnet School: Drawing Students to a Zoo's Living Classroom," *AAZPA Regional Conference Proceedings 1984*, pp. 513–18; "National Award to Be Presented at White House" (Buffalo: Buffalo Zoological Gardens Press Release, 26 September 1985); "New Bird Exhibit for the Children's Zoo," *Zoolog* (January/February 1985): 4; *Zoolog* 9 (May/June 1984): 2, 4, 6, 10, 11.

Canandaigua

ONTARIO COUNTY HISTORICAL SOCIETY, 55 North Main Street, Canandaigua, NY 14424. The Children's Museum Discovery Room opened on 12 October 1980 as part of a major building renovation. Located on the lower level, with 1,000 square feet of space, it has a pioneer kitchen and an exhibit/seating area. The museum offers children's programs and creates a special place for hands-on activities and access to artifacts. Discovery Boxes contain items and question cards related to industry, agriculture, and other topics of Ontario County history. There is an archaeological dig, a board game based upon local steamboat commerce in the 19th century which encourages role-playing and decision making, building blocks based on architectural styles, and a time capsule. These and other activities, which relate to exhibits located upstairs, are used to introduce visitors and classes from all grades to the museum. Program emphasis is on teaching how to "read" objects, buildings, and gravestones and fostering a greater understanding of local history. School loan kits have artifacts from the museum's collection, and slide shows can be sent or used by staff members, who present programs free of charge. In addition, there is a children's page in the society's newsletter, and the museum sponsors a summer day camp with history-related activities. Sixteen percent of the operating budget comes from memberships; 33 percent from local, state, and federal support; 20 percent from fund-raising and shop sales; and the remaining amount comes from gifts, investments, and reimbursements. A full-time education coordinator oversees the operation of the Discovery Room, which has approximately 2,130 visitors annually, most coming from nearby. The museum is open Tuesday through Saturday 10:00–5:00.

"Grant Awarded to Museum," *Daily Messenger*, 9 September 1979; Michael P. O'Lear, "Not for Children Only," *Regional Conference of Historical Agencies* 12, no. 7 (July 1982): 1–2; "A Spot Where Children Learn about History," *Daily Messenger*, 16 October 1980.

Cortland

CORTLAND COUNTY HISTORICAL SOCIETY, 25 Homer Avenue, Cortland, NY 13045. A Child's World opened in 1967 as the children's room and was renovated in 1984. It is filled with early 20th-century toys, games, and clothing. Set up like a child's playroom, it has a doll house modeled after one of Cortland's historical buildings, puzzles, board games, dolls, and try-on clothing. The society uses duplicates from the collection or reproductions and changes them periodically so that they remain fresh and the area continues to have appeal. Adults and children often visit together. In addition, kits which relate to the contents of the room are sent to schools; there are activity packets in the textile arts and kitchen crafts, speakers, slide/tape programs, and tours at the museum.

The society has 2 full-time and 4 part-time staff members who are assisted by 115 volunteers. The museum is open 1:00–4:00 Tuesday through Saturday, and morning tours are arranged by appointment. Support comes from memberships, grants, fund-raising, and donations. Last year a Child's World had approximately 11,000 visitors.

Michael P. O'Lear, "Not for Children Only," *Regional Conference of Historical Agencies* 12, no. 7 (July 1982): 2.

New York

THE AMERICAN MUSEUM OF NATURAL HISTORY, Central Park West at 79th Street, New York, NY 10024. The Peter Van Gerbig Natural Science Center for Young People, which opened in 1954 and lasted for several years, evolved into the Alexander M. White Natural Science Center. The current center, opened on 8 May 1974, is supported by an endowment and named after the museum's 6th president. It represents a physical expansion and a new focus on urban ecology, but the essentially hands-on character has been a constant since 1954. The 80-by-20-foot space is divided into various exhibit and teaching alcoves, all of which focus on the urban environment. There are a variety of natural, easily replaceable local plants, live animals, building materials, a cross section of a street showing what is under the sidewalk, and many participatory exhibits. Programs for grades 1 through 9 are held in the mornings on school days, and each group averages 30 in number. Pre-visit and post-visit materials are provided to teachers bringing their classes to the center. The general visitor may come in the afternoon and on the weekends although the target audience is ages 8–12. A museum instructor does the morning programs, and in the afternoons 1 or 2 volunteers assist in the room. The attendance averages 45,000 visitors per year including school classes. The very first children's room at the museum opened in 1909.

A Discovery Room, opened in 1977, was developed to provide hands-on, multisensory learning experiences in an informal setting for the visually handicapped and the general public. A foundation grant subsidized the renovation of a space adjacent to the Hall of Ocean Life, which was formerly used for meetings and storage. The 25-by-25-foot room has carpeted seating platforms and a ramp for wheelchair access. The collections used in the Discovery Room and for the boxes came from the Department of Education Collection, the various scientific departments, and an occasional purchase. The 24 boxes contain a variety of touchable, colorful materials organized around such themes as sand, wings, Eskimos, and weaving. They were developed to have minimal labeling and require maximum utilization of the senses; all have braille labels, and some are also in large type. The anthropology materials were chosen for their ability to communicate cultural change and some may be tried on. The Discovery Room is under the supervision of 1 museum instructor who is assisted by 3 volunteers per day who act as facilitators. Tuesday through Friday the room is reserved for groups of the disabled, children 2nd grade or above, or adults. Two classes per day with no more than 15 per group are scheduled. The weekends are for children 6 through 12 accompanied by adults. The ticket system limits attendance to 150 persons per day. Because the room was designed for casual family visits, sessions are limited to a half hour.

Malcolm Arth and Linda Claremon, "The Discovery Room," *Curator* 20, no. 3 (September 1977): 169–80; "Exploring the Winter World," *New York Times Magazine*, 19 December 1954, p. 26; Lois J. Hussey, "A Natural Science Center for Young People," *Curator* 4, no. 1 (1961): 29–38; Thomas D. Nicholson, "Volunteer Employment at the American Museum of Natural History," *Curator* 26, no. 3 (September 1983): 250; Catherine Pessino, "City Ecology for City Children," *Curator* 18, no. 1 (March 1975): 47–54; Bonnie Pitman-Gelles, *Museums, Magic & Children: Youth Education in Museums* (Washington, D.C.: Association of Science-Technology Centers, 1981), pp. 36–37.

THE CHILDREN'S MUSEUM OF MANHATTAN, 314 West 54 Street, New York, NY 10019. The idea for a neighborhood educational and arts center was conceived in 1972 by Bette Korman, and in May 1973 G.A.M.E. (Growth through Art and Museum Experience) opened in 2 basement storefronts. Initially it served a limited number of schools, acting as a cultural resource center which united school and museum programs. As G.A.M.E. caught on and more space was needed, the organization moved into a renovated 19th-century courthouse rented from the city. It opened in its new 3-story location, each floor about 150 by 60 feet, on 10 October 1979. At this time it changed its name to the Manhattan Laboratory Museum and expanded its program to serve the entire metropolitan area. Every 6 months the museum features a new participatory exhibit which relates to culture, art, and science. The permanent collection has a nature area with live animals and a miniature Central Park pond, costumes to try on, and a computer terminal. The 3 categories of programs offered by the museum include one for teachers and their classes, public programs after school and on the weekend for parents/children, and outreach programs in city schools. There are also performances, films, artists-in-residence programs, and intergenerational activities for teenagers and senior citizens. Since 1979 the museum has had a summer day camp consisting of 1-week sessions, each with a different theme, for children 5–12. A small staff is assisted by interns, college students, and volunteers, numbering in all approximately 55. Class visits, which must be reserved in advance, are Tuesday through Friday 10:00–2:00. The museum is open to the general public on Wednesday, Thursday, Friday, and Sunday 1:00–5:00 and on Saturday 1:00–5:00. There is an admission fee, and group rates vary depending upon the number of children and the program selected. The museum receives both public support and private funding and generates 25 percent of its income. Last year over 25,000 children and adults visited the museum. A new name, Children's Museum of Manhattan, was announced by the mayor in May 1985, and a search is on for larger quarters.

Educational Facilities Laboratories, *The Arts in Found Places* (New York: Educational Facilities Laboratories, 1976), pp. 17–19: ERIC Document Reproduction Service, ED 125 077; "A New Museum for Children," *New York Times*, 14 October 1979, p. 68; "A New Name for Museum and Fun Too," *New York Times*, 5 May 1985, sec. 1, p. 18; Barbara Y. Newsom and Adele Z. Silver, eds., *The Art Museum as Educator* (Berkeley: University of California Press, 1978), pp. 223, 298–99, 335, 336, 362, 373–78, 465, 680, 698–99; Bonnie Pitman-Gelles, *Museums, Magic & Children: Youth Education in Museums* (Washington, D.C.: Association of Science-Technology Centers, 1981), pp. 85, 123, 224.

Rochester

INTERNATIONAL MUSEUM OF PHOTOGRAPHY AT GEORGE EAST-MAN HOUSE, 900 East Avenue, Rochester, NY 14607. The Discovery Room, opened on 14 October 1983, encourages both children and adults to actively explore basic concepts related to photography and filmmaking. The room is a conscious effort by the museum to make its collections more accessible and understandable to the general public. In this 700-square-foot facility the exhibits, activities, and demonstrations provide visitors firsthand experiences with the history, technology, and art of photography. A camera obscura, where visitors can draw their own image; moving zoetropes and flipbooks; early cameras; treasure chests filled with various types of photographic images; and the opportunity to make a photogram/sunprint or watch a demonstration of how a photograph is developed are but a few of the experiences provided. The exhibits and activities change regularly to provide new insights and encourage return visits. The Discovery Room is located between the 2 main exhibition areas and can also serve as an introduction to these galleries. The director of education is responsible for the room and is assisted by 1 part-time person and a corps of 36 specially trained volunteers. There is an admission charge for the museum but no additional charge to visit the Discovery Room. During the school year, hours are Tuesday through Friday 10:00–4:00 by prior reservation, for groups only. There is no charge for Monroe County school classes. Weekend hours for the general public are 12:00–4:00. In July and August it is open to anyone Tuesday to Sunday 10:00–3:00. The museum is always closed on Mondays. The initial funds for the Discovery Room came from the Junior League, Wegman Foundation, Citibank, Ford Motor Company, the New York State Council on the Arts, and the National Endowment for the Arts. During the last year approximately 3,000 people visited the Discovery Room.

"Discovery at the Museum," *Democrat and Chronicle*, 7 October 1983, pp. 1C, 2C; Christopher Greenman, "Room for Discovery," *The Museologist* 46, no. 167 (Spring 1984): 11; "Now, a Place Where Children May 'Discover' Photography, Eastman House Collections . . . ," *Brighton-Pittsford Post*, 12 October 1983, p. 3B; "Rave Reviews from the Kids for 'Discovery Room,' " *Times-Union*, 18 October 1983, p. 3C; Kathleen

Wolkowicz, "The Discovery Room Project: 1982" (Rochester: George Eastman House, November 1982) (Typewritten).

Scotia

SCOTIA-GLENVILLE CHILDREN'S MUSEUM, PO Box 2178, Scotia, NY 12302. Founded by parents in January 1979, when field trips by schools were decreasing, the museum operates as a traveling facility. Since its inception, it has taken exhibits to schools, libraries, community centers, retirement homes, and other museums in a 6-county area. Currently, 16 programs in the areas of science, history, and creative arts are offered. Programs must be scheduled 2 weeks in advance, and when the date is confirmed, resource materials related to the exhibit are sent. Each presentation includes objects that can be touched, and audience participation is encouraged. Although programs are designed to accommodate 25 to 30 children, their flexible format allows them to be tailored to the special needs of the group. "Life on the Erie Canal" is a program aimed at 4th-grade children and can include a follow-up visit to the Schenectady County Historical Society. Three special puppet presentations are available for pre-schoolers. Other programs are recommended for age groups from preschool through junior high including "From Pulp to Paper," "The Ins and Outs of Weaving," "Mirror Math," "Weather or Not," and "Can You Build a Bird Nest?" In addition, field trips are scheduled, family workshops and Saturday morning classes are offered, and there is a special April event, "Something to Do Day," with exhibits and demonstrations. Both the director and program coordinator are paid and work part-time; 15 exhibit teachers present the traveling programs and are paid on a per-presentation basis, and there are about 50 volunteers. About 60 percent of the museum's support comes from exhibit income, 14 percent from memberships, and the rest from the April event and other sources. Last year the traveling museum reached about 9,000 people, mostly children.

"S-G District's Children's Museum Expands Tour for Other Districts," *Schenectady Gazette*, 24 January 1985; *Scotia-Glenville Children's Museum 1985–86: Traveling Exhibit Presentations* (Scotia: Scotia-Glenville Children's Museum, [1985]); Scotia-Glenville Children's Museum, "A Traveling Adventure," Scotia, NY, 1985 (Typewritten); " 'Something to Do' Thursday," *Schenectady Gazette*, 19 April 1985.

Seneca

SENECA FALLS HISTORICAL SOCIETY, 55 Cayuga Street, Seneca Falls, NY 13148. The Children's Suite is comprised of 3 rooms of the 23 in an 1880 Queen Anne mansion. After the Society moved into the home in 1961, volunteers began to design the rooms, which include a playroom with a stage, a Victorian nursery, and another small room which displays Schoenhut and Humpty-Dumpty circus toys. The collection is strongest in Victorian children's clothing, books, games, and toys. Programming for children includes work with the 4th-grade history curriculum, junior and senior high school clubs, scouts, and church youth groups. There are also tours, loan kits, speakers, and workshops. The Society has a full-time executive director, 3 part-time staff members, and 60 volunteers. Hours are Monday through Friday 9:00–5:00 for tours and other times by special request. Museum attendance is approximately 3,500 visitors per year. Financial support comes from federal and state grants, endowments, memberships, and donations.

Staten Island

STATEN ISLAND CHILDREN'S MUSEUM, Snug Harbor Cultural Center, 940 Richmond Terrace, Staten Island, NY 10301. Founded in 1974 by a group of interested citizens, the museum opened in 1976 in a storefront facility. The exhibits are participatory learning experiences designed for metro-area children 5–12 but attract all age groups from toddlers to seniors. Each year a new thematic exhibit creating a total environment is installed in the museum's main gallery. Previous shows have included communication, light, adaptations to winter, transformations of spring, EVERYBODY (an exploration of the human body), HO-CUS-FOCUS (art and visual perception), ONCE UPON AN ISLAND (4 centuries of Staten Island history), and an exhibition of sound and music SOUND-TRACKS. In 1983–84 ONCE UPON AN ISLAND was moved to a shopping mall where it reached a new audience. The museum provides outreach services, tours for classes, programs for those with special needs, and orientation sessions for teachers. In addition, there are classes, workshops, parent/child activities, concerts, and special events. The original Stapleton location was closed at the end of July 1985 and the museum reopened in January 1986 in a renovated 20,000-square-foot, 4-story, 1913 building at the Snug Harbor Cultural Center. A thematic exhibition about architecture and the built environment, BUILDING BUILDINGS, is the first installation in the 4,000-square-foot main gallery. Two other galleries, enlarged workshop space, a fully equipped theater, and a museum shop occupy the other 3 floors. One gallery will open with BIG TOP PUPPETS. There are a professional staff of 17, a volunteer staff of 30, and 15 interpreter/exhibition guides. The museum is open Tuesday through Friday 12:00–5:00, weekends 10:00–5:00, and the Mondays that are school holidays. There is a suggested contribution. About 40 percent of the museum's support comes from the New York City Department of Cultural Affairs, with other funding coming from the New York Council on the Arts and Department of Education, the Natural Heritage Trust Program, and various other corporations, foundations, and individual sources.

"Architectural Tinkering for Tots," *Metropolis: The Architecture & Design Magazine of New York* 5, no. 2 (September 1985): 10; "Children's Museum: It's More Than Fun," *Staten Island Advance*, 18 November 1983, sec. D, p. 1; Commission on Museums for a New Century, *Museums for a New Century* (Washington, D.C.: American Association of Museums, 1984), p. 112; "Kids Museum in Motion," *Daily News*, 7 June 1985; Bonnie Pitman-Gelles, *Museums, Magic & Children: Youth Education in Museums* (Washington, D.C.: Association of Science-Technology Centers, 1981), pp. 119, 208–09, 223–24; Lee Skolnick, "Once upon an Island: A Fantasy Exhibit at the Staten Island Children's Museum," *Interior Design* 53, no. 6 (June 1982): 222–25.

Syracuse

BURNET PARK ZOO, Syracuse, NY, PO Box 146, Liverpool, NY 13088. The Children's Zoo, first established in the mid–1950s, housed domestic animals and had a contact yard. Later enclosures for birds, a monkey island, and an aquarium were added. In 1979 the management of the zoo was assumed by Onondaga County, and in 1981 the County Legislature approved a master plan to construct a new, year-round facility on the 36-acre site. The ground-breaking ceremony was held on 21 December 1983, and the zoo, stressing North American wildlife, opened on 2 August 1986. The new zoo, designed as an educational institution, will have over 1,000 specimens in 3 major thematic areas: Evolution of Life on Earth, Animals of the Wild North, and a 2-part Animals and People Complex, which includes an international barnyard and an area devoted to animal care (kitchen, clinic, and surgery). The barnyard will include llamas, dairy cattle, sheep, goats, pigs, ponies, oxen, and elephants. This area is expected to have a special appeal to children with its mixture of demonstrations and contact experiences. In addition to daily management of their specimens, the 2 senior keepers and 6 keepers who have been assigned to the Animals and People complex will be heavily involved in the zoo's education program. They will be assisted by volunteers. Junior volunteers and an urban 4-H program will operate out of the Animals and People barn, caring for the livestock and presenting demonstrations. The zoo will be open daily, except Christmas and New Year's, from 10:00 to 4:30. Children under 5 and Onondaga County educational groups are admitted free. The zoo's operating support comes from the county and its capital expenses from county, state, federal, and private sources.

James F. Aiello, "Education as a Major Component in Planning a New Zoo," *AAZPA Regional Conference Proceedings 1984*, pp. 459–62; James Aiello, ed., *Little Tracks* (Winter 1984); Deborah A. Besch, ed., "Animaline: Burnet Park Zoo," *Animal Kingdom* 87, no. 2 (April/May 1984): 2; Rosl Kirchshofer, ed., *The World of Zoos: A Survey and Gazetteer* (New York: Viking, 1968), p. 257; *A New Breed of Zoo* (Syracuse: Friends of the Burnet Park Zoo Fund, n.d.).

THE DISCOVERY CENTER, 321 South Clinton, Syracuse, NY 13202. Opened to the public on 15 November 1981, the museum was developed by a coalition of 3 local groups, the Junior League, the National Council of Jewish Women, and the Technology Club. Currently there are 2,800 square feet of hands-on, participatory exhibits ranging from the life sciences to computers, with little emphasis on materials of artifactual value. The science arcade has 45 freestanding units, a large thematic exhibit on the respiratory system, and a planetarium which opened on 26 June 1982. A small Discovery Corner for very young children includes a small video theater and a changing selection of activity boxes on topics such as color, light, touch, magnets, and fossils. Each kit, designed for a child working with an adult, includes materials and suggestions for use. A special planetarium show, given the first Saturday of the month, was developed especially for children 2–6. The museum sponsors science fairs and lectures, holds workshops, provides loan kits, and conducts field trips. There is a small meeting room and a lecture hall which seats 70. Five full-time and 2 part-time staff members are assisted by about 125 volunteers. There are also teenage Explainers and summer interns. The Discovery Center is open Tuesday through Saturday 10:00–5:00 and Sunday 12:00–5:00. There is a small admission charge. Support comes 33 percent from earned income, 46 percent from corporate and individual contributions, and 21 percent from county, state, and federal sources. Half of the 53,000 annual visitors are children. Eleven percent of those who come to the museum travel a distance of more than 75 miles one way, and 90 percent of those visitors come to Syracuse specifically to visit the Discovery Center. Because of the increasing attendance the Discovery Center is currently looking for a larger facility.

"Discovery Center Finally Opens Today," *Syracuse Herald-American*, 15 November 1981, p. C–9; "Hands-On Experience for Teen Volunteers," *Syracuse Herald-American*, 10 October 1981; "Interim Site Sought for Science Center," *Syracuse Herald Journal*, 19 February 1981, p. D–5; "Science Center Opens in Syracuse," *ASTC Newsletter* 10, no. 1 (January/February 1982); "Universe Almost Ready for Visitors," *Syracuse Post Standard*, 18 June 1982, pp. C–1, C–2.

Troy

RENSSELAER COUNTY JUNIOR MUSEUM, 282 Fifth Avenue, Troy, NY 12182. The museum was founded in 1954 by the Junior League to provide a center for Troy-area children which emphasized art, history, and science. Until 1960 it was housed in the basement of the Rensselaer County Historical Society, and when more space was needed, it relocated in a Victorian house situated on a large lot. Volunteers did most of the renovation and landscaping, planned the galleries, and built the exhibits, a greenhouse, and a planetarium. The new facility allowed for increased programming and required a full-time staff. Besides school groups during the day and after-school and weekend activities at the museum, outreach programs were initiated to send kits and docents to schools. By the early 1970s another expansion was necessary, and in 1975 the museum renovated and moved into the historic J. J. Child Steamer House, a 1904 brick firehouse. The Family Gallery has hands-on science and natural science exhibits, including live snakes, reptiles, bees, an aquarium, dioramas, and a planetarium.

The Main Gallery has changing art, history, and science exhibits. There has been a steady increase in the variety of programs to schools and other groups, mobile exhibits, weekend and holiday activities for the general public, and most recently concerts, festivals, and bus trips. Three full-time and 2 permanent part-time staff members are assisted by 6 to 8 part-time guides and teachers, 2 senior aides, and 3 to 5 high school–age guides. Hours for the general public are Saturday through Wednesday 1:00–5:00, and for groups, any day by appointment. Support comes from the County Department for Youth, the city, United Way, the New York Council for the Arts, and the Natural Heritage Trust. The primary audience is children 4–12 and their families. The museum has approximately 26,000 visitors a year.

Mary Cuffe, "The Magnificent Illusion," *The Conservationist* 40, no. 4 (January/February 1986): 46–49; Educational Facilities Laboratories, *Hands- On Museums: Partners in Learning* (New York: Educational Facilities Laboratories, 1975), pp. 32–33: ERIC Document Reproduction Service, ED 113 832; Sherwood Davidson Kohn, "It's OK to Touch at the New-Style Hands- On Exhibits," *Smithsonian* 9, no. 6 (September 1978): 83; Sally M. Meneely, "The Garden Indoors: Living Dioramas," *Museum News* 41, no. 9 (May 1963): 17–20; Barbara Y. Newsom and Adele Z. Silver, eds., *The Art Museum as Educator* (Berkeley: University of California Press, 1978), p. 742.

Utica

CHILDREN'S MUSEUM, 311 Main Street, Utica, NY 13501. The museum was founded in 1963 by the Junior League as a Discovery Room at the Utica Public Library. It outgrew 3 sites before moving in 1980 to its present 5-story, newly renovated brick building that once was the home of Heiber Dry Goods Company. The museum currently is using 12,000 square feet of space and has another 18,000 square feet available for future development. Since its inception, the museum has been a participatory experience for children. The collections of the museum, strongest in the areas of local history and natural science, are used to support its programs. Exhibits include a life-size model of an Iroquois long-house, a giant bubble machine, a shadow box, and a "please touch" natural history corner. Educational programs are offered on a contract basis to school and youth groups in a 3-county area. There is a full-time staff of 5. The museum is open during the school year 1:00–5:00 Wednesday through Sunday, and during the summer 10:00–5:00 Tuesday through Friday and 1:00–5:00 weekends. Group programs are available by appointment. Financial support comes from the municipal, county, and state governments, memberships, and private and corporate donations. The museum has approximately 30,000 visitors a year.

Michael P. O'Lear, "Not for Children Only," *Regional Conference of Historical Agencies* 12, no. 7 (July 1982): 2–3.

NORTH CAROLINA

Asheville

THE HEALTH ADVENTURE, 501 Biltmore Avenue, Asheville, NC 28801. The Children's Health Museum was founded by the Buncombe County Medical Auxiliary in 1966 to provide health education for area youth. The first facility was located in the Medical Records Library on the grounds of Memorial Mission Hospital and volunteers gave tours. In 1974 the museum changed its name to the Asheville Health Education Museum and moved to a log cabin on the hospital grounds. After 6,000 feet of space was donated in 1978 by the Mountain Area Health Education Center, the Health Adventure again relocated and developed a more comprehensive program. The present facility includes a carpeted auditorium, individual teaching areas, and an observation booth. A transparent anatomical mannequin located in the theater is used as an introduction to all body systems and their functions. Visitors no longer tour the whole facility but select 1 or 2 programs in different learning areas. There are 30-minute sessions on 14 different topics from the brain, circulation, and senses to sports health and nutrition and 90-minute programs entitled "Life Patterns," "Substance Abuse," and "Peer Pressure." Some of these are adaptable for a variety of ages, while others are for a particular age group. There are also special topics, evening sessions for adults, and a series for senior citizens. At the present time all programs are given on-site by 3 professional health educators, assisted by trained volunteers, who use interactive hands-on techniques. While all ages participate in Health Adventure programs, the emphasis has been on children. In addition to school groups, there are scouts, preschoolers, church groups, and clubs. Museum hours are 8:30–5:00 Monday through Friday, and programs must be scheduled in advance. A 1-hour guided tour weekdays at 3:00, for which reservations are needed, gives visitors an overview of the Health Adventure and its lessons. There are a staff of 7 and a corps of over 100 volunteers. A small admission fee is charged, and support for the health museum comes half from public and half from private sources. The majority of the 25,000 yearly visitors come from Buncombe County and western North Carolina.

" 'Get Physical' Show at Health Adventure Can Give You a Test," *Asheville Citizen*, 17 June 1985, p. 3; "Here's to Your Health," *Southern Living* 20, no. 8 (August 1985): 30.

Charlotte

SCIENCE MUSEUMS OF CHARLOTTE, 301 North Tryon Street, Charlotte, NC 28202. Founded in 1947 with the support of the Junior League, the museum opened as the Charlotte Children's Nature Museum in a frame house belonging to the Charlotte Parks and Recreation Commission. An initial supporter and its first director, Laura Owens developed hands-on exhibits, discussion groups, and field trips. In 1951 the museum moved to a 31-acre wooded site donated by the Lions Club; the Junior League helped raise the money necessary for the 7,000-square-foot building; and the Parks and Recreation Commission provided half of the yearly operating expenses. Helmut Naumer, named director in 1960, was succeeded by Russell Peithman in February 1963. In 1966 the museum dropped the word "Children" from its name in order to appeal to a wider segment of the community, especially teenage youth, and provide students research opportunities. The museum expanded to include a planetarium and a health science wing; an environmental science van began to take programs out to disadvantaged children in 1969; and at the time of Charlotte's bicentennial in 1971, the museum opened an exhibit center which encompassed 200 years of local history. A close relationship developed with area schools; coordinators were assigned to the museum and its resources became an integral part of the earth science and health education curriculums.

To fulfill its goal of becoming a museum that would appeal to youth and serve the entire community, not just younger children, the museum proposed a downtown science and technology center. After almost 2 decades of planning, a bond referendum was approved by voters in 1977 and ground broken for the new facility in February 1978. Discovery Place opened 31 October 1981 in a 2-level, 80,000-square-foot facility at 301 North Tryon Street. It includes a LIFE CENTER (the functions of the human body, physics and chemistry areas); SCIENCE CIRCUS (hands-on exhibits); COLLECTIONS GALLERY (open storage display); science theater; rain forest habitat with plants, birds, and animals; an aquarium with wave tank, marine environments, and touch tank; and a trading post to identify and swap specimens. In 1985 it became a member of the Science Museum Exhibit Collaborative.

Discovery Place and the Nature Museum are now the Science Museums of Charlotte. The Nature Museum has exhibits, a live animal room, saltwater touch tank, planetarium, and nature trails. Local schools use a 4-acre trail to teach children about the Piedmont forest, and there are an additional 25 acres of undeveloped trails available to visitors. In the summer a Sciencelab travels to neighborhood centers, reaching about 3,000 children. A staff of 22, assisted by 90 volunteers, provides programs and services for 150,000 visitors annually. The Nature Museum is open Monday through Saturday 9:00–5:00 September through May, 9:00–6:00 June through August, 9:00–6:00 Saturday, and 1:00–6:00 Sunday. Discovery Place, a hands-on science and technology museum, also offers workshops, programs, and trips. It has a staff of 66 and 310 volunteers, who give over 20,000 hours each year. Hours are 9:00–5:00 weekdays September through May, 9:00–6:00 June through August, 9:00–6:00 Saturday, and 1:00–6:00 Sunday. Discovery Place cooperates with local schools, and museum staff members teach over 95,000 schoolchildren each year. There are 400,000 visitors annually. Support comes from admissions, fees, contributions, grants, and governmental support.

Educational Facilities Laboratories, *Hands-On Museums: Partners in Learning* (New York: Educational Facilities Laboratories, 1975), pp. 28–29: ERIC Document Reproduction Service, ED 113 832; Russell I. Peithman, "Live Animals in Museums," *Curator* 18, no. 2 (June 1975): 109–14; Russell Peithman, "The Place of a Children's Nature Museum in the Community," *Museum News* 45, no. 4 (December 1966): 33–34; Bonnie Pitman-Gelles, *Museums, Magic & Children: Youth Education in Museums* (Washington, D.C.: Association of Science-Technology Centers, 1981), pp. 9, 82, 134, 146; Alice Steinbach and Mark D. Selph, "Bond Issue Politics," *Museum News* 57, no. 5 (May/June 1979): 37, 40–42; Diane Young, "Look, Touch, and Learn at Discovery Place," *Southern Living* 17, no. 9 (September 1982): 131–33.

Raleigh

NORTH CAROLINA MUSEUM OF HISTORY, 109 East Jones Street, Raleigh, NC 27611. The Discovery Room was initially a component of the RALEIGH AND ROANOKE exhibit, which was installed at the museum from 8 March to 6 June 1985. When the exhibit closed, the Discovery Room remained over the summer, and in September 1985 portions of the room were reinstalled at a branch facility in Elizabeth City. The 650-square-foot hands-on area was designed to make both children and adults comfortable within the museum setting. Initially located adjacent to the exhibit's introductory section, the Discovery Room was another way to orient visitors and involve them in an active learning situation. A voyage from England started with mirror images where visitors saw themselves dressed as middle-class subjects, had an opportunity to try on armor, and examine reproductions of cumbersome 16th-century weapons. The travelers then moved aboard ship to hoist sails, use navigational instruments such as a cross-staff and knotline, identify parts of a cutaway sailing vessel, and play a navigational game. Arriving in the New World, they were introduced to Indian culture, learned a few Indian words, and made stone tools. The final discovery activity had visitors determine the fate of the 117 members of the Lost Colony. At the time of the RALEIGH AND ROANOKE exhibition there were films, special programs, family workshops, live presentations, and lectures. In addition, the museum had special evening hours on Monday, Tuesday, and Thursday. There was no admission charge, and during its 3-month stay the exhibition attracted 100,000 visitors.

Peggy Howe, "Cross the Atlantic in Half an Hour in the 'Discovery Room,' " *News* (Raleigh: North Carolina Department of Cultural Resources Press Release, 8 March 1985); "Major Exhibition Opens at History Museum," *Carolina Comments* 33, no. 2 (March 1985): 37–39; "Raleigh and Roanoke," *History News* 40, no. 3 (March 1985): 22; "Raleigh & Roanoke Exhibit Sent by British Library," *Library Journal* 110, no. 7 (15 April 1985): 11.

Winston-Salem

NATURE SCIENCE CENTER, Museum Drive, Winston-Salem, NC 27105. The Discovery Room opened in 1982 following a fund-raising campaign for the center. The 3,000-square-foot room is designed to explore physics with hands-on exhibits. There is a bicycle to generate electricity, parabolic dishes, optical illusions, shadow room, large kaleidoscope, Bernolli blower, and other exhibits that deal with eye-hand coordination and sound. Sea life in the 1,000-gallon tidal pool and the barnyard animals at the center may be touched. There are 31 acres of nature trails in addition to the 28,000-square-foot exhibit hall, 150-seat science theater, and planetarium. Lectures and workshops are held at the center, and outreach is delivered by Environvan's exhibits and programs and by Starlab, a portable, inflatable planetarium. Initially established in 1964 as a Junior League project in cooperation with the city, the center is now supported largely by city and county funds. There is no admission charge. Fifteen full-time and 3 part-time staff members are supported by many volunteers. The Nature Science Center is open Monday through Saturday 10:00–5:00 and Sunday 1:00–5:00. Separate attendance figures are not kept for the Discovery Room, but the center attracts approximately 86,000 visitors per year.

Bill Baughman, ed., "Our Museum World: Nature Science Center," *Explorer* 24, no. 4 (Winter 1982): 21; 25, no. 3 (Fall 1983): 18; Victor J. Danilov, *Science and Technology Centers* (Cambridge: MIT Press, 1982), pp. 47, 266.

OHIO

Akron

AKRON ZOOLOGICAL PARK, 500 Edgewood Avenue, Akron, OH 44307. When the zoo was established in 1952 as the Akron's Children's Zoo, it had a Mother Goose theme. Following growth in both audience and collections, the zoo developed a master plan in 1968 stating that it would specialize in animals of North and South America, the setting for the exhibits would be a major consideration, and education an important function, of the zoo. The 1-acre Ohio Farmyard, opened in 1975, was developed to provide a contact area where children could become acquainted and interact with domestic animals. A local trust donated funds for building an aviary for native American birds, and a zoomobile which travels to schools, civic centers, and churches was donated by the Teamsters Union. In 1978 the zoo's name was changed to reflect its broader audience and programming. There are 14 full-time and 18 seasonal employees and over 13,000 volunteer hours per year given by those 14 and older. The zoo is open from May through September 10:00–5:00, Monday through Saturday, and 10:00–6:00 Sunday and holidays. Because the outreach program operates throughout the year, the zoo serves 25,000 people through its education programs and has 60,000 visitors at the zoo. Support from the city of Akron covers part of the operating expenses with the zoo earning the remaining funds from memberships, admissions, concessions, and donations.

"Akron Children's Zoo," *Landscape Architecture* 66 (July 1976): 334–35; Michael J. Janis, "The Birth & Development of the Akron Zoological Park," *AAZPA Regional Conference Proceedings 1981*, pp. 133–34; Michael J. Janis, "Developing a Native Bird Aviary at the Akron Zoo," *AAZPA Regional Conference Proceedings 1979*, pp. 97–99; Roman C. Syroid, "Children's Zoo-Akron, Ohio," *Parks & Recreation* 37, no. 1 (January 1954): 18–20.

Cincinnati

CINCINNATI ART MUSEUM, Eden Park, Cincinnati, OH 45202. The Discovery Room, founded in the spring of 1980, was developed by museum staff, docents, and consultants to provide a hands-on facility for use in conjunction with children's guided tours. The 41-by-13-foot space includes an amphitheater, screen, projection booth, demonstration table, and individual activity stations. The Discovery Room does not have its own collection but draws from the works in the museum's permanent collection or commissions artists to create works specifically for its use. Stressing the creative process and elements of art, the programs involve demonstrations, slide presentations, and participatory activities which encourage individual discovery. The tour groups spend 20 minutes in the Discovery Room and 40 minutes in the galleries. Each program is developed and implemented by the Education and Docent Coordinators and a committee of 4 docents, with tours conducted by 80 trained docents. The programs change about every year and a half and have included "Discover: Painting," "Discover: Sculpture," "Discover: People," and "Discover: Color." The room, open during regular museum hours to scheduled groups, is visited by about 6,000 people a year. It is used primarily by children in the elementary and middle grades and other youth groups. The positive publicity the room has received has stimulated interest from adults and teachers in training. Occasionally on the weekends programs are offered for the public, and some have had special appeal to visitors who are blind. Initial funding came from the Junior League, the Frank E. Gannett Newspaper Foundation, the *Cincinnati Enquirer*, docents, the museum, and individual donors. Programs are supported by the museum's budget and supplemented with gifts and donations.

Katherine Guckenberger, " 'Discover: Sculpture' at the Cincinnati Art Museum," *School Arts* 84, no. 3 (November 1984): 10–11; "Museum Discovery Room a Work of Art," *Cincinnati Enquirer*, 27 April 1980; " 'Please Touch' Art Museum's Discovery Room," *Perspectives* [Junior League of Cincinnati] (June 1982): 4; " 'Please Touch' Art Program," *Arts & Activities* 91, no. 3 (April 1982): 6.

CINCINNATI ZOO, 3400 Vine Street, Cincinnati, OH 45220. The Children's Zoo opened in 1950 with a fairy garden theme and had a small admission. Over the years the area has displayed small animals and had a contact yard. It was expanded and totally rebuilt in the mid–1980s following a generous donation from Mrs. Ruth Spaulding. Opened on 1 June 1985, the 55,000-square-foot area is almost 3 times larger than the original children's zoo. Participatory, multi-sensory experiences allow the children to interact with the animals and the exhibits as they touch, compare, classify, weigh, measure, and move through, over, under, and inside the display areas. The facility was designed for a primary audience of 8–10 year olds. The Children's Zoo, with over 30 exhibits, is divided into an entry with penguins and flamingos, the zoo nursery, a contact area with domestic animals, a southwestern U.S. desert area, and an eastern U.S. wood-lands area. In addition, there is a special exhibit/classroom building for pre-schoolers and a Zoolab where children can study animals in more depth. Special features include an underground tunnel in the desert area where children can see eye to eye with prairie dogs and tortoises while adults view the habitat from an overhead walkway. In the woodland habitat, children can try to determine what a raccoon would eat by feeling hidden replicas of the raccoon's prey. Fossils can be dug from a cliff, and visitors can take a fossil home with them. Zoolab is an interpretive center filled with animal artifacts, games, stereoscopes, and magnifying lenses to promote discovery learning. The Kid's Center was designed to meet a need for preschool programs in the community. Here children can experience what it would be like to live in a tree. As they crawl through the tree, they pass flying squirrels living in a den, can try out a nest (bean bag), reach birds in an aviary at the top, and then exit down a 10-foot slide. Life-size footprints allow children to compare their feet to those of animals. Puppets, masks, and animal costumes add to the fantasy. In the summer, programs take place throughout the Children's Zoo. Puppet shows, animal demonstrations, animal contact, and talks are given daily in the amphitheatre and small alcoves located in several areas. The Children's Zoo has 3 full-time and 12 part-time employees and 200 volunteers. One hundred thirty of the volunteers are high school students who assist directly with animal care and programs. Since 1975 a 2-year Animal Care and Conservation program has been offered for high school juniors and seniors. Located at the zoo it is administered by a city vocational school. In addition, 24 children between 9 and 12 years old act as Ambassadors for 1 or 2 exhibits. The Children's Zoo is open 10:00–6:00 Memorial Day through Labor Day and 10:00–4:00 during the winter. An admission charge supports the Children's Zoo, which has about 1 million visitors annually.

Deborah A. Besch, comp., "Animaline: Cincinnati Zoo," *Animal Kingdom* 88, no. 5 (September/October 1985): 2; "Children's Zoo Full of Fun," *Morning News-Sun*, 15 June 1985; Cincinnati Zoo, *Joe H. Spaulding Children's Zoo*, Dedication, 1 June 1985; "Noah Never Had an Ark Like This," *News* [Dayton, OH], 24 June 1985; Bonnie Pitman-Gelles, *Museums, Magic & Children: Youth Education in Museums* (Washington, D.C.: Association of Science-Technology Centers, 1981), p. 174; Janet Ross, "Joe H. Spaulding Children's Zoo Plans Unveiled," *Zooviews* 3, no. 11 (January/February 1983):

1–2; "Vast New Improvements at Cincinnati Zoo," *Parks & Recreation* 33, no. 8 (August 1950): 283–84.

Cleveland

CLEVELAND CHILDREN'S MUSEUM, 10730 Euclid Avenue, Cleveland, OH 44106. Founded in 1982 following several years of interest, the museum opened in June 1986 in a 7,500-square-foot, remodeled Howard Johnson's restaurant. Half of its space is devoted to 3 exhibit areas of 1,800, 1,000, and 900 square feet. Before the museum moved into its permanent site, a director and staff were hired, and a traveling exhibit, BUILDING A HOUSE, toured the community. The target audience is children 3–12 and an area for younger children is being planned. Multidisciplinary in scope, the installations and programs will encompass the arts, humanities, science, and technology. The Children's Museum is based upon exhibit clusters utilizing dramatic environments that include hands-on manipulation, role-playing, social interaction, creative activities, and visual and aural experiences. The first installations include LITTLE HOUSE UNDER CONSTRUCTION, an expansion of its traveling exhibit BRIDGES, and OUT OF THE ORDINARY. Children will be involved in the design of the exhibit clusters through their participation in evaluation studies. School classes will be able to reserve an exhibit cluster for a 90-minute program, and pre- and post-visit materials will be provided for teachers and their classes. There are 7 full-time and several part-time staff members and a volunteer corps of more than 100. The museum is open 7 days a week. Hours are Monday through Saturday 10:00–5:00, Sunday and holidays 1:00–5:00, and closed on 3 major holidays. Admission is charged, but there are free hours on Tuesday and Thursday from 3:00 to 5:00. The Board of Trustees provides 13 percent of the museum's support, individuals 20 percent, foundations 43 percent, organizations 6 percent, and corporations 18 percent. Attendance during the first year has been projected to be 100,000.

"Bridges Will Be Theme of Children's Museum," *Cleveland Plain Dealer*, 26 May 1984, sec. D, p. 1; "Children Free to Touch in Their Museum," *Cleveland Plain Dealer*, 18 October 1982, sec. B, p. 1; Uriel Cohen and Ruth M. McMurtry, *Museums and Children: A Design Guide* (Milwaukee: Center for Architecture and Urban Planning Research, University of Wisconsin, 1985), pp. 15, 43; "Curator's Job Is Child's Play: A Museum for the Young," *Cleveland Plain Dealer*, 7 July 1985, sec. P, pp. 23, 29; "A Show of Hands at New Museum," *Cleveland Plain Dealer*, 1 June 1986, sec. P, pp. 31, 34.

CLEVELAND HEALTH EDUCATION MUSEUM, 8911 Euclid Avenue, Cleveland, OH 44106. The Children's Health Fair, opened in 1972, was designed specifically for children 3–8 years old. The 20-by-40-foot area is entered through child-sized portholes giving them sole access to the exhibits, which take advantage of many of the techniques utilized elsewhere in the museum. The Health

Fair has a transparent woman who delivers a program on body systems, a slide/ tape program, "The Poison Jungle," testing stations related to vision and nutrition, a giant 10-foot head, and a small puppet theater. In addition, animals teach children about the 5 senses, and there is a panorama that is changed periodically. Recognizing the value of family interaction, the Children's Health Fair is being replaced by the Family Discovery Center in late 1986. It will contain a variety of hands-on activities that children and adults can do together. More information will be presented about the body, including the need for exercise and fitness, and visitors will be able to listen to a heart and to test vision and hearing. There will be skeletons, an operating room with a plastic, take-apart body, mystery boxes, microscopes, computers, and a resource library. Since it opened to the public in 1940, the Cleveland Health Education Museum has been a pioneer in its use of anatomical models and audiovisual media including family-oriented TV programs and series for children. There is a small admission, but most of the museum's support comes from private, not tax, funds. Sources include memberships, grants, private contributions, and corporate support. The museum is open Monday through Friday 9:00–4:30 and weekends 12:00–6:00. No separate attendance figures are kept for the Children's Health Fair.

"Cleveland Health Museum, Cleveland (Ohio): Museum Education via Television," *Museum* [UNESCO] 8, no. 1 (1955): 69, and "Cleveland Health Museum, Cleveland (Ohio): Enseignement Télévisé du Musée d'Hygiène," ibid., pp. 69–70; Bruno Gebhard, "Health Museums in the United States: Review and Outlook," *Curator* 8, no. 2 (1965): 144–66; Paul Hoffman, ed., *American Museum Guides—Science* (New York: Macmillan, 1983), p. 149; Bonnie Pitman-Gelles, *Museums, Magic & Children: Youth Education in Museums* (Washington, D.C.: Association of Science-Technology Centers, 1981), pp. 42, 85, 154, 230.

Columbus

CENTER OF SCIENCE AND INDUSTRY (COSI), 280 E. Broad Street, Columbus, OH 43215. Kidspace, opened on 11 September 1984, is a 5,000-square-foot exhibit area designed specifically for children under 48 inches tall and their families. Developed over a 3-year period by a volunteer committee of early childhood experts from the community, Kidspace introduces young children to the museum environment and provides a place for parent and child to learn together. One hundred fifty people are allowed in Kidspace at any one time, and children are not permitted unattended. School groups may make a reservation to visit for an hour during regular center hours, and some space is always kept available for the public. The 5 thematic areas include SCIENCE-TECH, WATERWORKS, PERFORMING ARTS, ANIMALS, and STRUCTURES. Children have an opportunity to try things like computers, typewriters, a sound studio, video camera, makeup table, career costumes, puppets and a stage, building blocks, and animal lab with opportunities to observe and hold small animals. In October 1985 Phase II of Kidspace opened with a revised traffic flow, minor refinements to existing installations, and several additional ones including BUBBLES, KALEIDOSCOPE, CRYSTAL CLIMB, and SOUND STUDIO. In each area of the installation, free take-home sheets are available to enhance the museum experience. Four times a year Kidspace features an exhibit with additional activities related to the topic. Besides family and school groups, Brownies and other organizations are incorporating the area into their special activities at COSI. Kidspace has 2 full-time staff members Monday through Friday, 4 part-time weekend staff who alternate weekends, 2–3 adult volunteers present during the week between 9:00 and 2:00, and 4 high school student volunteers present on weekends and school vacations. Kidspace is open Monday through Saturday 10:00–5:30, Sunday 1:00–5:30, and closed major holidays. The exhibit has several corporate and foundation sponsors and also receives support from the COSI Women's Association. There is an admission charge to the center but no additional fee for Kidspace. Separate attendance figures are not kept for Kidspace, but COSI has 500,000 visitors annually.

"COSI Introduces a New Space for the 7-and-Under Set," *News Journal Sunday*, 18 November 1984, pp. 6H–7H; Victor J. Danilov, "Early Childhood Exhibits at Science Centers," *Curator* 27, no. 3 (September 1984): 183; Victor J. Danilov, "Discovery Rooms and Kidspaces: Museum Exhibits for Children," *Science and Children* 23, no. 4 (January 1986): 10; "Inquiring Minds Find Answers at COSI," *Ohio State Lantern*, 26 February 1985, p. 6; "Kidspace: A Place to Be Small," *Capital Magazine*, 17 November 1985, p. 6; "Kidspace 'Wows' Visitors," *Sights & Sounds* (October-December 1984): 1.

COLUMBUS ZOO, PO Box 400, 9990 Riverside Drive, Powell, OH 43065. The Children's Zoo, dedicated in the summer of 1972, covers over 5 acres and includes an animal nursery, barn with domesticated farm animals, several exhibits, and an amphitheater. The area attracts visitors of all ages who come to see the prairie dogs, capuchin monkeys, snow monkeys, lesser pandas, squirrel monkeys, porcupines, snow leopard, and deer. Except for the petting barn, the zoo has a no feeding policy. The endangered or threatened species found in the Children's Zoo are included in a special self-guided tour brochure, "Going, Going, Gone." The Children's Zoo is used by children 4–13 who participate in the summer day camps KinderZoo and Summer Experience. ZooKids, for 4–5 year olds, runs throughout the year in 1-week sessions and uses the Children's Zoo when it focuses on the barnyard. An education section opened at the zoo in 1973, and in 1981 a new education facility, the Exploration Center, became fully operational in what was formerly the giraffe building. Cracker Jack Paw Prints Park, an interactive area where children have the opportunity to compare themselves to animals, connects the Children's Zoo and the Exploration Center. The Children's Zoo has a staff of 8, assisted by 10 volunteers and additional zoo aides who run the petting barn. There are approximately 600,000 visitors a year. The zoo is open Memorial Day through Labor Day 10:00–6:00 and the rest of the year 10:00–5:00 daily. Admissions, memberships, grants, and concessions provide 58 percent of the zoo's support, and the remaining 42 percent comes from the city of Columbus.

Bring Out the Beast in You: Visit the Columbus Zoo—Education Programs for '85 (Columbus: Columbus Zoo, 1985); *History of the Columbus Zoo: Golden Anniversary 1927–1977* (Columbus, OH: Columbus Zoo, [1977]); Pauline Wessa, ed., *The Columbus Zoo Guidebook* (Columbus: Columbus Zoo, [1981]), pp. 5, 33, 36.

Toledo

TOLEDO ZOOLOGICAL GARDENS, 2700 Broadway Avenue, Toledo, OH 43609. The Children's Zoo opened in 1953 as a contact area with domestic and baby animals. Later a barn was added to the half-acre facility. In 1983 the original Children's Zoo was replaced with a new, year-round handicapped-accessible facility. There are 2 full-time and 11 part-time staff members who are assisted by 8 volunteers. The Toledo Zoo initiated credit classes for high school students in 1972. The technology-oriented program, open to junior and senior students, offers lab-related experiences and occupational job opportunities. These students spend some of their time working in the Children's Zoo maintaining the barn and animals and supervising the contact area. They also are involved with the outreach program.

On 8 September 1984 the 5,000-square-foot second phase of the Children's Zoo, the Diversity of Life, opened to the public in a renovated wing of the WPA-built Museum of Natural Sciences. This year-round zoo/museum was designed to illustrate the diversity of animal life, draw attention to the dangers our natural world faces, and actively involve the visitor. It contains live animals, a variety of exhibits designed for visitor participation and exploration, a 40-seat minitheater, animal nursery, graphic displays, 2 activity centers with 1 especially designed for young children, and specimens and other natural history materials to view and touch. A living stream complex provides a below-the-surface view, and stereomicroscopes with turntables are available to examine some aquatic plant and animal life. The theater is used for films, live animal demonstrations, and during school hours as a classroom. Young Exploration can accommodate about 20 youngsters at a time and provides animal masks for role-playing, a touch area with artifacts, games, and books. Adjacent to this room is an Activity Center for all ages with pull-out drawers filled with artifacts, magnifiers, and stereoscopes. Children can also make an animal footprint or an endangered species rubbing. Suitable for all ages, the zoo/museum installation is also designed to encourage parent/child learning. With reservations school and community groups can schedule live animal programs. The Diversity of Life has 2 full-time staff members, 1 exhibit technician, and 15 docents. The exhibit differs from a discovery room or zoolab because it is designed to operate unattended and be open to all visitors during regular zoo hours. Funding for the Diversity of Life came from a 1980 county capital improvement tax levy, and it is supported by zoo admissions. Hours are 10:00–6:00 in the summer and 10:00–5:00 in the winter. During the first year there were 200,000 visitors.

Michael Craden, "Educational Activities at Toledo, Ohio," *Newsletter International Association of Zoo Educators* 4 [1980]: 46–55; "The Diversity of Life," *Safari* 36, no. 4 (November 1984): 6–7; David Jenkins, "The Diversity of Life Continuing the Synergy of Zoo and Museum Design," *AAZPA Regional Conference Proceedings 1985*, pp. 338–43; David M. Jenkins, "A Survey of Interactive Technologies," *AAZPA 1985 Annual Conference Proceedings*, pp. 72, 75, 76, 77, 78, 83: ERIC Document Reproduction Service, ED 265 038; Pitman-Gelles, *Museums, Magic & Children: Youth Education in Museums* (Washington, D.C.: Association of Science-Technology Centers, 1981), p. 173; "Toledo Children's Zoo," *Parks & Recreation* 36, no. 11 (November 1953): 18.

OKLAHOMA

Fort Sill

U.S. ARMY FIELD ARTILLERY AND FORT SILL MUSEUM, Building 437, Fort Sill, OK 73503. Cricket's Corner opened in 1980 after the idea was proposed and developed by museum volunteers, mostly officers' wives. Initially known as the Children's Museum, the name was changed to Cricket's Corner in 1983, honoring a girl who lived at the fort in the late 19th century. The 25-by-50-foot facility occupies 2 rooms in the Visitor Center building. The displays consist of an Indian section with cultural artifacts including a tepee and photographs, a pioneer kitchen, a replica of an old school, and natural history specimens. The exhibit material is mainly items that have been deaccessioned from the collections or acquired by the volunteers themselves. A docent, assisted by 3 to 6 other volunteers, is in charge of Cricket's Corner and is responsible to a volunteer coordinator, who reports to the museum director. Cricket's Corner is open by appointment only, and the target audience is children 1st–5th grade. Attendance is sporadic and comes mainly from the post and town, but on occasion from as far as 50 miles away. About 2,000 children visit Cricket's Corner per year.

Oklahoma City

OKLAHOMA CITY ZOO, 2112 NE 50th Street, Oklahoma City, OK 73111. The Children's Zoo, opened in 1964, is 6 acres and includes a nocturnal building, an animal nursery with viewing windows for visitors, a prairie dog town, and a beaks and feet exhibit. A contact area with domestic animals is also open in the summer. The children's zoo is used with school groups and in summer programs, some of which are cosponsored with Omniplex (see next entry). Discovery Theater, an 800-square-foot area, was originally a combination classroom and holding facility for a teaching collection of live animals used by docents for weekend interpretive programs. With the opening of the 8,000-square-foot Rex Kennedy Rosser Education Center in the summer of 1983, Discovery Theater began operating full-time. It now includes an exhibit area with 12 displays covering geology, botany, zoology, and ecology, which are changed periodically, and 1 permanent display of birds' eggs. In 1984 grant funds were used to provide 4 discovery tables and a reading cubicle and to upgrade exhibit graphics. The zoo's large collection of mammal skulls, skins, invertebrates, and birds' nests and a collection of about 90 small animals are used in Discovery Theater and outreach programs. Docent interpretation with live animals remains the primary emphasis of the theater. There are 2 full-time educators, a volunteer coordinator, a part-time librarian, and a secretary who are assisted by 120 adult volunteers and 75 junior curators, 12–18 years old. General zoo attendance is about 500,000 annually with about 15 percent, or 75,000, participating in Discovery Theater or other educational programs. The zoo is open May through September 9:00–6:00 and October through April 9:00–5:00. Discovery Theater is open Tuesday through Sunday 1:00–5:00 and closed holidays. There is an admission charge, and support comes from generated revenue and city tax money.

Rosl Kirchshofer, ed., *The World of Zoos: A Survey and Gazetteer* (New York: Viking, 1968), pp. 247–48; *Teacher's Guide to the Oklahoma City Zoo* (Oklahoma City: Oklahoma City Zoo Education Department, August 1984).

OMNIPLEX, Kirkpatrick Center, 2100 NE 52nd Street, Oklahoma City, OK 73111. The Discovery Room, opened in 1982, is a 16-by-35-foot facility for nondirected study. The room contains many geology materials, including rock and mineral specimens, geologic time line set with paleo-plaques, a land forms puzzle, representative Oklahoma and comparative fossils, and a tape player with a variety of cassettes on geological topics. There are also shells, skeletons to compare, a mammal skull collection, typical Oklahoma birds' nests, a comparative butterfly collection, identification guides, a model of the solar system, globes, and simple machines. Thirty- to 45-minute science lab programs are held in the Discovery Room for grades 1–12 for no more than 15 students per hour. Reservations in advance insure exclusive use of the Discovery Room. The installation is available to everyone, with 3rd–6th grade children the largest visitor group. There is an admission to Omniplex but no extra charge for the Discovery Room. A science and nature day camp for 5–11 year olds is offered cooperatively by Omniplex and the Oklahoma City Zoo. Omniplex has a paid staff of 17 and 100 volunteers. There are over 200,000 visitors a year with approximately 30 percent being school groups with advance reservations. Hours are Monday through Saturday 10:00–5:00, Sunday 12:00–5:00, and closed Christmas and Thanksgiving. Support comes 65 percent from admissions and membership, 15 percent from donations, and 20 percent from grants.

Omniplex School Group Programs 1983–84 (Oklahoma City: Omniplex, [1983]), p. 4; "Summer Science and Nature," *Omniplex Omnigram* 2, no. 4 (April/May [1984]): 2.

OREGON

Newport

HATFIELD MARINE SCIENCE CENTER OF OREGON STATE UNIVERSITY, Marine Science Drive, Newport, OR 97365. The Touch Tank is one of the 16 saltwater tanks, ranging from 10 to 2,500 gallons, displaying animals native to the Oregon coast. The center, opened in 1965, was built with federal money made available by what was then the Area Redevelopment Agency. Besides the tanks, the 10,000-square-foot public wing has museum displays on various aspects of oceanography. There are also a variety of outdoor programs for school classes including tidepooling, an estuary field trip, and a tour of a commercial boat dock. Resource materials are available for teachers, and in the spring a marine biology skit, presented by drama student interns with the Oregon State University (OSU) Marine Science Center, goes to schools. During the summer there is a full schedule of programs for children and adults, including workshops, talks, walks, treks, and free films. A winter whale watch for families occurs between Christmas and New Years' and another during the 3rd week of March, coinciding with spring break. The public wing is part of a comprehensive 100,000-square-foot facility which includes labs, classrooms, a library, and governmental offices and is home port for a research vessel. The public wing staff includes 1 full-time and 2 part-time marine education specialists, 3 support staff members, and 10 volunteers. In the summer there are 4 additional interpretive aides. The center is open fall, winter, and spring 10:00–4:00, summer 10:00–6:00, and all holidays except Christmas. Approximately 350,000 visitors come to the center each year. There is no admission charge, but there is a small fee for some programs. The remaining support comes from OSU's Extension Marine Advisory Program, the OSU School of Oceanography, and the Sea Grant College Program.

Oregon State University's Marine Science Center on Yaquina Bay (Corvallis: Extension Service, U.S. Department of Agriculture, 1982); *Seataugua '86* (Corvallis: Oregon State University, [1986]); Frank J. Turkowski, "Education at Zoos and Aquariums in the United States," *BioScience* 22, no. 8 (August 1972): 472, 474.

Portland

PORTLAND CHILDREN'S MUSEUM, 3037 SW 2nd Avenue, Portland, OR 73503. The museum, founded in 1949 by the Park Department and the American Association of University Women, opened in a pioneer home. Two years later it moved to a 2-story brick building near downtown and now occupies 2 buildings with 15,000 square feet of space. Initially emphasizing good leisure-time activities, it gradually developed into a junior museum with live animals. Over the last 15 years it has moved from an arts-based education program to a participatory facility focusing on the young child and including classroom programs. Exhibits concentrate on real-life situations and hands-on experiences. The "Call an Artist" program helps teachers integrate the arts into the curriculum and offers students an opportunity to talk to artists about their work and participate in an activity. Programs by artists have included architecture/urban design, pottery, dance, printmaking, drawing, weaving, and sculpture. Special workshops for the gifted and talented have been offered during the school year for 4th–9th-grade students. The newspaper *Boing!* is published 5 times a year. There are 3 full-time and 3 part-time staff members, 15 to 20 instructors, and 20 to 30 volunteers. Support comes from the City Park Bureau, grants, and fees for classes. The museum is open Tuesday through Saturday 9:00–5:00, Sunday 11:00–5:00, and closed Mondays and holidays. The museum, with both an urban and suburban audience, serves 55,000 with its outreach program, 4,000 in classes, and has 46,000 visitors a year.

Call an Artist (Portland: Department of Public Affairs, [1980]); Yvonne Keck Holman, "An Investigation into the Dynamics of Children's Museums: A Case Study of Selected Museums" (Ph.D dissertation, Northern Illinois University, 1982), pp. 76, 81, 83, 86, 91–92, 94, 99, 101, 115, 119; Bonnie Pitman-Gelles, *Museums, Magic & Children: Youth Education in Museums* (Washington, D.C.: Association of Science-Technology Centers, 1981), pp. 176–77; Mary Alice Reed, "Creative Activities in a Junior Museum," *Recreation* 46, no. 9 (February 1953): 518–19.

WASHINGTON PARK ZOO, 4001 SW Canyon Road, Portland, OR 97221. The Children's Zoo opened in 1962 after the zoo moved to a new site. It occupies approximately 2 acres, half of which are covered or enclosed. The core of the children's zoo is the petting area with about 30 animals, including domestic goats, ducks, rabbits, and guinea pigs. There are nonpettable birds, tortoises, and lizards and a Dinosaur Park with replica dinosaurs and dinosaur bones. The 600-square-foot Cascades Nature Center, opened in 1980, has exhibits and activities related to the Cascade Mountain area. Interactive displays include an electronic matching game, question-and-answer lift panels, touchable furs, antlers, and touch boxes. Animals from the contact area are used for outreach programs to schools, the disabled, and nursing homes. The animal nursery is in the area but not technically a part of the children's zoo. The keeper from the children's zoo is the primary advisor to the Explorer Post. During the summer about 70 teenage volunteers learn the rudiments of zoo animal care in the children's zoo. There are 1 full-time and 1 part-time keeper, 2 summer volunteer supervisors who work with the teenage volunteers, and other adult volunteers who help supervise the petting corrals. Separate attendance figures are not kept, but it is estimated that the children's zoo has about 350,000 visitors a year, mainly young children with adults and school classes. Summer hours are 9:30–7:30 and winter hours are 9:30–4:00. The children's zoo receives its support from the zoo's overall budget, which is 50 percent tax-based and 50 percent revenue-based.

Warren Iliff, "Your Zoo in the 80's," *FOZ Newsletter* 3, no. 3 (September 1981): 3–5; Jan McCoy, "The Children's Zoo," *FOZ Newsletter* 3, no. 4 (Winter 1981): 3–4; Susan Plaisance, "Dinosaur Park: A Walk through the Zoo's Newest Exhibit," *Your Zoo* 6, no. 2 (Summer 1984): 8–10.

Winston

WILDLIFE SAFARI, Box 600, Winston, OR 97496. The Petting Zoo, opened in 1972, was included in the original plans for the 600-acre drive-through animal reserve. Located within the village area, the contact zoo features safari animals that, for various reasons, have been pulled from the drive-through part of the park. The exhibits change with the season and could include mouflon sheep, fallow deer, blackbuck, pygmy goats, donkeys, yak, and sheep. The corrals are arranged to allow interaction with the animals, and food can be purchased to feed them. In an adjacent area are various nonpettable exhibits. The village was refurbished in 1983, and the graphic displays have been redesigned. Wildlife Safari has a 4–H club for children 10–16; another group of youth 13–17 helps with the animals in the petting zoo; and docents (adults) also assist in the area. About 20 members participate in the youth volunteer groups, and there are 20 active docents. The contact area appeals to all age groups, particularly children, and approximately 85 percent of the 150,000 annual visitors experience the 1/6-acre children's zoo. It is open during park operating hours, summer 9:00–8:00 and winter 9:00–4:00. There is no additional fee for the Petting Zoo, which is supported by park revenues, animal food sales, and fund-raising events. An expansion initiated in the mid–1980s includes the development of a wildlife education center with exhibits, participatory displays, and 196-seat theater.

Cath Park, "Expansion and Development Plans," *Wildlife Safari Newsletter* 5, no. 3 (Fall/Winter 1985): 4; *Wildlife Safari* (Winston: Safari Game Search Foundation, 1985), pp. 15–16, 19–20.

PENNSYLVANIA

Harrisburg

MUSEUM OF SCIENTIFIC DISCOVERY, 3rd and Walnut Streets, 3rd Level, Strawberry Square, PO Box 934, Harrisburg, PA 17108. The museum opened on 16 February 1982 in 10,000 square feet of donated space in a new downtown shopping mall. Movement to establish a new museum downtown was started in 1977 by the Junior League. In 1979 the League sponsored a pilot project, SENSORAMA, in 2,000 square feet of space in the William Penn Memorial Museum. This venture was successful, and in 1980 the Junior League was joined by business and community leaders. Together they formed a board of directors, and the museum's name was changed to the Museum of Scientific Discovery. The museum has no collections, but it has grown from its original 34 exhibits to 55, all exploring various facets of science. Installations, workshops, and programs emphasize a hands-on experience. The most popular exhibits have been THE HEART OF HARRISBURG, a jungle gym where kids follow the path of blood through the heart, THE GRAVITY WELL, and GRAVITY TOWER. Classes and special programs have included computers, photography, preschool specials, lectures, teen programs, and a wide selection of 1-day and weekend sessions. In-service workshops for teachers were initiated in October 1983, and in 1985 outreach programs to schools began. There are 8 full-time staff members and about 150 volunteers. The museum is open Tuesday through Saturday 10:00–6:00, Sunday 1:00–6:00, and closed Monday. Support comes 28 percent from donations and grants, 26 percent from admissions, 24 percent from programs, 14 percent from the shop, and the remaining 8 percent from memberships and miscellaneous sources. The Museum of Scientific Discovery has about 70,000 visitors a year of all ages.

William R. Anderson and Herbert Sprouse, ''Museums in the Marketplace,'' *Museum News* 63, no. 1 (October 1984): 59–67; Commission on Museums for a New Century, *Museums for a New Century* (Washington, D.C.: American Association of Museums, 1984), pp. 92, 124; Dennis Zembower, *Cooperative Exhibit Development among Science Centers: Getting the Most for Your Dollars*, audiotape of panelists Marilynne Eichinger and Roger Smith, presented at meeting of the American Association of Museums, Washington, D.C., June 1984 (Shawnee Mission, KS: Vanguard Systems, 1984).

Philadelphia

THE ACADEMY OF NATURAL SCIENCES, Nineteenth and the Parkway, Philadelphia, PA 19103. Outside-In, the children's nature museum, opened on 17 March 1979 and was designed for 5–10 year olds. This special hands-on natural science area was developed following the departure of the Please Touch Museum from the academy, where it started as a pilot project in 1976 and 2 years later needed more space than the academy could provide. Open limited hours and supervised by specially trained staff members, Outside-In was an immediate success. Due to building renovations the facility relocated several times, but each move allowed for change and refinement. With funds from the William Penn Foundation and the McLean Contributionship, an enlarged 1,800-square-foot installation on the 3rd floor of the Academy, twice the size of the earlier ones, opened on 22 September 1984. The target audience is still primary-age children, but the area also appeals to preschoolers and adults. Exhibits were developed to be process-oriented and directly involve the visitor, demonstrate the interaction of living organisms, and address an urban audience unable to experience the natural environment by the creation of mini natural environments. Emphasizing Philadelphia and the Delaware Valley, Outside-In has a Jersey salt marsh with a beach, boardwalk, and saltwater aquarium, a working beehive, bald eagle's nest, stream and look-under pond with live animals and plants, giant beech tree, fossils, and a resource area. In addition, there are biweekly storytimes and monthly special demonstrations involving visitor participation. Outside-In has a full-time coordinator, 2 weekend managers, and 45 volunteer facilitators. Reservations are required for the 4 sessions of 30-minute lessons for classes beginning at 10:15 Monday through Friday. Families may come without reservations weekdays 1:00–4:00 and weekends and holidays 10:00–5:00. The Academy has an admission charge, and support for Outside-In comes from the general museum operating budget, foundations, corporations, and private individuals. The new Outside-In has approximately 95,000 visitors a year.

"Adults without Kids Barred from Outside-In Museum," *The Bulletin*, 16 March 1979; "Exhibit Is a Natural Pleasure," *Philadelphia Daily News*, 21 September 1984, p. 51; "Get the Inside Story on Outside Animals," *Philadelphia Daily News*, 20 March 1979; "Museum Offers Nature Tailored to a Child's Eye," *Philadelphia Inquirer*, 21 September 1984, sec. E, pp. 1, 22–23; "Outside-In," *Academy News* (Winter 1984): 2–3; "The Remodeled Academy Takes a Spring Fling," *Philadelphia Inquirer Weekend*, 28 March 1980, p. 24.

THE FRANKLIN INSTITUTE SCIENCE MUSEUM, 20th & The Parkway, Philadelphia, PA 19103. Opened to the public on 1 January 1934, the museum was modeled after the Deutsches Museum in Munich. Installations range from the historical to the future of science and technology, with an increasing emphasis being placed on the role and impact of science on society. The museum has 160,926 square feet of exhibit space, which includes both permanent and changing displays. It has always had hands-on exhibits, and many of these now involve the visitor in decision making and analysis. The target audience is children 7–14 and their families. The Institute has always worked closely with the Philadelphia schools, and each year the Board of Education assigns a few teachers to the museum to conduct classes for students. In response to the urban crisis of the 1960s, the museum developed 3 innovative educational programs, the Science Enrichment Program (PSSP), Project GOAL, and the Parkway Program. PSSP brought 6th-grade children from different backgrounds together at the museum to explore various science topics. GOAL was developed for 5th- and 6th-grade children at an overcrowded elementary school and functioned like an open classroom. The Parkway Program was a school without walls, and although it was headquartered at the Franklin Institute, the participating high school students also used the resources of other institutions.

Many science programs with a regional impact have been developed. In 1947 the museum held the first Philadelphia Science Fair for Young People and has continued to sponsor this annual event. Outreach programs were first offered in the 1940s and have been reshaped over the years to meet current needs. The Traveling Science Show, started in 1970, visits kindergarten through junior high students in school, scouts or other group meetings, and is available in the summer months for playgrounds, camps, and summer schools. Programs are designed for groups not larger than 300; small group sessions are available as a program follow-up; and the topics are suitable for a wide age range. A program to affect science education in the schools, the Science Enrichment Series (SES), produced kits focusing on a single concept for middle school teachers and their students. In addition to a program for gifted elementary and junior high students, the Institute offers a wide variety of classes, programs, and special events for youth and families including a special planetarium show for children 7 and under.

In the last decade the institute developed several innovative facilities and exhibits. In 1976 it opened Science Park, a 30,000-square-foot outdoor area with more than 40 exhibits, demonstrations, and experiments. From May through October, weather permitting, visitors can explore water, the sun, physics, and measurement in the museum's backyard. Museums-on-the-Mall, a gallery and demonstration space (1978–1982), was an outreach experiment in an urban shopping complex. The admission-free facility was open 7 days a week and offered live demonstrations, hands-on experiments, and displays. Museums-on-the-Mall attracted a more diverse audience than the parent facility, including fewer children and family groups and a much higher percentage of inner-city residents. For several years the Department of Museum Research studied visitor behavior, exhibit effectiveness, and learning in the museum setting. In late 1983 the Computer Activities Center with 20 terminals opened and offers computer classes for all age groups. A related area, the Science Arcade, opened in mid–1984 and contains a series of educational computer games which relate to the contents of the institute's exhibits. Each of the 10 programs is based upon a scientific principle. The arcade was developed to demonstrate ways that computers can be used effectively for educational purposes, especially science education.

There are a paid staff of 200 and about 100 volunteers. With a largely family audience, the museum has 600,000 visitors per year. Hours are Monday through Saturday 10:00–5:00 and Sunday 12:00–5:00. There is an admission charge. Support comes 23 percent from private corporations and foundations, 27 percent from individuals, 5 percent from the city, 3 percent from government grants, 7 percent from the State of Pennsylvania, and 35 percent from admissions.

Commission on Museums for a New Century, *Museums for a New Century* (Washington, D.C.: American Association of Museums, 1984), pp. 56, 62, 65, 69, 92, 112; Victor J. Danilov, "Science Museums as Education Centers," *Curator* 18, no. 2 (June 1975): 94–96; Bowen C. Dees, "The Franklin Institute: Commemorating a Great Interdisciplinary Scientist," *Interdisciplinary Science Reviews* 5, no. 2 (1980): 98–101; "Hall of Wonder for Young and Old," *New York Times*, 29 January 1961, sec. 2, p. 39; Bonnie Pitman-

Gelles, *Museums, Magic & Children: Youth Education in Museums* (Washington, D.C.: Association of Science-Technology Centers, 1981), pp. 40, 108, 124–25, 128, 175, 180; "Science beyond the Walls," in *Museum-School Partnerships: Plans and Programs*, Sourcebook #4, ed. Susan Nichols Lehman and Kathryn Igoe (Washington, D.C.: George Washington University, 1981), pp. 112–13: ERIC Document Reproduction Service, ED 216 945.

PHILADELPHIA ZOOLOGICAL SOCIETY, 34th Street & Girard Avenue, Philadelphia, PA 19104. The Children's Zoo, the first in the United States, opened in the summer of 1938 as the Baby-Pet Zoo and was immediately popular with visitors. It was a small barnyard area with pens and cages containing domestic animals that children under 12 were allowed to pet and feed. A trained animal show was also presented. There was a small fee to enter the children's area, which was screened off from the rest of the zoo. The Baby-Pet Zoo closed in 1944, and on 5 May 1957 a remodeled facility, the 2-acre Daniel W. Dietrich Memorial Children's Zoo, opened. It was developed to stimulate public interest in the zoo, educate visitors about the animal world, and generate income. Besides a contact area and controlled feeding it provided opportunities for close visual observation. In 1960 an outreach program, School Bus for Animals, was initiated; the children's zoo staff took small animals and made presentations in metro Philadelphia schools. This free service, operated from October to early March, was booked far in advance and was seen by about 35,000 children each year. In 1974 a dairy cow exhibit and in 1981 ZOO STOP, with artifacts and interactive exhibits, were added. In the mid–1980s the Daniel W. Dietrich Memorial Children's Zoo attracts 500,000 paid visitors per year, and another 40,000 to 50,000 are reached by off-premise programs. The area has a superintendent, an assistant superintendent, 3 keepers, 12 seasonal employees, and 25 volunteers. It is open weekdays 10:00–4:30 and weekends 10:00–5:30. Support comes from admissions, pony rides, and sale of animal food.

   In 1980 the designing of an additional facility began, and on 10 April 1985 the TREEHOUSE opened. This new 7,800-square-foot area, utilizing the original 1877 antelope house, was developed to cultivate a sense of wonder and appreciation of living things in young zoo visitors. Its primary purpose is not to transmit facts but to create impressions and perceptions about the basic themes of animal evolution and life cycles. A series of fabricated habitats includes a meadow, swamps, beaver pond, beehive, and ficus tree, and all are scaled so that the child is the same size as some animal found there. Each thematic environment involves all the senses with smells, recorded sounds, special lighting, slide shows, and interactive opportunities including making the dinosaur roar, climbing into a beaver lodge and sliding out, occupying a cocoon, and making a cricket call. The TREEHOUSE staff consists of a manager, a floor manager, and a corps of interns (4 are present at a time) supplemented with volunteers. Schools and other groups may make reservations; it is open to casual visitors weekdays 2:00–4:00 and weekends 10:00–5:00; and the facility can be rented for evening parties. Support for the planning design and development came from the City of Philadelphia, the George D. Widener Memorial Trust, and the William Penn Foundation.

"A Children's Zoo for Philadelphia," *New York Times*, 5 May 1957, p. 83; Deborah K. Dietsch, "Learning from Mother Nature," *Architectural Record* 173, no. 10 (September 1985): 120–25; Rosl Kirchshofer, ed., *The World of Zoos: A Survey and Gazetteer* (New York: Viking, 1968), p. 226; "May Day at the Philadelphia Zoo," *Parks & Recreation* 21, no. 11 (July 1938): 577–79; "New Children's Zoo at Philadelphia," *Parks & Recreation* 40, no. 9 (September 1957): 37–38; "The New Children's Zoo Creates a Habitat through Which to See the World the Way the Animals Do," *Architectural Record* 169, no. 12 (December 1981): 41; "Winter Educational Activities Philadelphia Zoo USA," in *International Zoo Yearbook* 4 (1962): 149–50, ed. Caroline Jarvis and Desmond Morris (London: The Zoological Society of London, 1962).

PLEASE TOUCH MUSEUM, 210 North 21st Street, Philadelphia, PA 19103. A planning group of teachers, designers, and parents formed in 1975, after perceiving a need for a cultural center to provide educational experiences for young children. The museum opened as a pilot project in October 1976 with 1,000 square feet of space donated by the Academy of Natural Sciences in Philadelphia (see entry under UNITED STATES/PENNSYLVANIA) and a volunteer staff led by Portia Hamilton Sperr. By the 2nd year programming increased to 40 hours per week. Needing more space, the museum began to look for a larger site, was asked to set up an exhibit in a shopping mall, and also found a larger place to rent. The museum maintained both the facilities until the spring of 1981, when it concentrated all its efforts in its 8,000-square-foot location and gave up the 1,600 square foot branch exhibit. Growth continued, making it again necessary to relocate. On 21 May 1983 the museum opened in a 30,000-square-foot, 3-story building it purchased. The target audience is children 7 and younger and handicapped children 12 and younger. Please Touch appeals to young children's perceptions of their world and stresses role-playing, participation, and play, and parents are encouraged to share play with their children. The collection is strongest in the areas of ethnic objects, costumes, masks, household objects from many cultures, toys with an emphasis on contemporary playthings, and natural science materials that can be touched. The permanent exhibits focus on the arts, cultures, sciences, technology, and the natural sciences. Each year there are 2 special changing exhibits which have included THE HEALTH CARE CENTER, CORNER STORE, PLEASE TOUCH CIRCUS 1984 and CHILDREN'S PLAY: PAST, PRESENT AND FUTURE. The museum also provides a discovery area called the Resource Center, outreach kits to Philadelphia schools and libraries, workshops, performances, and special events. In addition, the museum is developing a Childlife Center to record the history of childhood in the Delaware Valley through the collection of playthings, oral histories, and archival material including photographs. Please Touch is also sponsoring symposia on important issues related to children. There are 15 full-time and 15 part-time staff members who are assisted by approximately 60 volunteers. Admissions, store receipts, and memberships provide 72 percent of the museum's support, with the remaining 28 percent coming from foundations, corporations, individuals, and government agencies. Please Touch is open Tuesday through Saturday 10:00–4:30, Sunday 12:30–4:30, and closed Monday. Children must be accompanied by an adult. Annual attendance is about 120,000.

Victor J. Danilov, "Discovery Rooms and Kidspaces: Museum Exhibits for Children," *Science and Children* 23, no. 4 (January 1986): 2971; "For Youngsters, a Touchable Toy Exhibit," *New York Times*, 18 September 1985, sec. C, p. 1; Yvonne Keck Holman, "An Investigation into the Dynamics of Children's Museums: A Case Study of Selected Museums" (Ph.D. dissertation, Northern Illinois University, 1982), pp. 13, 36, 47, 57, 211–40, 282, 284–85, 286, 288, 290, 292, 295, 296, 297, 298, 299, 306; Jonathan Katz, *Philosophies and Methods of Youth Museums*, audiotape of panelists Steven Ling, Portia Sperr, and Michael Spock, presented at meeting of the American Association of Museums, Detroit, June 1985 (Shawnee Mission, KS: Vanguard Systems, 1985).

SCHUYLKILL VALLEY NATURE CENTER, 8480 Hagy's Mill Road, Philadelphia, PA 19128. The Discovery Room, opened in 1968, is 1,936 square feet. It carries out the center's mission of being a working classroom to promote an understanding of our responsibility to nature in face of growing urbanization. Established in July 1965, the 360-acre site has a bug house, nature center with classrooms and exhibit space, a weather station, and a special wing for the handicapped was added in 1975. The collection is strongest in mounted mammals and birds of the area, herbarium, insects, and natural history slides. Exhibits are geared for elementary-age children, constructed to be hands-on and participatory, and 2 new ones are installed each year. Programs for various age groups include "Natural Beginnings" for preschoolers, "Sunship Earth" and "Earth Journey" for school-age children, teacher environmental educational credit courses held in conjunction with area colleges, programs for senior citizens, and weekend public activities. The Nature Center also sponsors several clubs. Ten full-time and 2 part-time staff members including 3 educators are assisted by 35 volunteers. Hours are Monday through Saturday 8:30–5:00 and Sunday 1:00–5:00, except during August. Approximately 70,000 visitors come each year. The Schuylkill Valley Nature Center is supported by private memberships and corporate support.

"Come to Nature: Discover the Environment in Roxborough," *Philadelphia Inquirer*, 15 August 1985, p. B–1; Bill Newbold, "Schuylkill Valley Nature Center," *Parks & Recreation* 6, no. 2 (February 1971): 14–18, 54.

Pittsburgh

THE PITTSBURGH CHILDREN'S MUSEUM, One Landmarks Square, Allegheny Center, Pittsburgh, PA 15212. The museum was founded in April 1980 with Junior League support. It opened on 12 June 1983 in the basement of a historic old post office building and originally occupied about 5,900 square feet of space. The museum expanded in May 1985 when it took over the rest of the 22,000-square-foot building, which it leases from the Pittsburgh History and Landmarks Foundation. The target audience is children from infancy to 11. The museum encompasses participatory activities in local history, communications, science, health, and puppetry. Although not essentially a collections-oriented institution, the museum does have a major 280-item puppet collection and other collections. An exhibit, MYSTERY, MAGIC, AND MIRTH: A WORLD OF PUPPETS, contains hands-on components interspersed with hands-off displays, including donations and loans from Jim Henson, Fred Rogers, and the collection's major donor, Margo Lovelace. An innovative program and exhibit, PLAYPATH, has been developed to provide science-related activities for children under 2 and their parents. Learning aids and toys have been designed to stimulate sensory development in the child and increase parents' interaction with and awareness of their infant's development. The 9 full-time and 12 part-time staff members are assisted by approximately 80 volunteers. During the school year the museum is open Tuesday through Friday 9:30–2:30 for school groups and 2:30–5:00 for the general public. Monday and Saturday it is open 11:00–5:00 and Sunday 1:00–5:00. Support comes 45 percent from admissions, 44 percent from grants and contributions, 4 percent from memberships, 5 percent from retail sales, and 2 percent from earned income. The museum has about 115,000 visitors per year.

David Crosson, *How Can You Say No When Your Museum Says Yes? Collections in Participatory Museums*, audiotape of panelists Charles Howarth, Paul Richard, and Betsy Vincent, presented at meeting of the American Association of Museums, Detroit, June 1985 (Shawnee Mission, KS: Vanguard Systems, 1985); Victor J. Danilov, "Early Childhood Exhibits at Science Centers," *Curator* 27, no. 3 (September 1984): 186–88; Marcia Axtmann Smith, "A Mirror of the Past: Pittsburgh History and Landmarks Museum and Cultural Center," *Museum News* 59, no. 1 (September 1980): 55–57; Marcia Axtmann Smith, "Renewed Museums Revisited," *Museum News* 63, no. 4 (September 1985): 21–22.

RHODE ISLAND

Pawtucket

THE CHILDREN'S MUSEUM OF RHODE ISLAND, 58 Walcott Street, Pawtucket, RI 02860. Opened on 26 June 1977, the children's museum was initiated by the Pawtucket Jaycees in 1975. Renovation of the 5,500-square-foot, 1840s Pitcher-Goff Mansion was made possible by a grant from the Rhode Island Historic Preservation Commission and the vocational school students who provided the labor. Designed to provide educational experiences that are supplementary to home and school, the museum has a target audience of children 1–12 years old. There are 8 major hands-on exhibit areas, and each year 1 exhibit is changed. Current installations include storytelling and dramatic play, painting, a puzzle room, a house hunt which sends the children throughout the building to search architectural details, shape exploration, firefighting, great-grandmother's kitchen, and disabilities. In addition, there are a variety of workshops, performances, and special events. In 1984 the museum acquired its first collection, 40 hand made marionettes. In spring 1986 a mobile museum began traveling to libraries, schools, and shopping centers. In the fall of 1986 the museum installed THE STATE ROOM, a participatory exhibit in honor of Rhode Island's 350th anniversary. Four full-time and 6 part-time staff members are assisted by 80–90 volunteers. There are also student interns, currently 3 part-time and 1 full-time. The Kids' Advisory Committee, along with its other activities, assists with the publication of *Boing!*, which is distributed to 70,000 3rd–6th graders in their classrooms. The museum is open to groups by reservation weekday mornings, as well as during public hours, and teachers' packets are available prior to a visit. Public hours July 1 through Labor Day are Tuesday through Saturday 10:00–5:00, Sunday 1:00–5:00, and closed Monday. Winter hours are Wednesday and Thursday 1:00–5:00, Friday and Saturday 10:00–5:00, Sunday 1:00–5:00 and closed Monday, Tuesday, and major holidays. There is an admission charge. Support comes approximately 50 percent from earned income, 8 percent from state support, 14 percent from individual contributions, and 28 percent from foundations, contributions, and grants. The Rhode Island Children's Museum has about 34,000 visitors each year.

"Children Museum's Exhibit Will Show Young How It Feels to Be Handicapped," *Providence Evening Bulletin*, 20 July 1981; "For Some, Internships Are Child's Play," *Museprint* 2, no. 7 (March 1981): 1, 4; "Getting It Together at the Children's Museum," *East Side/West Side* 8, no. 24 (18 June 1981): 4; "Kids' Newspaper Competes with TV," *Evening Times*, 14 October 1980; "Stuff from Before You Were Born," *Providence Sunday Journal*, 26 June 1977, pp. 6–7, 9, 11; Eileen Wallen, "Children's Museums Come of Age," *Museum News* 58, no. 2 (November/December 1979): 46–49.

Providence

ROGER WILLIAMS PARK ZOO, Roger Williams Park, Providence, RI 02905. The Children's Nature Center, opened in 1981, is a multifaceted exhibit area of 1,100 square feet. Focusing on camouflage, the thematic displays include aquatic, tropical, and desert animals. There are a few additional exhibits, a working beehive, a glassed-in nursery, and a view of egg hatching. Adjacent to the center is ADAPTATIONS FOR MOVEMENT, where each display contains an animal representing an adaptation for locomotion and a few exhibit-related activities. Included are muntjac/hoofs, raccoons/climbing, prairie dogs/burrowing, view pond under water/swimming, and hawk/flight. At the New England Farm animals may be petted only if they come to the fence, and there is a no feeding policy. Studies have indicated that the zoo's graphics, 27 inches high and tilted at an angle, have encouraged family interaction. In 1985 a 10,000-square-foot Education Center opened in a restored, 100-year-old barn. Besides support areas for the zoo, a large classroom and a lecture hall occupy about one-third of the building space. The curator of education is assisted by 80 volunteers, and the Docent Council, founded in 1975, sponsors the Zoo Education Project. During the last 3 years 250,000 people have attended programs at the park or been reached by the zoomobile. The use of animal artifacts is being incorporated into programs to lessen the stress on the live collection that results from constant travel. In addition, an endangered species program for junior high youth has received permission to use confiscated goods for educational purposes. The zoo is open 7 days a week 10:00–4:00; and on Friday, Saturday, and Sunday from May 30 to September 4 the park stays open until 7:00 in the evening. Separate figures are not kept for the Children's Nature Center, but zoo attendance last year was 539,000. There is no admission charge, and the general operating support comes from the city of Providence. New projects and special exhibits are funded by the Rhode Island Zoological Society and private funds.

Robert Bendiner, *The Fall of the Wild, The Rise of the Zoo* (New York: E. P. Dutton, 1981), p. 114; Bonnie Pitman-Gelles, *Museums, Magic & Children: Youth Education in Museums* (Washington, D.C.: Association of Science-Technology Centers, 1981), pp. 108–09, 172–73; "Roger Williams Zoo: A Sanctum in the City Captivates the Young, Holds the Rest in Thrall," *Providence Journal*, 29 May 1985; "Zoos Are News," *Woman's Day*, 23 October 1984.

SOUTH DAKOTA

Sioux Falls

SIOUXLAND HERITAGE MUSEUMS, 200 West 6th Street, Sioux Falls, SD 57102. The Senses 5 Gallery in the Old Courthouse Museum was opened 15 March 1981 on a temporary basis to test the concept of a hands-on exhibit. The curator of education felt there was need for such a participatory area because the state had no children's museum. The initial installation, which emphasized history, natural history, and handicapped awareness, remained open until 6 December 1982. The pilot exhibit HANDS-ON was so popular that the museum joined with the Junior League to create a permanent children's gallery. The 983-square-foot Senses 5 Gallery, opened on 25 March 1983, focuses on science and explores the principles of sight, taste, smell, and hearing and touch. The collections used in the room are acquired specifically for the gallery. The Explainers, supplied by the Junior League, work with a museum educator and a museum interpreter. Approximately 20,000 visitors used the gallery last year. Senses 5 is open Monday through Saturday 9:00–5:00 and Sunday 2:00–5:00. There is no admission charge. The museum receives 45 percent of its support from the city, 45 percent from the county, and the remaining income from grants.

"Children's Morning at the Museum," *Siouxland Heritage Museums Community Report* 1, no. 3 [1983]: 3; *Senses 5: Sensory Expression as a Means of Communication* (Sioux Falls: Old Courthouse Museum, [1983]).

TENNESSEE

Knoxville

KNOXVILLE ZOOLOGICAL PARK, PO Box 6040, Knoxville, TN 37914. The Children's Zoo opened in 1971 and was remodeled in 1982. The quarter-acre facility has a contact area with African pygmy goats, white-tailed deer, mouflon sheep, minihorses, minipigs, donkey, a waterfowl pond, and hand-raised babies. Feeding is allowed with food purchased at the zoo. Children under 6 must be accompanied by an adult. Twenty to 25 volunteers work in the children's zoo, and 2 to 3 volunteers are always on duty. This area is open year-round, weather permitting, and has about 30,000 visitors per year. Animals from the petting zoo are sometimes used in outreach programs. There is a small admission charge for the children's zoo. Support for the zoo comes 75 percent from earned revenues and 25 percent from the city.

"Adjusting Priorities," *Expositor*, 10 October 1985; "Hey Kids! Let's Hear It for Baby," *Knoxville News-Sentinel*, 17 July 1983, pp. F1, F9.

Memphis

MEMPHIS BROOKS MUSEUM OF ART, Overton Park, Memphis TN 38112. The Artworks Gallery/Studio opened in the mid–1970s and was initially an audiovisual, movement, and art activities area for children. The 30-by-30-foot space is now used for structured art activities for tour groups and most recently has included ARTWORKS IN PROCESS, a 3-walled exhibit on media processes. Cases hung on the wall display tools, materials, and examples from the museum's permanent collections of painting, printmaking, and sculpture. The exhibit will rotate in the future to include other media, such as clay and fiber, and occasionally the area will be used for exhibits such as the annual juried student show. Tour groups receive basic art instruction in artworks related to the exhibitions, which the staff feels is the kind of programming that best meets the needs of students in area schools. Three full-time education department staff members are assisted by 45 docents; there are 15,000 student visitors annually. The wall exhibits are open to the public daily, except Mondays and holidays, and the art activities are conducted Tuesday through Friday and on scheduled weekends. Support for Artworks comes from the Memphis Brooks Museum of Art Foundation, other city money, and private funds.

Bartlett H. Hayes, Jr., *A Study of the Relation of Museum Art Exhibitions to Education: A Final Report* (Washington, D.C.: Office of Education, Bureau of Research, 1967), p. 47: ERIC Document Reproduction Service, ED 026 403; "How Art Works in Memphis," *Southern Living* 14, no. 10 (October 1979): 96, 98; Bonnie Pitman-Gelles, *Museums, Magic & Children: Youth Education in Museums* (Washington, D.C.: Association of Science-Technology Centers, 1981), p. 145.

Nashville

CUMBERLAND MUSEUM AND SCIENCE CENTER, 800 Ridley Boulevard, Nashville, TN 37303. Curiosity Corner, a Junior League project opened in February 1981, is a 1,800-square-foot participatory area designed specifically for children K–4 and families. For tactile exploration there are wonder boxes containing natural objects drawn from the collection and information cards which guide discovery and provide additional information. A tree in the center of the exhibit depicts life both above and below the ground with its fox den, spider home, view of a garden below the earth, and animal home matching game. A turn-of-the-century country store provides many opportunities for role-playing and contact with artifacts from another era. In 1982 a Japanese Room, sponsored by Nissan Motor Manufacturing U.S.A., was added. Children can experience traditional and modern Japan by trying on a kimono, doing origami, writing in Japanese, making a vegetable print, playing with a robot, or browsing books and watching a 7-minute videotape about Japanese life. The room may be closed to the general public on Tuesday, Wednesday, or Thursday mornings between 9:30 and 11:30 when special 1-hour programs for school groups are scheduled. On weekdays during the school year docents usually give the school programs, but on Saturdays and during the summers it is staffed with teenage Explainers who encourage visitor participation. Curiosity Corner is a reflection of the institution's continued commitment to children. Founded in June 1944 with the help of John Ripley Forbes, it opened in October 1945 as the Nashville Children's Museum in a historic 1853 building. In 1974, when the museum moved into a larger facility, its name was changed to Cumberland Museum and Science Center to reflect more diverse programming and an enlarged audience. Besides the permanent and temporary exhibits, live animals, computer lab and classes, planetarium, outreach programs, and clubs, there are in-service programs for teachers. There is a full-time staff of 27 assisted by over 200 volunteers. The museum is open Tuesday through Saturday 9:30–5:00, Sunday 12:30–5:30, and closed Monday (except in June, July, and August) and major holidays. Private funding provides 85 percent of the museum's support, and the rest comes from admissions and governmental sources. There were approximately 165,000 visitors last year, 42,000 of them schoolchildren.

Philbrook Crouch, "How Does the Name 'Children's Museum' Affect Finances?" *Museum News* 45, no. 9 (May 1967): 33–34; Edward Bryan Crutcher, "Museum Attendance of Children and Related Factors" (Ph.D. dissertation, George Peabody College for Teachers, 1966); "Curiosity Corner Touches the Child in All," *The Tennessean,* 19 February 1981, sec. E, pp. 1, 15; Louise Littleton Davis, *The Children's Museum of Nashville: The First Thirty Years* (Nashville: The Museum, 1973); Educational Facilities Laboratories, *Arts and the Handicapped: An Issue of Access* (New York: Educational Facilities Laboratories, 1975), p. 27: ERIC Document Reproduction Service, ED 117 829; *Educator's Guide 1982–83* (Nashville: Cumberland Museum and Science Center, [1982]).

Oak Ridge

CHILDREN'S MUSEUM OF OAK RIDGE, 461 West Outer Drive, Oak Ridge, TN 37830. The museum, founded on 11 March 1973, began as a project of local Senior Girl Scouts who believed a place was needed where adults and young people could learn together. In a little more than a decade it has grown into an educational and cultural center for the region. The museum occupies 30,000 square feet of a 54,000-square-foot building, a former elementary school built in 1943. It purchased the facility in 1983, and renovations, with the help of a National Endowment for the Humanities (NEH) Challenge Grant, are underway. Strongly oriented toward Appalachia, the collection also includes ethnic material donated by local residents, especially Liberian, Japanese, Chinese, and Korean. The museum also received material from the 1982 World's Fair. Exhibits include dolls, Indians, early medicine, pioneer living, grandma's attic, costumes, Civil War in Appalachia, early Oak Ridge, coal in Appalachia, a discovery room, rockets, Appalachian handcrafts, and gallery space. Programs revolve around the collections and exhibitions. From September through June docent-guided tours are available on weekdays by appointment. There is also a junior curator program for 6th-grade students. The museum produces curriculum materials, holds workshops, sponsors special events, and offers a wide variety of art and hobby classes on a quarterly basis for all age groups. In response to requests for learning opportunities for those who cannot attend day classes, the museum initiated a Thursday evening school in the fall of 1984. In addition, there are a regional Appalachian center library, archive and media center, and a TV news center with learning opportunities for junior and senior high students. Five full-time and 4 part-time staff members are assisted by 40 volunteers. The museum is open 9:00–5:00 weekdays and 1:30–4:30 weekends from September until mid-June. Summer hours include Tuesday evening 7:00–9:00 and closed Sunday. Support comes 16 percent from the United Way, 13 percent from classes and programs, 23 percent from rentals, 6 percent from tours, 10 percent from Oak Ridge and Anderson County Schools, 12 percent from grants, 8 percent from the museum shop, 8 percent from memberships, 1 percent from interest, and 3 percent from admissions. There are about 120,000 visitors annually, both children and adults.

Bonnie Pitman-Gelles, *Museums, Magic & Children: Youth Education in Museums* (Washington, D.C.: Association of Science-Technology Centers, 1981), pp. 122, 217; Jim Stokely and Jeff D. Johnson, eds., *An Appalachian Studies Teacher's Manual* (Oak Ridge: Children's Museum of Oak Ridge, 1981); Jim Stokely and Jeff D. Johnson, eds., *An Encyclopedia of East Tennessee* (Oak Ridge: Children's Museum of Oak Ridge, 1981); "A Touching Experience in Oak Ridge," *Southern Living* 20, no. 12 (December 1985), p. 9GA (Georgia) and p. 4SC (South Carolina).

TEXAS

Austin

AUSTIN CHILDREN'S MUSEUM, 702 Perry-Brooks Building, Austin, TX 78701. Founded in October 1983 by parents, educators, and others in the community, the museum was established to expand informal learning activities in the Central Texas region. In the fall of 1984 it began with 4 traveling exhibits in the humanities, everyday science and technology, and the human body. Currently operating as a museum without walls, it has an increasing demand for programs, multidisciplinary exhibits, and family activities. A downtown office serves as a base; a series of workshops brings small groups of families behind the scenes in laboratories, industries, and museums; and clubs and classes are in development. WHAT'S IN A TUNE began traveling in September 1985. SUN SIGNS AND SKY STORIES, a family festival focusing on the myths and sciences different cultures use to understand the sky, opened in the spring of 1986. Also scheduled is the Boston Children's Museum (see entry under UNITED STATES/Massachusetts) exhibit WHAT IF YOU COULDN'T. There are a part-time staff of 5 and about 75 volunteers. During its first 10 months it served about 14,000 children and adults. About a third of these were children under 6, a third were parents, and a third were older children. Hours vary depending upon the particular program or exhibit. No admission fees are charged for exhibits, and other fees vary with the program or activity. Support comes 40 percent from the community, 20 percent from private foundations, 35 percent from grants, and 5 percent from special benefit events.

"Austin's Children's Museum Takes Fun, Music around Town," *Austin American-Statesman*, 15 June 1985; "A Sound Smorgasbord for Kids," *Third Coast Magazine* (November 1985).

AUSTIN NATURE CENTER, 2416 Barton Springs Road, Austin, TX 78704. The Discovery Room, opened in 1973, was developed by the City Parks and Recreation Department due to community interest in the conservation of natural resources. The 20-by-30-foot facility at 401 Deep Eddy had a touch table with a variety of natural history materials, including bones, fur, feathers, skins, and mounted specimens. As a center for wildlife rehabilitation, the center had a collection of unreleasable animals available for use in on-site and outreach programs. In 1986 a Discovery Room was incorporated into the plans for new quarters expected to open in 1987. The 1,158-square-foot hands-on, participatory facility will be used as a large room or can be separated by a folding divider into 2 almost equal sections. One part will have child-sized furniture, lightweight, compartmentalized wooden boxes that focus on a single topic or concept, shelving with a lip to prevent indiscriminate exploration by younger children, and wall graphics. Trained volunteers will staff the room at all times. The other section will be for older children and adults interested in studying more extensive collections. Microscopes and magnifiers will be available and later may be added to the children's half. Volunteers will check material in and out. Both sides will have tables and chairs, carpeted risers, and the side for younger children will also have cloth-covered foam blocks. Groups will be able to schedule use of either section if they are led by an adult that has completed the training to be offered periodically for youth leaders and area educators. The Discovery Room will provide visitors the major access to the Austin Nature Center's collections. Funds for the exhibits in the new building are being provided by the Friends. The center has 8 staff members who are assisted by up to 40 volunteers a week. The Austin Nature Center is open Tuesday through Friday 8:00–5:00, Saturday 9:00–5:00, Sunday 1:00–5:00, and closed Monday. Support comes from the City of Austin Parks and Recreation Department.

"Babies and Beasties," *Soil and Water Conservation News* 5, no. 4 (July 1984): 6; "Budding Biologists Grow to Like Camp," *Austin American Statesman*, 8 September 1985, p. E4; "Fall Comes to the Nature Center," *Southern Living* 20, no. 9 (September 1985): 10, 14; Sally Y. Shelton, "The Discovery Room," Austin Nature Center, [1986] (Typewritten).

Brownsville

GLADYS PORTER ZOO, 500 Ringgold Street, Brownsville, TX 78520. The Children's Zoo is part of the nongeographic exhibits area of the 31.5-acre zoo, opened 3 September 1971, and occupies one-third acre. Displaying both domestic and wild animals, the children's zoo contains the baby animal nursery, primate playground, and a petting yard with African pygmy goats and assorted barnyard animals. Feeding is not permitted. The animal population in the children's zoo is always changing because of the nursery. The 4 full-time employees are assisted by 5 docents, and anyone 14 or older may take the training course. Docents also help with the school program and have assembled several discovery boxes using eggs, feathers, nests, horns, and snake shreds. All signs and graphics are produced in English and Spanish. The zoo is open daily from 9:00 to 1 hour before dusk. It has about 250,000 visitors a year, but no separate figures are kept on children's zoo attendance. There is an admission charge. Operating support comes 53 percent from foundations, grants, and the city and 47 percent comes from earned income. It also receives the continued support of the Earl C. Sams Foundation, which built, stocked, and equipped the Gladys Porter Zoo before giving it to the city of Brownsville.

Gladys Porter Zoo Animal Album, 2d ed. (Brownsville: Valley Zoological Society, 1983), pp. 4–5; Violet Springman, "Children's Zoo," *News from Gladys Porter Zoo* (December 1978); Violet Springman, "Gladys Porter Zoo Docent Program," *News from Gladys Porter Zoo* (December 1982).

Bryan

BRAZOS VALLEY MUSEUM, 3232 Briarcrest Drive, Bryan, TX 77802. The Discovery Room, opened in 1982, is 700 square feet and contains live animals, discovery boxes, and exhibits of interest to children. Schools use the Discovery Room, which can accommodate groups of up to 25 children. The museum, founded by the American Association of University Women in 1961, was originally known as the Junior Museum of Natural History. It broadened its audience to include adults and became the Brazos Valley Museum in 1983. The collection, which includes rocks and fossils, birds, and mammals, is used for educational purposes. The major exhibit, HOMETOWN OIL, covers the geology and technology of the petroleum business in the local area. The museum is located on a 30-acre site which remains in a natural state and contains trails. Programs on natural history are held on a regular basis. The audience is primarily young children and families, and annual attendance is 25,000. There are 4 full-time staff members, 4 more full-time in the summer, and about 20 volunteers. The museum is open Tuesday through Saturday 10:00–5:00, Sunday 1:00–5:00, and closed Monday. There is no admission charge, but for museum programs at school or the museum there is an hourly fee. The museum is privately funded.

1985–1986 School Programs, Brazos Valley Museum ([Bryan: Brazos Valley Museum, 1985]).

Dallas

DALLAS MUSEUM OF ART, 1717 North Harwood, Dallas, TX 75201. The Gateway Gallery opened on 29 January 1984 as an integral part of the museum's new building. Instrumental in the creation of the gallery was the Dallas Junior League, which for 8 years provided financial and volunteer support. The 8,500 square feet of space contains orientation areas, exhibit spaces, 2 large studios, and a multimedia library. There is interactive video and a series of 11 Discovery Boxes which contain self-directed art activities. Gateway Gallery exhibits change every 2 years. Its inaugural exhibition, LINE, COLOR, FORM AND TEXTURE—THE ELEMENTS OF ART, later traveled. INSIGHTS, an exhibit on perception and visual awareness, was installed in the summer of 1985 and will be on display through the summer of 1987. Through participatory components it teaches how to learn about art with all senses and tests the viewer's visual acumen. The Gateway Gallery offers classes, workshops, directed art activities Saturday afternoon, and demonstrations by artists Sunday afternoon. A staff of 2 supported by 80 volunteers serves an audience of 2,000 scheduled visitors and 2,500 other visitors per month. The Gallery is open 10:00–5:00 on Tuesday, Wednesday, Friday, and Saturday, 12:00–5:00 Sunday, 10:00–10:00 Thursday, and closed Mondays. Admission is free, and funding for the Gateway Gallery comes from the Dallas Museum of Art.

Gateway Gallery Gazette (Dallas: Dallas Museum of Art, 1984); *The Gateway Gallery Guide to the Elements of Art* (Dallas: Dallas Museum of Art, n.d.); Paul Rogers Harris, "Gateway Gallery Inaugural Exhibition: Line, Color, Form, and Texture," Dallas Museum of Art, 1984 (Typewritten); "Nine Lively Acres Downtown," *Time*, 13 February 1984, pp. 54, 57.

DALLAS ZOO, 621 East Clarendon Drive, Dallas, TX 75203. The Children's Zoo began in the early 1960s and had a contact area. Currently it occupies 12,000 square feet, half of it roofed, and is open during the summer season, June through mid-August. There are medium to small animals, and contact is closely supervised. Participatory exhibits focus on human/animal similarities and comparisons. "How Do You Measure Up?" has graphics the actual size of the animal, "Weighing In" includes a scale, and other current activities include "Texas Wildlife Hide and Seek," "Name that Bird," and "Junior Zookeeper." The children's classes at the zoo use the area. Staff includes an education coordinator, a keeper supervisor, 4 additional keepers in the summer (usually college students), and 2–3 volunteers per day used as interpreters. The children's zoo is currently being redesigned, and each year at least 2 exhibits will change. The renovation is expected to take 3 years. Separate attendance figures for the children's zoo, popular with the public, are not kept. The zoo is open Monday through Friday 10:00–5:00 and weekends 10:00–6:00. There is an admission to the zoo but no additional charge for the children's zoo. The zoo budget comes from city taxes with additional support coming from private donations.

P. A. Fontaine, "Braille Map of Children's Zoo at Dallas Zoo," in *International Zoo Yearbook* 7 (1967): 193, ed. Caroline Jarvis, (London: The Zoological Society of London, 1967); David M. Jenkins, "A Survey of Interactive Technologies," *AAZPA 1985 Annual Conference Proceedings*, pp. 73, 77, 80.

Houston

CHILDREN'S MUSEUM OF HOUSTON, 3201 Allen Parkway, Houston, TX 77019. Opened on 15 September 1985, the children's museum was initiated by a group of interested parents in 1980. Two temporary exhibits, KIDTECHNICS in June 1984 and OAXACA VILLAGE in February 1985, introduced Houston to the concept of a children's museum with participatory learning. The museum's first permanent facility has 11,000 square feet, 9,500 of which is display area and a classroom. Exhibits and related workshops, performances, and special events are taken from the arts, humanities, and science/technology. Besides the initial high-tech and re-created Mexican Indian village, installations included a Safeway minigrocery store (children role-play merchant and consumer), a Recycle Center, a room of collections children enjoy, and a space for rotating exhibits. In early 1986 the Mexican Indian village was replaced with a sesquicentennial exhibit, CHILDHOOD ON THE TEXAS FRONTIER, with a log cabin, store, and schoolhouse as well as artifacts. The museum anticipates 1 major thematic change per year and 3–4 enhancements of ongoing exhibits. The target audience is children, 3–12, their families and teachers. A professional staff of 9 is assisted by 200 adult and 60 junior volunteers. There is also an advisory council of 12 children. Advance reservations are required for groups, and children visiting the museum must be accompanied by an adult. Public hours are Tuesday through Thursday and Sunday 1:00–5:00, Friday 10:00–12:00, and Saturday 10:00–5:00. School tours are free with advance reservations Tuesday through Thursday 10:00–12:00. Support in 1986 is expected to come 14 percent from admissions, 7 percent from other earned income, 27 percent from individual contributions, 23 percent from foundations, 13 percent from corporate sources, 11 percent from government grants, and 5 percent from other sources. Annual attendance is projected to be 100,000.

"The Children's Museum: A Place That Encourages Kids To Look and Please Do," *Houston Post*, 1 July 1984, pp. 1G, 6G; "The Children's Museum: See, Touch, Play— A Place for Kids Opens," *Houston Post*, 13 September 1985, pp. 1E, 10E; "Museum New Kid on Block and Proud of It," *Houston Chronicle*, 10 September 1985, sec. 6, pp. 1, 4; "Profiles," *Houston* (August 1985): 51–56.

HOUSTON ZOOLOGICAL GARDENS, 1513 Outer Belt Drive, Houston, TX 77030. The Children's Zoo, opened on 15 November 1968, grew from a small pen of pettable goats to a 2.2-acre complex. It includes 2 contact areas, a hatchery, a Texas Wild Building, a 30,000-gallon aquarium with underwater viewing, 17 outside animal exhibits, a 200-seat amphitheater auditorium, and an activity area with a puppet stage. Docents assist in the interpretive program. Goat milking, wool spinning, and animal training are demonstrated, and lecture topics include local reptiles, birds of prey, and beasts of burden. Animals from the children's zoo are used in the outreach program which goes to schools and hospitalized children. The children's zoo is also used in the Wildlife Discovery Program, a cooperative venture of the Houston Independent School District and the Houston Zoo. Initiated in 1982, the program uses the zoo as a magnet school, integrating outdoor learning experiences into the 3rd-grade curriculum and bringing children of different ethnic backgrounds together. In May 1986 the children's zoo was renamed the Discovery Zoo to more clearly indicate its educational character and deemphasize the petting aspect. The classic zoo labels have been replaced with interactive displays. A Zoolab with discovery boxes, animal artifacts, and a staff member or docent to interpret was changed to a new, thematic lab that goes behind the scenes and shows the zoo from the keeper's point of view. A Texas wildlife exhibit installed in the former nursery is devoted to nocturnal animals. The 30-by-100-foot building has 9 glass-fronted cases, a video theater, and slide/tape programs; exhibits will be changed every 9 to 12 months. A buffalo bayou exhibit, made up of native fishes, has been installed in the aquarium. The Discovery Zoo has 15 full-time and 40 volunteer staff members and uses many of the 140 zoo docents. It is estimated that the children's zoo has 1,000,000 visitors annually. Open every day of the year, hours are Monday through Saturday 10:00–3:45 and Sunday 10:00–4:45. There is no admission charge. The zoo's operating expenses are paid by the city's general fund with remaining support coming from the Zoo Friends, the Zoological Society, and the Assistance League.

"Patients at the Texas Children's Hospital Are Visited," *HOU-ZOO* (October/November 1979): H4; Elyce Rodewald, "Multi-disciplinary Programming: The Wildlife Discovery Program at the Houston Zoo," *AAZPA Regional Conference Proceedings 1985*, pp. 18–19; J. E. Werler, "Children's Zoo in Houston Zoological Gardens," in *International Zoo Yearbook* 9 (1969): 66–69, ed. Joseph Lucas (London: The Zoological Society of London, 1969); *The Wildlife Discovery Program—A Third Grade Magnet School Cluster Center* (Houston: Houston Independent School District, n.d.).

San Antonio

SAN ANTONIO MUSEUM OF ART, 200 West Jones Avenue, PO Box 2601, San Antonio, TX 78229–2601. The Start Gallery, opened on 6 March 1982, was incorporated into the plans when the Lone Star Brewery was renovated for the museum. The Junior League of San Antonio provided the funding, and Margery Gordon of the Smithsonian's Explore Gallery (1974–1983) was project consultant. The 40-by-60-foot 1st-floor gallery provides an introduction to the basic elements of art with an emphasis on participation. A 7-foot-square touch wall covered with colors, shapes, and textures is designed for hands-on exploration, and a large enamel drawing surface is used for demonstrations, class projects, and individual experimentation. There are 20 Discovery Boxes, each focusing on a single topic, that include art-related materials and suggestions for projects that can be done at the museum or at home with found items. Four computers with programs in English and Spanish challenge visitors on a variety of art topics. The carpeted gallery wall provides space to exhibit works from the museum's permanent collection. There is also an amphitheater which provides a comfortable seating area for watching films, slides, or demonstrations. In November of 1985 the Start Gallery mounted a texture exhibit for the blind and sight-impaired. Workshops are offered on the history of art using works from the collection, audiovisual effects, and hands-on components. Other workshops deal with the basic elements of art. Working with the museum's educational staff, the Start Gallery has a full-time coordinator, 2 volunteer workshop leaders, and 15 docents from the San Antonio Junior League. The audience is primarily children and families. Each year there are about 12,000 children in school groups and 9,400 other visitors who drop in on an unscheduled basis. Hours are Tuesday through Saturday 10:00–5:00 with extended hours on Thursday until 9:00, Sunday 12:00–5:00, and closed Monday. There is a small admission charge, and support comes 59 percent from the San Antonio Museum Association, 40 percent from the San Antonio Junior League, and 1 percent from the Texas Commission for the Arts and Humanities.

"Creating a Tradition: Workshop Lets You Make Mexican Folk Art," *San Antonio Light*, 17 December 1985; "Museum Goes Oriental," *Express-News*, 25 February 1985, p. 4– D; Marcia Axtmann Smith, "Renewed Museums Revisited," *Museum News* 63, no. 4 (April 1985): 19–20; "START Gallery Fun for Kids of All Ages," *San Antonio Light*, [5 March 1985]; "START Gallery Opens," *News from SAMA* (San Antonio: San Antonio Museum Association Press Release, [1982]).

SAN ANTONIO ZOOLOGICAL GARDENS & AQUARIUM, 3903 North St. Mary's Street, San Antonio, TX 78212. The Children's Zoo, opened in 1982, occupies 2.8 acres and displays animals in representative habitats. Continents are presented as islands, and visitors can take a boat journey to the various parts of the world. Though the animals are best viewed from pedestrian walkways, the islands are best seen from the canals. At the entrance to the children's zoo are a visitor center, the nursery complex where many of the zoo's infant animals are raised in naturalistic environments, and the food preparation area. A board- walk crosses over a waterfowl pond and into the main exhibit section. Pelicans and cormorants are adjacent to Asian Island with its lesser pandas, muntjac deer, ducks, peafowl, and cranes. The South American continent has microhabitats with a shoreline, pond area, and a highland. Here are found squirrel monkeys, cavies, paca, capybara, llama, rhea, and agouti. There is an Everglades Swamp grass section and a boardwalk housing look-in exhibits that cannot be left in open view, a Galapagos Island, an African desert scene, and an Australian island which will include a Great Barrier Reef. The animal contact area is roofed over with a tentlike structure. It is adjacent to the zoo's large playground. A multipod education complex is used as an orientation facility for visiting groups, staff and volunteer training, and for classes, workshops, and lectures. Throughout the school year the children's zoo is used for class and group tours for more than 10,000 children. Teaching modules are available to aid teachers. In the summer there is a camp program for 150 students, and for the public, demonstrations using small animals and artifacts. The area has an education coordinator, 4 animal attendants, and 75 docents. The design of the children's zoo makes it attractive to all age groups, and it is seen by almost all of the zoo's 1,000,000 annual visitors. The zoo is open every day; summer hours are 9:30–6:30 and winter hours are 9:30–5:00. There is an admission fee, and support for 300 projects comes 90 percent from private donations and 10 percent from earned revenue.

Humane Education Projects Handbook (Ogden, UT: Junior League of Ogden, 1982), pp. 49–50: ERIC Document Reproduction Service, ED 229 247; *San Antonio Children's Zoo* (Mt. Prospect, IL: McFadzean, Everly and Associates, Park and Recreation Planning, 1979); "The San Antonio Children's Zoo," *News from the Zoo* 5, no. 5 (October 1979): 1–4.

UTAH

Salt Lake City

HOGLE ZOOLOGICAL GARDENS, 2600 Sunnyside Avenue, PO Box 8475, Salt Lake City, UT 84108. The Children's Zoo, opened during the summer of 1953, is centered around a small castle. On one side a barnyard and paddock, 50 by 100 feet, features domestic animals—donkeys, goats, and sheep—which are accessible to the public. This contact area is open daily during the spring, summer, and fall and is staffed by 5 high school or college students, who work part-time. In the summer of 1982 Zoolab opened in a 22-by-22-foot room inside the castle. It contains eggs, skins, feathers, horns and antlers, skulls, and skeletons arranged to emphasize the physiology of animals. An incubator enables visitors to observe birds' eggs hatching, and an automatic slide projector gives programs on various topics. Zoolab is open afternoons from Memorial Day until Labor Day and is staffed by 12 to 15 volunteers. Docents use both the children's zoo and Zoolab for a series of summer classes. Attendance is not recorded, but both areas are used by the general zoo visitor. The zoo has an admission charge, and support for these areas comes from the general operating budget and donations.

Rosl Kirchshofer, ed., *The World of Zoos: A Survey and Gazetteer* (New York: Viking, 1968), pp. 251–52; "Zoo Lab Opens," *Hogle Zoo News* 18, no. 3 (July 1983): 3; "Zoolab Reopens," *Hogle Zoo News* 19, no. 2 (June 1984): 3.

Springdale

ZION NATIONAL PARK, Springdale, UT 84767. The Zion Nature Center began in the summer of 1974 to provide an environmental education program for children 5–12. Initially known as the Zion Nature School, it was a cooperative effort involving the elementary education department of Southern Utah State College (SUSC), the Zion Natural History Association, and the National Park Service. SUSC thought that such a program would enhance its student teachers' chances of being hired, the Association paid the students' salaries, and the Park Service provided an unused park building. When supervisory funds were no longer available, SUSC dropped its participation, but the program has continued as a cooperative effort of the Association and the Park Service. The Old Zion Cafeteria, with a main room of about 20 by 40 feet, was renovated for educational purposes and now serves 6–12 year olds. Children are divided into 2 groups, each with its own teacher. Programs emphasize the history and natural history of Zion National Park. A ranger naturalist visits the classes each day to present a demonstration talk on some aspect of the park. In addition, the center uses a variety of touchable exhibits, and the Association has donated a small library. Three teachers are hired for ten weeks each year as employees of the Zion Natural

History Association. The program runs from June until early August. The teachers receive 1 week of area orientation and instruct 5 days a week, Tuesday through Saturday, for 9 weeks. There are 2 sessions daily, 9:00–11:30 and 1:30–4:00, with parents being responsible for their children during the lunch hour. Children may attend 1 or more sessions. Most of the children come from nearby campgrounds, motels, or the Zion Lodge. The Association pays all salaries and purchases most of the supplies, while the park provides a ranger, the building, utilities, and maintenance. There is no program fee. Approximately 1,000 children attend the center's program each year.

Janice Force DeMille, *Bushy's Secret Spot: A Child's Introduction to the Zion Nature School* (Springdale: Zion Natural History Association, 1981); "Park Activities," *Zion National Park, Utah* (Washington, D.C.: Government Printing Office, 1984); "Zion Nature Center" (Springdale: Zion National Park, n.d.) (Typewritten).

VERMONT

Essex Junction

DISCOVERY MUSEUM, 51 Park Street, Essex Junction, VT 05452. The museum was founded in October 1974 by a group of local citizens who perceived the need for supplemental educational opportunities for area children. The building, a converted home with about 1,000 square feet, has 5 major exhibit areas encompassing natural science, physical science, computers, art, and history. Programs are planned for children ages 2–12. Installations include WFUN (closed-circuit TV station to be a newscaster and forecast the weather using an official weather station), GRANDMOTHER'S ATTIC (try-on clothes), GET WELL MOTEL (health and human physiology), and an art gallery. Workshops related to the exhibits are held regularly for youth groups and the general public. Though not primarily a collection-oriented institution, the museum has a tool collection and another of mounted specimens. The museum is 1 of 2 rehabilitation centers for mammals and birds in Vermont. Initially staffed entirely by volunteers, the museum now has a paid staff of 4. Volunteers still play an active role in all aspects of the museum's operation. The floor volunteers handle their own recruitment and training, and teenage guides are now following this model for their organization. Income is generated by memberships, an admission charge for nonmembers, fund-raising events, and corporate contributions. From September through June hours are Tuesday through Friday and Sunday 1:00–4:30, Saturday 10:00–4:30. July and August hours are Tuesday through Saturday 10:00–4:30 and Sunday 1:00–4:30. The museum is always closed on Monday. Groups are welcome whenever the museum is open, but advance reservations are necessary. There are approximately 25,000 visitors per year from Vermont, northeastern New York, and the Quebec area.

Yvonne Keck Holman, "An Investigation into the Dynamics of Children's Museums: A Case Study of Selected Museums" (Ph.D. dissertation, Northern Illinois University, 1982), pp. 76, 81, 83, 85, 86, 101, 105, 108, 113, 119, 124, 125; Susan Noble, "The Discovery Museum," *Window of Vermont* 2, no. 1 (June/July 1983): 1; "Vermont's Museums," *Vermont Sunday Magazine*, 16 December 1984, pp. 5, 12.

VIRGINIA

Chesapeake

CHESAPEAKE PLANETARIUM, 300 Cedar Road, PO Box 15204, Chesapeake, VA 23320. The planetarium was established in 1962 following the launch of Sputnik, which stimulated an interest in science programs and facilities. The school system used funds made available by the National Defense Education Act (NDEA) to develop the planetarium. Opened in September 1963, it is situated in a separate building, has a 30-foot dome, and seats 120. The planetarium is used by grades K–12 and by local colleges; it also offers programs for the general public. All students grades 1–6 come once a year, and blocks of time are reserved for junior and senior high school classes. The planetarium is open weekdays 8:30–4:30 and Thursday evenings. There is 1 full-time staff member who is assisted by 3 volunteers. The planetarium receives its support from the school system, and there is no admission charge. There are 30,000 to 40,000 visitors annually.

Robert J. Hitt, *The Teacher's Planetarium Handbook* (Chesapeake: Chesapeake Public Schools, 1979); John B. Vance, "The Chesapeake Planetarium—A School and Community Venture," *Virginia Journal of Education* 58, no. 7 (March 1965): 20–21.

Norfolk

VIRGINIA ZOOLOGICAL PARK, 3500 Granby Street, Norfolk, VA 23504. The Children's Zoo, opened in 1978, is a quarter-acre farmyard with a large number of domestic animals. Besides being available to the general public, the farmyard has been used for a 4-H livestock program since 1983. This program, initially for 9–14 year olds, was expanded to include an advanced group and a group for younger children who have not previously participated. Meeting on Saturday mornings, the children's livestock program lasts 6 weeks. Beginners are restricted to the Saturday morning structured sessions, but the advanced group may come other days too. There are classes on different aspects of managing a farm, followed by cleaning the farmyard, and feeding and grooming the animals. Some animals are then available for visitor contact, with the child being responsible for the animals and interpretation. Occasional field trips are taken to operational farms, to observe sheep shearing or visit a rabbit breeder. The supervisor of animal services is assisted by 1 or 2 off-duty keepers.

In 1981 a children's garden program was started at the Virginia Zoological Park to give urban children an opportunity to experience horticulture. Park staff developed a 1-acre area into 15 10-by-10-foot plots. Children 7–11 years old may participate in the program; membership in the 4-H is required, but enrollment is free. From early March until late June weekly meetings are held at the zoo on Saturday mornings, and a midweek session is arranged to work the plots. Both vegetables and flowers are grown, classes cover a wide range of subject matter, and field trips are taken. In 1985 the children participated in a community project at a local senior citizens home. A program coordinator and the zoo horticulturist are assisted by a teen leader in directing the children's garden. Parents are encouraged to participate in both 4-H programs, and children completing the programs receive 4-H awards. The Children's Zoo and its related programs have a staff of 3 professionals who are assisted by 6 volunteers. The zoo has a small admission charge with the remaining support coming from the city, but admission every day from 10:00 to 11:00 is free. The zoo has about 400,000 visitors annually.

"Children Learn about Livestock on the Hoof," *Ledger-Star Zoom*, 10 May 1983; "Gardening for Youths Offered," *Ledger-Star Zoom*, 28 December 1983; Connie Sweet, "4-H Chapter—A Zoo Project," *AAZPA Regional Workshop Proceedings 1980*, pp. 178–79; "There's a Little Bit of Farmer in Everyone," *Ledger-Star Zoom*, 1 June 1982.

Portsmouth

CHILDREN'S MUSEUM, Court and High Streets, Portsmouth, VA 23704. The museum was founded in 1980 as a project of the Portsmouth Service League and opened with 1,600 square feet of space in the basement of the public library. In 1982 it was incorporated into the City of Portsmouth, Department of Museums. In 1985 the museum moved to the restored 1846 courthouse. The museum occupies the 2,500-square-foot ground floor and shares the building with the Fine Arts Gallery. The target audience is children 3–12. Current participatory installations include THE MAGIC EYE (optics, animation, shadows, and mirrors), THE CITY (occupational role-playing and uniforms from mail sorter, bus driver, and policeman to city planner), and HEALTHY SPACES—HELPING PLACES (dentist's and doctor's office, emergency room, and operating room). The health exhibit, sponsored by the Maryview Hospital, was designed to relieve the fears children sometimes have about medical settings and to encourage a healthy life-style. One major installation changes each year, and there is an exhibit area. The museum offers Showtime, a series of live performances, 1 show per month, during the school year. Programs have included folk singing, musicals, a vaudeville circus, folktales, and children's classic stories. In addition, there are 3 seasonal special events. Docents are available to greet visitors and help when needed, but no formal tours are given. Reservations are required for groups of more than 15, and families may come at any time. A staff of 3 is assisted by 20 volunteers. Hours are Tuesday through Saturday 9:00–5:00, Sunday 1:00–5:00, and closed Monday. The museum has about 40,000 visitors a year. There is a small admission charge, and the remaining support comes from the city of Portsmouth.

"Children's Museum Slates Program of 8 Kids' Shows," *Currents*, 17/18 September 1985, p. 12; "Rx for Knowledge: Exhibit at Children's Museum Eases Fear of Doctor, Hospital," *Virginia–Pilot and Ledger-Star*, 11 January 1986, pp. E1, E7.

Richmond

RICHMOND CHILDREN'S MUSEUM, 740 North Sixth Street, Richmond, VA 23219. Opened on 9 May 1981, the museum was established by local citizens to introduce children 3–12 to the arts and humanities. Located downtown in the old Navy Hill School acquired in 1980, the museum is 8,800 square feet. The first exhibit, BOXES, BLOCKS AND BLUEPRINTS, was an architectural installation which introduced design, structure, and craft skills and included the construction of a small house by visitors. COLOR! COLOR! COLOR! opened in October 1982 and was replaced in October 1983 by WHEN I GROW UP. With periodic changes of occupational components, it has a variety of workplaces, including a grocery, bank, TV station, drugstore, and industrial workshop. There are opportunities for adults to role-play with children. Workshops and special activities are held to complement the thematic exhibits. There are also a performing arts area and an art studio, and both are used for classes. The first traveling exhibit and a program, developed in 1983 in conjunction with the Women's Committee of the Richmond Symphony, introduced children to listening to music. In 1984 a theater troop was organized, and an exhibit on disabilities opened and later traveled. Six full-time staff members and 3 part-time program aides are assisted by volunteers. In addition, college students often work as interns as part of their studies. School groups can schedule 1-hour tours for 12 to 30 students, and packets for teachers are available. Hours are Tuesday through Friday 10:00–4:30, weekends 1:00–5:00, and closed Mondays. There is a small admission, and support comes 20 percent from earned income, 30 percent from corporate sources, 20 percent from grants, and 30 percent from donations. The 40,000 visitors a year are primarily school groups, families, and tourists.

"Children's Museum Is Russia-Richmond Art Connection," *Richmond News Leader*, 13 November 1985, p. 22; "Chinese See Supermarket, Museum," *Richmond Times-Dispatch*, 5 December 1985, sec. C, p. 1; "History of the Richmond Children's Museum," Richmond, January 1985 (Typewritten); *Richmond Children's Museum Annual Report 1984–1985* (Richmond: Richmond Children's Museum, [1985]).

SCIENCE MUSEUM OF VIRGINIA, 2500 West Broad Street, Richmond VA 23220. The Discovery Room, opened on 8 January 1977, was the museum's first exhibit area in its permanent facility, the former Broad Street Station. Established in 1970 by the Virginia General Assembly to improve public understanding and appreciation of science and technology, the museum existed for several years as a traveling exhibit, TRANSCIENCE I and later TRANSCIENCE II. Following building renovation, the first major permanent installation, CRYSTAL WORLD, opened in 1982, and in April 1983 the planetarium/space theater UNIVERSE opened. With the continued expansion of the facility, exhibitions, and programming, the Discovery Room was reshaped into a new gallery focusing on visual perception. The 2,500-square-foot area has interactive displays where visitors can experiment with illusions, perceptions, shadows, mystery boxes, and colors. There are plans for expanding the installation to include light and the eye. The exhibit, funded by the Memorial Foundation for Children and a grant from the Institute of Museum Services, was developed using a team approach. The exhibit areas are open Monday through Saturday 10:00–5:00 and Sunday 11:00–5:00. About half of the 241,000 annual visitors are school groups, and the other half are adults. The museum receives almost half of its support from the state of Virginia, 40 percent from generated revenues including admissions, 10 percent from contributions and volunteer services, and 3 percent from federal grants.

"Science Fills an Empty Train Station," *Southern Living* 18, no. 5 (May 1983): 46, 48; Elizabeth Sharpe, *Museum Research: How It Can Help You*, audiotape of panelists Paul Knappenberger, Patricia McNamara, Mary Ellen Munley, Paul Richard, Fath Davis Ruffins, and Robert Wolf, presented at meeting of the American Association of Museums, Washington, D.C., June 1984 (Shawnee Mission, KS: Vanguard Systems, 1985); Mary Timchick, ed., "Our Museum World: Science Museum of Virginia," *Explorer* 26, no. 2 (Summer 1984): 20.

WASHINGTON

Mount Vernon

BREAZEALE-PADILLA BAY INTERPRETIVE CENTER, 1043 Bayview-Edison Road, Mount Vernon, WA 98273. The Hands-On Room opened in 1982 and was recently enlarged to 1,200 square feet. There are discovery boxes, microscopes, marine life felt board, observation beehive, and quiz boards. The 11,600-acre Padilla Bay National Estuarine Sanctuary was established in 1980, and the center, built 2 years later, provides natural science education and offers opportunities for scientific research. There are exhibits of wildlife and habitats of the Padilla Bay area, and recently marine aquariums with local tidal life have been added. The center provides estuarine education curriculum for schools, youth programs for children 3–11, workshops, Sunday films, and winter kayak trips. There are 2 professional and 2 support staff members the supervisor of the Washington Conservation Corps and crew, and a part-time program assistant.

The center is open Wednesday through Sunday 10:00–5:00 and has about 25,000 visitors a year. Support comes 50 percent from the state and 50 percent from the National Oceanic and Atmospheric Administration.

Valerie Smith, "Take Part in Autumn Activities at Padilla Bay," *Washington Coastal Currents* 10, no. 5 (November 1985): 6–7.

Puyallup

PAUL H. KARSHNER MEMORIAL MUSEUM, 426 4th Street NE, Puyallup, WA 98371. The museum, founded in September 1930, is a teaching collection that is part of the Puyallup School District. It was established by Warner and Ella Karshner, in honor of their high school-age son who died of polio, with the express purpose of strengthening visual education. Initially located in the Puyallup High School, it relocated in 1965 to a 1920s brick school building with 7,000 square feet of space. The original collection of over 10,000 artifacts donated by the Karshners has been added to over the years by others in the community and is strongest in natural history, major Indian groups of North America, cultural artifacts from around the world, and local history materials. Programs are developed around the collection and are related to the curriculum and classroom studies for grades K–6. Kits are also available for use in the classroom. Beginning with kindergarten, the program areas now include "Self and Senses," "Man and Animal," "Fossils and Dinosaurs," "Indians in America," "Comparing Cultures," "Trade and Barter," and "Technology in Textiles." Exhibits are changed annually. There is also a library with rare books, periodicals, maps, documents, photographs, and original manuscripts. There are 2 paid staff members who are assisted by 4 volunteers. The museum is open 9:00–3:00 on school days and has approximately 6,000 elementary-age students annually for 350 classes. Community groups and local parochial schools and preschools are also allowed to visit the museum. Each spring there is an open house, and 2 public programs are held annually. Support comes from the school district and trust funds.

Paul H. Karshner Memorial Museum: A Teaching Museum of Puyallup Public Schools (Puyallup: Puyallup Public School District, [1984]).

Seattle

SEATTLE CHILDREN'S MUSEUM, Seattle Center, 305 Harrison, Seattle, WA 98109. Started in 1979 by a group of parents and educators, the museum began operating in December 1980. The founders were interested in developing a learning place for children and an educational resource center for parents and teachers. One exhibit, MINI CITY, toured the Seattle Public Library system, and another, A CHINESE CHILDREN'S PLACE, was installed at Seattle's

Wing Luke Museum. On 6 June 1981 the museum opened in a 2,200-square-foot facility in Pioneer Square. To highlight the ethnic diversity of the Pacific Northwest, the museum focused on the Chinese, Japanese, and Filipino cultures and produced activity books in support of its other activities. Outreach kits for classroom and group use were developed, and more are in process. In 1984 the search began for a larger facility to meet the increasing demand for programs and services. On 31 October 1985 the Seattle Children's Museum opened in its new 6,500-square-foot facility with 3 permanent exhibits. PLAYCENTER is both a play area for infants and toddlers and a resource center for adults. It has a community advisory board that reflects the ethnic and cultural diversity of the region. THE NEIGHBORHOOD has 2 houses, 1 with cutaway sections where children can build and repair, and the other a doctor's office. A schoolroom and fire station form another part of the neighborhood, which also includes a business district with a restaurant, grocery store, and bank, and city services such as telephone and electric company, post office, bus, police car, and traffic light. There are uniforms of various city workers to encourage occupational role-playing. Children can imitate what they have observed adults do by earning money, cashing checks, and buying goods and services. CURIOSITY CORNER includes natural history discovery materials, activity kits, and collections. An expanded version of an exhibit from the Pioneer Square location, BUBBLES, was moved to the new facility. In addition, the museum has gallery space and a seminar area. There are 9 full-time and 5 part-time professional staff members and a corps of 30 volunteers. The target audience is children under 9. There are no special hours for schools. The museum is open Wednesday through Saturday 9:30–5:00, Sunday 12:00–5:00, and closed Monday and Tuesday. Support comes 75 percent from admissions, fees, and memberships and 25 percent from private and corporate sources. In 1984 30,000 visitors came to the museum, and anticipated attendance in the new facility is expected to triple.

Charles A. Paxton, "The Children's Museum," *Puget Soundings* (December 1983): 45–46; "Small World: Seattle Children's Museum Opens Its Fun-Filled New Home at Seattle Center," *Seattle Times*, 1 November 1985, sec. E, pp. 1, 3; "Touch-and-Do Museum for Children Growing Up," *Seattle Post-Intelligencer*, 26 October 1985, sec. C, pp. 1, 2; Kathleen M. Wilson, "Seattle Children's Museum," *Going Places* (January 1986): 9; "Wow! A Museum for Kids Only," *Seattle Times Pacific*, 6 December 1981, pp. 23–24, 26–27, 29–30.

Tacoma

TACOMA ART MUSEUM, 12th and Pacific Avenue, Tacoma, WA 98402. The Children's Gallery was incorporated into the building plan when a 1920 bank building was converted to an art museum in 1971. Located in the basement, the 58-by-32-foot gallery includes a children's audiovisual theater in what was once a large vault. The area was maintained by Junior League for its first 2 years. Currently the gallery sponsors 2 exhibitions annually. The major exhibit is scheduled during the school year, and almost all of the exhibits are on loan. The themes change yearly, but all relate art to science or the humanities and have included EARTH, WATER, WIND AND FIRE, and DRAGONS, GARGOYLES, ETC. During the summer months art produced by local schoolchildren is displayed. Multimedia programs which include hands-on experiences and walk-through environments are offered, but no classes are held in the gallery. The head of education is assisted by approximately 25 volunteers. There are about 15,000 visitors per year. The Children's Gallery is open Monday through Saturday 10:00–4:00 and Sunday 12:00–5:00. Funding comes from the museum, which is supported by memberships and grants.

"December Is a Month for Children in the Puget Sound Area," *Sunset* 167 (December 1981): 32; "Dragons in Tacoma? Friendly Ones," *Sunset* 170 (January 1983): 6; Marcia Axtmann Smith, "Renewed Museums Revisited," *Museum News* 63, no. 4 (April 1985): 21; Marcia Axtmann Smith, "A Sound Investment: Tacoma Art Museum," *Museum News* 59, no. 1 (September 1980): 63–65.

WISCONSIN

Madison

MADISON CHILDREN'S MUSEUM, 1 North Bedford Street, Madison, WI 53703. The museum was founded in November 1980 by leaders in early childhood education and day care who felt Madison needed a children's museum like those in other cities. During the summers of 1981, 1982, and 1983 the museum built and sponsored traveling exhibits. On Saturdays during the winter and spring of 1981–1982 and 1982–1983 a pilot museum was operated in a 400-square-foot donated space. In the spring of 1983 a grant was received for an exhibit, a permanent site was located, and fund-raising was initiated. The museum opened on 1 April 1985 in a former warehouse. The facility has about 2,500 square feet of exhibit and demonstration space on the ground floor. The target audience is children 3–13, and a toddler area is being developed. Currently there is no collection, and exhibits will change every 9–15 months. Installations have included KIDS DAY SURGERY, IT'S PUZZLING (brainteasers, illusions, and computer games), IN TOUCH WITH INDIA (part of the official festival of India), and HOW HEAT GETS AROUND (an energy conservation exhibit). Workshops and special programs for children and adults are in the planning stage. The museum coordinator is assisted by part-time work-study students, interns, and 15 youth and 30 adult volunteers. Summer hours are Tuesday through Friday 1:00–4:00, Saturday 9:00–4:00, Sunday 1:00–4:00, and closed Monday. Groups of 10 or more children may visit the museum Wednesday through Friday mornings between 9:30 and 12:00 by prior arrangement. Winter hours are Friday and Saturday 9:30–4:30, Sunday 1:00–4:30, and Madison school holidays. Group visits are scheduled Tuesday through Thursday. There is a small admission fee, and support comes 50 percent from admissions and memberships, 40 percent from contributions and foundation grants, and 10 percent from government grants. About 2,000 people per month visit the Madison Children's Museum.

"At One Madison Museum, Learning Is Child's Play," *Milwaukee Journal*, 29 September 1985, p. 4; "Museum Needs Hand," *Wisconsin State Journal*, 8 November 1984, sec. 4, p. 1.

Milwaukee

MILWAUKEE COUNTY ZOOLOGICAL GARDENS, 10001 West Bluemound Road, Milwaukee, WI 53226. The Children's Zoo, opened on 15 July 1971, was the first nonanimal funding project undertaken by the Milwaukee County Zoological Society. The 6.2-acre facility initially had a circus theme and included a petting ring and 8 major exhibits. Gradually it has evolved into an educational facility with recreational areas and entertainment. Featuring North American domestic and wild animals, the zoo has a miniature farm, goat yard, chick hatchery, free-flight birdhouse, and petting ring which is a contact area. Visitors are encouraged to feed the goats and other farm animals with pellets sold in the children's zoo. There are peek holes to view minicritters, and touch carts with animal artifacts have been used. In the Discovery Center, opened in 1980, programs are offered including "Wild World of Wisconsin" for families with children 6 and older. It is presented 6 times per day, Monday through Saturday. The children's zoo is used in conjunction with the zoo's summer programs and includes a stage-bleacher facility seating 300. A birds-of-prey program was given in the children's zoo theater 3 times a day during the summer of 1985 and was repeated during the 1986 season. In addition, there are free mimecircus and magic shows. Construction began in March 1986 on a year-round, high-tech dairy complex to feature the dairy industry and its products. The facility will consist of 3 interconnected modules and include a cow barn and milking parlor, authentic 1896 Wisconsin octagonal barn (65 feet across with 3,400 square feet of floor space) housing an education center with participatory exhibits, and a dairy store with products for sale. This new dairy center is designed to serve all ages and will be available to school classes. The Children's Zoo is open Monday through Saturday 9:30–4:30 and Sundays and holidays 9:30–5:30 from Memorial Day through Labor Day. There are 2 full-time and 14 seasonal staff members. The zoo has an admission fee, but there is no additional charge for the Children's Zoo. Support comes from Milwaukee County and the Milwaukee County Zoological Society. The children's zoo has an annual attendance of approximately 600,000.

"Committee OKs Offer on Children's Zoo," *Milwaukee Journal*, 10 December 1970, p. 2; "Construction Set to Begin on High-Tech Dairy Complex," *Alive* (Fall 1985): 12–13; *Milwaukee County Zoo* (Milwaukee: Milwaukee County Zoo, [1985]), pp. 2, 3, 4,

30–31, 35; "Milwaukee Zoological Society Again Comes to the Rescue," *Milwaukee Journal*, 9 December 1970; "Speidel's Latest Masterwork: The Children's Zoo," *Zoological Society of Milwaukee County News Bulletin* 29 (August 1971): 1.

MILWAUKEE PUBLIC MUSEUM, 800 West Wells, Milwaukee, WI 53233. The Youth Center, opened in 1965 as a place for hands-on activities, evolved into the Discovery Center. The Center was initially oriented towards groups of children but later expanded to include participatory activities for families through the "Touch-Me-Do" program, which was available for 5 days in July 1975. There were casual activities similar to those found in a discovery room and a treasure hunt in a nearby exhibit. The Friends of the Museum began providing financial support the following year; the program ran for 4 weeks, Monday through Friday; and week-long themes were introduced that related to topics of current interest. This program became "Touch-Do-Discover" and offered expanded opportunities in the form of self-discovery activities and workshops. Musement Park, an area for children 4–7, opened in 1977 and was initially funded by the Junior League. Since 1980 the Friends of the Museum have continued the project. Park themes changed often and included communication, health, house building, and insect life. In November 1985 the 12,000-square-foot Wizard Wing opened; it includes the Discovery Center, Musement Park, theme section, and Pioneer Homestead. The Discovery Center now includes a culture quiz that uses artifacts from around the world, discovery boxes with natural history materials and artifacts, a collector's corner, and a wizardwood tree featuring information on the relationship between animals, insects, and the Wisconsin lumber industry. There are also books, games that the family can play together, and handouts. The theme section focuses on air, and Musement Park, now an area for 4–8 year olds, will have the same theme for the next 3 years. There is a staff of 4. Wizard Wing is suitable for small groups of 6–8 children with an adult and for family groups. School groups need a reservation for Musement Park. Hours are 10:00–3:00 daily. The general museum admission includes Wizard Wing, which was established with various grants and support from the Friends of the Museum. This new permanent exhibit area continues a tradition first initiated by the museum in about 1917 when, under Henry L. Ward, a special children's room was established. Though this children's room was short-lived, another was opened in 1925, again for a brief time.

"Air Takes Wing at the Museum: You'll See, Touch, Learn at Wizard Wing Displays," *Milwaukee Journal*, 4 November 1985, pp. 1, 7; Gerald T. Johnson, "Beyond Visual Learning," *Lore* 30, no. 2 (Summer 1980): 2–15; Nancy Oestreich Lurie, *A Special Style: The Milwaukee Public Museum 1882–1982* (Milwaukee: Milwaukee Public Museum, 1983), pp. 50, 61, 72, 112, 132; "The Milwaukee Public Museum's New Permanent Exhibition Area—The Wizard Wing," *Museum News* 64, no. 1 (October 1985): 77; Bonnie Pitman-Gelles, *Museums, Magic & Children: Youth Education in Museums* (Washington, D.C.: Association of Science-Technology Centers, 1981), pp. 118, 155.

VENEZUELA

CARACAS

MUSEO DE LOS NIÑOS (The Children's Museum), Parque Central, Edificio Tacagua, Apartado de Correos 14029, Candelaria, Caracas 1011A. The museum opened to the public on 7 August 1982 after almost a decade of planning. Recognizing the need for a new educational alternative for children and youth, the Children's Museum Foundation was formed in March 1974. The initial planning phase lasted until 1978, and in 1979 the Foundation implemented a program to secure financial support and locate an appropriate site. The Venezuelan government expressed an interest in the project and leased a building under construction in the central zone of Caracas. The staff was then hired and training visits were made to several institutions including the Exploratorium in San Francisco, the Boston Children's Museum (see entries under UNITED STATES/CALIFORNIA and MASSACHUSETTS), and the Ontario Science Center in Toronto, Canada. Upon returning to Venezuela, the staff formulated plans to focus on 4 basic areas: physics, biology, communications, and ecology. At the same time, architects and designers were adapting the building. There are 4,000 square meters of space on 4 levels; 3,000 square meters are devoted to participatory exhibits. The 67 biology displays encompass the body, brain, reproduction, microscopy, and health. To foster an understanding of communication as a human process, 53 exhibits cover language, the printed word, feedback, telephones, cordless transmission, television, computation, and photography. Ecology has 100 installations, including live animals and plants. The 150 physical science exhibits encompass light and color, perception, physics, mechanics, electricity, sound, and petroleum. The AUDIOVISUAL MAP OF VENEZUELA (a small theater) takes children on an imaginary trip through space to a country called Venezuela. The program acquaints children with the different regions of the country. In the "Exploring the Museum" program, guidesheets of 3 levels represented by 3 different colors provide information on the exhibits. Space is also available for temporary installations. The museum is for all children and hopes to reach out to those who have limited access to education. Though the target audience is children 7–13, some areas are suitable for younger children, and secondary school students have also become interested in the museum. Groups must make a reservation 2 weeks in advance. There are about 1,000 visitors a day, mainly schools, clubs, and family groups. The museum has a staff of 65 and 150 student guides. There is an admission charge, and support comes from the government, businesses, corporations, private institutions, and citizens.

"The Children's Museum of Caracas: A New Alternative in Education through Recreation," Caracas, [1983] (Typewritten); *Museo de los Niños* (Caracas: ARS Publicidad, [1982]).

ZIMBABWE

MARANDELLAS

MARONDERA CHILDREN'S LIBRARY MUSEUM, The Green, Marandellas. The museum was founded in 1970 by local residents who wanted a place
to display their private collections. Stone- and Iron-Age tools, pottery, and natural
history specimens, including butterflies, moths, birds, mammals, shells, rocks
and minerals, are exhibited. The collections are housed in a 17-by-25-foot room.
School classes come to the museum, and children also visit on their own. The
library staff maintains the children's museum with funds left for its upkeep by
an adult museum club no longer in existence. The library is open Tuesday through
Saturday 9:00–1:00 and 2:00–5:00.

Appendix 1
ALPHABETICAL LISTING
OF INSTITUTIONS

The Academy of Natural Sciences, Philadelphia, PA
African Lion Safari, Cambridge, ON, Canada
Akron Zoological Park, Akron, OH
Alexander Lindsay Junior Museum, Walnut Creek, CA
The American Museum of Natural History, New York, NY
The Ann Arbor Hands-On Museum, Ann Arbor, MI
Arizona Museum for Youth, Mesa, AZ
Art Gallery of Ontario, Toronto, ON, Canada
The Art Institute of Chicago, Chicago, IL
Audubon Park and Zoological Garden, New Orleans, LA
Austin Children's Museum, Austin, TX
Austin Nature Center, Austin, TX
Australian Science and Technology Centre, Canberra
Balzekas Museum of Lithuanian Culture, Chicago, IL
Bergen Museum of Art and Science, Paramus, NJ
Bernice Pauahi Bishop Museum, Honolulu, HI
Bethnal Green Museum of Childhood, London
Bode Museum, Berlin, German Democratic Republic
Brazos Valley Museum, Bryan, TX
Breazeale-Padilla Bay Interpretive Center, Mount Vernon, WA

The Brevard Museum, Cocoa, FL

Bronx Zoo, Bronx, NY

Brookfield Zoo, Brookfield, IL

Brooklyn Botanic Garden, Brooklyn, NY

The Brooklyn Children's Museum, Brooklyn, NY

Buffalo Museum of Science, Buffalo, NY

Buffalo Zoological Gardens, Buffalo, NY

Burnet Park Zoo, Syracuse, NY

The Calgary Zoo, Calgary, AL, Canada

California Academy of Sciences, San Francisco, CA

Capital Children's Museum, Washington, D.C.

Carl G. Fenner Arboretum, Lansing, MI

Center of Science and Industry (COSI), Columbus, OH

Chesapeake Planetarium, Chesapeake, VA

Chicago Historical Society, Chicago, IL

The Children's Discovery Museum, Acton, MA

Children's Discovery Museum of San Jose, San Jose, CA

Children's Museum, Boston, MA

Children's Museum, Detroit, MI

The Children's Museum, Hamilton, ON, Canada

The Children's Museum, Indianapolis, IN

Children's Museum, Lucknow, India

Children's Museum, Portsmouth, VA

The Children's Museum, Saint Paul, MN

The Children's Museum, South Dartmouth, MA

Children's Museum, Utica, NY

Children's Museum of Denver, Denver, CO

Children's Museum of Houston, Houston, TX

Children's Museum of Maine, Portland, ME

The Children's Museum of Manhattan, New York, NY

Children's Museum of Oak Ridge, Oak Ridge, TN

Children's Museum of Portsmouth, Portsmouth, NH

The Children's Museum of Rhode Island, Pawtucket, RI

The Children's Museum of San Diego, La Jolla, CA

The Children's Museum of Washington, Washington, D.C.

Chippewa Nature Center, Midland, MI

Cincinnati Art Museum, Cincinnati, OH

Cincinnati Zoo, Cincinnati, OH

Cité des Sciences et des Industries (La Villette), Paris, France

Cleveland Children's Museum, Cleveland, OH

Cleveland Health Education Museum, Cleveland, OH

Cobb County Youth Museum, Marietta, GA

Columbus Zoo, Powell, OH

Connecticut Children's Museum, New Haven, CT

Cora Hartshorn Arboretum, Short Hills, NJ

Cortland County Historical Society, Cortland, NY

Cranbrook Institute of Science, Bloomfield Hills, MI

Cumberland Museum and Science Center, Nashville, TN

Cylburn Nature Museum, Baltimore, MD

DAR Museum, Washington, D.C.

Dallas Museum of Art, Dallas, TX

Dallas Zoo, Dallas, TX

Delaware Museum of Natural History, Greenville, DE

Delaware Nature Education Society, Hockessin, DE

Des Moines Science Center, Des Moines, IA

The Discovery Center, Fort Lauderdale, FL

The Discovery Center, Syracuse, NY

Discovery Center Museum of Rockford, Rockford, IL

The Discovery Center of the Southern Tier, Binghamton, NY

Discovery Museum, Essex Junction, VT

The Discovery Place, Birmingham, AL

Discovery Theater of the Smithsonian Institution, Washington, D.C.

The Edmonton Art Gallery, Edmonton, AL, Canada

The Eugene Field House and Toy Museum, Saint Louis, MO

Evoluon, Eindhoven, Netherlands

The Exploratorium, San Francisco, CA

Express-Ways Children's Museum, Chicago, IL

Field Museum of Natural History, Chicago, IL

Florida State Museum, Gainesville, FL

Fort Wayne Children's Zoo, Fort Wayne, IN

Franklin Institute Science Museum, Philadelphia, PA

Gladys Porter Zoo, Brownsville, TX

Glen Oak Zoo, Peoria, IL

Government Museum, Madras, India

Granby Zoo, Granby, PQ, Canada

Hatfield Marine Science Center of Oregon State University, Newport, OR

The Health Adventure, Asheville, NC

High Museum of Art, Atlanta, GA

Hilltop, The Bloomington Youth Garden–Nature Center, Bloomington, IN

Himeji City Aquarium, Himeji City, Japan

Hiroshima City Culture & Science Museum for Children, Hiroshima, Japan

Hogle Zoological Gardens, Salt Lake City, UT

Houston Zoological Gardens, Houston, TX

Illinois State Museum, Springfield, IL

International Museum of Photography at George Eastman House, Rochester, NY

The Israel Museum, Jerusalem

Jackson Zoological Park, Jackson, MS

Jacksonville Museum of Arts and Sciences, Jacksonville, FL

James Ford Bell Museum of Natural History, Minneapolis, MN

John Ball Zoological Gardens, Grand Rapids, MI

Josephine D. Randall Junior Museum, San Francisco, CA

Judges' Lodgings Museum of Childhood, Lancaster, Great Britain

Kamloops Public Art Gallery, Kamloops, BC, Canada

Kidspace, Pasadena, CA

Kindermuseum TM Junior, Amsterdam, Netherlands

Knoxville Zoological Park, Knoxville, TN

Kohl Children's Museum, Wilmette, IL

La Habra Children's Museum, La Habra, CA

Lawrence Hall of Science, Berkeley, CA

Lilford Park, Peterborough, Great Britain

Lincoln Park Zoo, Chicago, IL

The Living Arts and Science Center, Lexington, KY

London Regional Children's Museum, London, ON, Canada

Lori Brock Junior Museum, Bakersfield, CA

Los Angeles Children's Museum, Los Angeles, CA

Louisiana Arts and Science Center, Baton Rouge, LA

Louisiana Nature and Science Center, New Orleans, LA

Louisville Art Gallery, Louisville, KY

Louisville Zoological Garden, Louisville, KY

Lutz Children's Museum, Manchester, CT

Madison Children's Museum, Madison, WI

The Magic House, Saint Louis, MO

Marondera Children's Library Museum, Marandellas, Zimbabwe

Memphis Brooks Museum of Art, Memphis, TN

Mesker Park Zoo, Evansville, IN

Metrozoo, Miami, FL

Miami Youth Museum, Miami, FL

Miller Park Zoo, Bloomington, IL

Milwaukee County Zoological Gardens, Milwaukee, WI

Milwaukee Public Museum, Milwaukee, WI

Minnesota Historical Society, Saint Paul, MN

Miramont Castle, Manitou Springs, CO

Monmouth Museum, Lincroft, NJ

Monterey Bay Aquarium, Monterey, CA

Morioka Children's Museum of Science, Morioka, Japan

Muncie Children's Museum, Muncie, IN

Le Musée des Enfants/Het Kindermuseum, Brussels, Belgium

Museo de los Niños, Caracas, Venezuela

Museum of Natural History, Regina, SK, Canada

Museum of Science, Boston, MA

Museum of Science and Industry, Chicago, IL

Museum of Scientific Discovery, Harrisburg, PA

Museum für Völkerkunde, Berlin, Federal Republic of Germany

National Aquarium in Baltimore, Baltimore, MD

National Centre for Children's and Young People's Art, Yerevan, USSR

National Children's Museum, New Delhi, India

National Museum of American History (Smithsonian), Washington, D.C.

National Museum of Natural History, New Delhi, India

National Museum of Natural History (Smithsonian), Washington, D.C.

National Science Museum, Tokyo, Japan

National Zoological Park (Smithsonian), Washington, D.C.

Nature Science Center, Winston-Salem, NC

Naturhistorisches Museum, Vienna, Austria

Nehru Children's Museum, Calcutta, India

New Britain Youth Museum, New Britain, CT

New England Aquarium, Boston, MA

New York Aquarium, Brooklyn, NY

The Newark Museum, Newark, NJ

Noorder Dierenpark Zoo, Emmen, Netherlands

North Carolina Museum of History, Raleigh, NC

Oatland Island Education Center, Savannah, GA

Oklahoma City Zoo, Oklahoma City, OK

Old State House Museum, Little Rock, AR

Omaha Children's Museum, Omaha, NE

Omniplex, Oklahoma City, OK

Ontario County Historical Society, Canandaigua, NY

Parque Zoologico Benito Juarez, Morelia, Mexico

Paul H. Karshner Memorial Museum, Puyallup, WA

Philadelphia Zoological Society, Philadelphia, PA

Phoenix Art Museum, Phoenix, AZ

The Pittsburgh Children's Museum, Pittsburgh, PA

Please Touch Museum, Philadelphia, PA

Plymouth Historical Museum, Plymouth, MI

Portland Children's Museum, Portland, OR

Rensselaer County Junior Museum, Troy, NY

Richmond Children's Museum, Richmond, VA

Rio Grande Zoological Park, Albuquerque, NM

Rock Creek Nature Center, Washington, D.C.

Roger Williams Park Zoo, Providence, RI

Rose Hill Manor Children's Museum, Frederick, MD

Royal Ontario Museum (ROM), Toronto, ON, Canada

Sacramento Science Center and Junior Museum, Sacramento, CA

Saginaw Children's Zoo, Saginaw, MI

Saint Louis Science Center, Saint Louis, MO

Saint Louis Zoological Park, Saint Louis, MO

San Antonio Museum of Art, San Antonio, TX

San Antonio Zoological Gardens & Aquarium, San Antonio, TX

San Francisco Zoological Gardens, San Francisco, CA

Schuylkill Valley Nature Center, Philadelphia, PA

Science Museum, Bangkok, Thailand

Science Museum, London

Science Museum of Connecticut, West Hartford, CT

Science Museum of Virginia, Richmond, VA

Science Museums of Charlotte, Charlotte, NC

Scotia-Glenville Children's Museum, Scotia, NY

Seattle Children's Museum, Seattle, WA

Seneca Falls Historical Society, Seneca Falls, NY

Shri Girdharbhai Children's Museum, Amreli, India

Singapore Zoological Gardens, Singapore

Siouxland Heritage Museums, Sioux Falls, SD

Sotome Museum of Child, Sotome, Japan

The South Florida Science Museum, West Palm Beach, FL

Staatliche Kunsthalle Karlsruhe, Karlsruhe, Federal Republic of Germany

Staten Island Children's Museum, Staten Island, NY

Sveriges Tekniska Museum, Stockholm, Sweden

Tacoma Art Museum, Tacoma, WA

Tallahassee Junior Museum, Tallahassee, FL

The Tampa Museum, Tampa, FL

Taronga Zoo, Sydney, Australia

The Thornton W. Burgess Museum, Sandwich, MA

Toledo Zoological Gardens, Toledo, OH

Topeka Zoological Park, Topeka, KS

University of Nebraska State Museum, Lincoln, NE

U.S. Army Field Artillery & Fort Sill Museum, Fort Sill, OK

Valley Zoo, Edmonton, AL, Canada

Vestlandske Skolemuseum, Stavanger, Norway

Virginia Zoological Park, Norfolk, VA

Washington Park Zoo, Portland, OR

Wetlands Institute, Stone Harbor, NJ

Wichita Art Association, Wichita, KS

Wichita Art Museum, Wichita, KS

Wichita Public Schools, Wichita, KS

Wildlife Safari, Winston, OR

Youth Museum of Charlotte County, Punta Gorda, FL

Zion National Park, Springdale, UT

Appendix 2
CHRONOLOGICAL LISTING OF INSTITUTIONS

If the children's museum or facility included in the book was established under another institutional name(s), it is given following the current name. All previous and current institutional names appear in the index. When a few years lapsed between founding and the first program or exhibit, the latter date is given.

1899	The Brooklyn Children's Museum
1913	Children's Museum, Boston
1914	Brooklyn Botanic Garden
1917	Children's Museum, Detroit
1925	The Children's Museum, Indianapolis
1925	Vestlandske Skolemuseum
1926	The Newark Museum
1927	Science Museum of Connecticut (formerly Children's Museum of Hartford)
1930	Paul H. Karshner Memorial Museum
1931	Science Museum, London
1934	Franklin Institute Science Museum
1936	The Eugene Field House and Toy Museum
1937	Josephine D. Randall Junior Museum (formerly Junior Recreation Museum)
1938	Philadelphia Zoological Society
1941	Bronx Zoo

1942	The Children's Museum of Washington
1947	Science Museums of Charlotte (formerly Charlotte Children's Nature Museum and later Charlotte Nature Museum)
1948	Hilltop, The Bloomington Youth Garden–Nature Center
1949	Portland Children's Museum
1950	Cincinnati Zoo
1950	Louisville Art Gallery (formerly Louisville Junior Art Gallery)
1951	Sacramento Science Center and Junior Museum (formerly California Junior Museum and later Sacramento Junior Museum)
1952	Akron Zoological Park (formerly Akron Children's Zoo)
1952	The Children's Museum, South Dartmouth
1952	Lincoln Park Zoo
1953	Brookfield Zoo
1953	Granby Zoo
1953	Hogle Zoological Gardens
1953	John Ball Zoological Gardens
1953	Lutz Children's Museum
1953	Toledo Zoological Gardens
1954	The American Museum of Natural History
1954	Cylburn Nature Museum
1954	Rensselaer County Junior Museum
1955	Alexander Lindsay Junior Museum (formerly Diablo Junior Museum)
1955	Burnet Park Zoo
1955	San Francisco Zoological Gardens
1955	Shri Girdharbhai Children's Museum
1956	Glen Oak Zoo
1956	New Britain Youth Museum
1956	Rock Creek Nature Center
1957	Children's Museum, Lucknow
1957	Crandon Park Zoo
1957	Saginaw Children's Zoo
1957	Tallahassee Junior Museum
1959	Valley Zoo
1960	Government Museum, Madras
1961	National Children's Museum, New Delhi
1961	Rio Grande Zoological Park
1961	Seneca Falls Historical Society
1962	Chesapeake Planetarium

1962	Cora Hartshorn Arboretum
1962	Dallas Zoo
1962	Washington Park Zoo
1963	Children's Museum, Utica
1964	The Art Institute of Chicago
1964	Oklahoma City Zoo
1965	Fort Wayne Children's Zoo
1965	Hatfield Marine Science Center of Oregon State University
1965	Milwaukee Public Museum
1965	Phoenix Art Museum
1966	Buffalo Zoological Gardens
1966	Evoluon
1966	The Health Adventure
1966	The Israel Museum
1967	Cortland County Historical Society
1967	Saginaw Children's Zoo
1968	High Museum of Art
1968	Houston Zoological Gardens
1968	The Living Arts and Science Center
1968	James Ford Bell Museum of Natural History
1968	Lawrence Hall of Science
1968	Schuylkill Valley Nature Center
1969	The Edmonton Art Gallery
1969	The Exploratorium
1969	Louisville Zoological Garden
1969	New England Aquarium
1969	Saint Louis Zoological Park
1969	Youth Museum of Charlotte County
1970	The Calgary Zoo
1970	Cobb County Youth Museum
1970	Marondera Children's Library Museum
1970	Minnesota Historical Society
1970	Museum für Völkerkunde
1970	National Centre for Children's and Young People's Art
1971	African Lion Safari
1971	Gladys Porter Zoo
1971	Tacoma Art Museum
1971	Milwaukee County Zoological Gardens

1971	Wichita Art Association
1972	Chicago Historical Society
1972	Cleveland Health Education Museum
1972	Columbus Zoo
1972	Lilford Park
1972	Miller Park Zoo
1972	Nehru Children's Museum
1972	New York Aquarium
1972	Rose Hill Manor Children's Museum
1972	Wetlands Institute
1972	Wildlife Safari
1973	Austin Nature Center
1973	Children's Museum of Denver
1973	The Children's Museum of Manhattan (formerly G.A.M.E. and later Manhattan Laboratory Museum)
1973	Children's Museum of Oak Ridge
1973	Connecticut Children's Museum
1973	Singapore Zoological Gardens
1973	Staatliche Kunsthalle Karlsruhe
1974	Art Gallery of Ontario
1974	Bethnal Green Museum of Childhood
1974	Bode Museum
1974	Discovery Museum
1974	Florida State Museum
1974	National Museum of Natural History (Smithsonian)
1974	Oatland Island Education Center
1974	Zion National Park
1975	Kindermuseum TM Junior
1975	Knoxville Zoological Park
1975	Memphis Brooks Museum of Art (formerly Brooks Memorial Art Gallery)
1975	Mesker Park Zoo
1975	Omaha Children's Museum
1975	Taronga Zoo
1975	Wichita Public Schools
1976	The Discovery Center (FL)
1976	Field Museum of Natural History
1976	Judges' Lodgings Museum of Childhood

1976	London Regional Children's Museum
1976	Lori Brock Junior Museum
1976	Le Musée des Enfants/Het Kindermuseum
1976	Please Touch Museum
1976	Staten Island Children's Museum
1977	California Academy of Sciences
1977	Capital Children's Museum
1977	Children's Museum of Maine
1977	The Children's Museum of Rhode Island
1977	Discovery Theater of the Smithsonian Institution
1977	Jackson Zoological Park
1977	Jacksonville Museum of Arts and Sciences
1977	Le Habra Children's Museum
1977	Muncie Children's Museum
1977	National Zoological Park (Smithsonian)
1977	Naturhistorisches Museum
1977	Royal Ontario Museum (ROM)
1977	Science Museum of Virginia
1978	Chippewa Nature Center
1978	The Children's Museum, Hamilton
1978	Monmouth Museum
1978	Museum of Science, Boston
1978	National Museum of Natural History, New Delhi
1978	Virginia Zoological Park (formerly Lafayette Zoological Park)
1979	The Academy of Natural Sciences
1979	Bernice Pauahi Bishop Museum
1979	Kamloops Public Art Gallery
1979	Los Angeles Children's Museum
1979	The Magic House
1979	Science Museum, Bangkok
1979	Scotia-Glenville Children's Museum
1979	The Tampa Museum
1980	Audubon Park and Zoological Garden
1980	Australian Science and Technology Centre (formerly Questacon Science Project)
1980	The Brevard Museum
1980	Buffalo Museum of Science
1980	Children's Museum, Portsmouth, VA

1980	Cincinnati Art Museum
1980	Hiroshima City Culture & Science Museum for Children
1980	Kidspace
1980	Louisiana Nature and Science Center
1980	Madison Children's Museum
1980	Ontario County Historical Society
1980	Parque Zoologico Benito Juarez
1980	Seattle Children's Museum
1980	U.S. Army Field Artillery & Fort Sill Museum
1980	University of Nebraska State Museum
1980	Wichita Art Museum
1981	Arizona Museum for Youth
1981	Balzekas Museum of Lithuanian Culture
1981	The Children's Museum, Saint Paul
1981	Cumberland Museum and Science Center
1981	Delaware Museum of Natural History
1981	The Discovery Center (NY)
1981	Discovery Center Museum of Rockford
1981	The Discovery Place
1981	Express-Ways Children's Museum
1981	Himeji City Aquarium
1981	Louisville Zoological Garden
1981	Metrozoo (formerly Crandon Park Zoo)
1981	National Aquarium in Baltimore
1981	Old State House Museum
1981	Richmond Children's Museum
1981	Roger Williams Park Zoo
1981	Siouxland Heritage Museums
1981	Topeka Zoological Park
1982	The Ann Arbor Hands-On Museum
1982	Breazeale-Padilla Bay Interpretive Center
1982	Brazos Valley Museum
1982	Bergen Museum of Art and Science (formerly Bergen Community Museum)
1982	Carl G. Fenner Arboretum
1982	The Children's Discovery Museum
1982	Cranbrook Institute of Science

1982	Delaware Nature Education Society
1982	Des Moines Science Center
1982	Illinois State Museum
1982	Miramont Castle
1982	Museo de los Niños
1982	Museum of Scientific Discovery
1982	Nature Science Center
1982	Noorder Dierenpark Zoo
1982	Omniplex
1982	Plymouth Historical Museum
1982	San Antonio Museum of Art
1982	San Antonio Zoological Gardens & Aquarium
1982	The South Florida Science Museum (formerly Science Museum and Planetarium of Palm Beach County)
1983	Austin Children's Museum
1983	Children's Museum of Portsmouth (NH)
1983	The Children's Museum of San Diego
1983	International Museum of Photography at George Eastman House
1983	Louisiana Arts and Science Center
1983	Morioka Children's Museum of Science
1983	Museum of Natural History, Regina
1983	The Pittsburgh Children's Museum
1983	Saint Louis Science Center
1983	Sotome Museum of Child
1984	Center of Science and Industry (COSI)
1984	Children's Discovery Museum of San Jose
1984	Children's Museum of Houston
1984	DAR Museum
1984	Dallas Museum of Art
1984	The Discovery Center of the Southern Tier
1984	Monterey Bay Aquarium
1984	Museum of Science and Industry
1984	The Thornton W. Burgess Museum
1985	Cleveland Children's Museum
1985	Kohl Children's Museum
1985	Miami Youth Museum
1985	National Museum of American History (Smithsonian)

1985	National Science Museum, Tokyo
1985	North Carolina Museum of History
1985	Sveriges Tekniska Museum
1986	Cité des Sciences et des Industries (La Villette)

Appendix 3
CLASSIFIED LISTING OF INSTITUTIONS

CHILDREN'S MUSEUMS (INCLUDING ARBORETUMS, EXHIBITS, GALLERIES, GARDENS, NATURE MUSEUMS, PLANETARIUMS, AND THEATERS)

The Academy of Natural Sciences

Alexander Lindsay Junior Museum

The American Museum of Natural History

The Ann Arbor Hands-On Museum

Arizona Museum for Youth

The Art Institute of Chicago

Austin Children's Museum

Australian Science and Technology Centre

Balzekas Museum of Lithuanian Culture

Bethnal Green Museum of Childhood

Bode Museum

Brooklyn Botanic Garden

The Brooklyn Children's Museum

Capital Children's Museum

Carl G. Fenner Arboretum

Center of Science and Industry (COSI)

Chesapeake Planetarium

The Children's Discovery Museum

Children's Discovery Museum of San Jose

Children's Museum, Boston

Children's Museum, Detroit

The Children's Museum, Hamilton

The Children's Museum, Indianapolis

Children's Museum, Lucknow

Children's Museum, Portsmouth (VA)

The Children's Museum, Saint Paul

The Children's Museum, South Dartmouth

Children's Museum, Utica

Children's Museum of Denver

Children's Museum of Houston

Children's Museum of Maine

The Children's Museum of Manhattan

Children's Museum of Oak Ridge

Children's Museum of Portsmouth (NH)

The Children's Museum of Rhode Island

The Children's Museum of San Diego

The Children's Museum of Washington

Cité des Sciences et des Industries

Cleveland Children's Museum

Cleveland Health Education Museum

Cobb County Youth Museum

Connecticut Children's Museum

Cora Hartshorn Arboretum

Cortland County Historical Society

Cylburn Nature Museum

Dallas Museum of Art

The Discovery Center (FL)

The Discovery Center (NY)

Discovery Center Museum of Rockford

The Discovery Center of the Southern Tier

Discovery Museum

The Discovery Place

Discovery Theater of the Smithsonian Institution

The Edmonton Art Gallery

The Eugene Field House and Toy Museum

Evoluon
The Exploratorium
Express-Ways Children's Museum
Franklin Institute Science Museum
Government Museum, Madras
The Health Adventure
High Museum of Art
Hilltop, The Bloomington Youth Garden–Nature Center
Hiroshima City Culture & Science Museum for Children
Israel Museum
Josephine D. Randall Junior Museum
Judges' Lodgings Museum of Childhood
Kamloops Public Art Gallery
Kidspace
Kindermuseum TM Junior
Kohl Children's Museum
La Habra Children's Museum
Lawrence Hall of Science
The Living Arts and Science Center
London Regional Children's Museum
Lori Brock Junior Museum
Los Angeles Children's Museum
Louisiana Arts and Science Center
Louisville Art Gallery
Lutz Children's Museum
Madison Children's Museum
The Magic House
Marondera Children's Library Museum
Memphis Brooks Museum of Art
Miami Youth Museum
Milwaukee Public Museum
Miramont Castle
Monmouth Museum
Morioka Children's Museum of Science
Muncie Children's Museum
Le Musée des Enfants/Het Kindermuseum
Museo des los Niños
Museum of Science and Industry

Museum of Scientific Discovery

Museum für Völkerkunde

National Centre for Children's and Young People's Art

National Children's Museum, New Dehli

Naturhistorisches Museum

Nehru Children's Museum

New Britain Youth Museum

The Newark Museum

Oatland Island Education Center

Omaha Children's Museum

Paul H. Karshner Memorial Museum

Philadelphia Zoological Society

Phoenix Art Museum

The Pittsburgh Children's Museum

Please Touch Museum

Portland Children's Museum

Rensselaer County Junior Museum

Richmond Children's Museum

Rock Creek Nature Center

Roger Williams Park Zoo

Rose Hill Manor Children's Museum

Sacramento Science Center and Junior Museum

Science Museum, London

Science Museum of Connecticut

Science Museums of Charlotte

Scotia-Glenville Children's Museum

Seattle Children's Museum

Seneca Falls Historical Society

Shri Girdharbhai Children's Museum

Sotome Museum of Child

Staatliche Kunsthalle Karlsruhe

Staten Island Children's Museum

Sveriges Tekniska Museum

Tacoma Art Museum

Tallahassee Junior Museum

The Tampa Museum

U.S. Army Field Artillery & Fort Sill Museum

Vestlandske Skolemuseum
Virginia Zoological Park
Wichita Art Association
Wichita Public Schools
Youth Museum of Charlotte County
Zion National Park

CHILDREN'S ZOOS AND AQUARIUM TOUCH TANKS/ CHILDREN'S COVES

African Lion Safari
Akron Zoological Park
Audubon Park and Zoological Garden
Bronx Zoo
Brookfield Zoo
Buffalo Zoological Gardens
Burnet Park Zoo
The Calgary Zoo
California Academy of Sciences
Cincinnati Zoo
Columbus Zoo
Dallas Zoo
Fort Wayne Children's Zoo
Gladys Porter Zoo
Glen Oak Zoo
Granby Zoo
Hatfield Marine Science Center of Oregon State University
Himeji City Aquarium
Hogle Zoological Gardens
Houston Zoological Gardens
Jackson Zoological Park
John Ball Zoological Gardens
Knoxville Zoological Park
Lilford Park
Lincoln Park Zoo
Louisville Zoological Garden
Mesker Park Zoo
Metrozoo
Miller Park Zoo

Milwaukee County Zoological Gardens

Monterey Bay Aquarium

National Aquarium in Baltimore

New England Aquarium

New York Aquarium

Noorder Dierenpark Zoo

Oklahoma City Zoo

Parque Zoologico Benito Juarez

Philadelphia Zoological Society

Rio Grande Zoological Park

Saginaw Children's Zoo

Saint Louis Zoological Park

San Antonio Zoological Gardens & Aquarium

San Francisco Zoological Gardens

Singapore Zoological Gardens

Taronga Zoo

Toledo Zoological Gardens

Topeka Zoological Park

Valley Zoo

Virginia Zoological Park

Washington Park Zoo

Wildlife Safari

DISCOVERY ROOMS, ZOOLABS, AND EDUCATIONAL/ LIBRARY RESOURCE CENTERS

This list contains those institutions included in the book *primarily* because they fit in one of the above categories. The index indicates all institutions with discovery rooms, zoolabs, or educational/library resource centers.

The American Museum of Natural History

Art Gallery of Ontario

Austin Nature Center

Bergen Museum of Art and Science

Bernice Pauahi Bishop Museum

Brazos Valley Museum

Breazeale-Padilla Bay Interpretive Center

The Brevard Museum

Buffalo Museum of Science

Buffalo Zoological Gardens
California Academy of Sciences
Chicago Historical Society
Chippewa Nature Center
Cincinnati Art Museum
Cité des Sciences et des Industries (La Villette)
Cranbrook Institute of Science
Cumberland Museum and Science Center
DAR Museum
Delaware Museum of Natural History
Delaware Nature Education Society
Des Moines Science Center
Field Museum of Natural History
Florida State Museum
Illinois State Museum
International Museum of Photography at George Eastman House
Jacksonville Museum of Arts and Sciences
James Ford Bell Museum of Natural History
John Ball Zoological Gardens
Louisiana Nature and Science Center
Louisville Zoological Garden
Milwaukee Public Museum
Museum of Natural History, Regina
Museum of Science, Boston
Museum of Science and Industry
National Museum of American History (Smithsonian)
National Museum of Natural History, New Delhi
National Museum of Natural History (Smithsonian)
National Science Museum, Tokyo
National Zoological Park (Smithsonian)
Nature Science Center
New York Aquarium
Noorder Dierenpark Zoo
North Carolina Museum of History
Old State House Museum
Omniplex
Ontario County Historical Society
Plymouth Historical Museum

Royal Ontario Museum (ROM)
Saint Louis Science Center
San Antonio Museum of Art
Schuylkill Valley Nature Center
Science Museum, Bangkok
Science Museum of Virginia
Siouxland Heritage Museums
Sveriges Tekniska Museum
The South Florida Science Museum
The Thornton W. Burgess Museum
Toledo Zoological Gardens
University of Nebraska State Museum
Wetlands Institute
Wichita Art Museum

SELECTED BIBLIOGRAPHY

"AAM: Children's Museum Section." *Museums Journal* 37, no. 5 (August 1937): 257.

Alexander, Edward P. *Museum Masters: Their Museums and Their Influence*. Nashville: The American Association for State and Local History, 1983.

Alexander, Edward P. *Museums in Motion: An Introduction to the History and Functions of Museums*. Nashville: The American Association for State and Local History, 1979.

Amanshauser, Hildegund and Wiesbauer, Elisabeth. "I Hear and I Forget, I See and I Remember, I Do and I Understand: Kindermuseen in den Vereinigten Staaten." *Mitteilungen & Materialien der Arbeitsgruppe Pädagogisches Museum* 15/16 (1982): 68–89.

American Association of Museums. *Museums: Their New Audience*. Washington, D.C.: American Association of Museums, 1972.

American Association of Museums. *A Statistical Survey of Museums in the United States and Canada*. Washington, D.C.: American Association of Museums, 1965; reprint ed., New York:Arno Press, 1976.

"American Zoos." *Parks & Recreation* 6, no. 7 (August 1971): 48–49, 100–01, 104.

Anderson, William R. and Sprouse, Herbert. "Museums in the Marketplace." *Museum News* 63, no. 1 (October 1984): 59–67.

Annual Report of the Board of Regents of the Smithsonian Institution—Year Ending June 30, 1904. Washington, D.C.: Government Printing Office, 1905.

Annual Report of the Smithsonian Institution 1901. Washington, D.C.: Government Printing Office, 1902.

Applewhite, E. J. "It's Not All on the Mall: A Personal Look at Washington's Other Museums." *Museum News* 62, no. 4 (April 1984): 20–31.

Arth, Malcolm. "A Century of Education at the American Museum of Natural History." *Roundtable Reports* 9, nos. 2 and 3 (Spring & Summer 1984): 8–10.

Arth, Malcolm. "The People Center—Anthropology for the Layman." *Curator* 18, no. 4 (December 1975): 315–25.

Arth, Malcolm and Claremon, Linda. "The Discovery Room." *Curator* 20, no. 3 (September 1977): 169–80.

"Art Notes: Appointment I." *New York Times*, 6 July 1969, sec. D, p. 21.

Ashton, Ray E., Jr. "Zoos and Museums: Working Together to Meet the Demands of a Changing Environment." *AAZPA Regional Workshop Proceedings 1977–78*, pp. 471–75.

Barry, Sharon L. "HERPlab: Prototype Materials for Families." *Newsletter International Association of Zoo Educators* 10 (1983): 16–17.

Baxi, Smita J. and Dwivedi, Vinod P. *Modern Museum: Organisation and Practice in India*. New Delhi: Abhinav, 1973.

Bay, Ann. "Getting Decent Docents." *Museum News* 52, no. 7 (April 1974): 25–29.

Bay, Ann. *Museum Programs for Young People*. Washington, D.C.: Smithsonian Institution, 1973: ERIC Document Reproduction Service, ED 090 116.

Besch, Deborah A., comp. "Animaline: Cincinnati Zoo and Philadelphia Zoo." *Animal Kingdom* 88, no. 5 (September/October 1985): 2.

Bitter, Gary G. "Electronic Publishing [Paint]." *Instructor* 92, no. 4 (November/December 1982): 152.

Bloom, Kathryn. "The Junior League and Children's Museums." *Museum News* 39, no. 7 (April 1961): 20–25.

Borun, Minda. *Measuring the Immeasurable: A Pilot Study of Museum Effectiveness*. Washington, D.C.: Association of Science-Technology Centers, 1977: ERIC Document Reproduction Service, ED 160 499.

Borun, Minda; Flexer, Barbara K.; Casey, Alice F.; and Baum, Lynn R., *Planets and Pulleys: Studies of Class Visits to Science Museums*. Washington, D.C.: Association of Science-Technology Centers, 1983.

Borun, Minda and Miller, Maryanne. *What's in a Name?: A Study of the Effectiveness of Explanatory Labels in a Science Museum*. Washington, D.C.: Association of Science-Technology Centers, 1980.

Brayton, Margaret M. "The Character of Children's Museums." *Recreation* 45, no. 6 (November 1951): 314–16.

Brayton, Margaret M. "Children's Museums in Science Education." *School Science and Mathematics* 56, no. 1 (February 1956): 121–24.

Brayton, Margaret M. "Children's Work in Museums." *Museum* [UNESCO] 1, nos. 3 and 4 (December 1948): 178–80, 217; and "Les Musées au Service de l'enfants," ibid., pp. 180–82, 217.

"Bringing the Masses to Culture: Ms. Pac-Man Packs Them in at Museum." *St. Petersburg Times*, 28 July 1982, pp. 1B, 6B.

Brodey, Patricia. "The LINKS-ZOO: A Recreational/Educational Facility for the Future." In *International Zoo Yearbook* 21 (1981): 63–68. Edited by P.J.S. Olney. London: The Zoological Society of London, 1981.

"Brooklyn Unveils Plan for Museum." *New York Times*, 19 May 1971, p. 38.

Brown, Robert A. "Why Children's Zoos?" In *International Zoo Yearbook* 13 (1973): 258–61. Edited by Nicole Dauplaix-Hall. London: The Zoological Society of London, 1973.

Bruman, Raymond. *Cookbook I*. 2d ed. with revisions. San Francisco: The Exploratorium, 1984.

Capital Children's Museum. *Paint*. Englewood Cliffs, NJ: Reston Publishing, 1982.

Cart, Germaine; Harrison, Molly; and Russell, Charles. *Museums and Young People*. Paris: International Council of Museums, 1952: ERIC Document Reproduction Service, ED 046 233.

Carter, Judith. "The Children's Museum." *Michigan Education Journal* 42, no. 4 (1 October 1964): 53.

Cheek, Neil H., Jr. "People at the Zoo." *Animal Kingdom* 76, no. 3 (June 1973): 9–14.

Cheney, Jane Burger. *Children's Museum: How to Start One*. Washington, D.C.: American Association of University Women, 1949.

Cheney, Jane Burger. "Focus on Children's Museums." *Museum News* 39, no. 7 (April 1961): 14–19.

Cherfas, Jeremy. *Zoo 2000: A Look beyond the Bars*. London: British Broadcasting Company, 1984.

"Children and the Museum." *Museum* [UNESCO] 1, nos. 3 and 4 (December 1948): 177, and "L'enfant et les Musées," ibid., p. 177.

"Children in Museums and Children's Museums." International Roundtable in Brussels, 17–18 February 1979. [Organized by the Brussels Children's Museum.] (Typewritten.)

"Children Learn That 'Dying Isn't a Vacation.' " *New York Times*, 26 August 1984, sec. 1, p. 25.

"Children Like Their Museum: Brooklyn Provides Place to Do Things As Well As See Things." *New York Times*, 8 January 1939, sec. 2, p. 5.

"Children Part of Show at Laboratory Museum." *New York Times*, 14 April 1981, sec. C, p. 12.

"Children's Gardens." *Recreation* 34, no. 1 (April 1940): 52, 54.

"Children's Museum, Boston, Mass." *Domus* 542 (January 1975): 11.

"Children's Museum: Boston's Unique 'Do Touch' Facility Is a New Kind of Classroom in Which All Learning Is Fun." *Architectural Forum* 135, no 2. (September 1971): 32–33.

"Children's Museum Boston." *L'Architecture d'Aujourd'hui* 154 (February/March 1971): LXXXIII 94–95.

"Children Museum." *Domus* 547 (June 1975): 37.

"Children's Museum Day Observed." *The Museum News* 17, no. 12 (15 December 1939): 1, 4.

"Children's Museum Moves 'Down by the Riverside.' " *This Week in Denver* (January 1984): 46.

"Children's Museum of Boston." *Museum Work* 3, no. 4 (January 1921): 106–07.

"Children's Museum 'Puzzle' Is Taking Shape." *Staten Island Advance*, 31 January 1985, p. A12.

"Children's Museums in the United States." *The Museum News* 30, no. 9 (1 November 1952): 3; 31, no. 20 (15 April 1954): 3–4; 32, no. 19 (1 April 1955): 3–4.

"Children's Museum Shows New Ideas." *New York Times* 24 March 1974, pp. 97, 112.

"Children's World of Wonder in Brooklyn." *New York Times*, 17 May 1977, p. 35.

"Children's Zoo." *New York Times*, 24 May 1941, p. 14.

"Children to Mark Museum Founding: La Guardia to Proclaim December as 40th Anniversary of the Brooklyn Institution." *New York Times*, 4 December 1939, p. 20.

Clark, Palmer Price. "A Historical Bibliography of Children's Museums and Work with Children in Adult Museums in the United States." Master's dissertation, Catholic University of America, 1957.

Cohen, Uriel and McMurtry, Ruth M. *Museums and Children: A Design Guide*. Milwaukee: Center for Architecture and Urban Planning Research, University of Wisconsin, 1985.

Cole, K. C. "The Art of Discovery in San Francisco—Exploratorium." *Saturday Review*, 14 October 1972, pp. 40–43.

Cole, Peggy, "Piaget in the Galleries." *Museum News* 63, no. 1 (October 1984): 9–15.

Coleman, Bettye Woods. "An Organizational Plan to Establish Children's Museums in Mississippi." Ph.D. dissertation, University of Mississippi, 1977.

Coleman, Laurence Vail. *Museum Buildings*. Washington, D.C.: American Association of Museums, 1950.

Coleman, Laurence Vail. *The Museum in America*. 3 vols. Washington, D.C.: American Association of Museums, 1939; reprint ed., Washington, D.C.: American Association of Museums, 1970.

Comer, Virginia Lee. "Junior Leagues Support Museum Programs for Children." *The Museum News* 26, no. 3 (1 June 1948): 7–8.

"Come to Philadelphia." *Parks & Recreation* 23, no. 1 (September 1939): 35–38.

Commission on Museums for a New Century. *Museums for a New Century*. Washington, D.C.: American Association of Museums, 1984.

Condit, Louise, "How Children's Museums Can Best Help Each Other." *The Museum News* 24, no. 18 (15 March 1947): 8.

Condit, Louise. "The Junior Museum at the Metropolitan." *Museum* [UNESCO] 1, nos. 3 and 4 (December 1948): 192–94; and "Le Musée des jeunes du Métropolitain," ibid., pp. 194–95, 219.

Condit, Louise. "A New Junior Museum." *Curator* 1, no. 2 (1959): 11–20.

Condit, Louise. "Points of View." *Museum News* 39, no. 7 (April 1961): 13.

"COSI's Kidspace Invites Young Children to Play and Explore." *ASTC Newsletter* 14, no. 2 (March/April 1986): 10.

Craig, Lois. "A Slice of the City in Cross Section: It Is the Centerpiece of Boston's New Children's Museum." *AIA Journal* 68, no. 12 (October 1979): 62–67.

Crask, Catherine. "An Art Library in a Junior Museum." *Library Journal* 71 (15 September 1946): 1170–72.

"A Cross-Country Guide to Museum Programs for Kids." *Black Enterprise* 15, no. 12 (July 1985): 63.

Crosson, David. *How Can You Say No When Your Museum Says Yes? Collections in Participatory Museums*. Audiotapes of panelists Charles Howarth, Paul Richard, and Betsy Vincent, presented at meeting of the American Association of Museums, Detroit, June 1985. Shawnee Mission, KS: Vanguard Systems, 1985.

Crouch, Philbrook. "How Does the Name 'Children's Museum' Affect Finances?" *Museum News* 45, no. 9 (May 1967): 33–34.

Crutcher, Edward Bryan. "Museum Attendance of Children and Related Factors." Ph.D dissertation, George Peabody College for Teachers, 1966.

Curzon, Rebecca E. "Children of the Castle." *Roundtable Reports* 5, no. 2 (1980): 1–3.

Dailey, Patricia M. "Buffalo's Science Magnet School: Drawing Students to a Zoo's

Living Classroom." *Newsletter International Association of Zoo Educators* 12 (1984): 20–23.

Danilov, Victor J. "Discovery Rooms and Kidspaces: Museum Exhibits for Children." *Sceince and Children* 23, no. 4 (January 1986): 6–11.

Danilov, Victor J. "Early Childhood Exhibits at Science Centers." *Curator* 27, no. 3 (September 1984): 173–88.

Danilov, Victor J. "European Science and Technology Museums." *Museum News* 54, no. 6 (July/August 1976): 34–37, 71–72.

Danilov, Victor J. "Push a Button, Turn a Crank." *American Education* 10, no. 5 (June 1974): 16–21.

Danilov, Victor J. *Science and Technology Centers*. Cambridge: The MIT Press, 1982.

Danilov, Victor J. *Science Center Planning Guide*. Washington, D.C.: Association of Science-Technology Centers, 1985.

Danilov, Victor J. "Science Museums as Education Centers." *Curator* 18, no. 2 (June 1975): 87–108.

Danilov, Victor J. "Under the Microscope." *Museum News* 52, no. 6 (March 1974): 37–44.

Dauphinee, David. "In Children's Museums, The Signs Say 'Please Touch.' " *Canadian Living* (April 1983): W12–W16.

"December Is the Month for Children in the Puget Sound Area." *Sunset* 167 (December 1981): 30, 32.

DeMartino, Marguerite. "Children Build the Brooklyn Bridge." *Design for Arts in Education* 85, no. 1 (September/October 1983): 17–19.

Dennis, Emily. "Seminar on Neighborhood Museums." *Museum News* 48, no. 5 (January 1970): 13–19.

Dietsch, Deborah K. "Learning from Mother Nature." *Architectural Record* 173, no. 10 (September 1985): 120–25.

"Digging into History: Children Go Back in Time at Indianapolis Museum." *Christian Science Monitor Home & Family*, 30 August 1985, p. 27.

"Discovery in the Suburbs." *Boston Globe Calendar*, 10 May 1984, p. 6.

The Discovery Room: An Introduction. Washington, D.C.: Office of Education, National Museum of Natural History, Smithsonian Institution, 1985. Slides/Script.

Douglas, Charles A. "A Museum for Children." *Museum Work* 3, no. 5 (February 1921): 158–62.

Draper, Miriam S. "The Children's Museum in Brooklyn." *Library Journal* 35, no. 4 (April 1910): 149–54.

Duff, John Carr. "Improving on Barnum: Plans for a Children's Museum." *The Nation's Schools* 14, no. 5 (November 1934): 21–26.

Dunitz, Robin J. "Interactive Museums." *Media & Methods* 21, no. 8 (May/June 1985): 8–11.

Earnshaw, Thomas Marvin. "Educational Activities in Selected Science Museums in the United States." Ph.D dissertation, Temple University, 1967.

Eason, Laurie and Friedman, Alan. "Elevator Exhibit." *Physics Teacher* 13, no. 8 (November 1975): 492–93.

Eason, Laurie and Linn, Marcia C. "Evaluation of the Effectiveness of Participatory Exhibits." *Curator* 19, no. 1 (March 1976): 45–62.

Eckhardt, Ferdinand. "Museums and Schools." *Museum* [UNESCO] 6, no. 4 (1953): 241–45; and "Le Musée et L'École," ibid., pp. 237–41.

Educational Facilities Laboratories. *Arts and the Handicapped: An Issue of Access*. New York: Educational Facilities Laboratories, 1975: ERIC Document Reproduction Service, ED 117 829.

Educational Facilities Laboratories. *The Arts in Found Places*. New York: Educational Facilities Laboratories, 1976: ERIC Document Reproduction Service, ED 125 077.

Educational Facilities Laboratories. *Hands-On Museums: Partners in Learning*. New York: Educational Facilities Laboratories, 1975: ERIC Document Reproduction Service, ED 113 832.

"Eight Teen-Agers Win Curators' Posts: Will Work at the Brooklyn Children's Museum on Saturdays for a Year." *New York Times*, 12 June 1960, p. 78.

Elwonger, Ruth. "Museums for Children." *Recreation* 39, no. 8 (November 1945): 398–401, 445–46.

Emery, Margaret. "Adventures in Leisure." *Museum News* 41, no. 5 (January 1963): 33–35.

"Environment Portfolio." *Industrial Design* 29, no. 4 (July/August 1982): 42–43.

Farb, Peter. "An 'Island of Nature' for Your Town." *National Parent-Teacher* 54, no. 8 (April 1960): 10–12.

Feasibility Study for the Children's Museum [Boston]. Boston: Robert J. Corcoran, May 1974. (Typewritten.)

Fertig, Barbara C., ed. *Volunteers in Museum Education*. Sourcebook #2. Washington, D.C.: George Washington University, 1979: ERIC Document Reproduction Service, ED 191 755.

Fialkoff, Kay. "The G.A.M.E. Plan." *Instructor* 84, no. 1 (August/September 1974): 93–94.

Fischman, Joshua. "Toys across Time: The Past, Present and Future of Child's Play." *Psychology Today* 19, no. 10 (October 1985): 56–63.

Fisher, Helen V. "Children's Museums: A Definition and a Credo." *Curator* 3, no. 2 (1960): 183–91.

Folsom, Arnott R. "How to Start a Children's Zoo." *Parks & Recreation* 1, no. 5 (May 1966): 430–32.

"For Youngsters, a Touchable Toy Exhibit." *New York Times*, 18 September 1985, sec. C, p. 1.

Forbes, John Ripley. "Children's Museum." *Journal of the National Education Association* 31, no. 2 (February 1942): 46–47.

Forbes, John Ripley. "Children's Museum for Every Community." *The Nation's Schools* 37, no. 5 (May 1946): 20–23.

Forbes, John Ripley. "A Museum for Your Children." *Recreation* 39, no. 7 (October 1945): 360–63, 391.

Ford, Kenneth W. "The Robert A. Millikan Lecture Award." *American Journal of Physics* 41, no. 12 (December 1973): 1309–10.

"Forget Big Convention Halls: Now Cities See Aquariums as Urban Renovation Tools." *Wall Street Journal*, 22 November 1985, p. 33.

"Four-Foot Eye Level Zoo at New York." *The Museum News* 19, no. 7 (1 October 1941): 2.

Friedman, Alan; Eason, Laurie P.; and Sneider, Cary I. "Star Games: A Participatory Astronomy Exhibit." *Planetarian* 8, no. 3 (Autumn 1979): 3–7.

Fuller, Melville W., Jr. "The Development and Status of Science Centers and Museums for Children in the United States." Ph.D. dissertation, University of North Carolina, Chapel Hill, 1970.

"A Funhouse Built in a Fun Structure." *New York Times*, 29 May 1977, sec. 2, p. 23.

Gabianelli, Vincent J. and Munyer, Edward A. "A Place to Learn." *Museum News* 53, no. 4 (December 1974): 28–33.

Gale, Francis Clair. "The Junior Museum and Its Program for the Education of Children." Ph.D. dissertation, Stanford University, 1957.

Gallup, Anna B. "Brooklyn Children's Museum." *School and Society* 32, no. 835 (20 December 1930): 865–66.

Gallup, Anna B. "Children's Museum, The Brooklyn Institute of Arts and Sciences." *Museum Work* 1, no. 5 (February 1919): 134–35.

Gallup, Anna B. "A Children's Museum and How Any Town Can Get One." *National Education Association Addresses and Proceedings* 64 (1926): 951–53.

Gallup, Anna B. "A Debt to the Child." *Museum Work* 5, no. 2 (July/August 1922): 30.

Gallup, Anna B. "The Essentials of a Children's Museum Building." *Proceedings of the American Association of Museums* 2 (1908): 84–93.

Gallup, Anna B. "The Work of the Children's Museum." *Proceedings of the American Association of Museums* 1 (1907): 144–49.

Gans, Susan. "Three Successful Programs Do Not a Museum Make." *Museum News* 52, no. 7 (April 1974): 14–19.

Garrison, Jane W. "The Brooklyn Children's Museum." *Brooklyn Museum Quarterly* 25, no. 2 (April 1938): 55–62.

Garrison, Mrs. Lloyd III. "Children's Museums." *Sierra Educational News* 36, no. 2 (February 1940): 33.

Garrison, Mrs. Lloyd III. "Nature for the City Child." *Recreation* 34, no. 1 (April 1940): 29–31.

Gaulding, Melissa. "HERPlab: A Cooperative Venture." *AAZPA Regional Conference Proceedings 1984*, pp. 9–11.

Giraudy, Danièle. "The Children's Museum, Marseille." *Museum* [UNESCO] 22, nos. 3 and 4 (1969): 226–29; and "Le Musée des enfants, Marseille," Ibid., pp. 230–34.

Glossling, Gloria. "A Children's Museum Changes Its Name." *Museum News* 45, no 9 (May 1967): 34–36.

Glover, Katherine. "Workshops of Wonder: Children's Museums Are Creative Laboratories of Leisure." *The Child* 13, no. 8 (February 1949): 114–18, 124–25.

Golden, Grace. "Children's Museum of Indianapolis." *Childhood Education* 15, no. 9 (May 1939): 408–12.

Goldman, Judith. "A Playground of Perceptions." *Art News* 74, no. 8 (October 1975): 82–83.

Goldman, Katherine J., ed. *Opportunities for Extending Museum Contributions to Pre-College Science Education*. Washington, D.C.: Smithsonian Institution, 1970: ERIC Document Reproduction Service, ED 046 215.

Gonis, George. "The Children's Museum of Indianapolis Emphasizes Historical Processes Rather Than Historical Facts in Its New Gallery." *History News* 40, no. 7 (July 1985): 12–15.

Goor, Ronald. "Has Your Museum Gone Buggy?" *Museum News* 51, no. 7 (March 1973): 13–16.

Gordon, Ayala. "Emotional Reactions to an Exhibition." *ICOM Education* 10 (1982/83): 13–14; and "Une exposition, source d'émotions," ibid., p. 15.

Gordon, Ayala. "The Museum's Junior Wing." *Ariel* 10 (Spring 1965): 49–53.

Gordon, Ayala. "Ten Years of Work in the Youth Wing." *Israel Museum Journal* 11 (1976): 27–34; reprinted as "Ten Years of Work in the Israel Museum Youth Wing." *ICOM Education* (1975/76): 42–44 and "Dix ans de travail à l'Aile des Jeunes du Musée d'Israël," ibid., pp. 45–47.

Gordon, Ayala. "Young People and the Museum." *Ariel* 60 (1985): 51–57.

Gordon, Ayala. "The Youth Wing: Aims and Methods." *Israel Museum Journal* 13 (1978): 12–20.

Gordon, Clyde. "A Children's Zoo Summary." *Parks & Recreation* 40, no. 3 (March 1957): 32.

Gordon, Margery. "The Art Museum as a Living Environment." *Design for Arts in Education* 81, no. 6 (September 1980): 16–19.

Gortzak, Henk Jan. "The Museum, Children and the Third World." *Museum* [UNESCO] 33, no. 1 (1981): 51–56.

"Grant for Children's Museum." *Washington Post*, 2 June 1979, sec. C. p. 7.

Graves, Melanie. "A Day at the Capital Children's Museum." *Classroom Computer News* 3, no. 1 (September/October 1982): 37–38, 74–75.

"Gray Power: Making Friends." *Washington Post*, 21 May 1980, sec. B, p. 5.

Griffen, Delia I. "History Study and Museum Exhibits." *Proceedings of the American Association of Museums* 10 (1916): 35–38.

Griffen, Delia I. "A Museum Experiment." *Proceedings of the American Association of Museums* 8 (1914): 46–51.

Grove, Richard. "Museums Come Alive." *American Education* 3, no. 4 (April 1967): 10–11.

"A Growing Phenomenon." *Boston Globe Calendar*, 18 April 1985, pp. 14–15.

Gurian, Elaine. "Adult Learning at Children's Museum of Boston." In *Museums, Adults and the Humanities: A Guide for Educational Programming*, pp. 271–96. Edited by Zipporah W. Collins. Washington, D.C.: American Association of Museums, 1981.

Gurian, Elaine Heumann and Kamien, Janet. "Interactive Exhibits at the Boston Children's Museum." *ICOM Education* 10 (1982/83): 9–11; and "Diversité et complémentarité des objects exposés au Musée des enfants de Boston," ibid., pp. 11–12.

Hancocks, David. *Animals and Architecture*. New York: Praeger, 1971.

Handbook of American Museums. Washington, D.C.: American Association of Museums, 1932.

" 'Hands On' Museums Find Backers, Skeptics." *Christian Science Monitor*, 12 May 1980, p. 18.

"Hands-on Policy." *Newsweek*, 3 December 1973, p. 82.

Harrison, Molly. "A New Approach to History in a London Museum." *Museum* [UNESCO] 1, nos. 3 and 4 (December 1948): 188–90, 218; and "Un Musée de Londres presente l'Histoire sous un jour nouveau." Ibid., pp. 191, 218–19.

Harvey, Emily Dennis and Freiberg, Bernard, eds. *A Museum for the People: Neighborhood Museums—A Report from the Brooklyn MUSE Seminar*. New York: Arno Press, 1972.

Hassler, William G. "Education and Youth Museums." *Museum News* 37, no. 3 (May 1959): 14–15.

Hayden, Carla D. "Museum of Science and Industry Library." *Science and Technology Libraries* 6, nos. 1/2 (1985): 47–53.

Hayes, Bartlett H., Jr. *A Study of the Relation of Museum Art Exhibitions to Education: Final Report*. Washington, D.C.: Office of Education, Bureau of Research, 1967: ERIC Document Reproduction Service, ED 026 403.

Hediger, Heini. *Man and Animal in the Zoo*. New York: Delacorte Press, 1969.

Heine, Aalbert. "Attendance, Population and the Junior Museum." *Museum News* 45, no. 9 (May 1967): 32–33.

Heine, Aalbert. "Making Glad the Heart of Childhood." *Museum News* 58, no. 2 (November/December 1979): 23–25.

Hensel, Karen A. "Aquariums & Marine Educators: Where Do We Go From Here?" *Current/The Journal of Marine Education* 1, no. 1 (1979): 10–12.

Hensel, Karen A. "Education in Zoos and Aquariums—Trends and Projections." *AAZPA 1978 Annual Conference Proceedings*, pp. 117–24.

Hensel, Karen Astrid. "Displays at Displays: Looking at the Family as Educator in the Context of a Living Museum—An Aquarium." Ph.D. dissertation, Columbia University, in progress [1987].

Hipschman, Ron. *Cookbook II*. San Francisco: The Exploratorium, 1980.

Hirshberg, Peter. "Compu-Tots and Other Joys of Museum Life." *Instructional Innovator* 26, no. 6 (September 1981): 28–30.

"History Update: The Boston Children's Museum and the Children's Museum of Rhode Island." *History News* 39, no. 5 (May 1984): 2.

Hodge, John C. "Museums and Children in Australia." *Museum* [UNESCO] 31, no. 3 (1979): 160–63.

Hodges, David Julian. "Museums, Anthropology, and Minorities: In Search of a New Relevance for Old Artifacts." *Anthropology and Education* 9, no. 2 (1978): 148–57.

Hoffman, Ellen, ed. *Impressions of Education in Japan: A Report of the Educational Staff Seminar Study Tour, December 3–20, 1973*. Washington, D.C.: George Washington University Institute for Educational Leadership, 1974: ERIC Document Reproduction Service, ED 134 509.

Hoffman, Paul, ed. *American Museum Guides—Science*. New York: Macmillan, 1983.

Holman, Yvonne Keck. "An Investigation into the Dynamics of Children's Museums: A Case Study of Selected Museums." Ph.D. dissertation, Northern Illinois University, 1982.

"Hoosier Tots Play and Learn in Their Own Museum." *Wall Street Journal*, 20 June 1985, p. 26.

"How Do Lasers Work? What Is Eye Logic? You and Your Children Tinker, Discover in the Exploratorium in San Francisco." *Sunset* 154 (February 1975): 40.

"How Visitors View Exhibitions." *Newsday*, 20 February 1983, sec. 2, pp. 21–22.

Hudson, Kenneth. *Museums for the 1980s: A Survey of World Trends*. New York: Holmes & Meier, 1977.

Hudson, Samuel. "A Child's Place." *Michigan History* 67, no. 5 (September/October 1983): 18–21.

Humane Education Projects Handbook. Ogden, UT: Junior League of Ogden, 1982: ERIC Document Reproduction Service, ED 229 247.

Hyams, Edward and MacQuitty, William. *Great Botanical Gardens of the World*. London: Thomas Nelson & Sons, 1969.

Iliff, Warren J. "A Storefront Insect Zoo." *Curator* 24, no. 2 (June 1981): 109–16.

"Indianapolis Children's Museum Embodies 'Hands-on' Concepts." *New York Times*, 3 October 1976, sec. 1, p. 53.

Irwin, Howard S. "Grocery Store Botany." *Curator* 20, no. 1 (1977): 5–14.

Jacobs, Betsy. *The Children's Garden*. New York: Brooklyn Botanic Garden, [1985].

Jenkins, David. "The Diversity of Life Continuing the Synergy of Zoo and Museum Design." *AAZPA Regional Conference Proceedings 1985*, pp. 338–43.

Jenkins, David M. "A Survey of Interactive Technologies." *AAZPA 1985 Annual Conference Proceedings*, pp. 72–83: ERIC Document Reproduction Service, ED 265 038.

Jewell, P. A. "Should Domestic Animals Be Kept in Zoos?" In *International Zoo Yearbook* 16 (1976): 229–31. Edited by P.J.S. Olney. London: The Zoological Society of London, 1976.

Johnson, Selina T. "Youth Museums Provide for Leisure Time." *Instructor* 65, no. 10 (June 1956): 34–35.

Johnson, Selina Tetzlaff. "Museums for Youth in the United States: A Study of Their Origins, Relationships, and Cultural Contributions." Ph.D. dissertation, New York University, 1962.

"Junior Museum Foundation Gets Grant, Changes Name." *Museum News* 37, no. 4 (June 1959): 24.

"Just-for-Kids Museum in Washington, D.C." *Sunset* 175 (May 1982): 72–73.

Kamien, Janet. *Is there Life after 50¢? A Guide to Building and Program Accessibility*. Boston: Children's Museum, 1980: ERIC Document Reproduction Service, ED 223 042.

Kamien, Janet. *Sensitive Subjects: Museums and Controversy*. Audiotape of panelists Linda Downs and Michael Hawfield, presented at meeting of the American Association of Museums, Detroit, June 1985. Shawnee Mission, KS: Vanguard Systems, 1985.

Kamien, Janet. *What If You Couldn't . . . ? A Book About Special Needs*. New York: Charles Scribner, 1979.

Kamien, Janet and Goldbas, Amy. *Museum Experiences for Families with Severely Disabled Kids. . . . A Program from the Boston Children's Museum*. Boston: Children's Museum, 1981: ERIC Document Reproduction Service, ED 223 044.

Katz, Herbert and Katz, Marjorie. *Museums, U.S.A.* Garden City, N.Y.: Doubleday, 1965.

Katz, Jonathan. *Philosophies and Methods of Youth Museums*. Audiotape of panelists Steven Ling, Portia Sperr, and Michael Spock, presented at meeting of the American Association of Museums, Detroit, June 1985. Shawnee Mission, KS: Vanguard Systems, 1985.

Kenny, David H. *Fifty Years Young: The Children's Museum*. Princeton, NJ: Princeton University Press for the Newcomen Society, 1975.

Kelly, Elizabeth. "New Services for the Disabled in American Museums." *Museums Journal* 82, no. 3 (December 1982): 157–59.

"A Kid Can Do Anything: Museum 'Touch-Feel' Exhibit Lets Them Take the Controls." *Chicago Sun-Times*, 15 November 1984, p. 36.

"Kid's Fort." *Architectural Review* 151 (January 1972): 123.

Kiefer, Michael. "A Most Curious Place: Where Toddlers Can Toy with Piaget Theory." *Chicago* 34, no. 4 (April 1985): 280.

Kimche, Lee. "American Museums: The Vital Statistics." *Museum News* 59, no. 2 (October 1980): 52–57.

Kimche, Lee. "Science Centers: A Potential for Learning." *Science* 199 (20 January 1978): 270–73.

"Kinder im Museum: Lernen Kann Ein Vergnügen Sein." *Die Frau* 50 (11 December 1982): 10–11.

Kirchshofer, Rosl, ed. *The World of Zoos: A Survey and Gazetteer.* New York: Viking, 1968.

Kline, Patricia. "Education Programme for Handicapped Children." In *International Zoo Yearbook* 5 (1965): 227–28. Edited by Caroline Jarvis. London: The Zoological Society of London, 1965.

Kohn, Sherwood Davidson. "It's OK to Touch at the New-Style Hands-on Exhibits." *Smithsonian* 9, no. 6 (September 1978): 78–84.

Kolar, Judith. "The Children's Zoo." *Animal Kingdom* 88, no. 3 (May/June 1985): LP6–7.

Kolb, Peter Leo. *Das Kindermuseum in den USA: Tatsachen, Deutungen und Vermittlungsmethoden.* Frankfurt am Main: Haag and Herchen, 1983.

Korty, Carol. "If I Were a Kid Back Then: Participatory Drama in a Museum Setting." *Children's Theater Review* 26, no. 4 (1977): 11–13.

Laetsch, Watson M.; Diamond, Judy; Gotfried, Jeffrey L.; and Rosenfeld, Sherman. "Children and Family Groups in Science Centers." *Science and Children* 17, no. 6 (March 1980): 14–17.

Larrabee, Eric, ed. *Museums and Education.* Washington, D.C.: Smithsonian Institution, 1968: ERIC Document Reproduction Service, ED 014 814.

"Last Saturday." *Recreation* 39, no. 6 (September 1945): 303–04.

"Las Vegas Gets Funding for Library/Children's Museum." *Library Journal* 110, no. 4 (1 March 1985): 32.

Lattis, Richard. "Animal Shows . . . An Educational Impact." *AAZPA Regional Conference Proceedings 1980*, pp. 146–49.

Lattis, Richard. "A New Idea in Children's Zoos." *Newsletter International Association of Zoo Educators* 7 (1981): 20–23.

Lattis, Richard. "Our Public Image: Starting with Children." *AAZPA 1983 Annual Conference Proceedings*, pp. 95–104.

"Learning the Fun Way." *Family Weekly*, 26 May 1985, p. 12.

Lehman, Susan Nichols and Igoe, Kathryn, eds. *Museum-School Partnerships: Plans and Programs.* Sourcebook #4. Washington, D.C.: George Washington University, 1981: ERIC Document Reproduction Service, ED 216 945.

Lerman, Doris. "50 Years of Humanizing the Arts: Victor D'Amico." *Roundtable Reports* 5, no. 2 (1980): 4–7.

Levin, Michael D. *The Modern Museum: Temple or Showroom.* Jerusalem: Dvir, 1983.

Lewin, Ann W. "The Nek Chand Garden at Capital Children's Museum." *The Hilltonian* (October/November 1985): 20–21.

Linn, Marcia C. "Exhibit Evaluation—Informed Decision Making." *Curator* 19, no. 4 (December 1976): 291–302.

Livingston, Bernard. *Zoo Animals, People, Places.* New York: Arbor House, 1974.

"Los Angeles Children's Museum: It's Child's Play." *Los Angeles Times*, 11 June 1979, pp. 1, 7.

Lurie, Nancy Oestreich. "An Era of Harmony." *Lore* 13, no. 2 (Summer 1983): 12–19.

Mabbatt, Frederic S. III. "San Diego's 'Zoo of the Future.' " *Museum News* 39, no. 4 (December 1960): 14–17.

McCarthy, Laura Flynn. "Children's Museums: Learning the Fun Way." *Family Weekly*, 26 May 1985, p. 12.

MacFadyen, J. Tevere. "A Japanese Roof Raising in Boston." *Asia* 2, no. 5 (January/February 1980): 12–19.

McGinty, Lawrence. "Exploratorium Cookbook II." *New Scientist* 92 (3 December 1981): 685.

McGlathery, Glenn and Hartmann, Martha N. "Here Come the Touch Carts." *Curator* 19, no. 3 (September 1976): 193–97.

McKie, Laura L. "Discovering Zoolab." *Roundtable Reports* (Winter 1978): 6.

Madden, Joan C. "Bridge Between Research and Exhibits—The Smithsonian Naturalist Center." *Curator* 21, no. 2 (June 1978): 159–67.

Madden, Joan C. "The Discovery Room: A Place for Learning." *Children Today* 11, no. 5 (September/October 1982): 7–11.

Marshall, Marilyn. "The Children's Museum." *Ebony Jr.* 11, no. 3 (August/September 1983): 9.

"Masterminding a 'Hands-On' Museum." *Boston Globe*, 29 October 1985, pp. 37–38.

"Match Boxes." *American Education* 3, no. 1 (December 1966): 9.

Matthai, Robert A. and Deaver, Neil E. "Child-Centered Learning." *Museum News* 54, no. 4 (March/April 1976): 15–19.

"May Day at the Philadelphia Zoo." *Parks & Recreation* 21, no. 11 (July 1938): 577–79.

Melnick, Ronnie Mae. "A Look at Children's Museums." *Studies in Museology* [Baroda] 9 (1973–74): 43–65.

Meng, William. "Children's Zoo." *Animal Kingdom* 73, no. 3 (June 1970): 14–15.

Mezhlumyan, Konstantin Sergeevich. "The Children's Art Centre in Yerevan." *Museum* [UNESCO] 36, no. 4 (1984): 199–203.

Miller, Julie Ann. "Hands On at the Museum." *Science News* 114, no. 11 (9 September 1978): 184–85.

Miner, Frances M. "Fingers in the Soil." *Plants & Gardens, Brooklyn Botanic Garden Record* 40, no. 3 (Autumn 1984): 11–13.

Monsen, Courtenay. "Museums Where Children May Touch as Well as Look." *California Journal of Elementary Education* 13 (February 1945): 172–82.

Montagu, Kyra. *Boston Children's Museum*. Boston: Children's Museum, 1984.

Moore, Donald. "Thirty Years of Museum Education: Some Reflections." *International Journal of Museum Management and Curatorship* 1, no. 3 (1982): 213–30.

Moore, Donald E. "A BBG Legend: Miss Ellen Eddy Shaw." *Plants & Gardens, Brooklyn Botanic Garden Record* 40, no. 3 (Autumn 1984): 14–18.

Moore, Eleanor M. *Youth in Museums*. Philadelphia: University of Pennsylvania Press, 1941.

Munari, Bruno. "Experimental Project of a Laboratory for Children at the Brera Art Gallery in Milan." *Museum* [UNESCO] 31, no. 3 (1979): 203–05.

Munyer, Edward A. "Museums and Their Discovery Rooms." *The Living Museum* 44, no. 3 (Summer 1982): 43–45.

"MUSE and the Brooklyn Children's Museum." *Design Quarterly* 90/91 (1974): 70–72.

"Musée pour enfants, Brooklyn, New York." *L'Architecture d'Aujourd'hui* 204 (September 1979): 71–73.

"Museum Beckons: 'Please Do Touch': Bedford-Stuyvesant Youth Get New Place to Learn." *New York Times*, 28 May 1968, p. 36.

"Museum Choosing 20 Curators (J.G.): Young Applicants Discourse on Pyramids and Roaches." *New York Times*, 26 May 1962, p. 22.

"A Museum Designed for the Children of Brooklyn." *Architectural Record* 151, no. 4 (April 1972): 114–15.

"Museum Doors Open on Learning Cornucopia." *Chicago Tribune Sunday*, 24 November 1985, sec. 18, pp. 3–5.

"A Museum for Children." *Museum Work* 3, no. 5 (February 1921): 158–62.

"A Museum for Children." *Recreation* 32, no. 6 (September 1938): 341–42.

"Museum for Kids Is Still Growing in Brooklyn." *New York Times*, 28 July 1978, sec. C, p. 13.

"Museum Play-In: Architect William Morgan Designs a Geometric Module to House the Ever-Growing Jacksonville Children's Museum." *Progressive Architecture* 51, no. 11 (November 1970): 64–69.

Museums, Imagination and Education. Museums and Monuments Series, no. 15. Paris: UNESCO, 1973.

"Museums & Kids." *Parents* 58 (September 1983): 42, 44.

"Museums Cater to Children." *Asbury Park Press*, 15 May 1984.

"Museums for Kids Say 'Please Touch.' " *USA Today*, 6 October 1983, p. 3D.

"Museums That Come to the Classroom." *Grade Teacher* 83, no. 9 (May/June 1966): 41–45.

"Museums to Teach By." *Mosaic* 10, no. 4 (July/August 1979): 17–25.

"A Museum Will Rise for Children." *New York Times*, 14 June 1972, p. 40.

Mutal, Sylvio. "Museums and Children in Latin America." *Museum* [UNESCO] 31, no. 3 (1979): 154–59.

N[ational] P[ublic] R[adio], "Options in Education: Libraries and Museums." Program Number 115, 3 April 1978: ERIC Document Reproduction Service, ED 167 073.

Natural Science for Youth Foundation. *A Natural Science Center for Your Community.* New York: Natural Science for Youth Foundation, [1960].

Naumer, Karina. "My Father Is the Director of a Children's Museum." *Jack and Jill* (January 1967): 28–32.

"Neighborhood MUSE." *Architectural Forum* 129, no. 2 (September 1968): 86–89.

Neill, Shirley Boes. "Exploring the Exploratorium." *American Education* 14, no. 10 (December 1978): 6–22.

"New Developments Highlighted at CIMUSET Meeting." *ICOM News* 39, no. 1 (1986): 10.

"New Fun with Science at S.F.'s Exploratorium." *Sunset* 167 (November 1981): 24.

"New Junior Museum." *Museum News* 47, no. 10 (June 1969): 4.

"New Metropolitan Junior Museum Open Oct. 16." *The Museum News* 19, no. 8 (15 October 1941): 1.

"A New Museum for Children." *Los Angeles Times*, 5 April 1979, pp. 1–2.

"A New Museum for Children." *New York Times*, 14 October 1979, sec. 1, p. 68.

"New Orientation Center Opening at Met Museum." *New York Times*, 22 January 1983, sec. 1, p. 10.

Newsom, Barbara Y. and Silver, Adele Z., eds. *The Art Museum as Educator*. Berkeley: University of California Press, 1978.

"New Theaters for Learning." *Time*, 25 July 1977, p. 56.

Nichols, Susan K., ed.; Alexander, Mary and Yellis, Ken, assoc. eds. *Museum Education Anthology 1973–1983: Perspectives on Informal Learning/A Decade of Roundtable Reports*. Washington, D.C.: Museum Education Roundtable, 1984: ERIC Document Reproduction Service, ED 248 883.

Nicol, Elizabeth H. *The Development of Validated Museum Exhibits*. Boston: The Children's Museum, 1969: ERIC Document Reproduction Service, ED 035 038.

Normandia, Susan. "The Bronx Zoo's Children's Zoo: A Case Study in Exhibit Design and Evaluation." Master's thesis, Cornell University, 1985.

O'Dea, William T. "Science Museums and Education." *Museum* [UNESCO] 8, no. 4 (1955): 242–45; and "Les Musées Scientifiques et l'Éducation," ibid., pp. 239–42.

Office of Museum Programs, Smithsonian Institution. *Proceedings of the Children in Museums International Symposium* [1979]. Washington, D.C.: Smithsonian Institution, 1982.

O'Lear, Michael P. "Not for Children Only." *Regional Conference of Historical Agencies* 12, no. 7 (July 1982): 1–3.

Olofsson, Ulla Keding, ed. *Museums and Children*. Paris: UNESCO, 1979.

Oppenheimer, Frank. "Exploration and Culture: Oppenheimer Receives Distinguished Service Award." *Museum News* 61, no. 2 (November/December 1982): 36–45. With an Introduction by Kenneth Starr.

Oppenheimer, Frank. "The Exploratorium: A Playful Museum Combines Perception and Art in Science Education." *American Journal of Physics* 40, no. 7 (July 1972): 978–84.

Oppenheimer, Frank. "The Exploratorium and Other Ways of Teaching Physics." *Physics Today* 28, no. 9 (September 1975): 9, 11, 13.

Oppenheimer, Frank. "A Rationale for a Science Museum." *Curator* 11, no. 3 (1968): 206–09.

Oppenheimer, Frank. "The Study of Perception as a Part of Teaching Physics." *American Journal of Physics* 42, no. 7 (July 1974): 531–37.

Oppenheimer, Frank. "Teaching and Learning." *American Journal of Physics* 41, no. 12 (December 1973): 1310–13.

"Out-of-School Science Education in Asia and the Pacific." *Bulletin of the UNESCO Regional Office for Education in Asia and the Pacific*. Special Issue. Bangkok: UNESCO, 1982: ERIC Document Reproduction Service, ED 226 989.

Paget, Oliver E. "The New Children's Hall at the Natural History Museum, Vienna." *Museum* [UNESCO] 30, no. 1 (1978): 55–58.

Paine, Albert Bigelow. "The Children's Room in the Smithsonian Institution." *Annual Report of the Smithsonian Institution—1901*. Washington, D.C.: Government Printing Office, 1902.

"Palace of Delights." *Aviso*, March 1982, p. 8.

Papageorge, Maria. "Celebrating IYC." *Museum News* 58, no. 2 (November/December 1979): 11–12, 15, 17.

Papageorge, Maria. "Children's Museum, Boston." *Museum News* 59, no. 6 (May/June 1981): 25, 27.

Papageorge, Maria. "An Experience in Community." *Museum News* 59, no. 7 (July/August 1981): 9–11.

Parr, A. E. "Why Children's Museums?" *Curator* 3, no. 3 (1960): 217–36.

Parsons, Beatrice. *Museums and Schools: Partners in Education.* Audiotape of panelists Janice Goffney, Philip Hanson, and Steven Ling, presented at meeting of the American Association of Museums, Detroit, June 1985. Shawnee Mission, KS: Vanguard Systems, 1985.

Pawley, Ray. "Children's Zoos: Whom Are They Reaching?" *Parks & Recreation* 3, no. 11 (November 1968): 18–21, 49–50.

Phillips, David. "Experiments in Visual Education: The Automatic Art Gallery." *Museums Journal* 82, no. 1 (June 1982): 11–13.

Pitman-Gelles, Bonnie. "Beyond Outreach: Museums and Community Organizations." *Museum News* 61, no. 6 (August 1983): 37–41.

Pitman-Gelles, Bonnie. *Museums, Magic & Children: Youth Education in Museums.* Washington, D.C.: Association of Science-Technology Centers, 1981.

"Plans of the New Museum." *The Museum* [Newark] 1, no. 2 (April 1925): 19.

Powell, David C. "New Tidepool Display at Sea World, San Diego." In *International Zoo Yearbook* 14 (1974): 220. Edited by Nicole Duplaix-Hall. London: The Zoological Society of London, 1974.

Preuss, Paul. "Please Touch: Museums That Make Magic with Science." *American Educator* 6, no. 1 (Spring 1982): 18–25.

Project for a "Children's Egyptian Museum." Turin: Rotary Club International, 1981.

"Projet de Musée pour enfants, Brooklyn, N. York." *L'Architecture d'Aujourd'hui* 170 (November/December 1973): 92–93.

Purwin, Louise. "Wonder—The Beginning of Wisdom." *Educational Forum* 8 (November 1943): 69–73.

Rabb, George B. "Man, Child, Animal." *Brookfield Bandarlog* 42 (Spring 1975): 14.

Ramsey, Grace Fisher. *Educational Work in Museums of the United States.* New York: H. W. Wilson, 1938.

Ranga, B. S. "Children's Museum in India—Its Scope and Functions." *Journal of Indian Museums* 36 (1980): 69–79.

Rathmann, Carl Gustav. "The Educational Museum of the Public School of St. Louis." *Proceedings of the American Association of Museums* 2 (1908): 39–56.

Rathmann, Carl Gustav. *The Educational Museum of the St. Louis Public Schools.* U.S. Bureau of Education Bulletin 1914, no. 48. Washington, D.C.: Government Printing Office, 1915.

Reece, Carolyn. "Exploring Art and Science." *Children Today* 3, no. 4 (July/August 1974): 18–21, 36.

Reece, Carolyn. "The Indianapolis Children's Museum." *Children Today* 7, no. 6 (November/December 1978): 10–13.

Reed, Pat. "Hardly What You'd Call Museums." *Design* [London] 349 (January 1978): 50–51.

Reising, Gert and Neysters, Silvia. "Drachen zum Weinen und Lachen: Notizen zu einer Ausstellung in Karlsruhe." *Zeitschrift für Kunstpädagogik* 2 (1981): 58–59.

Reuter-Rautenberg, Anne. "Der Erzieher als Ausstellungsmacher—Das Kindermuseum in der Staatlichen Kunsthalle Karlsruhe." Jerusalem ICOM Conference, March 1983. (Typewritten.)

Reuter-Rautenberg, Anneliese. "Ein Kindermuseum in einer Gemäldegalerie." *Museumskunde* 43, no. 3 (1978): 146–47.

Rivere, George Henri. Editorial. *Museum* [UNESCO] 31, no. 3 (1979): 146.

Roberts, David. "Making Fun Work." *Raytheon Magazine* (Winter 1984): 24–31.

Robinson, Jeri and Quinn, Patricia. *Playspace: Creating Family Spaces in Public Places.* Boston: Boston Children's Museum, 1984.

Rosenfeld, Sherman. "The Context of Informal Learning in Zoos." *Roundtable Reports* 4, no. 2 (Spring 1979): 1–3, 15–16.

Rosenfeld, Sherman and Terkel, Amelia. "A Naturalistic Study of Visitors at an Interactive Mini-Zoo." *Curator* 25, no. 3 (September 1982): 187–212.

Rosenthal, Mark A. and Fisher, Lester E. "The Farm-In-the-Zoo at Lincoln Park Zoo, Chicago." In *International Zoo Yearbook* 12 (1972): 226–27. Edited by Joseph Lucas and Nicole Duplaix-Hall. London: The Zoological Society of London, 1972.

Royal Ontario Museum. *Hands On: Setting Up a Discovery Room in Your Museum or School.* Toronto: Royal Ontario Museum, 1979.

Rubin, Victor and Medrich, Elliott A. *Children's Out-of-School Services and the Urban Fiscal Crisis.* Berkeley: University of California, 1980: ERIC Document Reproduction Service, ED 222 588.

Russell, Charles. *Museums and Our Children.* New York: Central Book Co., 1956.

Ryan, Jerry. "Creative Enjoyment at the Palo Alto Junior Museum." *School Arts* 47, no. 10 (June 1948): 334–37, 2a.

Ryder-Daves, P. "Small Domestic Animals in the Children's Zoo." In *International Zoo Yearbook* 16 (1976): 234–38. Edited by P.J.S. Olney. London: The Zoological Society of London, 1976.

Sahasrabudhe, Prabha. *A Children's Museum for India.* Baroda: University of Baroda Press, 1965.

Sands, Rose Mary. " 'Do Touch' Museums." *Recreation* 38, no. 8 (November 1944): 412–13, 442.

"San Francisco Museum Stresses Involvement." *Physics Today* 24, no. 6 (June 1971): 62.

"San Francisco's Scientific Fun House." *New York Times*, 9 July 1978, sec. 10, pp. 1, 13.

Saunders, John R. "Evaluation of Extension Work with Children." *Curator* 2, no. 1 (1959): 68–73.

Schatz, Dennis and Friedman, Alan. "Self-Discovery in Astronomy for the Public." *Sky and Telescope* 52, no. 4 (October 1976): 254–58.

Schlegel, Donna M. "Educating the General Zoo Visitor." *AAZPA 1982 Annual Conference Proceedings*, pp. 251–60.

Schlossberg, Edwin. "Outline and Brief Description of Participatory Learning Environment" and "Brief Description of Individual Elements of Learning Environment." [Brooklyn Children's Museum]. September 1972. (Mimeographed.)

Schneider, Gail. *Children's Zoos: Organization and Operation.* Management Aids Bulletin No. 87. Washington, D.C.: National Parks and Recreation Association, 1970.

Schneider, Gail. "Design Features of Children's Zoos" and "Husbandry in Children's Zoos." In *Zoological Park and Aquarium Fundamentals*, pp. 127–140, 311–20.

Edited by Karen Sausman. Wheeling, W.V.: American Association of Zoological Parks and Aquariums, 1982.

Schneider, Gail. "Domestication." *Brookfield Bandarlog* 42 (Spring 1975): 6–9.

Schneider, Gail. "Fall and Winter at Children's Zoo." *Brookfield Zoo Bison* 1, no. 4 (Fall 1984): 18–21.

Schneider, Gail. *1975–76 Children's Zoo Survey.* Wheeling, W.V.: American Association of Zoological Parks and Aquariums, [1976].

"Scholastic Science Fair." *Syracuse Herald-Journal*, 25 November 1981.

Schur, Susan E. "Museum Profiles: The Museum of Transportation & The Children's Museum of Boston." *Technology & Conservation* 4, no. 4 (Winter 1979): 26–32.

Schwartz, Alvin. "Junior Museum Teen-Age Art Class." *School Arts* 58, no. 10 (June 1959): 43.

"Science Museum to Offer Exhibit Design Program." *Physics Today* 32, no. 9 (September 1979): 108.

"Seattle Children's Museum Moves to Seattle Centerhouse." *Ovation Magazine* (October 1985): A–12.

"Seeing Science in Action." *Insight* 96 (July 1982): 2645–49.

Seidelman, James E. "A Junior Gallery within a Large Museum." *Museum News* 39, no. 7 (April 1961): 34–37.

Sharpe, Elizabeth. *Museum Research: How It Can Help You.* Audiotape of panelists Paul Knappenberger, Patricia McNamara, Mary Ellen Munley, Paul Richard, Fath Davis Ruffins, and Robert Wolf, presented at meeting of the American Association of Museums, Washington, D.C., June 1984. Shawnee Mission, KS: Vanguard Systems, 1984.

Shaw, Evelyn. "The Exploratorium." *Curator* 15, no. 1 (1972): 39–52.

Shuker, Nancy, ed. *Arts in Education Partners: Schools and Their Communities.* New York: Associated Councils of the Arts, 1977.

"Sick Kids Have Fun While They Wait." *New Haven Register*, 27 April 1985, p. 26.

Silverman, Fran. "Sharing the Wealth." *Museum News* 59, no. 3 (November/December 1980): 18–29.

Simon-Okshevsky, Ute. "The Royal Ontario Museum's Discovery Gallery—Not a Traditional Gallery." *Orbit 70* 15, no. 2 (April 1984): 24–25.

Simons, Robin; Miller, Lisa Farber; and Lengsfelder, Peter. *Nonprofit Piggy Goes to Market.* Denver: Children's Museum of Denver, 1984.

Smart, J. E. "Covering Up: An Exhibition of Protective Wear." *Curator* 27, no. 1 (March 1984): 11–22.

Smith, C. Ray. "The Great Museum Debate." *Progressive Architecture* 50, no. 12 (December 1969): 76–85.

Smith, C. Ray. "Museum Goes Underground: Some Neighbors Skeptical But Children Are Delighted." *Contract Interiors* 137 (June 1978): 116–19.

Smith, Marcia Axtmann. "A Joint Venture: Museum Wharf, Boston, Massachusetts." *Museum News* 59, no. 1 (September 1980): 24–31.

Smith, Marcia Axtmann. "Renewed Museums Revisited." *Museum News* 63, no. 4 (April 1985): 13–29.

Smithsonian Institution. *Museums and Handicapped Students: Guidelines for Educators.* Washington, D.C.: Smithsonian Institution, 1977: ERIC Document Reproduction Service, ED 152 062.

Smithsonian Institution. *The Smithsonian Experience*. Washington, D.C.: Smithsonian Institution, 1977.

Sneider, Cary and DeVore, Edna. "Halley's Comet and Beyond." *Classroom Computer Learning* 6, no. 4 (January 1986): 34–43.

Sneider, Cary; Kurlich, Kevin; Pulos, Steven; and Friedman, Alan. "Learning to Control Variables with Model Rockets: A Neo-Piagetian Study of Learning in Field Settings." *Science Education* 68, no. 4 (July 1984): 465–86.

Sneider, Cary; Pulos, Steven; Freenor, Evangeline; Porter, Joyce; and Templeton, Betty. "Understanding the Earth's Shape and Gravity." *Learning* 14, no. 6 (February 1986): 42–47.

Social Education and Its Administration in Japan. Tokyo: Social Education Bureau, Ministry of Education, 1972: ERIC Document Reproduction Service, ED 069 956.

The Sourcebook: Learning by Design. Washington, D.C.: American Institute of Architects, 1981.

"Speaking of Museums." *Museum News* 51, no. 3 (November 1972): 14–16.

"The Special Sounds of Old-Time Radio." *Chicago Tribune Friday*, 11 January 1985, sec. 7, p. 3.

"S[taten] I[sland] Children's Museum a Community Affair." *New York Times*, 11 August 1976, p. 40.

"Symphony on Pier 3." *Time*, 24 August 1981, pp. 45–48, 51.

Tappe, Dorothy. "Junior Museums with Special Reference to Bridgeport, Connecticut's Wonder Workshop Junior Museum." Master's thesis, Cornell University, 1953.

Taylor, Frank J. "Want to Borrow a Pet?" *Saturday Evening Post*, 26 June 1954, pp. 34–35, 112–14.

Thier, Herbert D. and Linn, Marcia C. "The Value of Interactive Learning Experiences." *Curator* 19, no. 3 (September 1976): 233–45.

Thomson, Peggy. *Museum People*. Englewood Cliffs, N.J.: Prentice-Hall, 1977.

Thomson, Peggy. "Please DO Touch These Exhibits." *Smithsonian* 5, no. 2 (May 1974): 92–95.

Tobias, John. "Reindeer as a Domestic Animal in the Children's Zoo." *AAZPA Regional Conference Proceedings 1985*, pp. 51–54.

Tressel, George W. "The Role of Museums in Science Education." *Science Education* 64, no. 2 (April 1980): 257–60.

Tullock, Margaret DeWolf. "The First Museum for Children." *Museums Journal* 51, no. 4 (July 1951): 90–94.

Tupper, Gene and Cox, Robert. "Growing with the Junior Museum." *School Arts* 52, no. 9 (May 1953): 295–97.

Turkowski, Frank J. "Education at Zoos and Aquariums in the United States." *BioScience* 22, no. 8 (August 1972): 468–75.

"2 Exhibits Show Children Factory Work, Life Cycle." *The Denver Post*, 30 November 1978, p. 56.

Uchida, Itaru and Asuke, Mitsunori. "The Touch Tank at the Himeji City Aquarium." In *International Zoo Yearbook* 22 (1982): 271–76. Edited by P.J.S. Olney. London: The Zoological Society of London, 1982.

Unsworth, Jean Morman. "Express-Ways." *Momentum* 14, no. 3 (September 1983): 42–43.

Vandorn, Bonnie. *Science Teacher Education at Museums.* Audiotape of panelists A. William Kochanczyck, Freda Nicholson, and Roy Shafer, presented at meeting of the American Association of Museums, Detroit, June 1985. Shawnee Mission, KS: Vanguard Systems, 1985.

Walker, Rowena Smith. "How Schools Use the Children's Museum." *The National Elementary Principals Thirteenth Yearbook* 13, no. 5 (June 1934): 261–66.

Wall, Roger. "A Museum Approach to Computer Learning." *Science and Children* 23, no. 4 (January 1986): 11–13.

Wallen, Eileen. "Children's Museums Come of Age." *Museum News* 58, no. 2 (November/December 1979): 46–49.

Walsh, Alexandra. "Fifteen Collaborative Ventures." *Museum News* 59, no. 3 (November/December 1980): 30–35.

Wasilewski, Marcy A. "Recycle for Museums/A Program Study." *Roundtable Reports*, Spring 1978.

Webster, Steven K. "Interactive Exhibits at the Monterey Bay Aquarium." *AAZPA 1985 Annual Conference Proceedings*, 63–68: ERIC Document Reproduction Service, ED 265 038.

Weeks, Brigitte. "Close Encounters of the Imaginative Kind: Capital Children's Museum." *Traveler* (Winter 1985/86): 116–23.

Wengen, Ger van. "Introduction." *Museum* [UNESCO] 31, no. 3 (1979): 148–52.

Weston, Ruth, "American Museums and the Child." *Museums Journal* (Supplement) 39, no. 2 (May 1939): 92–115.

White, Judith. *Developing Interactive Educational Materials: A Team Approach.* Audiotape of panelists Sharon Barry, Melissa Gaulding, and Dale Marcellini, presented at meeting of the American Association of Museums, Washington, D.C., June 1984. Shawnee Mission, KS: Vanguard Systems, 1984.

White, Judith. "Graphics—Reaching the Total Audience." *AAZPA 1978 Annual Conference Proceedings*, pp. 271–72.

White, Judith and Barry, Sharon. *Families, Frogs, and Fun: Developing a Family Learning Lab in a Zoo—HERPlab: A Case Study.* Washington, D.C.: Smithsonian Institution, 1984.

White, Judy and Girgus, Signe. "The How-to-Build-a-Better-Box Book." *Roundtable Reports* (Fall 1977): 11–17.

White-Marcellini, Judith. "Developing One Kind of Educational Program for Family Audiences," *Newsletter International Association of Zoo Educators.* Proceedings, 1982 Biennial Conference, 9 (1982): 28–31.

Williams, Henry Lionel. "Children's Museums: What They Are and How to Organize Them." *The Museum News* 15, no. 12 (15 December 1937): 7–12.

Winstanley, Barbara R. *Children and Museums.* Oxford: Basil Blackwell & Mott, 1967.

Wittlin, Alma S. "Junior Museums at the Crossroads: Forward to a New Era of Creativity or Backward to Obsoleteness?" *Curator* 6, no. 1 (1963): 58–63.

Wittlin, Alma S. *The Museum: Its History and Its Task in Education.* London: Routledge & Kegan Paul, 1949.

Wittlin, Alma S. *Museums: In Search of a Usable Future.* Cambridge, Mass: The MIT Press, 1970.

Wolf, Robert L.; Munley, Mary Ellen; and Tymitz, Barbara L. *The Pause That Refreshes: A Study of the Discovery Corners in the National Museum of History and Technology, Smithsonian Institution.* Washington, DC: Office of Museum Programs,

Smithsonian Institution, 1979: ERIC Document Reproduction Service, ED 196 772.

Wolf, Robert L. and Tymitz, Barbara L. *"Do Giraffes Ever Sit?": A Study of Visitor Perceptions at the National Zoological Park, Smithsonian Institution*. Washington, D.C.: Office of Museum Programs, Smithsonian Institution, 1979: ERIC Document Reproduction Service, ED 196 769.

Woodward, Ellen S. "WPA Museum Projects." *The Museum News* 15, no. 13 (1 January 1938): 7–8.

"A Working Paper on Exhibits." *Museum News* 54, no. 4 (March/April 1976): 27–31.

Workshop for Key Personnel Concerned with Out-of-School Scientific Activities by Young People: Report of a Regional Workshop (Bangkok, Thailand: August 24–September 2, 1982). Bangkok: UNESCO, 1982: ERIC Document Reproduction Service, ED 237 360.

Wrege, Rachael. "Hands On! For Kids and Adults, Computers Are Fast Becoming the Star Attractions at Amusement Parks and Museums." *Popular Computing* 1, no. 8 (June 1982): 110–23.

Yerke, Roger. "Families, What Are We Doing for Our Largest Audience?" *AAZPA 1984 Annual Conference Proceedings*, pp. 380–86.

Yerke, Roger. "Out of the Museum and onto the Zoo Grounds: Arthropod Discovery Boxes at the Washington Park Zoo." *AAZPA 1982 Annual Conference Proceedings*, pp. 344–64.

Yerke, Roger. "The Storefront Insect Zoo: An Effective Exhibit of Arthropods." *AAZPA Regional Conference Proceedings 1981*, pp. 183–86.

Young, Matilda. "A Children's Museum?" *Journal of the Education Association of the District of Columbia* 16, no. 3 (April 1947): offprint.

Zembower, Dennis. *Cooperative Exhibit Development Among Science Centers: Getting the Most for Your Dollars*. Audiotape of panelists Marilynne Eichinger and Roger Smith, presented at meeting of the American Association of Museums, Washington, D.C., June 1984. Shawnee Mission, KS: Vanguard Systems, 1984.

Zien, Jim. "Beyond the Generation Gap." *Museum News* 58, no. 2 (November/December 1979): 26–31.

"Zoos Are News." *Woman's Day*, 23 October 1984.

Zubrowski, Bernard. "Memoirs of a Bubble Blower." *Technology Review* 85, no. 8 (November/December 1982): 2–7.

Zucker, Barbara Fleisher. "Fifty Years of American Children's Zoos." *AAZPA 1986 Annual Conference Proceedings*, pp. 452–59.

INDEX

About the Author

BARBARA FLEISHER ZUCKER is Director of the Illinois Cooperative Conservation Program and serves as Visiting Professor at the Morris Library of Southern Illinois University at Carbondale. She has published articles in *Curator*, *Museum News*, and *Illinois Libraries*, and has presented numerous conference papers.